I0083722

ANGLO-IRANIAN RELATIONS
DURING WORLD WAR I

ANGLO-IRANIAN RELATIONS DURING WORLD WAR I

WM. J. OLSON

Routledge
Taylor & Francis Group

LONDON AND NEW YORK

First published 1984 by
FRANK CASS & CO. LTD.

Published 2013 by Routledge
2 Park Square, Milton Park, Abingdon, Oxfordshire OX14 4RN
711 Third Avenue, New York, NY, 10017, USA

First issued in paperback 2016

Routledge is an imprint of the Taylor & Francis Group, an informa business

Copyright © 1984 Wm J. Olson

British Library Cataloguing in Publication Data

Olson, Wm. J.
    Anglo-Iranian relations during World War I.
    1. World War, 1914–1918 – Diplomatic
    history   2. Great Britain – Foreign
    relations – Iran   3. Great Britain –
    Foreign relations – 1910–1936   4. Iran –
    Foreign relations – Great Britain
    I. Title
    327.41055   DA47.9.17

ISBN 13: 978-1-138-96354-2 (pbk)
ISBN 13: 978-0-7146-3178-3 (hbk)

*All rights reserved. No part of this publication may be reproduced
in any form or by any means, electronic, mechanical, photo-
copying, recording or otherwise, without the prior permission
of the publisher.*

To Lela, Anna Marie, and Addeane

CONTENTS

NOTE ON TRANSLITERATION

The problem of transliterating Persian words and names into English remains a subject of contention. I have used the system recommended by the *International Journal of Middle Eastern Studies*; however, I have dropped the various diacritical marks to reduce printing costs. In addition, place-names have been given the spellings most common in atlases and dictionaries.

PREFACE

... you know as well as we do that right, as the world
goes, is only in question between equals in power,
while the strong do what they can and the weak
suffer what they must.

Thucydides, the Athenians to the Melians

If nineteenth-century Persia had been a strong state, security-minded
officials in India would have worried. But Persia was weak and that,
too, concerned British officials because it invited the interference of
stronger powers. Persian weakness, therefore, became a liability for
Britain, largely because the British were unable or unwilling to take
adequate measures to compensate for it.

It was an anomalous situation for a nation to be in – its weakness
being a threat to the security of another state.

For a weak state such as Persia, caught in the crossfire of Great
Power rivalry without the ability to enforce respect for its integrity,
international relations became a part of the domestic political scene,
with the Powers able to make or break cabinets, to redirect the
economy to suit themselves, and to interfere directly in a variety of
internal affairs. As such the ministers of Britain and Russia, the two
principal powers, were more than accredited representatives in Persia;
they were virtually members of the cabinet with powers of veto. This
situation meant that the ministers of the two Powers became involved
in the machinations of various political factions and thus entangled
their nations' interests in petty internal squabbles. Given the personal
nature of politics in Iran, this type of meddling often meant that the
prestige or interests of the Powers depended upon the fate of a single
individual or small group; and given the insecurity in Persian domestic
politics, aggravated by Great Power rivalry, the security of interests
based on the tenure of personalities was correspondingly precarious
– a situation that in turn invited further meddling.

Paradoxically, Britain did not want to become involved in

Persian affairs; its interests would have been better served if Persia had been as devoid of people as the maps strategists studied when contemplating goals and national security. Indeed, a case could be made that one element in Britain's imperial expansion in similar situations was the result of an effort to reduce the number of independent variables in local areas so that key questions of security could be settled among the principals without constant reference to distinctive local circumstances. But for a variety of reasons, Persia could not be ignored or absorbed and so officials in London and India perforce had to concern themselves with local realities, something they were never comfortable with; and despite this necessity they continued to look on Persia more as an object rather than the subject of attention. Thus, a certain unreality dogged Anglo-Iranian relations. That unreality is the subject of this study.

* * *

To pick up a book on Iran now is a timely thing to do, even a book about a period over 60 years ago, partly because the actions of statesmen and ordinary people two generations distant had an impact on the way things are now, and partly because both author and reader must impart to their respective roles some sense of their own time. In all accounts of the past there is some of the present, and a temptation to read significance or moral both backward and forward. The original research for this work was done for a thesis in 1974 when Mohammad Reza Shah was still on his throne and Iran was an island of stability in the Middle East. Much has changed: the Shah is a memory and Iran a confused and confusing proposition which makes this author's task somewhat easier to find empathetic attention when he speaks of confusion and turmoil in Iranian affairs that disturbed the interests of the Great Powers at a distant time. But one must not confound the present with the past or assume too much by way of a present bias; and caution must be used in transposing the 'lessons' of history into contemporary situations. Such an approach impoverishes both the deed and understanding. But it is impossible not to see certain parallels, which, if not identical to present circumstances, invite comparison and have something to teach, even if that 'something' is nothing more than circumspection in the pursuit of international relations. It is a wonder that anyone reposes faith in the diplomatic process when one sees how seldom results match intentions, but at least it is a process that keeps us talking.

* * *

Today Iran is driven by domestic confusion and caught between the competing interests of the Super Powers. The country faces an uncertain future. So it was during the period covered by this book — a time when a young, impressionable religious student named Rouhallah Khomayni watched as his country suffered invasion and humiliation at the hands of foreign powers. The bitter lessons of these and subsequent years did much to shape the present Iranian distrust of alien forces.

The war years also graphically illustrate the problems that await the pursuit of great power interests in regional affairs. The quotation at the beginning of this preface succinctly puts the faith as held by those with power; but as the Greeks learned, power is not always a guarantee of outcome, and the use of power quite often involves the user in unanticipated and unwanted circumstances. Today, as seventy years ago, the super powers are bent on pursuing their own interests in the Middle East and look to client states for support. But the so-called clients, then and now, have interests of their own quite distinct from their patrons, interests that cannot be controlled by the patrons, and the pursuit of which is not always in the interest of the patron. The results can be very embarrassing. It is doubtful whether awareness that foolish mistakes have been made in the past will prevent similar mistakes from being repeated, but perhaps that consciousness will encourage people not to look at events in the Middle East with such a bipolar perspective. It should also remind us that the very efforts of the Super Powers to ensure their respective interests can be detrimental to those interests, creating further problems and destabilizing an area not known for its stability.

* * *

It is customary at this point to enumerate all the people to whom one owes a debt. It is also customary for readers to skip this part. That would be a mistake, for acknowledgements are more than perfunctory gestures: they are recognition of the community that goes into producing any piece of research no matter how individual. The majority of the research for this book was completed in Iran and Britain in 1974-75 thanks largely to a Fulbright-Hays research fellowship. A subsequent research trip in 1976 was made possible by grants from the History Department, the World Order Program, and the Middle East Center all at the University of Texas. In addition, a postdoctoral fellowship from the Leverhulme Trust and the kindness of Dr Roy Bridges and Professor John Hargreaves of the University of Aberdeen, Scotland, in 1977-78 made it possible to complete the research; and a generous fellowship from the University of Sydney, Australia, gave me the time to write. In the course of the research and writing I contracted numerous debts, though none who helped would see it this way. In particular I want to thank Dr Hafez Farmayan, my supervisor and friend, and Dr Wm. Roger Louis. I also owe a profound debt to Dr David Morgan and Johanna for their hospitality and tolerance. I have also benefited from discussions with Sandy Morton, Dr R. M. Burrell, Dr Richard Waterhouse, Dr Robert Blum, and Dr Richard Bosworth. I owe special thanks to Ann Moyal for reading sections of the book, and the reader owes her gratitude for the deletions her criticisms wrought. Joe Moyal, a polymath, also suffered through more than one discussion and, as always, had insightful observations. I also want to thank the Keeper of the Public Record Office, the India Office, the British Museum, and the Imperial Museum in London; the National Archives in Washington, D.C.; the National Library and Archives in Canberra, Australia; and the American Institute of Iranian Studies and the British Institute for Persian Studies, Tehran, for facilities in the course of my work. Most particularly I should like to thank Addeane Caelleigh for her editorial assistance. Having said all of that, it only remains for me to acknowledge that all the inadequacies of this work are entirely my own.

Washington, D.C.   WM. J. OLSON

CHAPTER ONE

INTRODUCTION

> Were it not for our possessing India, we should
> trouble ourselves but little over Persia.

As Lord Salisbury appreciated when he wrote this in 1889, Britain did possess India, and a proprietor's concern for security became the central and sustaining feature in the Anglo-Iranian connection.[1] One of the ironies of the relationship was that Iran was more the object of concern than the subject for relations. Apart from a rather limited trade, British interest or involvement in the kingdom of the Great Sophy arose out of an abiding concern for the defense of India's land frontier and the routes thither. Had the British been assured of the security of the strategic routes across the Middle East, and if they could have been reassured about the invulnerability of their vast continental possession, it is doubtful that Iran would have figured very prominently in British thinking. But one of the problems with security is that its mental frontiers always exceed the physical means for achieving security. A succession of Foreign Secretaries and Viceroys were never able to completely dismiss concern for or doubts about the security of India; nor were they ever able to solve the Persian puzzle – of finding a way to fit Iran into a scheme for imperial defense. This provoked one Foreign Secretary, Sir Edward Grey, to complain, 'Persia tried my patience more than any other subject.'[2] Hyperbole, perhaps, but considering the problems he had to deal with it reflects a sense of the frustration which was a constant feature of Anglo-Iranian relations.

It is not clear when maritime Britain first appreciated the consequences of being a continental power in India. Certainly by 1800 the British realized the vulnerability of India to invasion from the surrounding states. A Persian army, after all, had sacked Delhi barely fifty years before the British sacked Seringapatam, and Afghan tribes still preyed on northern India for their pocket money. The mildly fantastic Napoleonic scheme for marching overland to India in 1800 also contributed to Britain's fears that a European power with the support of local states could invade India.

Whatever its origins, some time in the late 18th or early 19th century, the awareness that India was exposed to a land approach took root in the British imagination and grew until it became the paramount imperial anxiety, remaining so until Germany began to develop its navy. Its very importance became its own problem, for it meant that a wide variety of British officials, often it seemed every British official, felt compelled to express an opinion on what the defense of India meant and how it should be achieved. Sorting through this welter of opinion for a clear policy taxed the abilities of British officials, the credulity of foreigners and the imaginations of subsequent historians.

The history of British policy towards Iran might be described as a failure that succeeded, with confusion and muddle attending the entire process. This stemmed largely from the nature of British rule in India. With India as virtually a separate country possessing its own civil service and army, its own peculiar domestic and international problems, and often its own foreign policy, British foreign policy had to toil its way through the conflicting interest groups of not one but two government structures; and then frequently had to seek coordination between two incompatible views – one held in India and one held in Britain. This meant that the British often had difficulty agreeing on a policy. As one Secretary of State for India put it, in an age more concerned with efficiency, 'The plain truth is ... that this country cannot have two foreign policies.'³ But that is what Britain did have for most of the nineteenth century, or at least a potential for two foreign policies that inhibited the formation of a clear policy.

Despite the confusion and struggle that attended Anglo-Iranian relations, four approaches evolved successively between 1800 and World War I for dealing with Iran. These may be loosely characterized as: seeking contact with Iran (1800-1830); hostility to Iran (1830-1870); strengthening Iran (1870-1890); and accommodation with Russia (1890-1917). These divisions were never discrete in practice for they were inter-related and they overlapped, with the recrudescense of older ideas amidst the new. And throughout the whole period there were endless wrangles between London and officials in India over policy, and even when a more or less consistent policy emerged there was always a significant opposition waiting to lead a revolt.⁴ Iran waxed and waned in British considerations, enjoying one moment 'a position of extravagant prominence,' as Lord Curzon put it, and 'unmerited obscurity' the next. Nonetheless these divisions approximate the main features of the development of British policy and governed the evolution of Anglo-Iranian relations.

The first policy, seeking contact with Iran between *c.* 1800 and 1830, relied on the neighboring states' support of or indifference to Britain's position in India. The initial British approaches to Iran in 1800 and in 1807, for example, sought Persia's assistance in frustrating Afghan tribal incursions into India, and in securing Persian promises to reject any connection with Napoleon. Even this policy, however, labored under the London-India dichotomy in British thinking, as two missions went to Iran to discuss the Napoleonic threat, one from the Home Government and one from India. It is debatable how seriously the British regarded Napoleon's fantasies, and if Iran in subsequent years had been able to maintain its own interests it is doubtful that Persia's relations with Britain or British India would have gone much further than pleasantries, apart from some commercial contact and unless, of course, the Iranians themselves became a threat. Britain was content to secure Iran's neutrality with offers of moral support and limited technical and monetary assistance, guaranteed by a treaty whose main purpose was to keep Iran friendly. The British were not prepared or able, with India still not completely subdued, to offer more material support. There was also another complication.[5]

Iran had its own preoccupation in 1800 when the first British mission arrived. At the same time that Britain wanted to close Persia to French schemes, Iran was involved in a struggle with Russia for control of the Transcaspian, an area, including Georgia, claimed by both countries, and the Persians wanted British support in their struggles. But since the British regarded Napoleon as their main enemy and Russia as one of their main allies against him, they were not prepared to seek Russian assistance against Napoleon in Europe while aiding Persia against Russia in Asia. The Russians might not have appreciated the subtlety of that diplomacy. A Persian alliance was not worth a Russian one. Even after Napoleon went into permanent exile Britain was still unprepared to support Iran against Russia, so that Iran was left to deal with the Russians alone, except for well-intentioned British offers to mediate the conflict.[6]

In 1826, after almost thirty years of intermittent war, Iran's struggle with Russia ended disastrously. Not only did Persia lose the Transcaspian provinces but the Persians also had to sign humiliating treaties that shattered the nation's military alternatives, weakened the government's financial solvency through indemnity, and established preferential trading rights and extra-territorial privileges for Russians that later enabled Russia to insinuate her interests into Iran's political and economic life. The defeats also rebounded to the detriment of Anglo-Iranian relations. They depreciated Iran's value as a British ally and at the same time convinced the British that Iran had become subservient to Russia. The second period of Anglo-Iranian relations grew out of this perception.

In the years after 1826 Russia loomed larger in British security worries over India. Russia's defeat of Iran and steady territorial expansion gave credence to the belief held by many British officials that Russia was the threat to prepare for.[7] But, as with virtually the whole history of British defense thinking, this opinion was not uniformly held, nor could those who held it agree on the best means of countering the Russian menace. The threat remained in the half-light of possibility, caught up in considerations of 'will they, won't they', 'can they, can't they.'

Appropriately enough, the policy that finally emerged has been characterized as 'masterly inactivity', a policy that concentrated on consolidation in India, affected indifference to the neighboring states except to punish troublemakers, and counselled watchfulness of Russia. But two ideas took hold, one being that *if* India were vulnerable to invasion the favored route would be through Herat, in western Afghanistan – the one area that Britain was prepared to defend.

The other idea maintained that the Russians, and because Russia presumably manipulated Iran, the Persians (who had claims to Herat quite apart from Russian incitement), must be kept from the vicinity of Herat as a means of protecting that approach to India.[8] How this was to be done was the subject of the familiar confusion, but between 1830 and 1870 Britain twice used punitive military force against Iran to stop Persian armies, and through them presumably Russia, from seizing Herat. The Persians were thus kept from Herat while the Russians continued to expand elsewhere in Central Asia, leaving Britain still with the problem of how to defend India. After 1870, however, the masterly inactivity school lost support to those favoring a more active policy. Inactivity had seen the Russians advance inexorably nearer to India with the commensurate deepening of British security anxiety. This meant a reconsideration of Indian defense which included a new view of Iran.

In the years of 'masterly inactivity' the predominant opinion, at least in the minds of the Liberal politicians who most favored a static defense, held that the territories and states between India and Russia formed a passive buffer, a safe geographical layer. To the Conservatives, however, this view and the consequent inactivity had been a positive mischief, and as they witnessed Russia's steady, seemingly inexorable growth they chafed to pursue a more active policy. In the years after 1870 their views gained favor both in India and Britain. More definitive plans for Indian defense developed and military authorities and politicians alike began casting about for some spot well beyond India that would be the best point to say to Russia, 'This far and no farther.' This effort was by no means smoothly conducted, but the policy of merely looking at the distant lands beyond India as a buffer began to give way to a policy of making those lands into a buffer. Thus it was that Britain took a more active interest in rehabilitating Iran, of bolstering it with British advice and economic support so that a rejuvenated Iran could occupy a useful role as a buffer for India. Since Britain was not prepared to assume direct responsibility for keeping the Russians out, a search began for some means that would accomplish the goal without expensive or embarrassing commitment. This effort occupied the British, most particularly the Third Marquis, Lord Salisbury, between 1870 and 1890, after which disillusionment set in.

Britain, being a trading nation, sought to improve Persia with various investment projects and the British also thought it only reasonable that Iran should benefit from advice on the needful administrative reforms to strengthen the state.[9] Not surprisingly, the British idea of improving Iran involved making it more like Britain in its economy and administration. Since the need for investment for internal development and an interest in reform coincided with Iranian efforts to rehabilitate their country, great things might have been anticipated. But all too often the foreign investments withered for lack of sufficient soil to nuture them, or the money disappeared into private pockets, or internal resistance and Russian opposition killed them. Many Iranians resented the invasion of foreign capital and the alien control it suggested, and the Russians resented British attempts to improve Persia for fear it would jeopardize Russia's interests. Russia wanted a weak Persia for the same reason Britain wanted a strong one: to facilitate the pursuit of their respective interests. It was an unfortunate position for the Persians, caught between competing

pressures in a situation where British-encouraged efforts at administrative or economic reform only seemed to increase the nation's
difficulties. This is not the place to discuss the permutations of that
stumbling policy in detail, but one example illustrates the point.

In the closing years of the nineteenth and the early years of the
twentieth century, Iran faced a variety of crises (see below, pp. 11-23)
among them a growing need for money. Until the end of the nineteenth century Iran had managed to avoid borrowing money to meet
its needs, but by the turn of the century the Government found itself
desperately short of funds and began to investigate the possibilities
of a foreign loan. The Persians would have preferred to borrow from
sources that did not have vital interest in Iran, i.e., *not* from Britain
and Russia. But both Russia and Britain knew the political advantages
of having Persia indebted to their respective chancellories, realizing
that giving money was another means of enhancing one's own position
while damaging that of the other. As with everything else in Iran in
the nineteenth century, or in Turkey or China for that matter, rivalry
to loan money ensued.[10]

The Persians, denied the recourse of borrowing from a third power
by the opposition of Britain and Russia, would have preferred a
British loan, partly because the Persians wanted to use the British to
counter-balance increasing Russian encroachment on Iran's independence, and partly because a loan from Russia would only increase
its already overbearing influence.

Salisbury, the British Prime Minister who also ran his own Foreign
Office, wanted to loan the money, and the British Minister in Tehran
felt it was essential; but the Treasury, arguing that the Shah really
had the money but would not release it and that the loan would only
incur more Russian activity to counter it, would not countenance
loaning the money or underwriting it even if some other acceptable
source (i.e., the Imperial Bank of Persia, a private British bank in
Iran with important connections in official circles in London) could
be found. The result was that the Russians were left as the only source
of funds for Iran and they were only too willing to supply them. In
1900 and again in 1902 Persia borrowed a total of almost £4 million,
most of which disappeared into private hands or went to finance the
cost of administering the loans, to repay other foreign loans, and to
enable the Shah to travel to Europe. In return, the Russians compelled
the Iranians to repay all outstanding foreign loans and to agree not
to contract any more except with Russia. The Russians also were able

to use the loans as an excuse for taking a more active role in Iran's internal affairs, demanding humiliating guarantees. As a result Russian influence increased at the expense of Iran's independence – developments contrary to British interests or intentions, but to a degree the outcome of British inconsistency or hesitation. These Russian successes and the British inability to agree on a policy that would strengthen Iran, and thereby convert it into an asset in imperial defense, produced the last stage in Anglo-Iranian relations before World War I.

The British in the Penjdeh crisis of the late 1880s had demonstrated that they were prepared to go to war over Afghanistan; but a similar attitude did not extend to Persia, not in the early 1800s and not at the turn of the century. If they had, things might have been simpler, for the Russians would have received their notice, the Persians would have been saved and Britain's security worries appeased – provided, of course, that Britain won. That was the rub. Every ruler from India to Constantinople, the British included, knew that prestige was a vital element in government in the East; without it only trouble would follow, and defeat meant irreparable damage to prestige. An alternative was necessary.

Short of war the British were willing to undertake some commitments to Persia, although these were ambiguous, but Russian pressure was not to be discouraged by Britain's efforts to bolster Iran. This reality brought the British hard up against their problem. The Russians remained a serious menace to India and no policy of using Iran as a buffer worked to hold them off. It remained, therefore, to try to reach some direct agreement with Russia or to continue to fret.

The idea of settling with Russia was not new. A variety of foreign secretaries, including Salisbury and Lord Lansdowne (Foreign Secretary, 1900-1905) had tried it, but the efforts always foundered: the Russians were impervious to British military and naval pressure, or so the British thought; and the British had nothing to offer, and so Russia remained indifferent to the idea. They disavowed any evil designs on India and continued creeping towards the frontier. It took the development of a common interest, a common enemy, and a Russian defeat and revolution to make the climate more favorable to an agreement.[11]

The common interest grew out of the menace from a common enemy, Germany. Germany's unification, vigorous industrial and economic power, and enthusiastic meddling in world politics alarmed most of Europe and went a long way towards promoting European unity — against Germany. The German menace encouraged France and Russia to seek closer ties, France and Britain to reconcile old animosities, and finally Britain and Russia to settle their mutual differences in Asia.[12]

The reconciliation between France and Britain (whereby they settled their differences over the British occupation of Egypt in 1882 with an agreement over Morocco in 1904) gave Britain and Russia (who had concluded an alliance with France in 1891) a mutual friend. But Britain's alliance with Japan, whom Russia considered an enemy, counter-balanced this and promoted bad blood between the two Powers when Russia went to war with Japan over Manchuria. To everyone's surprise, including Japan's ally, the Russians lost. The defeat aggravated Russia's financial difficulties which in turn abetted Russia's dissidents, who made a mildly successful revolution. With a shattered army to rebuild, a failing economy to rehabilitate, and a fractious populace to subdue, the Russian Government was more interested in calling a truce with Britain in Asia, especially with a powerful Germany to the west ready to take advantage of Russia's discomfiture. Thus Britain and Russia were able to find common ground to settle their differences in a convention signed in August, 1907.

The British had great hopes for the Agreement, which encompassed a reconciliation of various Anglo-Russian differences in Asia, particularly in Tibet, Afghanistan and Iran. With the Agreement the British Government believed it had secured the approaches to India, and hoped that the Agreement was a step towards easing Anglo-Russian relations which could be used to contain the greater German threat to British interests. This aspect was an unwritten article in the Convention and explains why Britain was prepared, after 1907, to tolerate increasing Russian violation of the spirit of the Agreement, the unwritten article being more important than the stated purpose.

The Agreement reflected Britain's and Russia's desire and need for a mutual accommodation, and did not include a contribution from the states whose interests were being disposed of; thus Iran, Afghanistan, and Tibet were not consulted. For Iran the Agreement meant division into spheres of influence and tacit British support for Russian activities. Since much of Iranian foreign policy had depended on playing off the interests of these two rivals, the Iranians regarded the Agreement as an unmitigated disaster. International rivalry may have created many of Iran's problems, but the continuance of that rivalry meant Persia had some means to check the demands of one power with those of the other; the Agreement, however, jeopardized the efficacy of that policy and opened up the dangers of partition. Iran suffered the fate of a small, weak state; caught between the interests of powerful rivals, its interests did not matter.

When the Europeans, represented mainly by Britain and Russia, began to arrive in force on the frontiers of Iran at the beginning of the nineteenth century, the Iranians found themselves with a problem – the European powers were stronger and better organized and because of this were better able to insist on their rights and privileges, to expect that things be done their way. It was Iran's misfortune to find its strength diminished by comparison; but weakness was no excuse in international politics in the nineteenth century; diplomacy, then, like nature, abhorred a vacuum. The result of comparative inability meant that Iran could not resist the economic or political encroachments of the British, who were consolidating their position in India, or of the Russians, who were expanding their state from Muscovy. The Persians had to surrender territories and privileges to these two Powers, to submit to an international political and economic system that reinforced their relative weakness, and to endure humiliations that undermined the power and prestige of the state among its own people and with the Europeans.[13]

Iran's decline, as with much of Asia, grew out of features inherent in the country's social, economic and political organization; much of that decline was only by contrast, that is, the arrival of the militarily and technologically superior Europeans converted previously acceptable institutions and methods into liabilities, but this very inability had pernicious results. Many of the problems were also the direct result of European interference in the internal affairs of the state – and a consequence of forcing Iran's pre-modern economic and political system into an international economic and political system based on European imperatives. The accumulation of these influences, internal and external, with the consequent disabilities they encouraged, undermined Iranian morale and affected Iran's ability to conceive and execute reforms.

The Iranians could not directly oppose foreign demands or prevent the Powers from becoming directly involved in Iranian internal affairs, and so diplomatic relations had a different meaning and developed along different lines than would the relations between equals. For the Iranians diplomacy became a domestic issue inextricably bound up with internal problems, with decline and humiliation and the desire for reform. This process was the unintended and perhaps unavoidable result of disparity in power, but the consequences – the habits that grew out of power and weakness – were real, and gave definition to Iranian political life and to Anglo-Iranian relations.

The influence of the two Powers entered Iran on two levels: at an international level, in a normal diplomatic fashion; and directly into internal affairs at the domestic level, when the Powers acquired semi-official interests within the country which they were prepared to protect directly, or when they supported individuals or groups within Iran who they felt would lobby for or protect their respective interests within the political framework. It has been customary to label these latter groups or individual politicians as 'pro-Russian' or 'pro-British', depending on which Power they supported. The British and Russians certainly applied these categories to describe such internal support and expected loyalty from them. And there were Iranians who believed either that their personal survival or that national benefit could only be secured by winning the support of one or the other of the Powers. But more complicated motives also applied.

In the system of personal authority prevalent in Iran, many officials were alert to any means of advancing their own personal influence or status. The injection of Russian and British interests into Iran, supported by the unstated power behind them, was a ready-made source of influence that attracted officials in the central Government, local governors, tribal leaders, and even merchants, to try to tap this vein of power for personal advantage – whether it be for security from arbitrary dismissal, relief from unwanted interference in local affairs, support for local autonomy, or protection from arbitrary exactions.

There were also less cynical or opportunistic reasons for deferring to the Powers. In the first place, since the Powers demanded to be consulted on issues of reform or investment, Persian officials could not ignore them. In the second place, much of Persian diplomacy for maintaining national integrity depended on playing the interests of the two rival Powers off against one another, and Persian diplomats often cultivated an image of favoring one Power only to court favor with the other in order to cancel out unwelcome demands. In addition, some statesmen believed that only by securing firm British support could the nation be saved from Russian pressure and so worked to achieve this by involving Britain in Iran's affairs. The effect of these various motives, however, meant that Anglo-Russian power and rivalry became another element in the internal domestic political equation, often to the detriment of central authority, either because it was unable to discipline internal elements that could appeal to one or other of the Powers for protection or because the Powers had interests to protect at Iranian expense. As a result, Iranian domestic politics became an issue in Anglo-Russian rivalry and that rivalry became an issue in Iranian domestic politics.

FROM THE 1907 AGREEMENT TO THE BEGINNING OF THE WAR

In 1899 George Curzon, then Viceroy of India, summarized British interests in Persia as 'commercial, political, strategical and telegraphic.' Although Curzon had a more enthusiastic interpretation about what needed to be done to uphold these interests than many of his contemporaries, his summary cannot be improved upon. Of these interests only the rather insignificant trade with Persia, amounting to less that £5,000,000 per year (a very rough-and-ready estimate) involved Anglo-Iranian interests directly and exclusively. The others – involving as they did the permutations of Great Power rivalry, questions of imperial defense and the security of imperial communications – went beyond the necessities of purely Anglo-Iranian relations, catching Persia up, willy nilly, in events beyond Persian interest or concern. This situation posed a variety of different but interrelated problems for British and Persian statesmen. For the British, as noted earlier, it meant trying to discover some means of fitting Iran comfortably into a system that ensured peace, stability, security, and trade. For the Persians it meant trying to accommodate and survive the pressures that contact with the British and Europe promoted. Unfortunately the pursuit of their respective needs often proved detrimental or contrary to smooth relations.

The Persians were interested in maintaining their own independence and integrity, in fending off the Russians, and in containing the threat of Turkish aggression. The Persians were not concerned with the worries, imperial or otherwise, that motivated British statesmen except when those affected Iran; in the legitimate pursuit of these interests, however, they often risked annoying the British. The realities of Iranian weakness and Britain's strength complicated this situation further. The Persians were in a double bond – their weakness, to some extent the result of contact with the West, invited the problems that worried the British and that weakness, in turn, meant they could not ignore demands to do something to alleviate British anxiety. The British wanted, if not overt support, at least assurances that Persia was not a threat to British interests. But since many of the threats lay with other European powers or in the minds of the British and were thus beyond Persia's control, the Persians were doomed to fall short of fulfilling Britain's needs and expectations. And the British were always to fall short of finding a way of making the Persians toe the mark or of removing the circumstances that made the effort necessary.

British interests in Iran were manifold. In a century of contact the British had acquired an ongoing commercial, political and strategic stake in the area that could not be easily disregarded. Although Anglo-Iranian commercial interests, that were spread throughout southern Iran, were small by international standards – between five and ten million pounds – the total British interest went beyond mere considerations of the value of trade. British interests owned the Imperial Bank of Persia, which had branches throughout the country. It also enjoyed the exclusive privilege of printing Iran's money, and was an unofficial instrument in British official policy and a source for maintaining British influence by making timely loans to the Persian Government. The British had also loaned money to the Persian Government, secured on the customs receipts of the Persian Gulf ports, that involved Britain in Iran's internal finances thus augmenting British concern for what happened in Iran. The oilfields in Arabistan (modern Khuzistan), which were developed by British capital and were since early 1914 largely owned by the Admiralty, added a further piquancy to British interest. In addition, the British had become involved in local Iranian politics, signing agreements with local tribes or interfering in local politics to secure interests or to uphold British prestige when the Persian Government would not or could not.

The British also regarded the Persian Gulf as a British preserve, Lord Lansdowne announcing this to the world in 1903, an attitude that even extended to the restriction or exclusion of the claims of the littoral states of the Gulf if they appeared to menace British interests. Lord Curzon as Viceroy of India had pushed for a declaration of British interests in the Gulf in 1899 and Lansdowne's pronouncement was the result of his urgings. Although the idea was to exclude political interests of other powers while acknowledging the right to pursue commercial goals, the British authorities on the spot found it difficult to disassociate commercial from political goals when people other than British subjects pursued them. British literature on the Gulf rings with phrases of the sacrifice of British treasure and blood to make the Gulf safe, so much so that it all has a slightly plagiaristic ring.

Underlying all this was the paramount issue, the security of the approaches to India. If for no other reason than that Iran and its environs might have been used as a fulcrum to pry India from Empire, British officials could not ignore the situation there.

Concern for the security of India, of the approaches to India and of the lines of communication with India formed the *basso continuo* of all British interest in Iran, in the Persian Gulf region and in much of the Middle East. The shortest routes to India ran through the Middle East and bordered Iran, one of the major telegraphic cables to India ran through Iran and was owned and operated by a British firm with British telegraphic traffic predominating; and the possibility that an enemy might steal a march on India through Iran with Persian connivance was a nightmare of British officials in the India Office and London. With this in mind British officers of the Indian Army had crisscrossed the country for years gathering intimate details on every conceivable subject. Iran was studied in a detail generally reserved for areas controlled by Britain; in fact, Iran and the Persian Gulf were better studied and their features more minutely catalogued than many areas within the empire – South Africa, Canada, or Australia, for example – the idea being to note routes of march, lines of supply, and geographic and demographic features in order to facilitate strategic planning and deployment in the event of a war that threatened India.

If these concerns were not enough, Iran was also a Muslim country and the British, claiming to govern the largest Muslim population in the world, did not feel they could disregard Muslim interests or the idea of pan-Islam for fear that the empire in India and elsewhere was open to sedition and revolution or an Islamic *jihad*. The accumulation of these features meant there was a considerable investment of British interest, both material and psychological, in Iranian affairs, and while Russian preponderance in the north was recognized the British were prepared to dispute all other encroachments on their interests.

In the seventy or so years after Napoleon's defeat, the British overseas empire had faced few challenges other than Russia in Asia. This freedom in Europe for much of the nineteenth century had allowed the British to become preoccupied with India as the *point d'appui* of imperial defense. But the rise of imperial competitors in France, Germany, and Italy in Europe, the U.S. in the New World and of Japan in Asia complicated the question of defense, a fact painfully demonstrated during the Boer War when it became obvious that imperial resources were limited and that the British Empire was not necessarily well-loved. A debate began in Britain over imperial defense priorities, over efficiency, over the best means of meeting the new threats to empire. New institutions such as the Committee of Imperial Defense developed to coordinate defense plans and the army and navy were reorganized and strengthened. The chief question was where to concentrate the effort, since the empire could not defend every point simultaneously. The rise of Germany and the German insistence on a navy apparently aimed exclusively at Britain seemed to answer that question. Thus, for significant sections of British opinion, Germany became the power, if not the enemy, to organize against. This imperative counselled British efforts to conclude an agreement with Russia and to keep it alive even in the face of Russian encroachment upon British interests. The Foreign Office of Sir Edward Grey and his chief permanent staff advisers believed in this point, and in the Anglo-Russian and Anglo-French ententes, as essential to British imperial defense, and made it a cardinal principle in their international policies, to the detriment of Iran's national independence and integrity.[14]

The Convention, as described previously, aimed at accommodating British and Russian interests in Persia, Afghanistan and Tibet, areas where Anglo-Russian interests had clashed and where future friction remained inherent. The British had long sought some agreement to ease anxiety about Russian advances and in 1907 the Russians favored an agreement to gain time to discipline their dissidents and recuperate from the defeat by Japan; both wanted the agreement because of increasing German competition and the military and naval threat it posed.

The preamble to the Convention is revealing and deserves to be noted in full:

The Governments of Great Britain and Russia have mutually engaged to respect the integrity and independence of Persia, and sincerely desiring the preservation of order throughout that country and its peaceful development, as well as the permanent establishment of equal advantages for the trade and industry of all other nations;

Considering that each of them has, for geographical and economic reasons, a special interest in the maintenance of peace and order in certain provinces of Persia adjoining, or in the neighbouring of, the Russian frontier on the one hand, and the frontiers of Afghanistan and Baluchistan on the other hand; and being desirous of avoiding all cause of conflict between their respective interests in the above-mentioned provinces of Persia; ...

Five articles followed. In Article I, Britain recognized a Russian sphere of influence in Iran's northern provinces and abjured political and commercial interference in that area. In Article II, the Russians recognized a similar British sphere of influence on the Persian-Indian-Baluchistan frontier that represented the minimal defense zone in Persia which the British had finally settled on after years of discussion and doubt on the subject. The remaining articles recognized existing concessions, established the right of each to pursue economic interests in the other's sphere, divided up Persian customs receipts pledged as security on their respective loans to Persia and agreed on the concept of consultation if it became necessary for one or the other of them to take more direct measures to secure the repayment of loans.[15]

The preamble and the accompanying five articles accomplished three things: Britain and Russia recognized Persian integrity; they recognized their mutual interests and right to protect them in areas of special interest; and they agreed to avoid conflicts in their pursuit of their interests. What the preamble did not do was to define 'independence and integrity' or set up a procedure whereby the two Powers could pursue and protect their interests without infringing Persian sovereignty and presumably Persian independence. But any such question was moot, for as Sir Edward Grey, the British Foreign Minister who concluded the agreement, noted in his memoirs years later, 'The real cause of the trouble [in Anglo-Russian, Anglo-Iranian relations], however, was that the independence and integrity of Persia, so tenderly cherished in the Preamble, did not in practice exist when the Agreement was made.'[16] The phrase was little more than a pious sop included to appease Persian sentiments that were, in any event, not consulted when the Agreement was under consideration. Respect for independence and integrity of another country is the normal state of international relations – at least among equals; that Britain and Russia disposed of this in a phrase before moving on to the real issues that concerned them was indicative of the fate of smaller weak nations caught between major rival powers in the international political system of the nineteenth and early twentieth centuries.

The agreement also did not set out a scheme for resolving differences between the two Powers; but the agreement was a self-denying ordinance and a statement of interest and intent, not a definitive program. Making it work was left to circumstances, to be settled as the need arose, and as it turned out a great many needs arose.

Between 1907 and 1914 the Convention underwent strains that nearly destroyed it. The agreement was unpopular with radical circles in Britain that did not like tying Britain to the reactionary Tsar; nor was it popular with an old guard of India-minded, Russian-menaced politicians such as Lord Curzon. These two usually mutually hostile groups were able to join forces over the Russian rapprochement and very nearly brought Grey and his agreement to grief over Russia's high-handed behaviour in Iran. The Russians added to this difficulty by resuming old habits of pursuing their interests in Persia at the expense of British ones, despite the agreement. They treated northern Iran as if it were a Russian province. They expelled or executed Persian dissidents, collected taxes, appointed local officials and kept the Persian government from interfering in its own business; and they harassed or interfered with legitimate British businesses. Grey had to warn the Russians more than once that their insensitivity to Persian feelings and to British interests and the political climate in Britain threatened the convention. But the German mirage meant that Grey's Foreign Office was willing to accept a very loose reading of the agreement, at least so far as northern Iran was concerned, to keep the entente alive.

The German threat, however, was not the sole or necessarily most important motivation behind the Convention. It freed Britain to deal with the Kaiser, but one of its essential features was the restraint it was hoped the Convention would place on Russian threats to areas of British influence and interest. Arthur Nicolson, the Permanent Under-Secretary of State in Grey's Foreign Office and one of the chief architects and defenders of the entente with Russia, consistently argued this point:

The maintenance of our understanding with Russia is of the very greatest importance to us both in Europe and in regard to India and our position generally in the Mid and Far East. Hardinge [the Viceroy] is constantly impressing upon me the urgent necessity of doing nothing which would in any way alienate the Russians from us, and I entirely agree ... She can hit us, if she becomes unfriendly, in localities where we are practically powerless, and she could do us an immensity of mischief without our being able to retaliate or even to defend ourselves ... The understanding with Russia is in reality of far more importance to us than it is to her, *and I am continually haunted with the fear that something may occur which may seriously impair that understanding.* [my emphasis]

This attitude, which was not shared with quite the same sense of hopelessness by Grey, was one of the factors that made Britain a party to the slow dismemberment of Persia.

In addition, the British had gradually come to the idea that there was really no hope of saving Persia from itself − an attitude that was hastened by the fact that the British had vital interests in the area that could not be ignored or left to the feeble Persian Government to defend. In the months before the war the idea of partitioning Persia began to creep into official despatches. In May 1914 Nicolson noted privately to George Buchanan, the British Ambassador to Russia, that:

I think you know my opinion, that is that I really have very little hope of Persia resuscitating herself by her own endeavours ... I am afraid we shall soon have to face the alternative, either of partitioning Persia, or placing every branch of her administration under European control and supervision.

Hardinge echoed these same sentiments in mid-October:

I have never for one instant believed − and nothing has ever arisen for me to modify my opinion − that Persia would be able by herself to establish an orderly government. *There are no men in Persia who are capable of achieving such an end, and I do not think the traditions and habits of centuries can be easily eradicated.* [my emphasis]

What these attitudes reveal is that many important British officials had, although they still dutifully intoned the homilies about respecting Persian independence and integrity, stopped thinking of Persia as an independent nation. Given the nature of international relations of the time and the pressure of circumstances − the need to forestall the Russians and protect vital interests − it is unlikely that the solecism between declaring Persia as independent and acting as if it were not would have survived for long had not the war intervened.[17]

The 1907 agreement merely acknowledged the obvious when it established a Russian sphere in north Persia, for the British had already determined there was nothing they could or would do to alter that fact − 'I had never expected that the Agreement would diminish

Russian activity in the north of Persia,' was Grey's admission. But the British did not surrender their own claims by recognizing Russian ones, and Grey constantly reminded the Russians (if in friendly terms made innocuous by Arthur Nicolson) that Britain had real interests in Persia that could not be ignored. Initially the main interest had been the defense zone in the southeast corner of Iran on the Indian border, but between 1907 and 1914 British interest expanded.

Increasing Russian domination of northern Iran, made strikingly manifest by the occupation of 1911, brought home to the British that Russian pressure southward was not necessarily going to respect the 1907 Convention. The British also appreciated that they had concerns in Iran apart from their rump sphere established by the Convention. The British had always regarded the Persian Gulf as a *mare clausum* and even with an agreement with Russia, they were not prepared to share the Gulf. Russian pressure also reminded Grey that Britain had a variety of economic interests in Iran he was not prepared to sacrifice. The discovery of oil in southern Iran, its development by British interests, and the need to have British-controlled sources of oil added a further concern.[18]

When the British concluded the 1907 Agreement, however, oil did not exist as a major consideration and when it did emerge it meant that a vital British interest was in the neutral zone outside the respective spheres of influence. Both Powers had equal rights to pursue interests in the neutral zone, but increasingly the British felt the area should be exclusively theirs, while Russia's high-handedness in the north and its seeming determination to push its interests and habits southward stiffened British resolve to gain exclusive rights in the neutral zone. By 1914 Grey was convinced that the 1907 Agreement would have to be renegotiated, although the Agreement itself remained fundamental to British interests. The German threat kept the necessity of the entente with Russia green, but a search for a way of accommodating the disparities had grown up in the intervening years.

This reality was a misfortune for Persia. The Agreement did nothing to halt Russia's steady abrasion of Iran's sovereignty while it added Britain's tacit support to it. The British may have regretted the fate of Persia, but the German threat chained them to the entente, a fact many Persians neither forgot nor forgave. The Convention came as a shock to the Persians, both to those who had tradition-ally looked to Britain as a protector against Russia and to those

Westernized intellectuals who regarded Britain as their model for liberal democracy. This shock soon turned to bitterness and alienation as Russian pressure increased and British acquiescence continued; as a result the Iranians began to cast about for new protectors and new models. It is not surprising that Britain's *bête noire*, Germany, should become for many Iranians the new champion of Iranian freedom.

German interests were never great in Persia, apart from limited banking interests, some steamer traffic, a carpet business, and mining concessions in the Gulf. But the German presence in Turkey and the development of the Baghdad Railway suggested a growing interest which, coupled with ability and the energy to make the most of the situation, alarmed Britain and Russia. German activity made the two Powers nervous and suspicious of Germany and of each other. The German menace helped to produce the 1907 Agreement on the one hand, and on the other, it made the two watchful of each other lest one made a deal with the Germans. The Persians, disappointed and embittered with Britain, appreciated the advantage of involving the Germans in local affairs if they could use this to balance the pressure of the two major Powers. The Persians also tried to interest the Americans in their affairs for the same reasons. But the Americans were not interested and the Germans, though interested, did not see enough advantage in Iran, per se, to take the Persian side vigorously. They were willing to exploit local tensions for advantage but this was hardly a policy designed to assist Iran; but the Persians, caught between the interests of the Great Powers, had to indulge in the 'sport', to use the British term at the time, of playing-off conflicting interests as the only game allowed them. In one of the ironies of such situations, it was also the only game designed to aggravate the situation further.

As noted earlier, one result of German pressure was the conclusion of the Anglo-Russian Convention in 1907, an instrument the British hoped would be a comprehensive solution to their problems in the East. It was this agreement and the efforts to keep it alive that governed the tone of international relations in Iran down to 1914. It settled differences with Russia, freed Britain's hands to deal with Germany and gave a semblance of recognition to Persian independence and integrity. To many Persians, however, the agreement between Britain and Russia was a national disaster, linking Iran's erstwhile friend with the country's worst enemy. But the country was prostrate and divided and had to suffer the ignominy of being parcelled into spheres of influence, seen by many as the prelude to partition and absorption into the two neighboring empires.

Between 1911 (the year the Russians occupied the north and forced the proroguing of the Majlis) and 1914, internal conditions deteriorated further. In the north there was a semblance of domestic order but it was imposed by Russian troops or the Russian-officered Cossack Brigade; and many of the government officials were Russian lackeys, especially in Azerbaijan. The Persian Government counted for little in the north, being unable even to send its own appointed governor to Azerbaijan. The situation in the south was, if anything, worse, for there was not even the semblance of order. Years of domestic unruliness, government weakness and regional self-assertiveness had reduced the south to near anarchy. The tribes – the Bakhtiari, the Qashqa'i, the Arabs of Khuzistan under Shaykh Khaz'al and the tribes of Baluchistan – had asserted virtual autonomy; brigands plagued trade and made ridiculous the government's efforts to disperse them. North of Isfahan brigand chiefs were virtually the only authority, and between Shiraz and the Persian Gulf brigand leaders or tribal chiefs little distinguishable from brigands imposed stiff 'tariffs' on commerce, to the annoyance of the British, who in 1909, 1911 and 1913 invoked naval and military measures to try to establish some law and order.

The British did not try to occupy the south as the Russians had the north, but their impatience with the Persian Government's inability to exercise convincing authority in the south caused them to take independent action, as mentioned above, as well as attempts to induce local tribal leaders to respect British, if not Persian Government interests. The British signed agreements with Shaykh Khaz'al of Mohammerah (modern Khorramshahr) and with the Bakhtiari, against the wishes of the Persian Government, that gave British recognition to the virtual autonomy of these groups; and they interfered in the tribal politics of the Qashqa'i, endeavoring to replace Sulat ud-Daula, a trouble-making tribal leader, with a candidate more favorable to British interests. The British undertook these approaches because the Persian Government was too weak to protect their interests; but however expedient the policy was it had unfortunate results for it further weakened the Persian Government in the eyes of its subjects, it embroiled the British in the niceties of Persian internal politics – winning dubious support from one group at the expense of alienating others – and it alienated further the sympathies of many Persians who resented foreign interference in Iran and who were already disillusioned by the Anglo-Russian agreement.

The British and the Persian Government tried to find a way out of this dilemma by establishing a competent police force to restore government authority and law and order. The Persians created a gendarmerie officered by Swedes (it was necessary to employ 'neutrals' because neither the Russians nor the British would accept officers from any of the Great Powers), financed largely by the British, that operated only in the south, since the Russians would not permit the Persian Government to assert its authority in this independent fashion in the north. Between 1912 and 1914 this force made progress towards restoring some of the government's authority, but this was limited and was denied in the areas where Britain had recognized the autonomy of local leaders.

Iran's problems were made worse by the complete lack of any internal political unity. Ever since the 1906 Revolution (a reform-minded movement composed of an unlikely union between westernizing elements, traditional merchants, and conservative religious leaders that removed a particularly bloody-minded monarch), the authority of the monarchy as a unifying force had been in abeyance, but no new mutually acceptable principle had replaced it. The various forces that made the Revolution of 1906 and defended it in 1909 had been united only in their opposition to the shah and arbitrary government; once he had been permanently dismissed that unity disappeared. The religious authorities, the old-style politicians, tribal leaders, and the more westernized elite, always a very small group, vied for power; while the majority of the population, who understood little of constitutional principles, struggled to survive.

The struggle for power meant that the government itself was hopelessly divided into mutually hostile and competitive groups, all of whom claimed the right to power, denied that anyone else had solutions to the problems, and who refused to compromise; a situation complicated even further by long-term political animosities, the consequences of a patronage-based political system, a conservative bureaucracy, financial insolvency, social unrest, foreign pressure and regionalism. It was little wonder that the Persian Government had trouble enforcing its will.

In 1911 Russian troops occupied northern Iran to force the Persians to dismiss Morgan Shuster, an American financial adviser who had not paid due deference to Russian sensibilities. This event only aggravated the situation further, for not only did the Russians occupy the north, but there was a further decline in the vestiges of national consensus. The circumstances of the Russian invasion forced the Persian Government to prorogue the Majlis and keep it closed. The Persian Government also had to recognize the validity of the Anglo-Russian Convention, something they had steadfastly refused to do, and to agree to consult the two Powers before appointing any more foreign advisers. However necessary, these measures drove significant portions of the politically aware and educated population into opposition. The Government fell heir to the view held of the monarchy – that it was a tool of foreign interests. Persian politicians in power had to work with the British and Russians, but they received little domestic understanding for this, and a division grew up within Persian politics in which anti-government and anti-foreign activity were often synonymous.

Along with these social and political divisions Iran lacked economic cohesiveness as well. The pattern of trade in the north, oriented as it was towards Russia, and in the south flowing towards Britain and India, plus the primitive state of inter-regional communication meant that the country had been drifting, economically speaking, into separate units for some time. When declining government authority, increasing foreign pressure and inherent regional biases joined with this, powerful centrifugal forces were unleashed within the country. Problems linked up and compounded at an ever increasing rate so that by 1914 Iran presented an image of imminent collapse.

The outbreak of World War I brought all these disparate features into bold relief, and into new perspective. It legitimized the Anglo-Russian entente, and it threatened to increase the pace of Iran's disintegration. At the same time, however, it opened up the possibility of great changes. War by its very uncertainty entertains the most extravagant hopes, the First World War in the Middle East and Persia being no exception. The British hoped to be released from their security worries, the Russians to preserve all the gains bought by sacrifice and suffering, the Turks and Persians to recover a true measure of their independence and integrity, and the Germans to win their place in the sun. Unfortunately for their respective hopes many of the goals were mutually exclusive, bought only at someone else's expense and lost to some else's gain. This fact made the war in the Middle East and elsewhere a spectacle of malice and cruelty, of self-aggrandisement and betrayal. It meant that Anglo-Iranian relations themselves remained a confusion of conflicting motives that denied satisfaction to everyone.

CHAPTER TWO

THE CRISIS OF WAR
AND NEUTRALITY
AUGUST, 1914 – JANUARY, 1915

> Anyone who has taken an important part in public
> affairs, looking backward after it is over, may be
> annoyed to see how far the results of what he did
> differ from what he intended them to be. He may
> well feel ... that he has been but an instrument for
> purposes of which he did not think ... and which
> are beyond his power to comprehend or fathom.
>
> Sir Edward Grey

Britain's position in Iran in August, 1914 was fairly straightforward
and British statesmen hoped that it would remain so, and that the
whole area would recline in inconsequence while the resources of
empire were marshalled to defeat Germany in Europe. This turned
out to be a wistful hope, for rivalries and hostilities, conflicting
interests and Iranian political collapse were intensified by the opportunities and uncertainties of war.

The Ottoman Empire's entrance into the war on the side of
Germany in later October, 1914 precipitated a major crisis for the
Allies. With the shelling of Russian Black Sea ports by the Turkish
navy (led by the fugitive German cruisers the *Goeben* and the *Braslau*,
renamed the *Yuvuz Sultan Selim* and the *Midilli* and therefore at least
Turkish in name) the European war spread beyond Europe.[1] Britain
had hoped to confine the war. Much of British pre-war strategic
thinking, the reorganization of the army, the redistribution of the fleet
had been conceived for a European conflict; but the Turks spoiled
the neatness of these dispositions; and the Germans, who had encouraged the Turks, were determined to strike at their enemies – to
make them bleed, as the Kaiser put it – where they might. Turkey
allied with the Central Powers made this possible, for Ottoman

territory bordered on Iran and the Persian Gulf, and in theory at least many of Britain's strategic interests were under Turkish suzerainty – Egypt, the Suez Canal, and the short routes to India through Mesopotamia. The Ottomans disposed a large, if uncertain army, and claimed to be the leader of the Muslim world, a claim accepted by many Muslims even in India. Thus the spectre of a *jihad*, a holy war, loomed, and the potential for an Islamic revolt in Egypt, Iran, Afghanistan and India could not be dismissed. The British had realized this danger even before Turkey entered the war, and although they remained committed to winning in Europe, they could not ignore the threat to their interests in the Middle East or Iran.[2]

Given the general nature of the disorder in Iran, it is doubtful whether any one of the interested parties could have achieved their goals without significant material force and military occupation. Only the Turks and the Russians had even the theoretical potential to do so, and the conditions of the war soon put it beyond their means. But each of the parties had the ability to keep the others from getting what they wanted and so conditions remained beyond control and confusion predominated.

THE NATURE OF THE PROBLEM IN IRAN

The main elements in this confusion were the competing goals of the British, the Russians, the Germans, the Turks, the Persian Government, and an assortment of Persian nationalists, tribes and opportunists. In some cases two or more interests would ally, but even then competition and caution were the dominate themes. This was particularly true for cooperative efforts between the Germans, Turks and Persian nationalists, among whom mutual hostility and petty infighting made a mockery of any unified purpose. The British and the Russians also had problems, as they had before the war, and continued to keep a jealous vigil on each other's intentions and their own respective interests. Within British official circles, as well, there was considerable squabbling and indecision, which, along with the vagaries of circumstance, cast a chill on any chance of consistency.

Under normal conditions before the war, British policy towards Iran passed under the scrutiny of officials in the Foreign Office, the Government of India, local representatives of both of these, the India Office, and if it required any expenditure, the Treasury. Even before the conclusion of the 1907 Agreement, Russian sentiments could not be ignored and occasionally Persian opinion had to be consulted.

The war changed none of this, except to add a sense of urgency to the process, as well as the necessity of consulting an array of military authorities in India, in Britain, and in Russia, as well as the ex-cathedra opinions of Lord Curzon, the pre-eminent Persian expert who at the beginning of the war was sitting in Parliament, and on occasion the mediation of the Cabinet to sort through the muddle generated by a cumbersome process of consultation. No consideration of Persian policy during the war escaped this process of criticism and struggle. Unfortunately during the war events often moved faster than the deliberations, and British policy in Iran was never able to bridge the gap between the development of problems and the implementation of remedies. What strikes one about the British Foreign Office before the war was its virtual independence in conducting foreign affairs. Before the reforms of the early twentieth century, direction of foreign affairs was largely left to the discretion of the Foreign Secretary, who consulted his country's best interests, public opinion, and his party's ideals. This latitude was somewhat reduced after Salisbury's departure, but even under Lord Lansdowne and Sir Edward Grey the consultative process that developed between the Foreign Secretary and his permanent officials was a 'family' affair and other members of the government outside the Foreign Office tended to respect this independence. Even Parliament and public opinion generally left the Foreign Office to conduct foreign affairs as it saw fit. In the East, however, a slightly different situation prevailed.

The presence of the empire in India and the existence of the Government of India, although a dependency of Britain, meant that British officials in India had their own interests to pursue, and the Government there conducted its own foreign policy, a fact that was largely respected in Britain. But after the Boer War and the realization that the empire needed a coordinated international policy, this independence declined as officials in Britain, in the Foreign Office and the India Office tamed it – a process hastened, perhaps, by the obstreperousness of the Curzon viceroyalty. The opinions of the Government of India became increasingly inert in the formation of overall imperial policy, but Indian Government opinion on events in areas bordering India could not be ignored. Iran fell within this purview and since the beginning of the Anglo-Iranian contact had occupied a sort of never-never land of divided responsibility in British eyes. In the late nineteenth century, however, a compromise was reached whereby authority was divided, with the Government of India appointing the Persian Gulf Resident (a political officer and overseer of British interests in the Gulf at Bushire) and half the consular establishment, while the Foreign Office appointed the minister at Tehran and conducted formal relations with the Persian Government. But even then a process of consultation, sometimes quite arduous, preceded every approach or consideration of policy. This process did not change with the diminution of Indian influence after 1900. On the contrary there was a brief revival of this influence at the beginning of the war which lasted until the disasters in Mesopotamia in 1916, where the Indian-run campaign faltered ignominiously at Kut al-Amara. Until this event, however, India had significant input into the formation of British wartime policy towards Iran and the Middle East, adding the weighty but often slow-developing opinion of the Viceroy and his establishment to the process of deliberation.[3]

The Foreign Office of Sir Edward Grey accepted this necessity but often with impatience and ill-humor, and a considerable interdepartmental struggle for influence between Foreign Office representatives and agents of the Government of India developed over policy formation for Iran, which had the effect of reducing the Foreign Office's independence. In addition, Grey believed that during the war foreign policy had to be sublimated to military requirements, a fact that tended to compromise the independence of the Foreign Office further and added a certain limpness to diplomacy. The erosion of Foreign Office independence continued throughout the war as it was invaded by Cabinet committees, the personal diplomacy of Lloyd George, and a host of military and political officials who took it upon themselves to express opinions. Foreign Office officials resisted this as much as possible and considerable interdepartmental rivalry developed over struggles to delimit authority. These demarcation disputes, plus the necessity of consulting a wide range of opinions, introduced a further degree of clumsiness into the execution of foreign policy which plagued Anglo-Iranian relations. After these intramurals, Russian opinion had to be consulted, which could and often did start the whole process of consultation all over again. Parenthetically, the Persians were occasionally consulted and their inconsistency could add significant delay or confusion. Quite often, once a policy was fortunate enough to escape this diplomatic mêlée, the conditions it was designed to meet had either disappeared or altered so as to make the policy redundant, and the whole process would have to be repeated — with similar results.

Furthermore, Grey's failing health and Arthur Nicolson's dislike of the Foreign Office, and the demands of work during the war retarded the development of policy towards Iran. The war placed heavy demands on the time and energies of the small permanent staff of the Foreign Office, and they resented the time taken from more pressing matters, and the frustration of having to deal with Persia, a country the Foreign Office considered to be a dilapidated Oriental monarchy staffed by vacillating incompetents, dilatory fools and mendacious schemers whose only aim was self-aggrandizement. Nor was the Foreign Office's understanding of events in Iran during the war helped by the fact that its representative there was not consistent in his opinions, or by the fact that Eyre Crowe, one of the most astute and informed members of the permanent staff was 'exiled' to obscurity in the commerce section until 1917 because he could not get along with his superiors. In combination these features freighted the development of policy towards Iran with considerable excess baggage, slowing the decision-making process.[4]

Had circumstances allowed, such a deliberate diplomacy might have suited, but a number of further factors made the process even more awkward. Chief among these was the incompetence of the Persian Government. Years of financial difficulties, political unrest and foreign encroachment had robbed Persian central authority of most of its vigor and authority. Whole provinces existed in virtual autonomy, and the Government could not even claim the loyalty of its own limited armed force. The Persian Cossack Brigade, reputedly the best equipped force, was small and officered by Russians, who were not encumbered with an excess of loyalty to the Persian Government. The Swedish-officered, British-financed gendarmes were only newly organized and of doubtful efficiency. And the Persian regular army, under-supplied, over-officered and untrained, had been the subject of rude jokes for fifty years. In addition, significant elements of the politically astute population regarded the Government as little more than a pawn of Britain and Russia, so that resistance to foreign encroachment was closely allied if not synonymous with opposition to the Government.

The political factionalism of the revolutionary period did not subside in the period between the proroguing of the Majlis in 1911 and the war, although it was subdued, and in mid-1914 it broke out afresh. Even as the Europeans stumbled into war, elections for a new Majlis liberated all the pent-up emotions and frustrations festering since 1911. The avowedly nationalistic, anti-Russian Democrats secured a majority of support in this Third Majlis and in coalition with many of the Moderates, who shared their ideas, they were in a position to influence strongly if not control the Government. The main goal of this coalition was the removal of all foreign influences from Iran and the clear establishment of Iran's independence. In their eyes the Russians were the main offenders, but the British shared the opprobrium by signing the 1907 Agreement and by allying themselves with Russia. The coalition's political objective was to evict both Britain and Russia; but given Iran's internal disunity and lack of substantial force they had little hope of success. The war, however, presented them with an apparent opportunity to secure the assistance necessary to realize their goal.

It had long been an object of Iranian diplomacy to enlist the aid of some third power in Iranian affairs as a means to counter-balance Russian pressure. Britain had proved a poor choice and so the Persians had sought to involve the French, the Germans, and the Americans, with no notable success. Iran was too unimportant to these other powers. However, the war made Iran more interesting to Germany. Although the Germans did not suffer a conversion to Persia's cause, they did suddenly discover a usefulness in Iranian hatred of Russia. The Persians, for their part, did not suddenly become pro-German, but they became interested in a German victory in so far as it would hurt Russia and Britain and promote Iran's independence. The war sponsored a marriage of convenience between Persian nationalists and the Germans.

The Persian Government, many of whose members shared the desire to rid Iran of foreign influence, were, however, not as free to act on these sentiments. The Government had to face hard facts: Russian troops in the northern provinces within easy reach of Tehran; lack of a reliable military force; British troops in India and the Persian Gulf; lack of internal unity; lack of any German force to counter the Russians and the British; and the unproven ability of Ottoman forces joined to a healthy Persian suspicion of Ottoman motives. If the Persian Government were going to declare for the Central Powers they wanted something more tangible than diffuse expression of sympathetic affection and support.

The Persian Government tried to avoid involvement, perhaps like the Italians playing for time to see which way things were going, by declaring its neutrality when it became obvious that the Ottomans were joining the conflict. But this neutrality was compromised from the beginning. First, Russian troops occupied northwestern Iran, presenting a threat to Turkey by menacing invasion along the relatively easier route from Iran rather than through the mountains of the Russian Caucasus. The Russians denied they posed any threat to Turkey, raising the somewhat tactless argument that since they had been in Iran since 1911 they were not violating Persian neutrality, but the Turks were not reassured. Second, the Turks themselves were not overly solicitous of Persian sentiments nor could they afford to ignore the presence of Russian troops in Azerbaijan. Third, the Germans were not disposed to take Persian neutrality seriously. They were out to bag Persia and regarded the declaration of neutrality as a quaint homily, and they were abetted in this view by the activities of Persian nationalists. Nor were the British prepared simply to stand by and let their many interests be jeopardized. The whole affair was made more confusing by the fact that the Persian Government's sympathies were equivocal at best, and they lacked the necessary internal authority to see that neutrality was observed. Individual Persians, political factions, and tribal groups were at liberty to pursue their own interests, which they did with a particular zest, while the other forces concerned – the Allies, the Central Powers, etc. – tunnelled past the insignificant obstruction raised by Persian neutrality. As a result, by early 1915 Turkish forces were in Azerbaijan (at one point occupying Tabriz), Russian forces were operating throughout the north, small numbers of British troops were occupying areas along the Gulf, German agents were busy recruiting support in Iran to challenge the Allies, Persian nationalists were busy coordinating anti-Allied activities, the Swedish officers and most of the gendarmes defected to the Germans and nationalists, and a host of petty officials and tribal leaders were trying to figure out the best means of making the situation pay. It was a state of affairs that satisfied no one, and in trying to rectify it the various competing interests only succeeded in making matters worse.

Much of the complexity of the situation in Iran stemmed from the erosion of Iranian independence and the parallel decline in government authority, with a corollary increase in foreign interference and regional autonomy. To understand the political-diplomatic situation it is perhaps best temporarily to suspend consideration of Iran as a nation at all. It had geographical extent, as delineated by Western political necessities and boundary commissions, and there was a degree of cultural identity, but after that there was little cohesion. The Persian Government could claim to represent the country but could not pretend to govern it, and within the government political in-fighting for personal advantage still predominated over a spirit of compromise or institutional loyalty. The Majlis was largely a consultative body appended to the governmental system rather than an integral element, but it was a focal point in the political process for internal dissension and rivalry, both between factions in the Majlis and between the interests of the Majlis as a body and the Government — the bureaucracy and the cabinet.

These latter two groups were by no means free of rivalry either. The bureaucracy was encumbered with sinecures and place-servers who jealously protected their interests, while the cabinet itself was largely the battle ground for power struggles within a small coterie of public men. The other major component of the Iranian political scene, the monarchy, was at the start of the war a much reduced factor. Since 1909 a minor had occupied the throne under a Regency. The young ruler, Ahmad Shah, did not reach his majority until 1914 and his coronation in July, 1914 coincided with the European crisis.[5] The revolution and civil war, plus the youth of the shah, had significantly diminished the power of the monarchy to govern, but did not eliminate the monarch as a focal point of influence-peddling and political rivalry. Thus none of the institutions of government were free of strife or were able to govern effectively, and mutual hostility and place-serving remained the predominant atmosphere, a feature replicated throughout the country as tribal leaders and local officials competed for influence and jealously husbanded their positions.

In this atmosphere international relations took on peculiar qualities. The weakness of the Government and the lack of an effective army had allowed or invited the insinuation of British and Russian interests directly into the national life, by-passing the normal channels of diplomacy. A duality developed as a result: on the one hand, the Powers dealt with the Persian Government as the political representative of an independent nation; on the other, they recognized that the Persian Government was a negligible factor and so they conducted their own affairs in Iran as if they themselves had a patent for government, making deals with Iranians without reference to the Persian Government and supervising their interests with troops if necessary. In this fashion the interests of the Powers became caught up in the domestic political confusion.

EARLY DEVELOPMENT OF BRITISH POLICY IN IRAN

British wartime policy towards the Middle East in general and Iran in particular was slow to develop, subject to fits and starts and until 1917 not subject to anything approaching an overall conception, other than the determination to defend the empire and defeat the Germans. Since the British were committed to fighting in Europe, policy in the Middle East and Persia fell under the shadow of the European conflict, but Britain had too many interests and too long an involvement simply to ignore the Middle East. The British problem was lack of general agreement on just how important the Middle East was, how much should be done to protect the position there, and how it would be accomplished. Nothing illustrates this better than the haphazard development of the campaign in Mesopotamia or the attempts to control the situation in Iran.

On August 18, as the armies in Europe moved into position, Lord Crewe, the Secretary of State for India, asked the Viceroy, Lord Hardinge of Penhurst, to consider plans for securing British life and property in the Persian Gulf should the Turks join the Germans. No one at this point was sure that the Turks intended to join either side and Louis Mallet, the British ambassador in Constantinople, was optimistic about keeping the Turks neutral; but neither did anyone want to abandon British interests. Had Mallet or any other British official known that the Turks had already signed a defensive alliance with the Germans they might have been less sanguine, but no one knew, and no one wanted to take precipitous action that might drive the Ottomans into the German embrace. Thus, military displays were kept to a minimum (further necessitated by the demands for concentration in Europe), Turkish territory was scrupulously respected, and the diplomats worked to keep the Turks at peace. No similar solicitude, however, manifested itself in Britain's relations with Iran. The Ottomans at least had an army and a navy, if of uncertain value, and as titular leaders of the Sunni Muslim world were in a position, theoretically, to claim the loyalty of even the Muslims in India, not to mention Egypt, which was still nominally a part of the Ottoman Empire. The Persians, by contrast, were Shi'ites and therefore apart from the majority of Muslims, and they had no army and no navy – although there was an admiral – and the writ of the Persian Government hardly reached the city limits of Tehran. Thus while the British took care not to antagonize the Turks, a similar attitude did not extend to the Persians.[6]

This difference in attitude toward Turkey and Iran had been true of the decade before the war as well. On two occasions, in 1906 and 1910, the British had contemplated using force against the Ottomans to protect British interests and prestige in the Gulf, but careful consideration had ruled this out. The British did not want to precipitate a dismemberment of the Ottoman Empire and they feared a war against the Turk would aggravate Muslim opinion in India. But a slightly different attitude prevailed in relations with Iran, where the British had not stopped short of armed intervention in 1909, 1911, and 1913. The sundry punitive expedition against domestic brigands was not intended as anything other than an expedient use of force in the absence of Iranian governmental authority, but it signified an important feature of the political situation in the Middle East − the Ottomans were still taken seriously while the Persians were fast becoming a nonentity, no longer a government and a nation but a situation.

Thus, while the British took pains to avoid violating Turkish territory, in early August the Government of India (hereafter referred to as 'India') despatched a warship and one hundred sepoys to Abadan in South Persia, where the oil refinery of the Anglo-Persian Oil Company (A.P.O.C.) was located; and later, in October, when a more extensive military force was moved into the Gulf as relations with the Porte deteriorated, a force landed at Bahrein, close to Mesopotamia rather than in Persia where it was first considered sending them, only because the British were still hoping to avoid pushing the Ottomans over the brink. A few weeks later when war came and the British landed troops in Mesopotamia, elements of this force moved into Persian territory to protect the oil fields and the pipelines without reference to Persian wishes. The only real concern expressed by India or London was that they did not want to appear to be violating Persian neutrality.[7]

In British calculations about what to do in the event of war with the Turks, an assortment of Arab leaders received more serious attention than the Persian Government. In the years before the war the British had made treaties with Arab leaders in most of the Gulf states, including Shaykh Khaz'al of Mohammerah (modern Khorramshahr) in southwestern Iran where the oilfields lay, and maintained contact with others. Well before war became a certainty, plans were mooted for inciting the Arabs against the Turks if they should join the Germans. But even after the war began in earnest, no similar idea developed for securing Persian support. In fact in early September the Foreign Office rejected a Russian proposal to bribe the Persians with Najaf and Karbala, religious sites in Iraq sacred to Shi'ites. The Russians were aware of anti-Allied sentiments in Iran and they thought to reverse this by showing generosity to the Persians – with Ottoman territory. The Foreign Office rejected the scheme because of plans to mobilize Arab support and it was felt that concessions to Shi'ites might offend Sunni sentiments.

There was also another telling objection to the Russian idea, one that, understandably, was not mentioned to the Russians. When the Russians first made their suggestions, Sir Edward Grey had solicited the opinions of various officials, among them his trusted friend Charles Hardinge, the Viceroy of India. On September 9, Hardinge sent an interesting reply to Grey denigrating the Russian proposal. The Viceroy did not think Britain should be generous in giving away Ottoman territory not because the Turks were still neutral, but because in the event of war he foresaw Britain retaining that part of Mesopotamia south of Baghdad, and he did not want to see an inconvenient Persian enclave west of the Tigris, for two very good reasons.

First, such a gesture as Russia had in mind would offend Sunnis, who after all were the majority sect in Islam; and second, because 'in the event of ultimate partition of Persia Russia might conceivably claim that enclave should appertain to [the] Russian sphere.' And no one wanted that. Not only is this one of the earliest mentions of a British sphere in Mesopotamia, anticipating the war by two months, it also exposes a curious aspect of Britain's alliance with Russia. Although Hardinge was somewhat ahead of his contemporaries in seeing a British presence in Mesopotamia (no formal declaration of British intentions there being made until 1917), the tenor of competition with Russia suggested by the Viceroy's remarks, despite the recognized necessity of the alliance with Russia, was by no means an isolated sentiment.[8] And though the British and the Russians, along with France, agreed in September 1914 that there would be no annexations until after the war, each power kept an eye on those areas it intended to keep or keep the other out of. To paraphrase the Zionist attitude towards cooperation with Britain against Germany in World War II – the British were prepared to fight the Germans with Russia as an ally as if there were no empire, and to keep an eye on their imperial interests against the Russians as if there were no war.

An anomolous position, but the ability of governments to be true to contradictions is expansive and perhaps explains why the British were able without too much blushing to make so many conflicting promises during the war.

The Viceroy's telegram also contained a neat summation of the role that Persia was expected to play. Hardinge felt that it was in Persia's best interest to remain friendly. 'We are,' wrote Hardinge,

... of [the] opinion that as far as we are concerned her [Persia's] own interests should keep her neutral and that nothing further is called for to that end than the exertion and influence of H. M. Minister and renewed assurance that our steadfast policy will be to preserve her integrity and actively support her administration in the South.

If, however, Persia were foolish enough to overlook this view, Hardinge did not expect too serious repercussions. He expected that the inland missions might suffer, but 'we should at once occupy Gulf ports and close one of her chief sources of revenue and it does not appear that she could add seriously to our difficulties.' Since this was the traditional way of dealing with Persia and it had worked well before, Hardinge felt that no real effort needed to be wasted on Persia itself, a view shared by the Foreign Office, where it was decided to let the Russian suggestion die a natural death, to let the matter 'sleep'.[9] Six weeks later the Turks entered the war and the picture changed.

The British had long sought to avoid a war with the Ottomans because as rulers of a large Muslim population themselves they did not want to be placed in the invidious position of making war on the paramount Islamic state. When the Ottomans forced the issue, though, officials in India and at the Foreign Office had to deal with its moral effect on Britain's Muslim subjects, and so it became important to ensure that the Ottoman case was isolated, to avoid an Islamic domino effect. Missions to the Arabs were one approach for diffusing the threat of *jihad*; another was to ensure the neutrality of Persia. But there was considerable difficulty in deciding how this latter objective might be achieved.

Part of this problem stemmed from the alliance with the Russians, who had to be consulted and their position considered, if for no other reason than because the Russians would have to supply the main Allied military force against the Turks, and because growing numbers of Russian troops occupied northern Iran, compromising Iran's neutrality at the outset. No one seriously believed that the Persians could restore authority in Azerbaijan and the Russians were not in any rush to find out, being in a position in Azerbaijan analogous to that of the British in Egypt, but without the same qualms of conscience. When the Persians renewed suggestions in late September 1914 that the Russians should evacuate Azerbaijan (bolstering their case with the argument that the danger of war between the Turks and Russians would threaten Iran if the Russians remained, but that if Persian sovereignty were restored the danger would cease) they were politely but firmly informed by the Allies that Russian troops in Iran were defensive in character and no menace to the Turks, that they had been there since 1911 protecting Russian interests and were, therefore, not violating Persian neutrality, and that if war came the Turks could not be trusted to stay out of Iran and therefore the Russian troops were necessary to preclude a Turkish invasion. The answer did not satisfy the Persians and presumably did not reassure the Turks.

This was another feature that made it difficult for the Allies to secure Persian neutrality. The Persians wanted the Russians out and the Russians would not leave; the Persians hated the Russians and their ally and only evacuation might have eased this, but evacuation was the one thing the Russians were not prepared to do. Short of that it was difficult to devise a means of appeasing the Persians. The problem was complicated further because the Russians and the British could not quite coordinate their ideas on what to do. The Russian offer of August had fallen on dead soil, but that was before Ottoman participation was clear. In November the British were more interested in winning a favorable attitude in Persia, or at least not being seen to violate Persian neutrality first. The Russians accepted the necessity but this agreement on principle did not produce a substantive approach.

The Foreign Office may have realized that some change in dealing with Persia was necessary, but they were not prepared to be hustled into a line of policy, least of all a Russian one. They were prepared to cooperate with the Russians, not to submit to them. Yet no one had exactly made up his mind just what to do. This deliberate diplomacy was in contrast to the effervescence of Russian diplomacy. The British were to be embarrassed more than once by Russian fickleness — one minute all vigor, the next complete torpor; at one time conciliatory and cooperative, at another hostile and moody. Bismarck had said Russia 'was more an elemental force than a government, more a mastadon than a diplomatic entity, and she must be treated like bad weather until things were different.' More than one British official would have reason to comprehend this opinion during the course of the war. But the cumbersomeness and caution of British policy making was little better.

But it was difficult to know what to do in Persia, and in the opening months of the war, when everyone believed that it would be a short, sharp affair, there was no reason to be concerned, or to undertake new initiatives or ponder changes in policy; for that matter, even well into the war, the Foreign Office did not see the necessity for any major departures in the pattern of relations with Iran, except to increase British influence. The main objectives in August, 1914 were to shelve any problems with Russia until after the war so that the alliance could proceed harmoniously with the defeat of Germany; and to husband local interests, insulating them from European reverberations.

As noted earlier, the Foreign Office would have preferred not to concern itself over events in Iran. This had been true before the war, and became more pronounced during the war. The pressure of work falling on the small, though professional, band of men who made the Foreign Office work, had grown steadily, as had the problems, before the war; and the various departments had been hard put to deal adequately with the volume of work. The war added immeasurably to that volume, and it structured the minds of the men in the Foreign Office to see the world with clearer priorities. Germany and winning the war in Europe became the prime concern, and the overworked men at the FO wanted to concentrate on that enterprise. They resented distractions. Persia was one of the distractions and what attention was spared for Iran was grudging.

Grey, who had little reason to love Iran since it had provoked endless complications with Russia and had almost cost him his job in 1911, barely mentions the place in his memoirs during the war years. Indeed, Grey's comments are rare in the despatches after 1914; Arthur Nicolson, George Clerk, head of the Eastern Department, Lancelot Oliphant, a senior clerk, and a variety of junior clerks being the most prominent writers of minutes in the first years of the war. And throughout the despatches a tone of asperity and impatience predominates.

In the early months of the war, when it still seemed as if it could be confined to Europe, Persia received little attention, but between

September, 1914 and January, 1915, the picture underwent a gradual change. The main cause of that change, of course, was the increasing likelihood that the Ottomans would not remain neutral.

The immediate problem for Grey's Foreign Office in that event was how to keep Persia neutral and thus minimize the propaganda effect on Muslims if the Turks joined the Germans. As with most British initiatives in Persia, the main concern dealt not with Persia, but with larger issues that might affect Britain's position in the region. At the same time, the Foreign Office did not want to embark on innovations during the war that might give Russia greater influence in the region, or place constraints on possible British interests after the war. Thus, there was very little maneuvering room in Britain's thinking on Persia. These limitations were illustrated in early September when the Russians broached the subject of giving Persia territory in Mesopotamia as a means of winning its benevolent neutrality. The Foreign Office and India banished that idea quickly, and in early September there seemed no real need to make any serious effort in Persia, the opinion being that it was in Iran's best interests, as viewed from London and Simla, to remain neutral and pro-Allies. Instead of offering something directly to the Persians, Grey decided it would be more beneficial if the Russians could make conciliatory noises to placate sentiments in Persia. This had the advantage of costing nothing. But the Russians were not overly cooperative.

The main issue disturbing Russo-Persian relations was the presence of Russian forces in northern Persia. When war broke out in Europe, the Persians stepped up their efforts to persuade the British and the Russians that Russian troops in Persia increased the risks of a clash with the Turks; the Persian Government of Mustaufi ul-Mamalik also worked to convince the Porte that Russian troops in Persia posed no threat to the Ottomans. Throughout September and October, Ala as-Saltana, the Minister for Foreign Affairs, a long-time political figure whose advanced age raised Allied doubts about his abilities, made repeated efforts to establish Persian neutrality as a believable reality. But as long as Russian troops remained in Azerbaijan, a province bordering Turkey which offered an easier invasion route than from the more mountainous Russian Transcaucasus, the Foreign Minister had little hope of reassuring the Porte, even if the Turks had been prepared to listen. Nor were the Russians willing to end their occupation. They had ignored Persian protests since 1911, and now that a confrontation with the Ottomans seemed likely, they felt even less inclined to withdraw. They rejected a Persian suggestion that the Persian Crown Prince go to Azerbaijan to raise a local force of 20,000 to protect the province, and they then reinforced their own presence in the province; and, to add insult to injury, began to raise a Persian force under their own auspices.[10] In addition, local Russian agents began threatening enemy nationals – Germans and Austrians – in the province, encouraging them to leave – actions that indicated that the Russians regarded themselves as the legitimate governors of Azerbaijan.[11]

At the same time, the Turks began encouraging Kurdish tribes in the eastern portion of the empire to make raids on Persian villages (usually Christian and under Russian protection) and isolated Russian detachments. The Turks also had begun to mobilize their army in August and to reinforce their forces in the provinces bordering Russia and Iran; actions the Russians and Persians regarded as ominous.[12]

Realizing that war was likely and that Azerbaijan would suffer, Mustafi ul-Mamalik and Ala as-Saltana tried to convince Sir Walter Townley, the British minister, that the Persians should be left to defend Azerbaijan on their own, a project they felt would alleviate the dangers of war. But Townley, though sympathetic, could not alter his own government's determination to support the Russian ally, nor could his government, had it been amenable, have done much to change Russian policy. Nor did Persia have anything to offer that would have made their proposals worth considering; the Russians were not about to surrender control over Azerbaijan to any hastily organized, dilapidated force the Persians could muster.[13]

Grey tended to agree. Past experience had convinced him that little could be done for or expected of Persia. He therefore felt that since there could be no changes in Anglo-Russian interests, the best course was to create a conciliatory climate, diffusing Persian hostility by getting the Russians to act with restraint, whatever that meant, since the Russians were not prepared to give up anything. Indeed, by early October, Sazanov was taking an even harder line. He was annoyed at the Persian Government's repeated representations over Azerbaijan. He rightly felt that these efforts were inspired by anti-Russian sentiments, but he went even further, believing that the Persian Government was acting as a Turkish agent in the matter rather than from a desire to see their country free of foreign troops. In either case, Sazanov was not prepared to tolerate Persian interference. He was convinced that fighting was unavoidable in Azerbaijan and that the

Persians were completely incapable of self-defense, and more importantly, of safeguarding Russian interests. He forcefully emphasized to George Buchanan, Britain's ambassador to Russia, that Persia was a liability, and spoke of the 'uselessness of pretending any longer to regard her as a Sovereign Power.' This was a far cry from the September offer of Ottoman territory, but it indicated a solidifying of the Russian position as war became more likely. It also made the Foreign Office's efforts at effecting a conciliatory attitude toward Persia more difficult. Lancelot Oliphant noted that Sazanov's remarks were 'not very happy and in the hands of our enemies might be used with considerable effect for propaganda purposes.' [14] But Grey's policy was rightly concerned with the necessity of the Russian alliance and so there was not much that the Foreign Office could do, except to try to blunt the edge of Russian animosity, and to hope that if war came the enemy would be the first to violate Persian neutrality – an already much discredited and abused commodity.

On October 29 the Ottomans ended the suspense over the prospects of the war spreading to the Middle East by shelling Russian ports on the Black Sea. Within days the Ottomans were at war with Britain and Russia. The Persian Government greeted the news of the event by declaring its country's neutrality, but the stage had already been set, and the homely fiction of neutrality was casually brushed aside.

Grey, however, was concerned that Ottoman actions might have a profound effect on Muslim sentiments in India and elsewhere, and he wanted to minimize the damage as much as possible. This meant a new effort at Petrograd and Tehran to ameliorate Russo-Persian hostilities. This new effort was not accompanied by any new substantive ideas of how to achieve this rapprochement, but Buchanan was instructed to inform Sazanov that since fighting was likely between Turkish and Russian forces in Persia it was important to offset this by conciliatory gestures toward Tehran, to be floated on the old, reliable assurances of respect for Persian independence and integrity. [15]

Sazanov responded favorably to the idea, and on November 7 outlined a plan for winning over Persia. He made it clear that the necessity of defending Russian interests would render Persian neutrality fictitious, and that this might aggravate Muslim sentiments. He proposed, therefore, to encourage Persia to join the Allies, and revived the idea of offering Najaf and Karbala as inducements. [16] This was more than Grey had had in mind.

He responded on November 10. He agreed that it was a good idea to get Persia on the Allied side, but, recalling earlier objections to territorial offers, he felt that offering territory in Arabia (the Foreign Office sometimes referred to Mesopotamia as 'Arabia') to Shi'ites would offend Sunni opinion. He added, though, that 'any other inducements, political, territorial, or economic ... will receive our most favourable consideration.' He failed, however, to suggest any substantive alternatives, but he did express the hope that Persian neutrality could be respected at least until Persian participation could be secured or the Turks had violated it first.[17]

This fluctuation from denigrating the necessity of Persian support to actively seeking their assistance which was manifested during the crisis of Turkish entry into the war, repeated itself many times in the following years as new crises arose to jeopardize the Allied position. This inability to decide on any policy except one of responding to crises hampered all Allied dealings with Persia. They could never reach a clear decision on how much they needed Persian assistance, whether it were required, and how they planned to secure it if it were. In the first three months of the war the Russians had already considered securing Persian assistance twice, and their opinion was about to change again.

On November 12, Sazanov informed London that, in Russia's view, Turkey had already violated Persian neutrality by encouraging and supplying Kurdish tribes that had attacked Russian forces in Persia in early October, well before the shelling of the Black Sea ports. He added yet again that Russian forces had been in Azerbaijan a long time and therefore were not in violation of neutrality. Russia returned to the idea that they need not conciliate the Persians since the Turks were violating Persian neutrality and that the Allies need not, therefore, be overly solicitous of it.[18] Grey agreed:

... the sole cause of our wish to avoid a violation of Persia's neutrality is the embarrassment, which would result, if our action in attacking Turkey were to appear in any way analogous to that of when the latter [Germany] violated Belgian neutrality in order to attack France.[19]

Grey felt that Turkey's actions justified Russian countermeasures to protect Azerbaijan from incursion. Thus almost as quickly as it had developed, Russian concern for securing Persian participation dwindled.

Instead, only one week after his original proposal, Sazanov suggested that Persia develop a special neutrality, one that would be so favorable to the Allied cause as to make an alliance, with unwelcome concessions, unnecessary. On November 14, he told Buchanan that Persia would probably not join the Allies anyway and even if it did it had no army and would be exposed to attack where neither Russia nor Britain had troops. Sazanov suggested, as an alternative, that Britain and Russia ought to encourage Persia to become a benevolent neutral, as it had been during the Russo-Turkish War of 1877. He proposed that Britain and Russia promise certain compensations if the Allies won, but he added he was willing not to mention this if Britain decided it would bind them to financial assistance later.[20]

It is not clear why Sazanov changed his mind so suddenly. The objections he raised over Persian cooperation existed when he made his original proposal and presumably he had been aware of them. The British had not raised major objections to seeking Persian assistance and the situation in the East had not changed dramatically in favor of Russia. Yet the Russians performed a *volte face*. Perhaps they felt they could handle the situation and were worried that a Persian alliance might prove politically embarrassing and make it impossible to maintain the pre-war stance *vis-à-vis* Persia. In any event, the Russians dropped the idea. Furthermore, they became less willing to placate Persian sensibilities. In the next few weeks Russia began pursuing a policy that aggravated the Persian situation further and, to a considerable degree, caused disaster in Azerbaijan. In mid-November the Russian Caucasian Army began a campaign against the Turks. Russian troops in Azerbaijan joined this campaign and moved toward Lake Van, thus making Iran a base for military actions against Turkey. In addition, the Russians reinforced their position in Azerbaijan and began to raise and equip a local force under one of their Iranian proteges. In late November the Russians brought Samad Khan Shuja ud-Daula from exile in Tiflis to Maragheh, south of Tabriz, the capital of Azerbaijan, where he began organizing a force to supplement Russian troops defending Azerbaijan. Samad Khan had been the Russian instrument for governing Azerbaijan after they occupied the province in 1911 until he fled to Russia in early 1914, after his tyrannical, arbitrary rule had alienated the local population. Shuja ud-Daula's return re-opened old animosities, embarrassed the Persian Government, and further compromised Persian neutrality.[21]

The Turks were well aware of these arrangements and informed the Persian Government that while Turkey was willing to observe Persian neutrality, they could not ignore Russian activity or Shuja ud-Daula's recruitment of an Iranian force under Russian auspices.

The Turkish Ambassador stressed that Turkey would have to take measures they judged sufficient to defend their frontiers if these activities did not cease. The Persian Government appreciated the position and repeatedly protested to Russia, pointing out that Samad Khan's activities endangered Iran's neutrality.[22] But the Allied position had hardened. The Russians were taking a hard line, and without consulting their ally it seems. On November 21, Townley informed Grey that the Russian Minister for Foreign Affairs expected Persia to observe benevolent neutrality, to do its best to prevent Turkish incursions and to adopt a position similar to that in 1877. He further added that Russia's future attitude toward Persia would depend upon the latter's behavior now.

The Russian Minister, Korostovetz, informed Townley that this marked a new phase in Russian-Persian relations and was an official declaration; but when the Russian Legation's First Secretary objected, the Minister changed his remark and said that it was only his Government's point of view. The abruptness of the Russian action, taken without reference to Britain, caused Grey to remind Sazanov of the necessity of communicating with the British ambassador in Tehran if the two governments were going to act in concert.[23] The British wanted to support Russia but they also wanted to exercise some restraint to keep from offending Persian sympathies.

In the meantime, the Persian Government's approach underwent some modification. In a note to Townley the Government said that they were in doubt as to which party was the first aggressor in Azerbaijan but they felt that Russia's act of strengthening forces in Azerbaijan and marching troops off in the direction of Lake Van before Turkey moved was evidence of their intentions to use Persia for incursions into Turkey. A further note pointed out that they knew what would happen if Russia did not withdraw and that they wanted assurances of integrity and a promise that Persia would be compensated for losses and that troops would withdraw after the war.[24] The Government also tried to get some favorable adjustments elsewhere. Townley informed the Foreign Office on November 24 that the Persians had expressed their regret that Russia had not withdrawn from Azerbaijan; but they appreciated that they could not do so now. Therefore, they requested that all other Russian troops in north Persia be withdrawn, arguing that this would quieten hostile opinion, recently augmented by the opening of the Majlis with its collection of anti-Russian nationalists. Townley had informed Grey earlier that an anti-Allied party was active although currently ineffective, but that it only needed an untoward situation to arouse hostility. The Foreign Office was also aware that a new Majlis was preparing to meet and that there was the possibility of a coalition between Democrats and Moderates. This and the need not to alienate Persia overtly inclined them to urge the Russians to conciliate Persia on this point. The Russians, however, rejected the idea, arguing that their forces in Mazanderan and Khorasan, two northern provinces, were really nothing more than reinforced consular guards whose presence discouraged anti-Russian sentiment and kept order, while the forces in Azerbaijan, as everyone knew, were necessary to protect legitimate interests. The Russians became even less inclined to conciliate Persia as they were convinced, on no apparent grounds, that the Persian Government was acting on the instigation of the Turks.[25]

In December the Russians reinforced their position in Azerbaijan by sending elements of the Persian Cossack Brigade, a nominal Persian force, to join Shuja ud-Daula. This antagonized Persian public opinion. Britain realized that such activities inflamed public sentiment and threatened to alienate Persia but they were unable to moderate the Russian position. The intransigence of the Russians embarrassed the Persian Government and Britain. The Persian Government was unable to obtain any concessions that might have strengthened their position *vis-à-vis* anti-Allied activists. As a result, the British found themselves supporting the Persian Cabinet against Russia, which wanted a change of cabinets.

Townley informed Grey in late December that he felt he could induce Persia to join the Allies if it were desired, adding that he would have to act alone because of the dislike and distrust of Russia. He also added that Persia could raise a force of 4,000 Bakhtiari, Lur, and Sinjabi tribes in western Iran, under British officers, and could protect those areas of Persia undefended by Russia and Britain.[26] The Foreign Office was still not particularly eager to have Persia as an ally, but they were alive to the fact that the Russian stance endangered the situation in the East. They hoped to defuse the situation without a quarrel and without a Persian alliance. However, the closing weeks of 1914 not only brought no relief, but generated a new, more serious crisis for Allied and British diplomacy when the Turks pushed the Russians out of most of Azerbaijan.

THE CRISIS OF RUSSIAN DEFEAT IN AZERBAIJAN

Russian determination to use Shuja ud-Daula had continued to exacerbate the internal situation, and the Persian Government continued to protest his presence as a threat to public peace. The Government pointed out that they had been willing to send the Crown Prince to Azerbaijan to raise a force to restore order, an idea opposed by Russia, who then turned to Samad Khan, a virtual rebel whose presence undermined governmental authority and compromised Persian neutrality. The Government maintained that his presence plus Russian troops encouraged support for Turkey and prevented the Government from being able to enforce its authority. But these arguments were of no avail. The Russians continued their activities and the Turks responded by moving against the Russian position in Azerbaijan in late December, supported by local tribes and Iranian nationalists. Russian forces were unable to stop the combined forces and Samad Khan's force in particular was completely routed south of Lake Urumia. The Russian position disintegrated and in January 1915 the Turks and their allies forced the Russians to withdraw from most of Azerbaijan.[27]

The Persian Government and Foreign Minister Ala us-Saltana could not help pointing out to Townley, with some irony, that the Russians had allowed Shuja ud-Daula's return, thus putting their trust in the very forces which they had maintained could not keep order when the Persian Government suggested a similar force under complete Persian control. They asserted that if Russia had accorded with Iran's wishes by evacuating Azerbaijan and agreeing to the formation of a Persian force, the situation in Azerbaijan would not have developed; but that affairs were now out of hand.[28]

Such statements by the Persian Government only served to annoy the Russians, who believed the Persians were abetting the Turks and capitalizing on Russia's difficulties. Russian hostility made it difficult for Britain to secure any settlement in Iran that would put Allied security on firm ground. Townley was not particularly pleased with this situation, which he felt the necessity of cooperating with Russia had created. In summarizing the situation in January 1915, he vented his feelings:

It is unfortunate that the Russian Government is so suspicious of the present Cabinet, as I am convinced that there is not the smallest foundation for such suspicions. I can understand that Petrograd has been annoyed by repeated requests, perhaps somewhat injudiciously preferred with over much insistance, that the Russian troops should be withdrawn from Persia, and that it may have been thought that too great keenness was being shown to turn the present situation to good account, but it is but fair, I think, to bear in mind that the Persians have for long been endeavouring to get the Russians out of Persia, and that it is only human to seek to profit from a chance occasion. There is very little to prove the Russian contention that there would be disorders if the Russian troops were withdrawn, and Persia has not been allowed to take any steps to prepare for the preservation of order on the country being evacuated. That the presence of foreign troops in the country is provocative of disorder was, I think, abundantly proved in our own case at Shiraz, where the withdrawal of the Central India Horse had the best possible effect.

Korostovetz himself openly avowed to the Persians in my presence that strategic necessities, and not the maintenance of order and the protection of Russian interests, made it imperative to keep Russian troops in North Persia for the last two years. In any case, had the troops been withdrawn last October when the Persian Government first asked that they might be, our position and that of Russia would have been a much better one than it is today. We have a mighty weight to carry here in our Russian ally which makes it no easy task to guarantee that Persia will not listen to Turco-German blandishments, whilst Russia has become little better than the laughing stock of the thoughtless Persians who do not trouble to look ahead, and only rejoice to see their hated enemy apparently forced to leave Persia by their brother Mussulmans. Had Russia been able to maintain her position in Azerbaijan, all would have been well, and if she now comes back, as is more than probable she will in pursuit of the fleeing Turks, the situation will become a hopeless one for Persia, however well it may suit Russia, and we shall suffer in public estimation with our allies.[29]

Townley's sentiments, however, could not alter the essential fact that Britain needed the alliance with Russia and was not prepared to make concessions to Persia that it felt would only hurt British interests or benefit the Russians at British expense. The ambivalence that this view injected into British thinking remained a consideration as long as the alliance with Russia remained vital – a fact that encumbered all British approaches to Iran.

In early 1915, though, a possibility developed that suggested a way to placate the Persians. Russian reverses in the face of a vigorous Turkish offensive in the Caucasus and in Azerbaijan inclined the Russians to become more conciliatory towards Iran, and elicited the possibility of a Russian withdrawal from north Persia altogether.

On January 1, Sir Walter Townley informed the Persians, upon a request by Korostovetz, that Russia was planning to withdraw its troops from northern Iran. The announcement was unofficial and curiously delivered – Korostovetz had approached Townley at a New

Year's Eve party at the British Legation and asked him to inform the
Persian Government on Russia's behalf of Russian intentions – but
it gave the Persian Government reason to hope that neutrality might
be saved.[30] These hopes were not discouraged when Prime Minister
Mustaufi ul-Mamalik saw the Turkish Ambassador, who repeated
Turkish promises to respect Iranian neutrality if the Russians
withdrew, although the Ambassador added that a verbal announcement of Russian intentions was insufficient evidence. On January 4,
Foreign Minister Ala us-Saltana wrote to the Porte and asked them,
in light of Russia's intention to evacuate Azerbaijan, to withdraw their
troops and respect the frontier. On January 6, Ala us-Saltana wrote
to the Persian Minister in London informing him of Russian intentions and asking him to press the point that Persia wanted complete
Russian evacuation of the north; and the next day Ala us-Saltana
informed the Persian Minister to the Porte of Russia's intention of
withdrawing from Iran and asked him to get the Turks to withdraw
as well. However, the Persian Government's actions were premature,
which became clear when they tried to get the Russians to formalize
their verbal statements.[31]

Although the Russian Minister Korostovetz had confirmed his
Government's intentions on January 4, and both he and Townley had
asked the Persian Government to outline their program for restoring
order, protecting life and property, and securing the withdrawal of
the Turks, there was still no official declaration. As the Persian
Government continued to press the Russians for some official sign of
their intent, they also reminded them that the situation in Azerbaijan
was the result of their failure to heed the Persian Government's advice
in the first place. They pointed out that the Government was now
almost incapable of defending the province because the Russians had
given all available military stores to Shuja ud-Daula, who had
promptly lost them to enemy forces, thus arming the enemy and
compromising Persian neutrality further. The Russians did not
appreciate such expressions, however true, and resented these repeated
reminders, rightly suspecting the Persian Government of trying to take
advantage of Russian difficulties if not actually colluding with the
Turks to cause them.[32]

The British, especially Townley, did not believe this latter point
but found themselves caught in the middle. They wanted to cooperate
with the Russians but did not want to alienate all Persian sympathies,
with the implicit dangers that suggested. And although the two goals

were not particularly compatible, the Foreign Office was bound to try. In the meantime the Persian Government continued its efforts to restore the situation in Azerbaijan. They returned to the idea of sending the Valiahd (Crown Prince) to Azerbaijan and opened discussions with Britain concerning the funds necessary to help organize an army and to meet government operating costs.

But ominous signs were developing. Despite repeated attempts, Foreign Minister Ala us-Saltana had been unable to get the Russians to commit themselves formally to withdrawal. The Persian Government had regarded this as essential but they proceeded as if it were only a question of time. By January 14, only two weeks after the initial verbal offer, that bubble burst. Russian military forces were beginning to restore the military balance in the Caucasus as the Turkish offensive lost steam and if the Russians had ever really intended to withdraw, this turn of events made them reconsider. On January 11, the Minister of Foreign Affairs received the disturbing news from the *Karguzar* (a local Persian official employed by the Persian foreign ministry) at Qazvin in the northwest that Russian troops were going to re-enter the city. At the same time the Persian Ambassador to Britain alerted Ala us-Saltana that Russian military authorities had no intention of evacuating Iran and that Korostovetz had made a mistake; as if to confirm this, on January 14 the *Karguzar* at Qazvin reported that Russian troops were indeed reoccupying the city. The Persian Ambassador at Constantinople added a further depressing note when he reported that the Porte saw Russian withdrawal as the result of Turkish military operations and not the result of Persian diplomacy or Russian good will.[33] The Turkish Minister of Foreign Affairs said that Turkey had the best intentions regarding Persian integrity and that the army would respect lives and property but would not withdraw. There was little Ala us-Saltana could do. Although he continued to try to get neutrality respected he had to see Azerbaijan torn by war, with further Russian animosity as the only significant result of his diplomatic efforts.

Sir Walter Townley, who had initially informed the Persians of Russia's intentions, made some scathing remarks about this particular action of his country's ally. Although he discounted the feelings of his colleagues in the diplomatic corps that the Russians had meant to put him in a 'hole,' he viewed the Russians with no great favor. To some extent Townley sympathized with the Persians and held the view that many of the problems in Azerbaijan and for the Allied cause could have been avoided if Russia had withdrawn in October 1914 as originally requested by the Persian Government. In a personal letter to Grey on January 18, he aired his feelings at length. He voiced his aggravation over the Russian attitude in Persia and the activities of the 'junior' members of the Russian diplomatic establishment who were pursuing a forward policy in Persia to Britain's detriment. He expressed a deep distrust of Russian intentions and his remarks betrayed a coloring more becoming to pre-1907 Anglo-Russian relations than to that spirit of cooperation needed between allies in war time. Townly regarded Russia's friendship as a handicap and a threat to British interests:

, ... the more I study the question the more convinced I become that, unless Russia is willing to agree to a mutual 'hands off Persia' policy no agreement [he is speaking of a revision of the 1907 Convention] can be made that will guarantee us from an ever-present danger of friction between ourselves and Russia except some form of partition, or at least a much clearer cut definition of our respective pretensions than is the case at present. As things are today, the junior members of the Russian Legation (in other words, the Consuls of tomorrow), who, despite all official denials to the contrary, really shape Russia's policy in Persia ... are plotting schemes for the expansion of Russian influences in the South.[34]

But Townley's sentiments were not echoed in the Foreign Office. Grey, as the architect of the original Anglo-Russian entente, was determined that the Persian situation should not jeopardize Anglo-Russian cooperation. This may have been one of the key factors that later decided Grey to replace Townley with Sir Charles Marling, who had served at Tehran before and who, coming fresh upon the scene, might be more committed to Anglo-Russian cooperation. Grey appreciated the implicit dangers of driving Iran into enemy hands and he still hoped to find means of reconciling Persia and Russia, at least until the danger of war passed. His main concern, however, was never Persia.

THE CRISIS OF ANTI-ALLIED EFFORTS

To understand the nature of the problems confronting the Allies and the Persian Government, why events went so far beyond their control, it is necessary to recall for a moment the prevailing political situation in Iran in 1914 and the fact that Allied interests and activities were matched by anti-Allied Persian nationalists, the Germans, and the

Turks. Even as early as July the Germans had considered sending agents to stir up sedition in India and, shortly after the war began, a number of German army officers were seconded to Turkey to make preparations for spreading propaganda in India and Afghanistan. Although elements of this party, divided up into small groups to avoid capture, did not begin arriving in Iran until early 1915 (delayed by petty squabbles over leadership with the Turks), German consular agents in Iran had already begun to meet with Iranian nationalists and to inflame anti-Allied sentiments. The Turks got in the act too, as mentioned before, by encouraging Kurdish tribes on Ottoman territory to attack Russian positions in Iran well before they joined the war. And Iranian nationalists had by no means been idle either. Drawing on the well of anti-Russian sentiment in the country, they were able to arouse elements of the population and challenge the Allies for control of the Persian Government; and in cooperation with the Turks and Germans (itself a much-troubled partnership) they threatened to drag Persia into the war.

The Germans were aware of the potentials of appealing to Islamic and nationalist sympathies and they also realized that a rebellion in the East could divert large numbers of British forces from Europe and perhaps cripple the entire war effort. Although the Middle East theater was minor militarily, the game played there was for the highest political stakes.* When Turkey joined the Central Powers only two independent Muslim countries remained uncommitted – Iran and Afghanistan – and both sides knew the potential if yet another Muslim country could be persuaded or maneuvered into war. Militarily the best ally was Afghanistan but it was remote and its sentiments unknown. Persia was negligible militarily, but from the point of view of the Central Powers it was more accessible; furthermore the road to Afghanistan lay across Persia. Thus Iran attracted the attentions of the belligerents, but unfortunately for Iran neither side was particularly interested in Persian opinions, conditions, or aspirations. They regarded Iran as a military resource, a weapon to be exploited to settle their international quarrels.

The political picture in Iran was also far from clear. The Persian cabinet endeavored to protect neutrality but it was not apparent, to

---

* The British, like the Germans, made plans to encourage such sentiments. The Arab revolt against Turkey was a measure of British attempts to encourage subversives into action that would cripple the war effort of the enemy. In the Middle East the British were much more successful than the Central Powers.

the Allies anyway, how sincere these efforts were. The Russians, in particular, suspected the cabinet of being in league with the rabidly anti-Russian Democratic party. Furthermore, the Government was weak and there were considerable elements in Persia, some of them politically active, that favored the Germans. Many newspapers and private presses published anti-Allied declarations and appeals to Muslim brotherhood; some of them endorsed *jihad* and publicly sympathized with Germany.

In Isfahan, for example, the Habl ul-Matin press, which published a Persian reform newspaper, published a long circular in response to an official telegram issued by the British Consul outlining British views of the war and reasons for fighting Turkey. The circular questioned British claims to being a friend of Islam and of fighting the war for high moral issues, and accused Britain of perfidy and imperial aggression. It pursued several Iranian themes, reminding its readers of the 1907 Agreement and of British partnership with Russia:

When a Mussulman, and especially a Persia[n], for the many years has heard and seen the friendship, worship of truth, faithfulness, justice, kindness, etc, etc, of England and Russia towards the countries which have been under their influence operations and communications especially his home Persia particularly in these last years owing to our unlimited helplessness they have interfered openly in our affairs [sic]. They did whatever they liked. One day without our knowledge they divided our country into spheres of influence, another day they sent troops into our country &c. &c. What Persian is there who is not heartbroken by the heartrending events in Azerbaijan, Kasvin, Resht, Holy Meshed and the overbearing acts of the Russians towards the honoured sacred enclosure of eighth Imam? Is the unjust and unnecessary interference of the representatives of the two nations and the subject making games of the Consuls and Agents (to which Blue Books testify) forgotten? This is why the Persian who remembers these above mentioned sad events and also ponders this telegram is compelled to say that he is seeing a dream ...[35]

It is not clear how far such ideas and publications went toward encouraging anti-Allied activity, but this circular and others like it pinpoint the attitude common to many Persians, some of whom were willing to act. As a consequence the Germans were able to find support which the British had to counter if they meant to protect their situation in the East.

Although slow to get off the ground, the activities of the Germans and the nationalists ranged from creating an ongoing political crisis in Tehran and elsewhere, to organizing armed actions against British and Russian interests, especially in the south, the north, and the west.

The Germans hoped to use nationalist support and the Democratic party apparatus. One of their main aims was to get to Afghanistan and they were well aware that the only feasible route to Afghanistan lay across Iran, although it presented certain problems. In addition to the distance, this route exposed the attenuated German lines of communication to British and Russian attack, so they hoped to use their contacts in Iran to provide the necessary equipment, guides and protection. The Germans also hoped to stir up local sympathies against the Allies; they tried to suborn local officials and encouraged, with financial and moral support, the formation of anti-Allied political groups. In some areas they also began hiring and arming local toughs, brigands, and tribal groups to act as para-military forces and to give added protection to their lines of communications. One of the most successful operations in this direction was that of Wassmuss. Wilhelm Wassmuss, a former consul on the Persian Gulf and originally a member of the German expedition to Afghanistan, began organizing local forces in south Persia in 1914. During the next four years his activities caused the British considerable embarrassment, so much so that he is often considered to be the German 'Lawrence of Arabia'. All these activities were contrary to Persian neutrality but the Germans were no more scrupulous than others in observing a fact that they regarded as a cumbersome fiction. Throughout, the Germans were abetted by Iranians eager to free their country from Russia and Britain or to fatten their purses.

The Democrats in Tehran were quite prepared to work with the Germans to put an end to Russian and British imperialism.* The Democratic party had no elaborate, well-organized party structure but they did have a better articulated apparatus than other political groups; and they had supporters in all levels of government, including the cabinet. As a result of the election of the Third Majlis held in late 1914, the Democratic party held a real, though small, majority – they were represented by thirty-one members to the twenty-nine of the Moderates, and enjoyed the support of twenty non-committed delegates. In addition, the Moderate party, the main political opponent of the Democrats, was not united and nearly half of its

* In foregoing sections the terms 'nationalist' and 'democrat' have been used fairly synonymously.

supporters tended to side with the Democratic party.[36] The Democratic party also enjoyed the support of many local groups and individuals and made an effort to direct, control and discipline these local interests, so that they were able to follow local events and to an extent get local groups to act in accordance with the views of the central committee of the party. It was not altogether a coincidence that many Iranian telegraph operators were Democrats or that the Democratic party endeavored to get its supporters employed in foreign embassies and government agencies as a means of keeping up with events. The party aimed at liberating the country from Britain and Russia and the leaders were prepared to work with the Germans to achieve this end.

Taken all together this meant that the leaders of the Democrats had a broad, if shallow, base of support among politically active Iranians. No Persian Government could overlook this fact, and the British had to find means of counteracting the Democrats if they intended to keep Persia neutral. The Germans, on the other hand, hoped to translate Democratic strength into significant anti-Allied action. The Democrats hoped to use their power plus German support to rid the country of Russian and British influence. Thus the stage was set for the maneuvering for position and struggle for power that characterized the World War in Iran.

* * *

Thus only five months after war broke out in Europe, the British found themselves in a morass in Iran. Faced with an unreliable and belligerent ally, a weak but tenacious Persian government, and an aggressively anti-Allied Democratic Party spurred on by German agents all over the country, the British had to control the situation in Iran or risk *jihad*, danger to India, and a further spread of the war. The struggle that ensued for the rest was a three-cornered affair and occurred on two levels. The main elements in the struggle were the Allies, their opposition, and the Persian Government (or rather 'governments,' as cabinets tended to change with tidal regularity). Given the lack of central authority, the distances between cities, the problems of travel and communication, and the fragmented nature of social and political life, the efforts of all concerned tended to occur in a series of isolated pockets with confusion and improbability attending the whole process. Thus it is difficult to develop any comprehensive picture of what was happening at any given time, but very easy to understand why frustration was the common emotion shared by all the rival groups. It is also easier to understand why the British, with all the disadvantages of the alliance with Russia and their own cumbersome decision-making process, found it so difficult to achieve any, not to mention enduring, respite in Iran.

In attempting to reach a settlement in Iran, the British employed four separate, but interrelated, approaches. First, they considered some sort of agreement with the Persian Government; second, they considered arrangements with local officials and tribal leaders in the absence of governmental authority or willingness to cooperate; third, they considered raising local levies from Persian tribes or other groups; and finally they resorted to direct force when all else failed – which it did with predictable regularity. None of the efforts produced the desired easing of Britain's security worries. The Persian Government was elusive and the Allies were generally unwilling to pay Persia's price – and no Persian Government could have survived a deal with the Allies without substantial concessions. Local officials and tribal leaders were not reliable since their loyalty was negotiable, and there too the British were reluctant to make concessions that might tie their hands after the war. Raising local levies achieved only limited success and in one instance made matters considerably worse (see Chapter VI), since Persian martial spirit left something to be desired and Persian hostility to Russia meant that the levy forces were always open to sedition. And, of course, all these efforts were challenged by the activities of the Germans, Turks and nationalists and placed at risk by Russian cooperation. Despite repeated frustrations British authorities continued these four policies, separately or in various combinations, throughout the war, and only the blundering incompetence of their opponents came to the rescue.

Another factor characterized the subsequent British effort in Iran. The instability of the political situation, the support the Germans seemed to enjoy, and the lack of effective action from a succession of Persian cabinets (which averaged four a year) caused the British to put increasing reliance on securing favorable men in public office. For years the British had brought pressure on the Persian Government to appoint acceptable officials in the area of British interest, but during the war the British stepped up their efforts to secure favorable officials and cabinets by threat or bribery. When unsuccessful they tended to let matters drift in Tehran while they pursued the alternatives of local leaders, local levies, or direct intervention. It is understandable that British officials did not want to support a hostile cabinet, since their experience in Turkey worked as a reminder of the consequences, but they began to regard any but a virtual British creature as hostile. In the fever of war any action that did not meet with British approval was regarded as anti-Allied and pro-German. Every situation was measured by the yardstick of loyalty and even groups such as the tribes in the south, whom the British had antagonized for years and who had caused trouble long before the war, suddenly became pro-German agents in British eyes. Extended to the cabinet this meant that only the clearest demonstrations of loyalty were accepted, and without them the cabinet was left to sink or swim or was actively undermined. The consequence was to tie the success or failure of British policy to the tenure of this or that political figure. In doing so the British accentuated the internal political divisions and isolated their policy and potential supporters.

CHAPTER THREE

THE SEARCH FOR AN ACCOMMODATION: THE MORATORIUM MARCH, 1915 TO NOVEMBER, 1916

... we shall no doubt continue to receive expressions
of conflicting views.

The failure to keep the Ottoman Empire neutral opened up the possibility of a pan-Islamic holy war against the Allies, with Britain having the most to lose. This, plus the fact that by early 1915 the war in Europe was obviously bogged down, the race of armies and trench lines to the north having ended in a dead heat, encouraged some British officials to look outside Europe for means to break the stalemate or to protect existing interests. In combination these events were enough to divert Britain's concentration from the war in Europe, but they were not sufficient to make clear the line of policy to pursue. Even in Europe the Liberal Asquith government stumbled along with pre-war organization, which meant limited coordination between departments, and difficulty in deciding what to do and how to do it. It is not surprising, then, that in the Middle East dithering should have been an essential element in decision-making.

The main problem for the British in Iran started with the fact that no one wanted to give Persia any serious consideration. Once that no longer seemed possible, deciding on what to do summoned up all the cumbersome mechanisms for consultation. The decision that evolved in the first months of the war fluctuated between bolstering the Persian Government with money – the favored policy – and formally binding Persia to the Allied cause. The problem with the former approach was that the Persian Government needed more than money to restore its authority while the latter approach kept falling foul of individual British or Russian interests. Neither Power could forget its position in Iran and both were reluctant to make commitments or concessions that would limit their maneuverability after the war. Only major crises forced their hands — but any crisis that forced the Allies to consider concessions to Iran precluded the possibility that the Persian Government could survive an arrangement with the Allies. On more than one occasion the Allies would reach an agreement with a Persian cabinet only to have that cabinet collapse and take the agreement down with it. It might be summarized thus: if the climate were impossible for making an agreement, offers were made; and if the situation were favorable to a settlement, there was a retrenchment until the next crisis.

During the war the British made numerous proposals but few substantive offers. There were, however, two major agreements, one for money and one that tried to bind the Persians to the Allies in a semi-defensive alliance. The first, called the Moratorium, staggered into life between March and November of 1915. The second, the Sipahsalar or August Agreement, was reached in August 1916. Neither agreement, however, notably eased Britain's security worries, and to some extent they worked to the detriment of those interests.

THE IDEA OF A MORATORIUM

It is not clear when the idea of giving the Persians money to be still first gained acceptance. And exactly what it meant eluded everyone concerned, for even much later in the war, officials in the India Office and the Foreign Office were puzzling over what they had done.

Basically the idea was to supply the Persian Government with funds to meet its operating costs so that the Government could maintain its authority and therefore its neutrality. The confusion developed from trying to construct the loan so that it would not look like a loan. The Persian Government needed the money and the Allies, after some hesitation, wanted to give it, but a direct loan would have required the sanction of the Majlis. Since the nationalists dominated the parliament, neither the Persian cabinet nor the Allies wanted to excite a public debate on the subject of money, and so they resorted to a subterfuge. The Allies agreed to suspend the collection of interest on their respective loans, secured on Persia's customs revenues, and to give the Persians in monthly installments a sum equivalent to the monthly customs revenues. In order to by-pass the Majlis the arrangement was presented as a moratorium on the collection of

Persia's debts. In obscuring the issue to deceive the Majlis, the British also confused themselves, as is revealed by a series of telegrams and letters that passed back and forth between India, the Foreign Office, the India Office, the Treasury and the minister in Tehran trying to make clear what was meant. It took the Foreign Office eleven months to secure the agreement and once it was finally reached, it was too late to prevent serious difficulties in Tehran.

Why this preoccupation with money? No one wrote down the exact reasons, but giving financial aid was a favored British method for bolstering shaky governments to promote British interests; and the Foreign Office recognized that the Persian Government needed money to meet its obligations, and that if the Allies supplied it then Persian gratitude might thereby be secured. To some extent money was Britain's main leverage at Tehran, since the capital was well within the Russian sphere and removed from Britain's sources of power in the south; and since Persia was still nominally independent and neutral, money (unlike troops) did not have the disadvantage of openly violating Persia's integrity. In addition, the Persians most persistently asked for money and it was easier to pay out funds than to concede the other demands that always accompanied the requests for money. And the Foreign Office, the India Office and the Government of India believed that Persians were overly fond of money anyway and that providing it, even if it did not win popularity, would at least procure quiet. And finally, money was more readily available than the men and materials that might have been required if the situation in Persia were allowed to get out of hand.

Several obstacles had to be overcome, though, before the British were actually able or prepared to pay out anything. One of the obstacles was, of course, the Russians, who took a lot of convincing before they were prepared to see any Persian Government strengthened. Another problem was getting a Persian Government that the Allies trusted to agree on terms for accepting money. In doing this, the Allies not only had to counter the activities of the Persian nationalists and Germans who opposed them and who were out to seize control of the government or so compromise Iran as to force it into the war; but they also had to winnow the host of unacceptable Persian desiderata, and negotiate their way through the convolutions of Persian politics. Finally, not the least of the obstacles in settling to pay the Persians was the difficulties British authorities had in deciding among themselves on whom to pay, how much, and in what manner. Nor was the situation helped by the fact that everyone realized that the Persian Government was not in complete charge and that paying them was only an interim or partial solution. Events in Persia seemed to demand other actions that interfered with or precluded any reliance on money and under these circumstances it was difficult to be consistent. But giving money seemed, if not ideal, at least worth a try and the Foreign Office endeavored to find a way of making it work.

The actual payments of the moratorium began in October after last minute Russian additions were avoided and Persian amendments accommodated. The fund eventually available for subsidizing the Persian Government was in two forms: a retroactive sum of £240,000 (figured to January 1914), and a monthly subvention of £30,000 or 200,000 tumans shared evenly between Britain and Russia. The fall of the relative value of the pound to the tuman added to the actual sum the Allies had to pay, the exchange rate being subsequently at 5·5 tumans to the pound. The sums were payable at the discretion of the British Minister through the Imperial Bank of Persia and were paid on request to successive Persian Governments until May 1917 when political uncertainties in Iran and the Russian Revolution caused the British to suspend paying the subvention while they reconsidered their position in Iran. Early in 1916 the Russians defaulted on their share and Britain took over paying the whole sum. Also in 1916 the Allies forced the Persian Government to accept a degree of financial supervision, in the form of a Mixed Financial Commission (see Chapter IV). In 1918 when the British hoped to secure a favorable government in Persia the moratorium was recalculated and to it was added a further 100,000 tumans.

In September 1918 Britain began paying a total figure of 350,000 tumans per month, arrived at by adding the £30,000 of the moratorium (at 5·5 tumans per pound) plus 150,000 tumans from the arrears of the moratorium (payable for six months) plus a subsidy of 100,000 tumans. This sum was the minimum the Persian Government of the day felt it needed to meet all its obligations and continue in office, something the British wanted; for past experience, plus a series of cabinet changes and frustrated agreements throughout the war, convinced the Foreign Office to do everything in its power — so far as paying out money was concerned — to get and keep a favorable government in power. One of the essential characteristics of British policy in Iran was a reliance on particular individuals or groups. In part this was a reflection of the realities of the Persian political environment, but however expedient it was it meant tying the fate of a particular policy to the fate of particular individuals or to the power of various groups. In effect British policy subscribed to the wild uncertainties of the Persian political environment.

The earliest suggestion of the idea of a moratorium seems to have come from Ala us-Saltana in late September or early October 1914 in reply to a memorandum from Townley about the possibility of purchasing certain islands in the Persian Gulf.[1] The Persian Foreign Minister said nothing of the islands but he did indicate that his government needed money and he suggested that Britain forego payments on debts secured on Persia's southern customs receipts for one year and that the Allies give Persia £500,000 with which to equip a force to preserve order in Azerbaijan. Townley dismissed the idea as preposterous, and the Russians were in no mood to give the Persians money, especially to a cabinet they distrusted, or see them raise an army. The idea lapsed. But Turkey's entrance into the war, the Russian reverses in Azerbaijan and the danger that Iran might join the Central Powers added a new dimension to the value of securing Persia's cooperation; the British became more interested in giving the Persians money, but the Russians opposed the idea. Sazanov did not want to support a government that continually raised difficulties about the Russian presence and he was somewhat petulant over the state of Anglo-Russian relations.

NEGOTIATIONS WITH THE RUSSIANS

On January 11, Sazanov told George Buchanan, the veteran British representative at Petrograd, that he was depressed over the state of Anglo-Russian relations. He said that he assumed the Agreement of 1907 had meant that in the future neither side was entitled to interfere with what the other did in its respective sphere; but, he said, England had never observed this, and had constantly protested Russian measures to secure their legitimate interests. Buchanan demurred. He believed that the Russians had missed the point. Russia had signed an agreement to protect Persian integrity and independence; and 'We,' Buchanan went on to say,

did not dispute Russia's predominant position in North Persia and if she would only respect legitimate Persian sensibilities of the Persian Government,

Russia's interest then would be amply safeguarded without a word of complaint on our part.

Buchanan stressed that the Persian Government was not motivated by anti-Russian sentiments but by a genuine regard to see Azerbaijan spared.[2] However, both Buchanan and Grey hastened to add that this did not mean Britain was taking Persia's side.

Grey tried to make this clear on January 18. He wanted Sazanov to understand that his only interest was to prevent a quarrel that might prove beneficial to the enemy.

For me the sole consideration is whether policy pursued in Persia is likely to help or hinder the progress of the war. During the war the Persian question does not exist for me, apart from its effect on the war.

Grey wanted to guarantee the security of British-Russian interests and he was willing to purchase it if necessary. The Persian Government, still having financial difficulties, gave him an opening when they renewed requests for monetary support, asking for a loan of £100,000. And by late February Grey began to feel that it was the only choice: 'Diplomatically I can see nothing except to attach the Persian Government to our side by meeting the pressing request that they are making for an advance of £100,000.' He proposed, then, that Russia and Britain share the cost of buying-off Persia.[3] But Sazanov was reluctant and so long as he opposed the government at Tehran, a settlement with the Persians remained a different prospect.

Lord Crewe, the Secretary of State for India, in a note to the Foreign Office on the subject of Russian obduracy, noted that although the Russians were more conciliatory after their return to Tabriz at the end of January, having stopped and then routed the Turkish offensive that had almost driven them from Azerbaijan, their attitude was still troublesome. Crewe wanted Grey to impress on Russia that 'the attitude of Persia cannot be a matter of indifference to them, unless they are prepared to see Great Britain's power to help her Allies on land crippled.'[4] Grey appreciated this fact and continued efforts to mitigate Russian hostility.

But Sazanov remained adamant in his opposition to financial support for Persia.[5] He believed Mustaufi ul-Mamalik, the Persian Prime Minister, was anti-Russian and he wanted a change of cabinets before agreeing to give any money, perhaps hoping in this way to shut off constant requests for the evacuation of Azerbaijan. Grey, however, was not so eager to change in mid-stream. Britain had no reason to love the Persian cabinet but the Foreign Office was not at all confident of securing favorable appointments or of keeping the Germans and Democrats from capturing a new cabinet. As a result British-Russian cooperation reached an impasse.

But the Foreign Office believed that cooperation was essential. To promote this and thereby hopefully be more able to act decisively in Iran, the Foreign Office in February arranged with the Russians to replace their respective representatives at Tehran. The Russian minister, M. Korostovetz had never been popular with the British and it was clear to the Foreign Office that Townley – who, according to the French Ambassador's wife, had gone so far as to express his ill-feelings about Russia publicly – and the Russians were pulling against one another. The Russians agreed to send M. de Etter, the counsellor at the Russian embassy in London and someone the Foreign Office knew and could work with, while Charles Marling, a career diplomat who had served in Tehran before the war, replaced Townley. The Persians objected to the change, feeling it represented a change of intentions as well as ministers, but the Allies were more concerned with their own harmonious relations than with Persian approval, although they assured the Persians that they had every intention of respecting Persian integrity. The Foreign Office recognized that Marling was not the most acceptable candidate, if only because he was taking on more responsibility than he had previously handled, but he was reliable, had experience in Iran and, it was believed, would get on well with the Russians. The new representatives did not reach Iran immediately, Marling not arriving until mid-April, and de Etter in May.

The Foreign Office meanwhile worked towards an arrangement of another kind with Russia that they hoped would promote more harmonious relations – over the question of the possession of Constantinople and control of the Straits into the Black Sea. Control of the Straits had been a long-term Russian goal, an objective most steadfastly resisted by Britain. But the alliance and the war made a resolution more likely. The Russians had been pursuing the idea since late 1914 and in February and March 1915 the British Government, aware of the need to keep Russian goodwill, were prepared to concede control to Russia, in return for certain guarantees concerning access to the Straits and a promise that the holy places in Mesopotamia and Arabia would remain in Muslim hands. At the last minute Grey added a further demand. In the months before the war the Foreign Office had become increasingly aware of the need to revise the terms of the 1907 Agreement and especially to get control of the neutral zone in Persia. The bargaining over the Straits opened the doors to a trade and Grey added control of the neutral zone as a requirement to complete the settlement, to which the Russians, although hesitant, consented, with the stipulation that Russia would have a free hand in their sphere, presumably free from the constant harassment mentioned by Sazanov in January. The Foreign Office knew this settlement was only the first step in a searching discussion with Russia about a comprehensive settlement in Asia, but it was a beginning and with the arrangement in Persia and the replacement of the representatives it was hoped that more harmony would develop at Tehran between the two Powers.

As in 1907 the two Powers purchased their harmony in Persian coin. But, although the Foreign Office recognized the fact that Persia's integrity was now insubstantial, they did not want to obliterate it completely, '... it is very necessary,' Nicolson informed Buchanan, 'in view of our mussulman subjects and our general interests throughout the moslem world that we should keep up as long as it is possible the integrity of that benighted country.'[6] And Nicolson hoped that Marling and de Etter would work out a way whereby Britain and Russia could protect their mutual economic and political interests without unduly encroaching on Persian independence, at least during the war, for Nicolson and others had already made up their minds about Persia's ability to stand on its own. Only the concern that abrupt actions in Persia during the war would have adversely affected Britain's Muslim subjects prevented the Allies from making dispositions in Persia resonant with their interests and attitudes.

No one at the Foreign Office, though, was clear on how they intended to square the litany of respect for Persia's independence and integrity with the constant violation of it in practice. It was not mere cynicism that caused Nicolson, or Grey, to repeat the magic phrases, but there was considerable distance between the piety of the sentiments and the realities of politics. The Persians were weak, the Russians were absorbing the north, and Britain did have interests that could not be discarded for the sake of sentiment if the Persians could not stand up for themselves. The pressure of circumstances, not deliberate policy, forced Britain to participate in the partition of Persia.

TIDING THINGS OVER

For the British the Persian Government's inability during the war to protect its frontiers against the armed intervention by the Turks or to suppress the anti-Allied activities of its own subjects in cooperation with an assortment of German agents clearly demonstrated the weakness and unreliability of Persia and underscored the necessity for direct action, either unilaterally or in conjunction with the Russians. But the British did not give up on making some arrangement with the existing Persian Government – hoping that in conjunction with the other measures, this would tide things over during the war.

In pursuing such an arrangement, given Russia's hostility, Grey considered an approach that did not require the Russians. On February 18 he asked Townley to sound out the Persians on the idea of neutrality – or Persia's price. Grey, in return for Persia's neutrality was willing to: (1) remove all British troops from Ahwaz, where British troops had been since the start of the war to protect the oilfields, when the military situation permitted; (2) secure better treatment of Persians at Najaf and Karbala and secure a Shi'a governor there; and (3) grant a large loan on security of certain Gulf islands without interest other than the average revenue of the islands. At the same time Grey instructed Buchanan to make it clear to Sazanov that these proposals contained nothing detrimental to Russian interests, even if it did not involve them in the solution.[7]

Townley, however, felt such proposals were too vague and inconsequential. First, he pointed out that making conditional statements about military withdrawal might arouse Persian suspicions about troop withdrawal, especially with the Russian example in the north. Second, Townley felt that most thinking Persians already appreciated that a British administration of the holy places would mean more favorable treatment of Shi'a interests and this was, therefore, not a real bargaining point. Finally, he suggested that the Foreign Office would have to be more specific about money, and he cautioned that the offer over the islands should be cast as a mortgage because an actual occupation would strengthen the pro-German party who could point to British aggression.

In short the Foreign Office had to come up with something more solid – and expensive – to secure Persian favor. In spite of Russian hostility and Mustaufi ul-Mamalik's unsatisfactory cabinet, Grey felt some approach was necessary. In a minute to Townley's remarks Grey noted that:

Persian neutrality has little material value, but it has great moral value for if Persia departed from neutrality and the Persian Government officially and openly made common cause with Turkey and joined the jehad it would affect Afghanistan against us.[8]

Everyone knew what potential lay there. It would, however, be some months and several crises before there would be anything approaching a solution, at least in Tehran. One crisis after another would overwhelm a series of Persian governments and any hope of a settlement had to wait on prospects of a return to normality.

CABINET CRISIS

One reason for the difficulties was the feebleness of the Persian cabinet, or its susceptibility to adverse pressure. In early 1915 Mirza Hasan Khan, Mustaufi ul-Mamalik, a long-time Persian politician of indifferent capabilities, headed the Persian Government. He had assumed office in the summer of 1914 and like most Persian politicians of the time who held important positions in the cabinet his energies were spent trying to balance all the forces seeking to propel him from office. The security of his tenure was not improved by Russian hostility nor by the fact that, although he may have sympathized with the nationalists, he could not afford to go too far in encouraging them. His balancing act became even more precarious in November 1914 when the Majlis convened and unleashed all the political turmoil that consultative democracy in Iran provoked.

Mustaufi ul-Mamalik's government was in a shaky position. Although Iran had declared neutrality no one had taken it seriously, and so the country was invaded by Turks to fight the occupying Russians, and the British had moved troops into the south to protect the oilfields and their flank in Mesopotamia, while the Germans ignored the neutrality in their own fashion. These actions excited Iranian sympathies and the Government received much of the blame for not stopping the incursions. In addition the nationalists and their German allies, though personally favoring Mustaufi ul-Mamalik, who appeared sympathetic, were determined to capture control of the cabinet. Townley recognized the ambiguity of the Prime Minister's position and the fact that he was so concerned to maintain his personal popularity that he shrank from offending anyone. 'You can imagine,' Townley wrote to Arthur Nicolson, Permanent Under-Secretary at the Foreign Office, 'what this leads to in a place like Persia where everyone is seeking the furtherance of his own interests.'[9] But Townley was not convinced that any agreement was possible so long as Mustaufi ul-Mamalik remained Prime Minister.

The atmosphere in Persia made it very difficult to satisfy anyone. In such a situation the Government, given its relative weakness, had only one alternative when faced with recalcitrant opposition or overbearing foreign pressures – resignation. It is difficult to prove, but one suspects that this recourse was used as a negotiating point by a variety of Persian Governments, who traded on their viability and indispensability to the various factions and political interests as well as to the Powers as the symbol of legitimate authority to stay in power. It is also difficult to substantiate but one is inclined to suspect that in the upper levels of government there was a degree of collusion between the various candidates for Prime Minister, who supposedly represented different parties, or the interests of one of the Powers, to coordinate loosely a line of policy favorable to Persia.

Although the cabinet changed some sixteen times during the course of the war, the demands of the respective governments were remarkably consistent and the personnel staffing the cabinets came from a limited pool of candidates. In fact, changes of government were often little more than cabinet reshuffles with the key offices passing back and forth between small groups of the elite. Mustaufi ul-Mamalik himself was four times Prime Minister, a fact that may have depended on his ability to straddle more fences than anyone else, being all things to all parties, while the other leading political figures were more clearly associated with one particular party or interest.

There were ten posts, though all positions were not always filled in the cabinet, the four main ones being the portfolios of Prime Minister, Minister of Interior, Minister of Foreign Affairs and Minister of War. The tax minister was generally an expert and the officials in the other minor posts were filled by a small group of recurring personnel, while the top posts were filled by the leading politicians, the Shah appointing the Prime Minister from the available candidates. Rarely did political rivals occupy the four top positions at the same time, the Prime Minister filling those posts with his closest associates, but the number of officials remained small – only fifty-one individuals filled the 158 posts available during the war,* with the Prime Minister's office passing back and forth among eight individuals, three of whom held the office more than twice.

During the war the cabinet changed with depressing frequency, but given the small number of actual changes as opposed to reconstitutions, there was much greater continuity between Persian cabinets, say, than between changes of government in Britain. This fact escaped notice at the time, made more obscure by the fact that Persian politicians were deft at playing off competing interests and tended to cast themselves in the role of favoring first one group, then another. A look at each of the successive cabinets reveals that in each there was a mix of interests representing the major influences on the political scene and each time the cabinet changed it was in response to a crisis, with the new Prime Minister appearing to favor the faction or Power that had the upper hand.

Of course, there are other ways to account for the mixed composition of the cabinet and their frequent demise under pressure. Given the ambiguity of the Persian political scene it would have been difficult to fill a cabinet with individuals sharing the same or similar opinions; the cabinet, therefore, tended to reflect the diversity of politics without conscious choice. Cabinets were also weak by their nature, susceptible to the sudden chills of the Persian political climate, and so change in a crisis was a reflection of the instability of government and the pressures placed on it. But looking at the small numbers involved and the consistency of Persian demands, as will be seen later, the conclusion that more than just accident or coincidence governed the changes is not so rash. It is impossible to prove but it bears holding in mind that when the demands on a particular cabinet became too great it resigned or threatened to in order to moderate the pressure or to win concessions; and that if this failed, they did resign, with the new cabinet tending to lean in the direction of greatest pressure. This is one possible explanation of why none of the Powers was able to win a firm, enduring agreement with any Persian Government, and yet why successive Persian cabinets managed to get so much, mainly money, from them. It might account for Townley's observation to Arthur Nicolson that

---

* The figure is derived by multiplying the number of cabinet offices times the number of cabinet changes during the war.

The situation [the political and strategic situation in Iran in late 1914] is outwardly more critical than I have ever seen it, but I am tired of crying wolf, as this wretched people [the Persians] always continue to emerge from the most hopeless positions, if badly crippled, yet smiling fatuously at having saved their skins.[10]

The weakness of the Persian Government and its questionable loyalties did not inspire the Foreign Office with confidence, nor were the British in control of the situation.

In Tehran the Germans and the Democrats lobbied for support with influential individuals and made plans for using their considerable power within the Majlis to embarrass the Allies. This included ideas for eliminating the Belgians, who had come to Iran in the late nineteenth century to reform the finances and who had become a symbol of foreign interference, from financial affairs, and for enlarging the gendarmerie, whose Swedish and Iranian officers could be counted on to support the nationalists.

Various leaders of the Democratic party, such as Mirza Qasim Khan, Sur Israfil, the editor of an influential Tehran newspaper, Sulayman Mirza, the head of the Democratic Party in the Majlis, and Vahid ul-Mulk Shaybani, met regularly with von Kardorff, the German Chargé d'Affaires, to discuss courses of action. They visited the Shah, the Valiahd (Crown Prince) and cabinet officials and continued their embassies to important public figures, such as Ali Quli Khan, Sardar As'ad, an influential Bakhtiari Khan, seeking their sympathy or support.[11] Towards the middle of Janaury 1915 Sur Israfil visited von Kardorff and outlined plans for using their sizeable footing in the Majlis to get pro-Allied supporters removed from influence.

The plan was a rather neat piece of work. First they planned to challenge the credentials of deputies they did not like and use their majority support to remove them; next they planned to get possible opponents removed from any position in the Government. According to the Constitution, a Majlis deputy could not hold a cabinet post simultaneously, although in practice this was ignored. What the Democrats proposed to do was force those cabinet members who were also deputies to give up their seats in the Majlis and then force a change of cabinet. Then, by using their majority, they could guarantee that only Democratic-approved individuals obtained posts in the new government. In this manner they hoped to rid Parliament and the government of pro-Allied leaders and fashion a political weapon to bring Persia into the war. But the plan had flaws.[12]

At first the Democrats had some success and at least one deputy was forced out; but there were problems with the plan to force a change of government. Mustaufi ul-Mamalik was both Prime Minister and a deputy; forcing the issue could cause him to resign both positions. Not all nationalists wanted Mustaufi ul-Mamalik, but the Germans and many of the Democratic leaders believed he favored their cause and feared that forcing the cabinet issue would lose his support. In addition, like the British, they were apprehensive of being able to control the selection of a new cabinet. Thus von Kardorff and the Democratic leadership were solicitous of the Prime Minister's position and acted cautiously.

Indeed, when Hosayn Pirnia, Mutamin ul-Mulk, the President of Majlis, informed von Kardorff on January 17 that the Prime Minister was contemplating resignation, the German Chargé paid the Prime Minister a visit in order to persuade him to remain. The Prime Minister availed himself of the occasion to air some of his 'burdens.' He complained to von Kardorff of the activities of the Swedish officers of the gendarmerie, who were acting contrary to the Government's wishes and who expressed pro-German sympathies in public. Mustaufi ul-Mamalik said he knew that the Swedes were under direct German influence and that they did nothing without checking with the German legation. He wanted von Kardorff to admonish the Swedes so that they would comply with Government orders. He then informed von Kardorff that he did not like the state of things and was planning to resign. The German Chargé tried to talk him out of it and suggested a cabinet reshuffle instead.[13] Mustaufi ul-Mamalik made no decisions, but he was interested enough in von Kardorff's views to send Mirza Sulayman Khan Mikada, the assistant Minister of War and a Democrat, to visit the German Legation and sound out the Chargé's opinion concerning the cabinet.

Mirza Sulayman Khan told von Kardorff that the Prime Minister wanted support to strengthen his cabinet and welcomed suggestions on new members. Mirza Sulayman Khan also took the opportunity to express his personal opinion that only von Kardorff could convince the Prime Minister to remain. The German Chargé replied by recommending that Ain ud-Daula be made Minister of the Interior and that Mushir ul-Mulk become Minister of Foreign Affairs,[14] choices who were felt to be at least not pro-Allied, if not pro-German.

In the meantime, a crisis loomed as the Democratic plan to force the issue of Majlis-Cabinet membership took shape. The Democrats and others realized that this might cause Mustaufi ul-Mamalik's resignation and on the evening of January 23, Mirza Muhammad Sadiq Tabataba'i (the leader of the Moderates), Sulayman Mirza, Sur Israfil and Arbab Kaikhusrau worked on him for four hours trying to keep him in office. No decisions were reached, however, and the crisis continued. Meanwhile other forces concerned themselves with the Persian cabinet's composition.

Townley had suggested a cabinet reshuffle in early January. In a meeting with the Prime Minister, Townley referred to doubts in certain quarters about the cabinet's ability to meet the situation – a euphemism for Russian dislike for the cabinet. Townley, hoping to add a more pro-Allied seasoning, suggested that Mustaufi ul-Mamalik appoint Farman-Farma as Minister of the Interior and that Vusuq ud-Daula replace Foreign Minister Ala us-Saltana, whose age was making it difficult for him to carry out his duties. Townley had confidence in both his candidates, who had been friendly in the past, and he may also have been trying to get one of the burrs from under the Russian saddle. But Mustaufi ul-Mamalik was giving up nothing. He expressed his concern over the Russian attitude but stated his conviction that Russian not Persian actions would precipitate a crisis for the Allies. He rejected Farman-Farma and Vusuq ud-Daula, his political rivals, on the grounds that their ideas and his were incompatible, and he declared complete confidence in Ala us-Saltana. He did indicate an interest in finding someone to replace himself as Minister of the Interior, an office he was holding simultaneously – a not uncommon practice – but he was not in a conciliatory mood.[15]

These actions were somewhat curious. In discussions with von Kardorff he had mooted his imminent retirement and then discussed German support and asked their recommendations. In his conversations with Townley he pursued a similar course. After taking a firm stand on the composition of his cabinet – at least on the membership of Farman-Farma and Vusuq ud-Daula – he followed up almost immediately by telling Townley he was determined to resign and stressed the recalcitrance of the Russians as the cause. Why? Perhaps Mustaufi ul-Mamalik felt indispensable and planned to use this to gain leverage. He certainly balanced his intentions of resignation with demands for support or assistance. Whatever his intentions his wavering attitude contributed to the unstable political atmosphere in Tehran and a cabinet crisis developed.

MORE CABINET CRISES

The cabinet crisis continued until Mustaufi ul-Mamalik finally agreed to form a new cabinet in mid-February. Only then did the political situation, relatively speaking, return to its normal confusion. None of the basic problems were resolved but the Prime Minister received enough reassurances to feel that he could continue in office. The various forces at work did not regard him as ideal but no one felt sure enough of controlling the character of his replacement to risk a change. The British were not pleased with the new cabinet. Mustaufi ul-Mamalik appointed Ain ud-Daula as Minister of the Interior, and Mukhbir us-Saltana as Minister of Justice against Townley's recommendation. As a consequence, the British considered the new cabinet unreliable, if not hostile,*[16] and too much under the influence of the Germans and the Democrats. They could not, however, completely write-off the cabinet because that would mean abandoning the position to the enemy.

No sooner was this cabinet crisis over, however, before another started, this time precipitated by British actions in the Gulf and south Persia. The British wanted to work with the cabinet, but they also recognized its weakness and knew that the Germans were taking no notice of Persia's neutrality. It was clear that the Swedish-officered gendarmerie was becoming increasingly pro-German and German agents were busy in almost every major city, meeting with local nationalists and encouraging *jihad*. One agent in particular, Captain Wilhelm Wassmuss, a former consul in south Persia before the war, became the subject of special concern.** The British tried to arrest him

---

* Mukhbir us-Saltana was Governor-General of Fars. The British had a special dislike for him because of his more than candid disapproval of British interference in Persian affairs. The British also suspected him of harboring pro-German sympathies and wanted him removed from Fars, one of the main areas of British interest. They exerted continual pressure on the Central Government to remove this thorn. The appointment of Mukhbir us-Saltana as Minister of Justice may have been Mustaufi ul-Mamalik's way of recalling Mukhbir us-Saltana without embarrassing him or seeming to give in to the Allied pressure, but Mukhbir us-Saltana did not assume his duties in Tehran nor was he removed from Fars. This move was even more unpopular with the British, who did not want to see a problem moved from one area to another.

** Wassmuss became Britain's special nemesis. He had been in south Persia before the war as consul at Bushire and was familiar with the region and its inhabitants. He spoke fluent Persian and was physically active and outgoing. He had many friends among the tribal leaders around Bushire and when war broke out he returned to south Persia to try to use these contacts to encourage anti-British activities. He had only marginal success but his activities frightened the British, who began seeing his influence

after he arrived in the south but Wassmuss escaped to Shiraz where the local Governor-General, Mukhbir us-Saltana, accorded him protection, arguing that Wassmuss was in a neutral country and entitled to protection, and that the British had no right to arrest him. The Governor-General's position was legally correct but the British never forgave him and began exerting pressure at Tehran to have him recalled. The British were not prepared to stand by and let the Germans and their Persian sympathizers simply hustle Iran into the war. In response they began making contacts with various tribal leaders, offering them money and support if they would act against the Germans and nationalists, and they also arrested all the other Germans in south Persia they could lay their hands on and deported them to India, and sent more troops to Ahwaz to protect the oilfields. The combination of these pressures, plus the open contraventions of Persia's neutrality, forced Mustaufi ul-Mamalik to resign on March 10.

He had been unable to control the situation. He had to deal constantly with British demands to stop the Germans and to placate a hostile, obstreperous Parliament. His Government needed money, but because of Russian hostility he could not hope for relief from the Allies and any deals with the Germans would mean an Allied occupation. If all this was not enough, he had a war in Azerbaijan, where

---

everywhere. The War Office, for example, printed a map indicating its ideas of the distribution of all enemy forces in the East. On one such map, covering all of south Persia, printed in large red letters was the one word 'Wassmuss.' So worrisome did he become that the British violated Persian neutrality in efforts to arrest him. When they failed Sir Percy Cox even offered a reward for Wassmuss – alive or dead. The Foreign Office, however, was horrified at the prospect of political assassination and the idea was suppressed – Arthur Nicolson called the idea repugnant and the Viceroy ordered its mention expurged from the original dispatches. Cox, however, had a measure of revenge. Later, when India had occasion to ask him if there was not something to be done to stop Wassmuss, he could only reply, 'The risk which we incur of exciting [the] abhorrence [of] His Majesty's Government together with the inability of the Indian Government to authorize any practical form [of] support to Haidar Khan after his arrest of Linders and after his abortive endeavour to arrest Wassmuss, render it very difficult to do anything which would have effect.' (Cox-SSI, 6/27/15, FO 371/2430) Wassmuss continued his activities in south Persia right through the war, and although after 1916 his threat was much diminished, his presence continued to menace British security in the south. For more complete information on Herr Wassmuss, see Christopher Sykes, *Wassmuss*; Howard Sachar, *The Emergence of the Middle East*; A. J. Barker, *The Neglected War*; Percy Sykes, *A History of Persia*, II; Ferdinand Tuohy, *The Craters of Mars* and *The Secret Corps: A Tale of 'Intelligence' on All Fronts*; and Frederick O'Connor, *On the Frontiers and Beyond: A Record of Thirty Years' Service* and *Things Mortal*, which is little more than a new edition of *On the Frontiers*.

some Persian subjects were in open revolt. In addition, German agents at Isfahan, Kermanshah and Shiraz were encouraging *jihad* and hiring local toughs; and the Ottomans had brought Salar ud-Daula (the brother of the deposed Muhammad Ali Shah and uncle to Ahmad Shah) to the western borders of Iran in hopes that his presence would cause more local tribes to flock to their side. Finally, British actions in the south proved too much and on March 10 the Cabinet resigned. Ahmad Shah accepted the resignation, perhaps realizing that a change of personnel might find new solutions or defuse hostilities.[17] This time no one seemed distraught at Mustaufi ul-Mamalik's departure.

When the Shah accepted the resignation, he instructed Mutamin ul-Mulk, President of the Majlis, to discover whom the Majlis favored as a successor. The various factions unanimously picked Mushir ud-Daula,[18] and on March 11 the Shah, acting upon the consensus of the Majlis, ordered him to form a government. The appointment of Mushir ud-Daula may have been an attempt to placate all the various parties. He was a recognized reformer and patriot and well respected by all political parties within the country. He was not identifiably attached to any side and he had considerable cabinet experience as well as having been Persian Ambassador to Britain and Russia. The Shah and those who favored neutrality may have hoped that Mushir ud-Daula could save Persia from being dragged into the war.

Mushir ud-Daula was not any more popular with the Allies than his predecessor. He was a bit too independent and included individuals in his cabinet that Townley and the Foreign Office felt were pro-German. And the Russians were still disinclined to make conciliatory gestures to any Persian Government.

Townley in Tehran and Sir Percy Cox (a recognized expert on Arab affairs and the Persian Gulf Resident detached as Political Officer to Force 'D', as the expeditionary force in Mesopotamia was called) both encouraged conversations with tribal leaders to give British interests the muscle they needed to control Persian internal affairs in the absence of the government's willingness or ability to satisfy the British. And both favored strong representations to the Persian Government regarding the activities of the gendarmes and the Governor-General of Fars, and concerning the activities of German agents, who had started to appear in various parts of the country as self-proclaimed consuls, and of Iranian nationalists who were preaching *jihad* and forming armed bands. The idea of intervening in a more direct fashion also began to grow because of the inability to get anything done through the Persian Government, with Cox urging the use of troops and Lord Crewe at the India Office raising a similar idea. But the Foreign Office wanted to avoid any direct action that would play into enemy hands, hence the talks with tribal leaders and the menacing language used on Mushir ud-Daula. (Both direct military intervention and arrangements with tribal leaders are discussed in Chapter VI.)

BRINGING PRESSURE TO BEAR

Throughout March, while pursuing the possibility of local arrangements, Townley had continued to press the Persian Government to check the activities of Wassmuss and other German agents, bluntly informing Mu'avin ud-Daula, the Persian Minister for Foreign Affairs, that 'men that acted in this way behaved like pirates, and were as much open to treatment of belligerents in neutral state as if they had weapons in their hands ...'[19] and he reiterated Britain's determination to check such agents by direct measures if necessary. Furthermore, he said that his Goverment had reason to believe that the Governor-General of Fars, Mukhbir us-Saltana, and the gendarmerie were involved in a plot to seize the British consulate at Shiraz (Consul-General O'Connor reported the plot and asked Townley for permission to burn his cyphers, to which Townley agreed.) He pressed the Persian Government to recall Mukhbir us-Saltana from Fars and to replace Major Pravitz, the Swedish commandant of the gendarmerie, as well. Mushir ud-Daula merely hinted that if the Russians withdrew it might be possible to discuss the recall of Mukhbir us-Saltana.[20] This did not sit well with the Allies and as a result Townley, Korostovetz and the French Minister called on the Prime Minister on March 21, and strongly urged him to: (1) recall Mukhbir us-Saltana and Pravitz, (2) cease protesting the presence of troops, and (3) stop enemy intrigues. They assured him that this was only a gesture of solidarity and not an ultimatum,[21] but they were determined, nevertheless, to find some settlement. Mushir ud-Daula was willing to settle outstanding difficulties; he was not ready to give in. He returned to the theme of Russian evacuation and stressed that only this would make it possible for a Persian Government to reach an agreement with the Allies. On March 23 he saw Townley at a party and took the opportunity to observe that Persia had three courses: (1) to side with the Allies; (2) to side with Germany; (3) to remain neutral. He said public opinion would not allow the first option; and although public opinion would approve the second course the Government did not. The Prime Minister felt that Persia's best course was to remain neutral, but he said this would be impossible if Russia did not withdraw from the north and stop the arrival of new troops.[22] Townley had already made clear what the Allies thought of withdrawal. He felt that German intrigues were the source of the troubles and that the presence of Russian troops was one of the few resources the Allies had in view of the Persian Government's inaction or inability to guarantee its neutrality. Although their respective positions remained irreconcilable, Townley began applying telling pressure on the Prime Minister.

In early April, Townley pointed to incidents where the Government had on the one hand not checked German activities while on the other it had done nothing to encourage pro-Allied officials.[23] He stressed to Mushir ud-Daula that Persian actions, or inaction, were endangering Britain's faith in the Persian Government, leaving the Prime Minister to assume what consequences might follow as a result. Such statements began to have an effect on the Prime Minister, who informed Townley that he would speak to the Majlis, the press and the *ulama* concerning the importance of England's friendship and the need for close ties. Indeed, he backed off his position so far as to agree to drop the question of Russian withdrawal and to promise more active measures to stop internal intrigue.[24] In this context he brought up the question of his Government's need for money and for the third time the subject of a moratorium appeared. The Prime Minister asked that the Allies assist Persia by suspending the service on foreign loans − a moratorium − so that the Government could have funds to operate.[25] At last, it seemed, there was an opening that could be exploited to reach an agreement, but despite this apparent opportunity, the Foreign Office did not rush to make an agreement. There was, however, a gradual shift in attitude.

Late in March, when the fever of strong action seemed to be in everyone's counsels, Cox had suggested that British officials in Iran publish lists of German agents and call on all patriotic Persians 'wishing to safeguard neutrality of their country to do all they can to show their disapprobation of them.'[26] The India Office, too, favored such a project and wanted to encourage friendly Iranians to help capture and deport troublesome Germans.

As might be expected, the Foreign Office worried that such actions would aggravate Persian opinion or that they could be construed by international opinion as violations of Persia's neutrality and so wanted to proceed more cautiously. The India Office could not suggest any alternatives, but Lancelot Oliphant and G. P. Clerk, senior clerks at the Foreign Office who believed that the project of strong action and bribing local Persians was futile and unhelpful, brought up the subject of the moratorium. In addition, Townley opposed the Cox plan on the grounds that it might produce bad results; he said that the fervor for Germany had declined and that Turkish high-handedness in the west, especially during the occupation of Qasr-i Shirin, a small border town, had inflamed Persian public opinion and might produce a war between Turkey and Persia.[27] Consequently the Foreign Office, while not giving up local negotiations, decided to take advantage of the more favorable climate at Tehran and returned to the idea of reaching a settlement with the central Government. Events in western Iran seemed to have turned Persian opinion against the Turks, thus making a general settlement more likely.

In mid- and late-April Turkish forces under Rauf Bey began occupying areas of western Persia. The presence of these troops, coupled with the activities of German agents and the return of the German and Austrian ministers (who had been in Europe on leave when the war began), excited local sentiment against the Allies as well as the Central Powers. The British and Russian consuls at Kermanshah, near the border with Mesopotamia and in the area affected by Turkish invasion and German agitation, considered the situation serious enough to evacuate the town, leaving it to Schunemann, one of the newly minted German consuls and the chief German agitator in western Iran, and his Persian supporters.[28]

NEW OPPORTUNITIES

At the same time, however, news of Turkish activities and rumors of high-handedness at Kerbela, a religious center sacred to Shi'a Muslims, aggravated Persian nationalist and religious sentiments. Turkish forces clashed with the Sinjabi — a close-knit, influential Kurdish tribe headquartered at Mahadasht in western Iran — and Rauf Bey demanded that the Persian Government punish them. Such aggressive actions caused Mustishar ud-Daula, the pro-German Minister of the Interior, to complain to Assim Bey, the Turkish Minister. Sir Charles Marling, the new British Minister who had just arrived in Persia, was able to report that these actions had embarrassed Assim Bey, who had asked Constantinople to keep Rauf Bey in check. British officials saw an opportunity of capitalizing on the changed climate of Persian opinion and as a result the sentiment for strong action began to wane.[29]

The Government of India now modified its opinion, something it and other British officials did with some frequency. In early March the Viceroy had expressed the opinion that only a victory in Mesopotamia would have the desired effect in Iran; although he had been in favor of small cash outlays to help the Persian finances if the Government would give something in return — such as refusing to recognize fresh appointments of German consuls in areas where Germany never had commercial interests. In early April, however, as *jihad* sentiment spread and enemy activities menaced south Persia, the Viceroy decided that, if the Persian Government was still wavering, Britain and India should not rely on stop-gap measures, but should offer a large loan — £300,000 — without interest, with certain Gulf islands as security. (The Viceroy suggested this sum be doled out in monthly installments of £25,000 and repaid in £50,000 annual installments.) At the same time Mushir ul-Mulk, Persian Ambassador to London and brother of the Prime Minister, complained that the Allies had done little to demonstrate their support and reminded the Foreign Office of the moratorium.[30]

Grey telegraphed Townley* on April 16 that the Allies were willing to support Persia.[31] Even Cox sensed a change in conditions because of Turkish actions and asked if the time had not come to renew 'any tempting' inducement to secure Persian support.

I take it for granted that we contemplate annexation of Basra Vilayet and also possibility of having to occupy Baghdad Vilayet for a time even if we intend ultimately to resign it to some less direct form of control. Consequently I presume that we still consider it necessary and expedient to offer Persia a footing in the Holy Places in prospect of our conquering Iraq.[32]

If not this, Cox suggested giving the Holy Places a Shi'a governor.**

---

* Sir Charles Marling replaced Sir Walter Townley as British Minister on April 15, but the cable was sent under Townley's name.

** It is difficult to understand where Cox acquired the notion that the Foreign Office still considered it 'necessary and expedient to offer Persia a footing in the Holy Places.' If there was one point on which the Foreign Office maintained a fixed opinion it was on giving a footing in Iraq to Persia. They had responded coldly to the idea when raised by Russia in 1914 and had again dismissed it in February 1915 when it was raised by

There seemed to be some possibility of reaching a settlement. But as Lord Crewe observed, 'The Persian atmosphere seems adverse to the retention of consistent views,'* for before any serious negotiations could begin with Mushir ud-Daula's Government, the Prime Minister resigned, after only two months in office, precipitating a new cabinet crisis. He had been caught in a crossfire, unsuccessful in his dealings with the Allies and in his efforts to control internal factors. He had to deal with constant British pressure to dismiss local officials and pursue pro-British policies in a situation where much of his support came from strongly anti-British sources. In addition German actions embarrassed his Government and gave the Allies reason to complain. The British, for example, discovered that Baron Ruess, the German Minister who was returning from leave in Europe, was transporting arms and ammunition in his personal luggage. The British insisted that the Persian Government seize this material. The Persian Government could only respond, and properly, that Ruess was entitled to diplomatic immunity.[33] One final factor that may have contributed to Mushir ud-Daula's resignation was the arrival in mid-April of Sir Charles Marling as the new British Minister. Persian rumor had it that Marling disliked Mushir ud-Daula and his hostility made it impossible for him to remain effective, although Marling had been minister only seven days. In any event, on April 22 the Prime Minister resigned and a scramble began to determine his successor.

Oliphant as a means of securing Persian assistance. (Minute by Oliphant to Townley-Grey, 2.12.14, FO 371/2428)

* It was not only the Persian atmosphere that affected consistency. On April 23, for example, the Viceroy reversed himself on the idea of a loan for Persia. In his opinion Persia had exaggerated views of its importance and had under German-Turkish insistence made unacceptable demands. The Viceroy referred the Persian Government to one of his messages urging them not to be drawn into the war. The Persian Government replied that if the British desired Persian neutrality, which was important, they should refrain from questionable acts – such as closing Persian telegraph offices, arresting German consuls on Persian soil, and troop landings. The Persian Government expressed the concern that, 'If difficulties should continue to be created as before, Persian Government regret that they will be powerless to deal with situation and disturbances will occur in Persia in consequence of which peace will depart from British possession ...' (Persian MFA-Government of India, 4/24/15, FO 371/2427) The Viceroy did not appreciate this reply and expressed the opinion that a loan offer would be a sign of weakness. (Viceroy-10, 4/24/15, FO 371/2427) Marling, too, believed that the Persian Government was too weak to benefit from monetary support. (Marling-Grey, 4/22/15, FO 371/2427)

YET MORE CABINET CRISES

The Germans tried to capitalize on the situation by embarrassing the mainstay of Britain's economic position – the Imperial Bank of Persia.* The German Legation withdrew 60,000 tumans [about £12,000] in silver and incited a run on the Bank. Under the Bank's charter it was obligated to cover its paper currency with silver upon demand; but when the Germans began the run the Bank was only able to cover 30 per cent of its note issue – because bad roads and insecurity had kept coinage from coming in from the provinces and because the Persian Government had not repaid heavy advances. As a result of the unexpected demands the Bank was in danger of having to close, an event that would have angered Persians and undermined Britain's position and prestige.[34] The Allies were not prepared to see such a situation develop and they, like the Germans and nationalists, considered strategy.

Marling met with the French Minister and Russian Chargé d'Affaires (who stood in for the new minister who was to replace Korostovetz but had not arrived) and they agreed to press Ahmad Shah to form a strong cabinet. Mirza Javad Khan, Sa'd ud-Daula; Sultan Abd ul-Majid Mirza, Ain ud-Daula; and Abd ul-Husayn Mirza, Farman-Farma, had expressed an interest in forming a government and the Allies agreed that these three men, with Sa'd ud-Daula as Prime Minister, would be the best candidates for a cabinet. Marling informed London that he would press for this. He also got reasonable assurances that the Government would introduce a bill in the Majlis that would declare bank notes legal tender – if the bank advanced money to the Government. This would relieve the pressure on the bank and frustrate the run, but Marling was concerned about the situation. The imminent return of the German minister, who had been in Germany on leave when the war began, and the activities of German agitators had created excitement in Tehran. The Swedes, in charge of the police force, were unreliable and the run on the Bank indicated the possibilities of unchecked German actions. Marling expressed the

---

* A private bank chartered to Baron de Reuter to compensate him for his loss of a more comprehensive concession in the late nineteenth century, the Imperial Bank of Persia became the chief banking institution in Persia. It had the sole authority to print money and it was the financial channel through which the British Government loaned money to the Persian Government to meet its obligations. See Firuz Kazamzadeh, *Russia and Britain in Persia, 1864-1914* and Marvin Entner, *Russo-Persian Commercial Relations, 1828-1914* on this institution.

opinion, one he would raise and drop many times, that Russian troops at Qazvin should be brought to Tehran and reinforcements should be held ready at Resht. He felt their presence would strengthen the Allied bargaining position and hold the situation together. The Foreign Office, however, continued its opposition to overt acts that might play into German hands. In a minute to Marling's telegram, Nicolson reiterated the Foreign Office belief: 'It should be the aim of the Allies to do nothing which should appear like a violation of Persian neutrality or which would give encouragement to our ill-wishers in Persia.' The Foreign Office remained alive to the threat of the situation and they wanted a solution – thus they were willing to support a new cabinet – but they wanted to avoid military actions. Grey informed the Russians of this sentiment and with this in mind, Marling visited the Shah to press for Sa'd ud-Daula's appointment as Prime Minister.[35]

The nationalists learned of this visit and panicked. The nationalists suspected Sa'd ud-Daula of being in the pocket of foreign interests and since the constitutional revolution many regarded him as a re-actionary. He was another long-time politician who had originally sided with the constitutionalists in 1905-6 against Muhammad Ali Shah, but who later changed sides, and the constitutionalists never forgot it. Sa'd ud-Daula was also associated in the popular mind with the Russians and the British and the prospect of seeing a man so clearly in one camp raised the image of a coup. To make matters worse, a courtier* informed the Democrats that Marling was not only pressing for Sa'd ud-Daula as Prime Minister but he also wanted the Shah to close the Majlis, shut down the anti-Allied press, expel the Swedes and stop German activities – in effect, an anti-Democratic coup.

The nationalists began considering counter-measures. Von Kardorff was unavailable when the news came in and so the nationalists, who were coordinating their activities with the German embassy, sought out Swedish officers of the gendarmes, who sympathized with Persia's cause, for advice. Proposals ranged from kidnapping the Shah to arresting the Allied ministers. They finally decided to wait on von Kardorff. When the German learned of the Allied pressure on Ahmad Shah, he and Assim Bey, the Turkish Ambassador, went to

---

* Von Kardorff created a secret organization at the start of the war which included many influential figures as well as courtiers, deputies, ministers, local officials, and even Iranian employees of foreign embassies. This organization was able to supply him with information on Allied plans and actions.

see the Shah, and, in a session that lasted until 3:00 in the morning, they convinced him not to appoint Sa'd ud-Daula; they settled on Ain ud-Daula, instead, who was a more neutral figure, although another long-time politician[36] and the Shah's uncle by marriage.

Marling reported to London that even with the support of the two legations Sa'd ud-Daula had been unable to form a cabinet. The Shah and Ain ud-Daula had raised objections and no influential men who might have served as cabinet members were prepared to enter the government of a man as unpopular as Sa'd ud-Daula. Ain ud-Daula emerged as the prime candidate and Marling accepted the inevitable because he appeared to have good relations with the Majlis[37] and was not openly hostile to the Allies or partial to the nationalists and Germans. But, in an effort to have some men in the cabinet that the Allies regarded as real supporters, Marling pressed the Shah to include Farman-Farma and Mirza Hasan Khan, Vusuq ud-Daula. He believed that Ain ud-Daula's appointment would be read in Petrograd as a British victory, since he had before the war been more friendly to the British, and so Marling wanted to see Farman-Farma and Vusuq ud-Daula included because it was believed they were strongly pro-Russian.*

On April 26 the Shah instructed Ain ud-Daula to form a new cabinet, the fourth since August 1914. He began his tenure under difficult circumstances. The previous cabinet had collapsed under pressure from political factions and the Turkish invasion, and his own cabinet had been forged from the clash of opposing interests. He was in power as everyone's compromise, unable to rely on broad support in the Majlis, and he had to depend on persuasion and circumspection.

Soon after his appointment Ain ud-Daula went to see Ruess, the German Minister, who had finally made a near-triumphal return to Tehran amid pro-German demonstrations and cries of 'Khuda mujazat dihad – Inglistan ra! [God will punish England].' The new Prime Minister talked about the pressures from Russia and Britain and explained to the German Minister why it was not possible to name his whole cabinet from pro-German politicians. According to one source he apologized for appointing Farman-Farma and promised to include Hakim ul-Mulk, a Germanophile, to balance the cabinet's complexion.[38] At the same time Ain ud-Daula had to keep the Allies

---

* A curious fact because now these two men have the reputation for having been pro-British. It is more likely that their 'loyalty' to one Power or the other was based on the necessities of the moment.

contented and operate his Government against internal opposition – partly from nationalists who wanted to force issues and partly from long-lived political rivalries and jealousies that punctuated the life of all Persian cabinets. But he was not without resources. He did have some following and the various sides had at least allowed him to form a government. He was able to capitalize on this only by careful balancing.

He appeared friendly to the Germans and conciliatory to the British. The run on the Imperial Bank of Persia had promised serious political repercussions for British interests and Ain ud-Daula agreed to get a bill passed that would relieve the situation. He also promised to check German-nationalist intrigue and to recall Mukhbir us-Saltana, the troublesome Governor-General of Fars. But he wanted financial support in return. His Government needed funds to meet expenses and the Prime Minister, not without hope, believed Britain would help. Once again it was the Persian Government that opened up the possibility of financial support.[39]

Marling, although somewhat equivocal, supported the idea to London. He considered the new cabinet more reliable, although it had done nothing to substantiate the feeling other than make vague gestures. But Marling felt that this cabinet was not so dubious as its two predecessors and was less likely to make impossible demands. He believed it would need financial aid, but he had not given Ain ud-Daula any hope unless he gave 'satisfactory evidence that his administration deserves it.'

Marling was less guarded in his remarks to London, however. The newly reconstituted cabinet gave Britain a more favorable position which Marling believed was maintainable with a 'reasonable measure of financial support'; but he warned, 'if we refuse to assist, that position would be worse than thrown away.'[40] The Foreign Office took the hint, since it was in line with its own thinking, and informed Marling of their willingness to support the cabinet. Grey instructed Marling to explore the Persian position, but he wanted to make it clear to the Prime Minister that Britain was in no way committing itself 'until the Cabinet shall have shown definitely that it merits our support.'[41] But no sooner had Marling expressed confidence in the new cabinet than he reversed himself.

Marling had not given up on the idea that Russian troops at Qazvin were the only real way of giving the cabinet the backbone it needed to stand up to all the forces loose in Tehran. He was not, however, always consistent in his positions, part of which can be explained by the circumstances he had to cope with. But there was more inconsistency in his opinions than events supported. Hardinge, who had reason to dislike Marling, described him as 'a queer fellow of dyspeptic nature [who] seems to jump at conclusions for which there is no solid foundation.'[42] He also tended to exaggerate conditions in Iran, as if he had to over-sell his position to get what he felt British policy needed. Given the number of different official views that had to be coordinated before any decisions could be reached, Marling may have developed the habit of shouting to be heard over the chorus. In the following months he would disparage every opinion emanating from officials of the Indian Government, unless they concurred with his, and then he had modifications to suggest; and he would become involved in bitter power struggles with the Viceroy and others over the direction of policy in Iran. His antipathy to certain Persian statesmen and the negative opinions he shared with many other British officials about Persians generally and about nationalist sentiments, made him less than the best choice as minister to Persia. (Perhaps his most enduring gesture was the gift of various Persian antiques, collected while he was in Iran, to the Victoria and Albert Museum in London.)

When Ain ud-Daula made his proposals for financial support Marling urged them on London, but he did not believe that any one solution would give British interests the security they needed and he believed troops were the only way to give the cabinet the strength to maintain the country's neutrality. Unlike the Foreign Office he felt that the presence of troops would show the Persians that the Allies had a limit to their patience and that it would not cause them to abandon neutrality, but would probably prevent the Germans and nationalists from jockeying the country into war. On May 12, Marling again urged the need for troops and in view of this insistence Grey instructed Buchanan to encourage the Russians to send more troops to Enzeli, the main Persian port on the Caspian. But Buchanan hardly had time to raise the point before Marling suggested a different approach. He did not rule out the need for troops, but an opportunity to secure the active support of the Persian Government developed and he wanted to exploit it. The Persians were still making noises about a moratorium.[43]

Marling and de Etter met with Ain ud-Daula and Muhtashim us-Saltana, the Minister for Foreign Affairs, on May 13, and discussed the situation. Muhtashim us-Saltana asked for (1) a moratorium; and (2) settlement of various questions with Russia in Persia's favor – viz., collection of revenues in Azerbaijan by Russian consuls, protection given to Persian subjects by Russia, and the rights of Russian subjects to own property in Persia. The Russian Minister, with Marling's support, ruled out a moratorium but he expressed a willingness to discuss the other topics. Marling also pointed out that neutrality was important to Persia and he suggested that the Persian Government draw up a list of their financial proposals. In presenting the Persian Government's position, the Prime Minister professed a readiness to pursue a neutral policy and to combat intrigue, and also retreated from the moratorium idea. He admitted his Government's financial need but he did not ask for a large lump sum; instead, he suggested a scheme whereby the Allies would strengthen his position financially as his Government achieved results. Marling approved the idea and arranged to secure 40,000 tumans [about £7,500] through the Imperial Bank of Persia as an installment in this process. In return Ain ud-Daula promised to recall the Governor-General of Fars and to appoint Qavam ul-Mulk, a tribal leader in Fars, his temporary successor. In addition, the Prime Minister expressed confidence in his ability to control the Majlis, or at least to get them to adjourn for a long holiday.[44]

This seemed to convince Marling of the benefits of Ain ud-Daula's Government and on May 16 he informed the Foreign Office that it was time to make definite financial proposals. He also reversed himself on the need for troops, whose arrival he now felt might make the Germans nervous enough to do something desperate. As a result, on May 18 Grey instructed Buchanan to ask the Russians not to send troops but to hold two or three thousand men in readiness just in case they were needed after all. Marling had not secured a definite agreement but he was able to feel he was gaining 'over the noisy and mischievous self-seekers who call themselves the Democratic party.'[45] His confidence was premature.

On the evening of May 18 a group of assassins attacked and murdered M. von Kaver, the Russian bank manager at Isfahan.[46] Rumor suggested that the Germans had instigated the attack and on the following day Ain ud-Daula, pressured from all sides, resigned. Britain found itself without a clear line of action. Marling had wanted troops, only to change his mind because he thought the situation was better. Now there was a new crisis, Marling's gains evaporated and Britain still had not managed to reach a settlement.

RENEWED DIFFICULTIES

The Shah and the Majlis prevailed on Ain ud-Daula to stay, but the situation, at least for Britain, continued to deteriorate. On May 20 Marling was back on the theme of troops. This time, however, he felt that the two or three thousand men that might have had an effect if landed at Enzeli earlier would have to be increased to at least 6,000. He was also convinced that if Ain ud-Daula fell the new cabinet would be a German-nationalist creature – with the obvious consequences.[47] In addition to these worries Marling began having trouble with Ain ud-Daula himself.

Ain ud-Daula faced a dilemma. His government was not united and much of it was actively supporting actions opposed to his policy. He wanted to avoid difficulties with the Allies, but he felt that their actions, especially when coupled with the ingrained Iranian dislike for things Russian, made a shambles of his attempts to maintain order. His efforts to point this out aggravated the Russians and convinced the British he was playing the old game of taking advantage of British-Russian rivalry.

Despite repeated reminders Ain ud-Daula delayed submitting his financial proposals and when he did present them, on May 28, they were largely a reiteration of earlier proposals. They even returned to the idea that the Allies should supply Persia with a moderate sum to finance a small force – an idea raised by Mustaufi ul-Mamalik in 1914.[48] Furthermore, Ain ud-Daula did not, at least in Marling's opinion, take very active measures to check intrigues and he did not recall Mukhbir us-Saltana. Marling was perplexed by the fact that he could not even get the Prime Minister to withdraw the 40,000 tumans that he had arranged through the Imperial Bank of Persia to ease the Government's financial problems. Ain ud-Daula returned to the question of Russian withdrawal and he procrastinated in holding talks with de Etter over property rights and tax collection by consuls, despite Russian willingness to discuss the matter.[49] In short, he had not proved very reliable after all. In the meantime conditions grew more tense and the Viceroy felt obliged to outline India's policy in the event of Persia joining the enemy.

The Viceroy had already proposed abandoning the hinterland of

Persia and holding only Bushire on the Gulf in the event of war when he rejected a proposal by Cox to create a virtual British enclave in southern Persia based on tribal support.[50] As the situation declined further he elaborated on these plans. In the event of war the Viceroy intended to: (1) leave Persia as a whole severely alone, taking only the action necessary to extract British legation and consular personnel; (2) endeavor to protect oil installations, with offers of large sums to local tribes; (3) if possible hold Bushire, Jask and Charbar (Gulf ports through which ran the British telegraph line to India), and blockade Persia's southern ports.[51]

While the Viceroy formulated these measures the Foreign Office continued to hope for a settlement. They dissuaded the Russians from pressing their claims for compensation over the murder of von Kaver — partly because the necessary force was lacking, partly because they did not want to weaken the Persian Government further, and partly because they did not want to alienate the Bakhtiari, a tribal group that governed Isfahan. The Russians wanted to dismiss the Bakhtiari governor of Isfahan and Marling supported the idea, but Grey was not enthusiastic. He was willing to support it if the Persian Government were willing to take the action, but he did not want to risk alienating the khans, whose support, after all, Britain might need if affairs in Tehran got out of hand. The Russians, however, insisted that the Persian Government at least replace the Bakhtiari governor, Sardar-i Muhtashim, with a more active Bakhtiari khan who would take stronger actions to defend Allied interests. The appointment of a new governor made the Russians happy but did little to alter the situation. Isfahan remained one of the centers of Germany activity. In the meantime Marling continued to press Ain ud-Daula to come up with financial proposals, since he considered the most recent presentations as mere fishing.[52]

On June 3 Ain ud-Daula presented a new *aide memoire* that was not markedly different from earlier versions, except that he dropped the reference to Russian withdrawal or settlement of Russian-Persian differences, and once again expressed an interest in a moratorium, for three years. Marling was not pleased with the new proposal — he had already rejected the moratorium idea and here it was again. He and de Etter decided not to respond to the new note.[53] As a result Ain ud-Daula went to see Marling, who disparaged the moratorium as unlikely and one of three years as out of the question. The Prime Minister did not give up, though, assuring Marling that he could not get along without such a commitment. But Marling worried that the Democrats would wait until Britain paid over the money and then turn the cabinet out so they could get it. Ain ud-Daula responded by suggesting that if Britain believed this they could stipulate that payment could be terminated at British discretion.[54] No agreements were reached but neither had spoken the final word. The Persians shifted the scene of their approaches.

On June 12 the Persian Minister in London, Mirza Mihdi Khan, Mushir ul-Mulk, indicated that his Government would like some material proof of Britain's goodwill and Grey asked Marling for further details on Persia's needs.[55] Marling had more or less consistently deprecated the moratorium idea to the Persians, but Persia's insistence and the need for some solution to the problems in Persia began to make the moratorium more attractive. The Foreign Office began seriously to consider arranging for a moratorium along the lines asked for by the Persian Government and on June 21 even Marling recommended that the Foreign Office accept the moratorium as presented by the Persian Government.[56] Theoretically this meant a suspension of Iran's payments on its debts to Britain and Russia, but in fact it amounted to a monthly subsidy to the Persian Government to meet operating costs. The proposal called for the release of £10,500 monthly from the customs receipts of Persia's southern ports and £20,000 from the northern ports.* In addition the Allies were not to press for payment of arrears. When he passed along these proposals, Marling deprecated the idea that Britain would be able to exact any control over the money because this would make the arrangement unacceptable to any Persian cabinet, although he held out some hopes for establishing guidelines for the expenditure.

Surprisingly the Russians were not opposed to the idea, though they complicated the issue by insisting they could only pay in rubles, a problem since the ruble was in trouble and its buying power in Iran greatly reduced. The manager of the Imperial Bank of Persia saw the moratorium as an attempt by the Russians to unload large quantities of paper money at someone else's expense and he was not eager for such an arrangment. This was a minor point, however, and Grey presented the proposals to Austen Chamberlain, Secretary of State

---

* Russia and Britain acquired control of the customs revenues as security on various loans floated by Persia in the late nineteenth and early twentieth century. See Kazamzadeh, *Britain and Russia*, and Entner, *Russo-Persian Commercial Relations*.

for India, with the explanation that this approach seemed the most likely means of strengthening the Persian Government.[57] On July 2 the Foreign Office broached the idea with the Treasury, pointing out the importance attached to an early decision, for they had reason to believe that this money would strengthen the Cabinet and give Britain the looked-for solution for combating German activities.[58]

The Treasury, however, did not move with haste.* The Foreign Office pressed for an answer, which seemed essential given the situation at Tehran and the fact that the Persian Government was looking for support. The Persians had already approached the French, and the Foreign Office knew that the Germans would be willing to come up with funds if they were asked. But the Treasury delayed. The Foreign Office pressed for an immediate answer, arguing that the moratorium was not a loan of money but a foregoing of receiving it.

Meanwhile conditions throughout the country continued to cause alarm and an agonized tone began to appear in Foreign Office minutes. It had taken the Foreign Office several months to decide on the moratorium as the best means of securing the situation and it was impatient with the Treasury for taking its time in deciding. The Foreign Office hoped that bolstering the Persians would forestall a disaster, and it was impatient because events in Tehran and throughout the country were growing more dangerous and delay seemed fatal.

DECLINING PROSPECTS

The political situation in Tehran had been growing steadily worse and the consuls at Isfahan, Shiraz and elsewhere had little if any encouraging news. German activities at Kermanshah forced the British consul to flee to Hamadan, where the situation was little better; and Frederick O'Connor, the consul at Shiraz, continually reported a bleak political atmosphere, with the exception that Qavam ul-Mulk and Sulat

---

* The Chancellor of the Exchequer had assured the House of Commons that none of the money voted by them would go to foreign countries without their sanction. At the beginning of the war Parliament voted the Government the right to spend money on the war effort for the duration of the war plus six months without having to refer constantly to Parliament for sanction on every item of the war budget. There were, however, certain limitations. The question arose whether to regard the moratorium as a foreign loan and the need for deliberation caused a delay.

ud-Daula, two powerful tribal leaders of the Khamsih and the Qashqu'i, respectively, had agreed to bury their differences and maintain neutrality if the Government did not. But Wassmuss continued his activities in the south. He tried to bribe Sulat ud-Daula and he enlisted armed supporters, including some of Sulat ud-Daula's disaffected brothers and various other khans between Shiraz and the Gulf.[59]

The Germans at Isfahan continued their subversive activities and a small party of Germans and Iranian supporters, headed by two Germans, Doctor Zugmayer and Lieutenant Gresinger, set off for Kerman in early June to spread German propaganda. Another party also left Isfahan for Khorasan and Afghanistan. Throughout the summer of 1915 various German parties arrived in and departed from Isfahan, the main center of activities, bound for various parts of Iran or Afghanistan.[60] These groups were often joined by Iranian sympathizers and armed men, posing a serious problem to British policy because they had the potential of compromising Persian neutrality to the point of war. In late June and early July as the internal political situation began to decline and various German parties began pushing in earnest for Afghanistan, the Government of India, not relying on the success of the moratorium idea, began to consider courses of action to alleviate the dangers.

India had initially dismissed the threat posed by the German missions, but as it became obvious that such parties could rely on local supporters and that the political situation in Afghanistan might be fertile ground for German intrigue, they became alarmed. In addition, disturbing reports from the area south of Shiraz indicated that Wassmuss had succeeded in raising considerable support and that several local khans were planning an attack on Bushire and British holdings in the south.

In the absence of sufficient Indian forces to cover the approaches to Afghanistan or protect British lives and property in Iran, the Viceroy considered alternatives. Securing local support seemed the best answer, and in keeping with the early determination not to make long-term commitments to regional leaders he decided to rely on money. On July 2 he instructed the consuls at Bushire, Mashad and Sistan (the latter two locations are in northeastern and southeastern Iran, respectively) that under no circumstances were German parties to be allowed to enter Afghanistan. He then authorized them to raise local forces and to make punitive use of them, if necessary, to stop the German advance.[61] The Viceroy instructed the consul of Kerman to use secret service funds 'freely' with the object of putting leading men against such parties, getting them boycotted, and collecting information on their number, movements and armaments. More boldly, he instructed the Governor-General of Baluchistan to authorize the political officers of the Persian-Baluchistan frontier to collect information and to 'proceed against any party of German agents approaching the frontier with militia and such local forces as may be available and to destroy them.' Furthermore, British troops were to operate out of Rabat (located in Indian Baluchistan near the confluence of the Persian-Afghanistan-Baluchistan border) in co-operation with Russian troops from the north in order to cordon off the approaches to Afghanistan – an operation eventually known as the Eastern Cordon.[62]

The Viceroy's actions drew immediate comment. The Foreign Office and Marling put their hopes in the moratorium and wanted to avoid actions that would embarrass the Persian Government. Marling opposed the idea completely. He was surprised at India's concern, since they had never given grounds to doubt the Amir of Afghanistan or to fear the German advance before. Furthermore, he believed that the use of British troops in Persia would give an impetus to German agitation and so wanted to avoid direct action and to work through the Persian Government, who had promised to advise local officials to halt the Germans. He had seen how effectively German money had encouraged support at Tehran, and he felt certain that Britain could enjoy similar support in the Majlis and the cabinet if certain scruples were overcome.[63] The India Office did not completely close the door to such a recourse. They respected Marling's assessment but Chamberlain informed the Foreign Office that he presumed

... that what His Majesty's Government are concerned about is not so much the neutrality of Persia – which has already been violated by Germany and Turkey and which the Persian Government has shown itself unable to maintain – as the possibility that military action on our part may, in the given circumstances, afford the pro-German party in Persia the excuse and the opportunity for dragging the Persian Government into the conflict.[64]

While the India Office accepted this view, wanting to avoid direct action, Chamberlain hoped that the Foreign Office would keep India informed if Marling decided that military action to stop the Germans was the only alternative after all.[65] The India Office instructed the

Viceroy to direct the consuls and political officers not to raise local forces, to avoid confrontations, and to work through regular Persian officials to stop the Germans.[66] India complied but not without taking a parting shot. Marling, said the Viceroy, had misunderstood India's view of the Afghanistan situation. India had not acted because it distrusted the Amir but because it was unclear whether he could control his fanatical followers.[67] Nevertheless India rescinded the orders. However, circumstances would soon make the Viceroy's plan more attractive and Marling, who was not always consistent in his recommendations, would have cause to change his mind.

Meanwhile, Marling tried to secure the Persian Government's active support with the moratorium. But the nationalists dominated the Majlis, kept the political atmosphere heated, and gave Marling no leisure to reach an agreement. In late June they renewed their attempts to remove unsatisfactory cabinet members. This time the attack centered on Farman-Farma, the Minister of the Interior, whom the British and the Russians favored. The Democrats regarded Farman-Farma as pro-Allied and his efforts on their behalf to stifle local intrigues and incidents reinforced their prejudice. As a result they used the fact of the Turkish invasion as a device to question the Government's and Farman-Farma's failure to defend the country.*[68] Ain ud-Daula defended his cabinet and Farman-Farma, but he let it be known that he was going to resign, perhaps as a tactic to test for support. Marling and de Etter, who had hopes of reaching an agreement with the cabinet, did not want to see Ain ud-Daula's resignation and they backed him. Some Majlis deputies also wanted him to stay, but the majority of the Democrats wanted to replace him.

Ain ud-Daula was aware of this position and tried to find a compromise. He informed a Majlis group that he was willing to replace Farman-Farma as Minister of the Interior, moving him to the War Ministry — a virtually powerless sinecure since Persia had no army — but the Democrats wanted him completely out of the Government. Ain ud-Daula was caught between this pressure and Marling's determination to keep Farman-Farma in the Government; but he finally gave in to the Democrats' pressure and promised to replace Farman-Farma if his cabinet received a vote of confidence. Sulayman Mirza, the leader of the Democrats, reluctantly agreed.[69] Other

* Many of Farman-Farma's private estates were located in the area of the Turkish advance and some of his property was looted or burned by the Turks.

members of the cabinet, however, indicated they would resign if Farman-Farma were replaced and so the crisis continued.

Farman-Farma tried to mend his fences. He visited Democratic leaders and entertained Ruess, the German Minister, letting it be known that he was not anti-German.[70] But the Democrats remained intractable and tried to force the issue even though the Germans did not want to see Ain ud-Daula's fall lest the Russians use the occasion to become more aggressive. But even this unsuspected support could not avert the crisis.

Marling was aware of the attack on the Minister of the Interior and of Ain ud-Daula's willingness to sacrifice Farman-Farma. He and the Foreign Office regarded this with dismay, and Marling informed the Prime Minister that any move to replace the Minister of the Interior would be regarded as a sign that German pressure had prevailed, and if that were the case he could no longer count on British support. He went so far as to say that the moratorium depended upon Farman-Farma remaining in the cabinet. Marling attached great importance to Farman-Farma's retention and expressed to Grey the opinion that Britain could do without Ain ud-Daula altogether.[71] Privately, Farman-Farma also received £1,000 from the Allies to use to win over public opinion and help secure Ain ud-Daula's position for himself if the government fell. The Allies were not trying to bring down Ain ud-Daula's government, but they were trying to store up goodwill for the inevitable change.[72]

Despite this, though, Marling tried to rescue Ain ud-Daula, believing any alternative might prove worse. He visited the Shah and pointed out the dangers of drifting into enemy hands, informing Ahmad Shah that His Majesty's Government would regard the resignation of the cabinet as the bidding of a minority and as a sign that Persia was under enemy influence. He wanted the Shah to use his influence to retain the cabinet or face the likelihood that Britain would have to take direct action to protect its interests. The Shah, however, indicated that the cabinet had already resolved to resign and doubted his chances of preserving it.[73] The only hope for the cabinet rested on the fact that no one group had enough support to determine his successor.

The Majlis established a commission to study possible successors but there was no agreement among the various factions. Some favored Ain ud-Daula, some Mustaufi ul-Mamalik, and others Mushir ud-Daula. The cabinet crisis intensified and the debate over successors spread to the various Tehran newspapers – each of which upheld the opinion and candidate of the faction it represented. The only thing that united the various elements was a general opposition to Farman-Farma, but no one could count on a consensus to form a government. The situation continued to deteriorate. The collapse of the cabinet undermined Marling's plan to get the Persian Government to stop the German missions to Afghanistan and his sporadic efforts to tie the cabinet to the Allies by means of the moratorium. Marling was not prepared to give up on the return of Ain ud-Daula's cabinet but he now recognized that local Persian authorities would be unable to stop the German parties and he recommended that British and Russian troops in eastern Persia be ready to take direct action to stop them. In the meantime events elsewhere in the country precipitated a new crisis and on July 12 Ain ud-Daula resigned.[74]

THE BUSHIRE INCIDENT

Wassmuss' activities in the south finally produced the long-awaited attack.[75] Several minor khans in south Persia in an area called Tangistan responded to his blandishments and began moving their followers into the vicinity of Bushire, the main British base in the Gulf. On July 12 a small British reconnaissance party stumbled into a party of these tribesmen and two British officers were killed. Several minor engagements followed in which the tribesmen made feeble attacks on British outposts around Bushire. By the 13th, however, these attacks had petered out and advancing British troops found that all enemy forces had disappeared.[76] Nonetheless, the incident was serious, for a German agent had finally succeeded in moving Persians to violent action. The Persian Government was in a state of collapse and German agents were pressing on Afghanistan. In the face of this situation all British indecision disappeared; it only remained to decide what to do.

The attack caused Marling to reverse his position again. He now felt that Britain had perfect justification for using any necessary force to prevent the Germans from reaching Afghanistan and that the death of the two British officers was justification for Britain to adopt 'similar' means and 'employ steady tribesmen to attack their [German] emmissaries.'[77] Marling also returned to the theme of vigorous action. He no longer believed Ain ud-Daula could be relied upon and he wanted the Russians to reinforce their troops by five thousand men and for Britain to occupy Bushire, Bandar Abbas, Lingeh, Mohammerah, and Hormuz in the south until Persia made reparation and stopped German activities. He saw these as the actions that could reverse the situation: 'If we fail to do this we must be prepared to see the Germans free to do what they like, except where we are able to use our own resources and be exposed to the possibility of further outrages.' The Foreign Office was inclined to agree and informed the India Office of this opinion.[78] But it was now India's turn to be cautious.

The Government of India agreed that some action was necessary and that Russia should be encouraged, but they felt Marling's suggestions would endanger relations with Persia and excite the tribes further:

Although action of some kind seems to us to be absolutely necessary for the purpose of making the Persian Government realize that it is impossible to allow the hostile machinations of Germany and Austria to proceed unchecked in Persia, our eyes must not be closed to the fact that if in consequence war should be declared by Persia on Great Britain and Russia, although she herself is a negligible quantity and impotent, the task of the Ameer in maintaining his neutral position in opposition to the warlike tendencies of the Afghans will certainly be made much more difficult and unrest and bitterness of feelings amongst his own Mohammedan population will probably result.

In view of this India proposed that Britain assume control of Bushire and demand from the Persian Government, if they were unwilling to protect British interests, the punishment of the offending khans and a payment of £500 and £100 for each sepoy killed or wounded, respectively. They also wanted action taken to stop the Germans and the recall of Mukhbir us-Saltana from Shiraz. If not, then Britain would reconsider its options. The Viceroy was opposed, however, to any action outside Bushire unless it were an attack on Dilwar, a village controlled by one of the offending khans.[79]

Marling was somewhat disappointed by this attitude. He felt that most Persian opinion already saw Bushire as controlled by Britain and that its occupation would accomplish nothing. He believed it was imperative that either Britain or Russia make some demonstrative show of strength. He recommended that Britain demand an apology and that Persia pay £20,000 indemnity, recall the Governor-General of Fars, punish the offenders, arrest and expel Wassmuss and other German agents and intern Austrian prisoners-of-war who had escaped from Russia and were joining forces with enemy activists in Iran.

Cox, too, wanted vigorous action, including the arrest of all Germans and the assumption of total control of Bushire Customs House if the Persian Government did not accept British terms. The Government of India, however, hesitated. They worried about the repercussions, and lacked the necessary troops for extensive action. Operations in Mesopotamia employed India's available field forces and any operations in south Persia, even the occupation of Bushire, would require a diversion of men and material. Therefore, military authorities decided to delay action until operations in Mesopotamia permitted a moderate diversion. In the meantime the Admiralty assembled a small naval force to assist in the contemplated occupation of Bushire and bombardment of Dilwar.[80]

Marling was unhappy with these events. He felt that India had misled him regarding the German threat and that their actions in the Gulf were completely inadequate. In a private letter to Arthur Nicolson on July 21 he vented his disgust:

We have been doing something very like living in a fool's paradise, and were rudely aroused from it by the Indian Government's tardy avowal that they were by no means sure of the situation either in Afghanistan or even in India. I should be sorry to say that if we, I mean Etter and myself, had known of it earlier we could have done more for it hardly depended on us, but we could have tried and I should have insisted very much more strongly on the necessity of a much larger number of Russian troops being sent to Kazvin than were actually despatched. The 750 or 800 men sent were, I felt, not sufficient to give the Cabinet the backbone necessary to deal with the Germans, tho[ugh] their arrival did for a time produce an effect, i.e., that of making Ruess transfer his centre of active operations from Tehran to Isfahan; and in face of the unwillingness of both governments to impose a cabinet on Persia — and with India's apparent feelings of security ... I considered that the worse that was to be feared was that Persia would be jockeyed into war, and even that possibility had at one time been regarded by India as nothing terrible. Well, all that is past now but I fear that India has told the truth to us too late ...[81]

He went on to paint a gloomy picture of the political situation in Tehran. He termed the occupation of Bushire ineffectual and expressed the opinion that only the arrival of Russian troops would save the Allied position: '... if no Russian troops arrive there is no hope. *We must show strength*' [Marling's emphasis].[82] The show of strength was slow in coming and it was not what Marling had hoped for.

The necessary troops for the operations at Bushire did not arrive until August 4 and they did not move ashore from the destroyer *Juno* until August 8. The attack on Dilwar occurred five days later when British troops stormed ashore under the cover of naval fire and destroyed the unoccupied village and its palm groves.[83]

Under the circumstances the moratorium idea retreated rapidly into obscurity and even if the British had been ready to take up the matter, there was no Persian Government with which to negotiate. The moratorium or any new approach had to wait on events.

PERSIA WITHOUT A GOVERNMENT

While Whitehall, India and the Legation at Tehran debated the merits of a show of force, the crisis that had overwhelmed Ain ud-Daula's Government continued. The Shah had accepted his resignation but Ain ud-Daula had not given up attempts to remain Prime Minister. He had been unable to control Majlis opposition to Farman-Farma and he may have resigned to create a crisis to make his recall necessary, for it was obvious that no candidate could rely on majority support, and so the position would go to the man of the hour. The Majlis met in long sessions and discussed various candidates for Prime Minister, the main contenders being Ain ud-Daula, Mushir ud-Daula, and Mustaufi ul-Mamalik. No candidate had majority support, however, and these discussions produced more friction than resolution. Ain ud-Daula insisted that if he were to resume office all opposition must cease and his former cabinet had to be returned *in toto*.[84] This was totally unacceptable to the Democrats, who had not engineered the initial crisis to see Farman-Farma back in office. As a result, on January 20 Ain ud-Daula could only reaffirm his resignation, and on July 21 the Shah asked Mushir ud-Daula to form a government. Mushir ud-Daula asked for time to investigate the majority will and to plumb for candidates. He then tried to form a coalition cabinet that would have included Ain ud-Daula and Mustaufi ul-Mamalik.[85] But neither of the former prime ministers seemed interested in accepting a cabinet post under someone else and these efforts fell through.

Mushir ud-Daula's failure made Mustaufi ul-Mamalik the likely candidate and on July 28 he began considering the idea. On August 2 he visited Mushir ud-Daula and invited him to join his cabinet. Mushir ud-Daula refused, but Mustaufi ul-Mamalik continued his efforts and on August 4 promised the Majlis he would introduce his cabinet in a few days.* In the meantime rumors of an advance of Russian troops on Tehran caused considerable excitement. Crowds gathered in mosques throughout the city and deputations of frightened citizens approached the Majlis for action. Ruess even suggested that the Shah move the capital to Isfahan.[86] Continuing his efforts to form a government in this climate, Mustaufi ul-Mamalik finally succeeded in putting together a cabinet on August 17, which he introduced to the Majlis on August 19, more than a month after Ain ud-Daula's resignation. The Democrats, who supported him, regarded this a victory, but Mustaufi ul-Mamalik was by no means an anti-Allied activist. Like its predecessors, the new cabinet contained individuals representing the political spectrum, and the Prime Minister, although favored by Democrats, had not gone out of his way to favor them in his cabinet. In his previous tenure as Prime Minister he had tried to maintain Persia's neutrality and upon his return he soon let the Germans know that he did not appreciate the activities of their agents. His cabinet was the legitimate government and he resented German agents carrying on relations with private individuals.[87] Neither was his Government prepared to accept the British occupation of Bushire or the actions of British officials in local areas who also by-passed regular government channels and who busied themselves with raising armed forces on Persian soil. Unfortunately for Mustaufi ul-Mamalik, as for his predecessors and successors, the wishes and writ of the government counted for little.

Since Mustaufi ul-Mamalik had first assumed office in August 1914 there had been four cabinet changes, the longest cabinet holding office for only six months while two had been in office barely one month. This deprived the central government of any stability, and when Mustaufi ul-Mamalik assumed office this time the country had been without a government for some time and in the interim events had moved rapidly. German agents pushed for Afghanistan and stirred up anti-Allied activities at Kerman, Isfahan, Shiraz, Kermanshah, Tehran and Yezd.** Turkish troops pillaged villages

---

* Mushir ud-Daula was not pleased with these actions. Mustaufi ul-Mamalik had refused to join the cabinet and by so doing had ruined the chances of a coalition government. Instead he had remained aloof until circumstances made it possible to form a cabinet himself. (Sipihr, *Jang-i Buzurg*, p. 194)

** British authorities tried to keep continuing tabs on German movements. They noted the arrival of Zugmayer at Kerman on July 4 and the arrival and departure of numerous

in the north, keeping public opinion in ferment; and British forces occupied Bushire, which embarrassed the Government and fueled resentment against the Allies. Internally, rebellious tribal elements defied Government authority, interrupted trade or supported the Germans to get their gold. Furthermore, the Prime Minister stood at the head of a factious government that enjoyed little respect, one which Britain suspected and Russia hated. Indeed, even before he introduced his Cabinet the Russians had tried to sabotage it by exerting pressure on Muhammad Vali Khan, Sipahsalar A'zam [or Sipahdar, a variant of the same title] to refuse the appointment as Minister of War.[88]

THE RETURN OF MUSTAUFI UL-MAMALIK

Nor was Marling's opinion of the Prime Minister favorable. He believed Mustaufi ul-Mamalik was in office because the Democrats realized he was the best they could get since they could not control the Government outright. Marling felt he was sincere and well-meaning but ineffectual and weak. He regarded the new Government merely as a means to an end, since he had no confidence in the new cabinet and only hoped to hold the situation together as long as possible to forestall any political situation that would drag Persia into the war. He saw his task as far from easy, and pessimism crept into his remarks. He regretted India's lack of vigor over Bushire, and in late August informed Grey that he and de Etter shared the view that the Germans and their supporters were gaining mastery in the major centers and elsewhere and that they intended to create a state of disorder that would require the British consuls and even the Legation to quit the country.[89] Britain's position was far from secure and Marling's pessimism was not wholly misplaced.

It was becoming painfully obvious that measures in eastern Persia were too late to stop the Germans, and the Treasury's tardy response

---

parties from Isfahan and other cities; Marling estimated that more than 400 men in all were despatched to Afghanistan. Wassmuss continued his activities in the south and Zugmayer got in touch with local Democrats on reaching Kerman, began hiring armed men and tried to incite *jihad* spirit. Schunemann in the west expanded his forces and openly defied Persian Government authority. He also used his armed followers actively to oppose attempts on the part of the British and Russian consuls to return to Kermanshah. In the absence of a government, the British could get no instructions sent to local governors so that German agents were able to carry out their activities without even that feeble harassment.

to the Foreign Office moratorium plan had left Marling without the opportunity of using the offer as a device for supporting Ain ud-Daula through the July crisis. Furthermore, the Bushire incident and subsequent British occupation complicated Anglo-Persian relations because it introduced new tensions between the two Governments and aroused anti-British sentiments. Incidents at Bushire and elsewhere proved the Germans could organize or instigate offensive actions against British interests and underlined the divisions over policy among the British themselves, with Marling and India barely speaking to one another. In addition, cooperation with the Russians had not produced encouraging results.* Russian jealousy had prevented the British from organizing a levy force at Mashad that might have stopped the German missions to Afghanistan, and Russian tardiness in sending troops to Khorasan made it possible for the Germans to cross the frontier. The troops they finally did send only aggravated local Iranian sentiment by quartering in mosques and insulting religious figures and women.[90]

Nor were efforts to secure local support among the tribes rewarded with any success (see Chapter VI). Wassmuss had more luck in that direction, even though that was a puny affair for all the noise it generated. In short, things were in a mess and no one seemed to know what to do.

In this atmosphere Mustaufi ul-Mamalik resurrected the idea of the moratorium, which had by now become a favorite theme of a succession of cabinets. But the British were not enthusiastic about the Persian proposals. Marling did not reject the moratorium, but he did not encourage the Prime Minister to believe that Britain would give money to a cabinet made by the Democrats unless the Prime Minister could give more convincing proof that Persia merited the money. But he did not completely slam the door in Mustaufi ul-Mamalik's face because, although he believed nothing substantial could be obtained, he had decided to play for time, to forestall what he felt was an inevitable anti-Allied coup until the Russians could provide troops or until arrangements with the tribes in the south had

---

* Buchanan had urged Saznov to find some Russian troops for use in Persia but the Viceroy of the Caucasus needed every available man to fight the Turks. The Foreign Minister did, however, hint that Russia might save the situation by allowing the ex-Shah, Muhammad Ali, to return. (Buchanan-Grey, 8/10/15, FO 371/2433) Under different circumstances the Foreign Office might have found this humorous, but given the situation they were not amused. The plan was dropped.

secured British interests. Marling also was ready to exploit any possible advantages in the interim. As he explained to Grey, 'our present endeavour is to get what we can out of the Cabinet before it falls.'[91]

The situation throughout the country was not reassuring. The Persian Government had done very little to check German activities and the British consul in Kermanshah actually had to leave his post. Nor were conditions at Shiraz, Isfahan or in the other major cities encouraging, with the exception of Tabriz and Mashad where the Russians had troops. O'Connor, the consul at Shiraz, predicted an attack on the consulate and had even asked permission to burn his cyphers, while Grahame at Isfahan was discussing the likelihood of having to evacuate the British community there. The run on the Imperial Bank, engineered by the Germans, the attack on Bushire organized by Wassmuss, and continuing trouble in Tehran pointed to the increasing insecurity. And on September 1 German inspired agents attacked Grahame, the Consul-General at Isfahan, wounding him and killing his Indian orderly. There was also another attack on Bushire, repulsed with ridiculous ease, but upsetting nonetheless.[92]

Under more normal circumstances the British would have demanded compensation for these outrages, but the Foreign Office and Marling did not want to push the point and drive the Persians over the brink. They decided instead to let the matters wait, as they had with other outrages, as in a similar vein they had restrained the Russians over the murder of the Russian bank manager at Isfahan earlier in the year. The attack on Grahame, however, emphasized the delicate state throughout the country and Marling returned to the theme of decisive action. In the discussions that followed the idea of a moratorium came up again, this time proposed by the Foreign Office.

RETURN TO STRONG ACTION

On September 3 Marling's Russian colleague, de Etter, had an interview with the Shah. He came away with the impression that the Shah was 'very much under enemy influence.' Marling added his belief that the Persian Government was doing nothing to check the Germans because it wanted to use its activities as a lever to squeeze concessions from Britain. In view of this and the aggravated state of affairs at Isfahan and Shiraz he once again urged strong action; this time, however, he wanted to go even further, both applying pressure and offering substantial inducements to bring the Persian Government to its senses. He wanted an ultimatum.[93]

Marling did not favor occupying any more Gulf ports, for that had only added fuel to the fire. He also opposed the idea of more Russian troops at Qazvin − unless it were 15,000 or more − as taking too long. Under the circumstances he felt that the only course was to give Persia a choice of declaring war for or against the Allies. If they agreed to declare war against the enemy, then the Allies would agree to a moratorium from that point until some time after the war (Marling suggested three years). If Persia chose not to do this, then the two Legations and their respective diplomatic establishments would quit the country. He wanted to give the Persian Government forty-eight hours to decide and he believed they might accept if the Allies were willing to offer money, military assistance and territorial guarantees. Marling and de Etter agreed that unless some such drastic measures were taken, or a decisive victory won to shake the image of German invincibleness, 'we shall not be able to remain at Tehran ... and it would at least be less damaging to our prestige to depart by our own doing than to be driven out.'[94]

This opinion came as somewhat of a surprise to India and to the Foreign Office. The Viceroy responded immediately:

We most emphatically deprecate ultimatum proposed by Minister, which would simply be playing Germany's game. In improbable event of Persian Government deciding to enter war on side of Great Britain she would, unless supported by considerable military force from Russia and ourselves [an action neither power had the ability to undertake], be powerless to stamp out German intrigues which would continue to inflame populace and create state of anarchy if not actual revolution. Our Consuls and British community would be in greater danger than at present, while to secure this result British Government would certainly have to incur heavy financial obligations besides possibly other embarrassing guarantees.

These were eventualities India hoped to avoid. To these considerations the Viceroy added that such a course of action would expose the oilfields to greater danger, drawing troops from Mesopotamia for their protection, and give the enemy a political weapon to use, if Persia should side with them, to consolidate their appeal for a general Muslim uprising in Afghanistan and India. 'For these reasons,' continued the Viceroy, 'we infinitely prefer for the present [a] policy of drifting.' India did not believe Persia was inclined to act against

Britain unless pushed, and so they favored a wait-and-see attitude, placing hope in the success of the Dardanelles campaign, then underway, as a counter to German intrigues.[95]

Marling rejected India's thinking and launched a vigorous if pessimistic counter attack. He too was aware of the inherent dangers and while admitting that his proposal invoked 'no small element of chance ...,' he could not see 'how the policy of drift, which Government of India advocate, can meet the difficulty.' In Marling's opinion India's objections did not pertain because the Germans already controlled the situation and were employing techniques that would, willy nilly, precipitate the crisis India hoped to avoid. It was not a question of drifting 'but of how long the Germans will hold their hand ...' Marling would not even accept India's opinion of the value of victory in the Dardanelles; he deprecated the idea that the Germans would wait to see if Britain forced the Dardanelles – although he took the opportunity to express the opinion that the capture of Baghdad would have more effect. He did not bother to explain why the Germans would be any more willing to wait for victory there.

Despite this vehemence Marling did not offer his plan without reservation. He believed that Britain's only advantage lay in the fact that the Persian Government did not want to see the legations depart. He wanted to exploit that sentiment, but he was not sanguine over the opportunities for success of his own plan:

... we believe that the course we suggest, by utilising the only element of the situation that tells in our favour, and at the same time promising financial assistance and other inducements, offers a chance of pulling the chestnuts out of the fire. The chance is but a small one, for, in spite of half-hints from Persian Government that they would at a price become our Allies, I can scarcely believe that ... so flabby a Minister as Mustaufi would find courage to put his name to a declaration of war against Germany, to say nothing of Turkey.

If Britain were not willing to pursue this course Marling saw only one other alternative to drifting, namely 'to confess to surrender and allow ourselves to be mercilessly blackmailed.' In other words, Britain would have to offer inducements of arms and money and settle the Bushire question in Persia's favor. Marling warned that any inducements would have to be large and made immediately without waiting for Russian assent.[96] Obviously, though, Marling felt his original suggestions were the best answer.

The Foreign Office regarded Marling's initial plan as a bit

precipitous. Even though an additional outrage had occurred – an assassin had killed the Persian who was the British vice-consul in Shiraz – the Foreign Office did not want to undertake drastic measures. They sought a middle course, and on September 9 they authorized Marling to inform Persia of Britain's surprise that such events were allowed to happen and to express their concern that such occurrences undermined those friendly feelings toward Iran that Britain had maintained throughout the previous century (a slight exaggeration!). Marling was to inquire about the steps the Persian Government intended to take to prevent such incidents and that if the reply were satisfactory he could express Britain's willingness to grant a moratorium from then until six months after the end of the war, and to pay a subsidy of £50,000 per month during the war or so long as Persia's attitude remained satisfactory. Confidentially Grey authorized Marling to offer as much as £100,000 per month but he 'greatly' hoped the smaller amount would suffice. In the event that the Persian response was not satisfactory, Marling was to remind Mustaufi ul-Mamalik that if the two legations were once withdrawn the 'probable result might be that the two Powers would never again be represented in Persia by two diplomatic missions accredited to an independent and neutral court.'[97] However, this strong language did not conceal the fact that the Foreign Office placed considerable hopes in a financial solution to the situation. This optimism was not wholly misplaced, for the Persian Government suddenly gave in over the Bushire question.

SETTLING THE BUSHIRE EPISODE

The Bushire incident of July had complicated Anglo-Persian relations because the British refused to withdraw until they acquired some satisfactory assurances that the situation would not deteriorate further – and the Persian Government refused to consider British proposals until all troops had withdrawn. The Persian Government protested the violation of Persian neutrality and reiterated that such actions only antagonized public opinion, making it harder for the Government to protect British interests. Marling, on the other hand, virtually accused the Persian Government of criminal negligence and insisted that the Persians recall Mukhbir us-Saltana, the Governor-General of Fars; punish the khans who led the attack; and take effective measures to prevent the 'pernicious activities of German agents and pay an indemnity for the loss of life.' Impasse resulted. Then, on September 8, Mustaufi ul-Mamalik saw Marling and agreed to recall Mukhbir us-Saltana, to appoint Qavam ul-Mulk as temporary governor until a British-appointed candidate was named, to punish the offending khans, and to check German intrigue. No mention was made of compensation for the British lives lost, but Marling assumed that the Persians tacitly agreed to pay. In return the British were to restore Persian authority at Bushire.[98]

It is not clear why the Persians capitulated. Marling believed it was because fresh Russian troops arrived at Enzeli,[99] but it may have resulted from Mustaufi ul-Mamalik's realization that the British were not going to give in over Bushire and that their presence there was creating a dangerous situation. Internal dissidents and tribal leaders were using the situation to advantage and the Government's authority was further weakened. Furthermore, by capitulating he not only eased the political situation but also enhanced the possibilities of securing needed funds for his administration, something he had been trying to achieve since assuming office. In any event, this cleared the way for Grey's offer of a moratorium and subsidy. It only remained to reach a settlement.

Marling did not object to the Foreign Office's plan, but he did have some suggestions to offer. First, the moratorium should be granted on the southern customs as planned, but he thought he could employ all or part of the proposed subsidy more directly in Britain's interests if he rather than the Persian cabinet controlled it. The Foreign Office agreed and on September 12 urged the Treasury to approve the plans.[100]

While the Treasury considered these proposals Mustaufi ul-Mamalik approached Marling again over the idea of financial support. He asked for 200,000 tumans (£30,000) per month, retroactive to January, plus arms and ammunitions. Marling and de Etter approved this idea and recommended its acceptance with the comment that, although there was little the Persian Government could do against the Germans even with money, the moral effect of the Cabinet (a pro-German creation) asking and receiving money from the Allies might be considerable.[101]

On September 16 the Treasury reluctantly agreed to the Foreign Office proposal, but recommended that Marling's expenditures should be charged as other secret service payments and not appear as part of the subsidy to the Persian Government.[102] They also suggested that the Government of India pay a larger portion of the financial outlay involved in the subsidy, although normally expenditures of this type were evenly divided. This attempt at economy evoked an irate reply from the India Office:

Mr. Chamberlain is not aware of any precedent for an unequal division in such a case, and he sees no justification for it in the circumstances of the advance now in contemplation, the object of which is to prevent the critical situation in Persia from developing in a manner which would be prejudicial to the interests of Great Britain at least as much as to those of India ...[103]

The India Office agreed to pay half of the subsidy and the matter was dropped.

The Foreign Office then informed Marling that his Government was prepared to accept the Persian Government's appeal and agreed to a suspension of the services of loans to the extent of £30,000 per month. A few days later de Etter informed Marling that his Government favored participation in the plan in principle and it only remained for the proper occasion to inform the Persian Government and to decide whether or not to make retroactive payments to January. The latter point required attention because the Manager of the Imperial Bank of Persia had reported that retroactive payments to January might prove dangerous for the bank, which would handle the transfer of funds, especially considering the rumors of a renewed run on the bank. As a consequence the Foreign Office decided to make payments from March, reducing the amount of cash the bank would have to make available. The Foreign Office still approached the Treasury to approve payments from January, to be used in case it were needed, which was finally approved. Because of this the moratorium had a dual nature − the monthly £30,000 subsidy plus a retroactive fund that could be dispensed to the Persian Government on the basis of need and at Marling's discretion.[104]

The situation seemed to be taking a definite turn for the better and on September 17 Marling wrote that the attitude of the Persian Government had undergone a marked change as a result of genuine fears over German intrigues. Marling was also able to tell Grey that the Persian Government had finally dismissed Mukhbir us-Saltana from Fars and appointed Qavam ul-Mulk as acting governor.[105]

MORE FAVORABLE CLIMATE FOR THE MORATORIUM

The negotiations were proceeding well and although the Germans were still in a seemingly powerful position the idea of reaching a settlement with the Persian Government seemed to reduce the threat. It is not clear how much Marling or the Foreign Office believed they could gain by paying a cabinet that only recently had been so suspect – they may have still been playing for time – but there were advantages to be gained. An agreement would at least legitimize Britain's position in Iran and make it easier to justify their actions there, weakening the impression that Britain was violating a neutral or, in the event of a German-engineered coup, making war on a Muslim country. The Persian Government, despite all its weakness, still had influence throughout the country and if it were to back the British or be supported by Britain it would possibly ease the job of securing cooperation from Persian officials or tribal leaders who still kept one eye on what the government said and did. With these ideas in the background the negotiations proceeded with uncharacteristic speed.

On September 25, Marling and de Etter submitted their proposals to their respective Governments and reassured Mustaufi ul-Mamalik that his proposals were receiving due consideration.[106] On September 28 the Foreign Office approved the plans and on September 30 they informed Marling that the Russian Minister of Finance, who was in London for a conference, also agreed to the proposals.[107] But there was no positive word from Sazanov; and de Etter, who was instructed not to proceed without special instructions, was unable to act. Grey wired Buchanan on October 3 hoping to get the matter settled speedily but there was no immediate response from Sazanov.[108]

Meanwhile in London, the Treasury took a turn at being obtuse and wanted to know why, if the Persians were farming the southern customs to Britain, the British Government should pay a full share of £30,000 instead of the difference between the customs revenues and £30,000. This confusion was not exactly erased by the Foreign Office's explanation that the moratorium was a fiction to avoid reference to the Majlis and was really a further loan, but the Treasury agreed to pay their share – £7,500 – while India paid the other half of Britain's total share.

The Foreign Office continued to press Petrograd for an answer and on October 10, after repeated urging, Sazanov finally sent de Etter permission to proceed, but his instructions included a stipulation that, in Marling's opinion, threatened to make it impossible for the Persian Government to accept the offer.[109] Marling was exasperated at what he considered Russian obtuseness:

The use of the words 'moratorium' and 'suspension of service' seem to have created the impression, more especially at Petrograd, that the operation is a very complicated one, but then once it is realized that it consists in nothing more than a monthly subvention, shared equally by the two Governments, the payment of which is implicitly served on the customs receipt, all obscurity vanishes.[110]

In reality the moratorium was a subvention disguised as a suspension of services on the Persian debt so as to allow the Persian Government to accept and use the money without submitting the measure to the Majlis. Sazanov had not grasped this fact and wanted to insert in the penultimate paragraph of the notice of terms to be presented to the Persian Government a sentence to the effect that the money was to be 'in form of a new advance' and repaid on the same conditions as preceding advances. Furthermore, he wanted to omit that part of the notice which entrusted the Imperial Bank of Persia with the financial arrangements. De Etter was exasperated because he had carefully explained to his Government that the formula of the notice enabled him to insist on reasonable conditions through the Imperial Bank of Persia; in addition, both he and Marling felt that Sazanov's modification would mean that the Persian Government could not accept without submitting the proposals to the Majlis, something everyone wanted to avoid. Therefore, after some discussion Marling convinced de Etter to send the notice to the Persian Government, omitting the unfortunate sentence and the reference to the Imperial Bank of Persia while he, Marling, sent a similar notice with but minor changes from the original. In this manner they avoided delay and the spirit of Sazanov's instruction. Marling regretted this stratagem but the notes were not contradictory and he argued that his note could be represented to the Persian Government as supplementary to de Etter's because it contained the method for implementing the agreement, namely through the Imperial Bank of Persia.

The notices informed the Persian Government that the two Governments were placing at its disposal £30,000 per month in the form of a suspension of services on Persian debts to Britain and Russia, secured on the customs receipts of the northern and southern ports, retroactive to March 1915. The Persians did not respond with undue haste. Muhtashim us-Saltana, the Minister for Foreign Affairs, objected to the fact that the notice reserved to the two Governments the right to terminate the arrangement at any moment which made it one-sided, and he maintained that it was unnecessary since it would be administered by the Imperial Bank of Persia and could be stopped at any time anyway. Muhtashim us-Saltana did not press the issue with Marling, who pointed out that all his previous statements linked the continuation of moratorium payments with proofs that the Persian Government was taking satisfactory steps to protect Allied interests. Instead Muhtashim us-Saltana approached de Etter and urged him to suppress the conditions while he informed Marling that he was working through the Persian ministers in London and Petrograd to the same effect. In view of this, Marling, who felt a quick conclusion was necessary to give a weak cabinet at least some opportunity to remedy the critical situation, recommended that the Foreign Office accept. Meanwhile, Sazanov instructed de Etter to send the notice again in its original form, omitting only the offending paragraph. Marling, who had not heard from the Foreign Office, went along. The moratorium was an accomplished fact. Or was it? As with other experience in Iran the accomplished fact was often more imaginary than real. Although the Allies and the Persian Government had agreed on money terms it remained to translate that arrangement into some practical means of controlling the internal situation. Things came unstuck quickly.[111]

MISSED OPPORTUNITY

Although all the stumbling blocks finally disappeared, it had taken over a month and in that time the Germans had managed to aggravate the situation further. Even though the Foreign Office notified Marling that the Treasury had agreed to retroactive moratorium payments to January the delay seemed fatal.[112] Marling wrote privately to Oliphant that the situation was going from bad to worse.

As you know I never had much hope that giving the Government money would be of much use and the amazing way in which the Russians have managed to delay the giving has given the Boches time to strengthen their position so considerably that our financial support is only now worth 50% of what it would have had [sic] a month ago. It is always the same old story of 'too late.'[113]

The delay caused by the Russians gave the Germans time to discover the true nature of the moratorium, enabling them to organize an attempt to get it submitted to the Majlis, which the Allies had hoped to avoid.[114] The delay also allowed other problems to grow. Marling outlined the troubles, ranging from German import of rifles to the spending of vast quantities of money – Wassmuss alone reportedly spending £50,000 like sand – to incite anti-Allied activity. Marling felt this was being done to facilitate a German-dominated military take-over of the major cities and Tehran itself. He returned to the theme of the need for Russian troops, adding that the Russians would probably send them too late. He berated the Persian Government which had brought negotiations to a standstill by raising objections over the wording of the 'moratorium.' He was unhappy with the Prime Minister, whom he characterized as having as much backbone as a worm, but felt obliged to support his cabinet because the Germans were trying to undermine it. However, he added that: '... if I could be sure of bringing in something better *without delay* [Marling's emphasis] I would help them like a shot. But cabinet making is so much harder than Cabinet wrecking.'[115]

The complications seemed endless. The Persian Government continued objecting to the wording of the moratorium notice, and at the same time returned to the idea of using some of the money to finance a national army, a force the Persians had suggested before and an idea which Marling had discouraged. These events caused him to reiterate the theme of immediate, large reinforcements of the Russian garrison at Qazvin.[116] In Marling's opinion the Persian Government seemed to be retreating from the moratorium altogether, especially after Mustaufi ul-Mamalik began insisting that the Imperial Bank of Persia make available the entire amount of the retroactive portion of the moratorium – some 1,800,000 tumans (about £300,000) – to meet arrears in salaries in various government departments.

On October 25 Marling saw the Prime Minister and discussed these points, as well as a rumor that the Persian Government was negotiating with the German Minister. The Prime Minister vehemently denied the rumor* and insisted that the Bank could find the money. Marling,

---

* There is some confusion over this supposed agreement. The Russian Minister reported news of it to Marling, who first heard of it from Grey and who then reported that he had heard the Persians had definitely signed an agreement. Marling urged an ultimatum to prevent its implementation (Marling-Grey, 10/28/15, FO 371/2436). The Foreign Office felt this precipitate and wanted confirmation; but the most that seemed available were rumors from 'reliable sources.' Mustaufi ul-Mamalik denied that there was such

however, reminded the Prime Minister that while the Allies were willing to support the Government they wanted and expected some sign from them that German intrigue would be stopped. Marling pointed out that there were indications that some Iranian officials were actively supporting the Germans and in some instances smuggling escaped German and Austrian prisoners of war out of Russia. In Marling's opinion the Persians were trying to get all they could to line their pockets. He did not believe that Mustaufi ul-Mamalik had the nerve actually to sign an agreement with the Germans but he was not sure of a new cabinet and so he instructed the Imperial Bank of Persia not to release any money to the Persian Government until the situation became clearer. At the same time, however, he recommended that the Foreign Office consider offering Persia a defensive alliance to counter any German moves in that direction. He was hoping that if nothing else this might give the Russians time to send troops.[117]

Buchanan reported from Petrograd on October 28 that Sazanov had tried to influence the situation. The Russian Minister of Foreign Affairs called in the Persian Ambassador and informed him that the Anglo-Russian Convention of 1907 guaranteeing Persian integrity was conservative in character and that in the event that Persia sided with Germany 'that instrument would be used in an entirely contrary sense that would be fatal to Persia.'[118] In other words, the Allies would

---

an agreement and told Muvarrikh ud-Daula, who worked in the German Legation, that an Iranian interested in creating a crisis had forged an agreement and slipped it to the Russians. Still he did hold discussions on possible German assistance with Ruess from September to November (Sipahr, *Jang-i Buzurg*, p. 237). He was very upset with the Germans but was willing at least to enter into discussions concerning an alliance serious enough to cause Reuss to get Berlin to transfer von Kardorff to Isfahan so that he could not share in the responsibility for it. The Persians, however, were in no more of a hurry to come to terms with the Germans than with the Allies and they wanted to preserve at least the appearance of neutrality until a German army actually arrived (Sipahr, ibid.). According to Ulrich Gehrke, who has made an extensive study of the German documents, an agreement was reached that provided for a twenty-year alliance. But the agreement put the whole responsibility of preparing Persia for war on the Germans, and left open the date of Persia's participation. Everyone knew that Persia would do nothing unless a German army were to appear in the area. The Persians negotiated with the Allies and with the Germans, perhaps waiting to see who would come up with the most, and which side would win (see Gehrke, *Germany and Persia up to 1919*). Furthermore, given the divided nature of the cabinet it is possible that some members of the Government discussed possibilities with the Germans, without informing Mustaufi ul-Mamalik, in the hopes that his ministry would fall and a new cabinet would take more decisive action. The Democrats were not happy with Mustaufi ul-Mamalik and were endeavoring to bring him down. It was rumored that he considered proroguing the Majlis to prevent this.

cease to be concerned about preserving even the image of respecting Persia's independence and integrity. This produced results in Persia. The Persian Minister of Foreign Affairs once again denied, disingenuously, that there were any negotiations with the Germans, and stated that the Persian Government would respond in a satisfactory sense to the moratorium.

RAISING THE STAKES

On November 1 the Persian Minister of Foreign Affairs called on de Etter and indicated that his Government might consider changing their strict neutrality to benevolent neutrality, favoring the Allies, and he responded favorably to the moratorium. With these signs of contrition, Marling recommended that the Persians be allowed to draw £40,000 on the account,[119] but in his very next telegram he once again described a hopeless situation. He felt that the Persians would make impossible demands for benevolence and that the weakness of the cabinet precluded any real arrangements. He favored moratorium payments simply as a means of gaining time and urged the speedy reinforcement of Russian troops as the only real salvation.[120] In fact, the Foreign Office repeatedly urged the Russians throughout October to send troops. At the same time the idea of a British advance on Baghdad to demonstrate Allied strength in the Middle East gained ground.

The continuing state of alarm, the frustration of every attempt to control the situation and the ominous possibilities of a German coup alarmed British authorities, and perhaps added an exaggerated sense of urgency. The impending disaster at Gallipoli and the need to make sure of the Arabs only added to their anxiety, so that the British authorities began to consider actions that would resolve all doubts in one bold gesture.

Originally, the campaign in Mesopotamia had been intended as a demonstration to the Arabs of Britain's support and a protective measure for the oilfields. But the 'demonstration' had achieved striking successes and by late 1915 the British achievement in Mesopotamia was almost the only bright spot for the Allied war effort. By late 1915 the British could almost see Baghdad, the heart of Mesopotamia, just over the horizon – an easy prey for just a little more effort. Failure in Europe had encouraged planners to look elsewhere for possible successes and easy victories, and although military authorities did not favor large diversions of men and material for peripheral endeavors, Mesopotamia seemed ideal to some because of the ease of past successes. The stakes seemed to demand boldness, but unfortunately in this instance boldness exceeded prudence.

The genesis of the advance on Baghdad is not germane to cover in depth here, but an important role must be assigned to Persia in any description of the motives behind it. The political implications of Persia joining the enemy were a potent influence in persuading British authorities to favor an advance on Baghdad as a means of swaying events in Persia, or at least the situation there gave added weight to the arguments of those who wanted an advance. On October 21, as the situation in Persia approached critical proportions and the moratorium agreement seemed doubtful, the India Office informed the Viceroy that it was prepared to order General Nixon to advance on Baghdad, especially since the War Office was willing to release two Indian divisions from Europe; and intelligence reports indicated that the Turks would only offer minimal resistance in the immediate future. The India Office stated why they were ready for this step:

At present moment it seems that German attempt to break through to Constantinople will succeed, and our position and prospects in Gallipoli are most uncertain. Persia seems drifting into war on German side whilst Arabs are wavering, and unless we can offer them great inducement will probably join Turks. We are, therefore, in great need of striking success in the East both to check Persian movement and to win Arabs.

The Viceroy concurred, replying on October 23 that:

Your description of the situation in the Near East proves conclusively the necessity for action in the Middle East in order to prevent if possible Persia and Afghanistan declaring against [us].[121]

REVERSES IN SHIRAZ AND THE ADVANCE OF RUSSIAN TROOPS

While British authorities considered the Mesopotamia campaign, the situation in Iran worsened and an incident at Shiraz seemed to confirm the worst British fears about the consequences of German activity. On November 10 a group calling itself the National Committee for the Protection of Persian Independence seized control of Shiraz with the aid of the gendarmes, and arrested O'Connor, the British Consul, and the local representatives of the Imperial Bank and the Indo-European Telegraph Company, along with their families. O'Connor and the other male British citizens were hustled out of Shiraz and entrusted to the care of the khans of Tangistan (who had attacked Bushire), where they remained for the next fourteen months.[122]

Furthermore, the advent of Muharram, a holy month in which religious fervor could reach fanatical proportions, added another sinister feature. As a result, with all avenues of negotiation or arbitration apparently closed, the only resource seemed to be the despatch of troops – Marling's long-called-for decisive action. The Russians succeeded in finding a few squadrons of cavalry and some infantry battalions and rushed these to Qazvin, 125 miles west of Tehran. The exact utility of these forces was uncertain, but they were now available for action should the Germans and nationalists try to start the rumored uprising at Tehran and elsewhere.

Meanwhile Marling had finally approved moratorium payments to buy time until the move on Baghdad would resolve the dilemma, and while the Russians raised more troops. At the same time Marling and de Etter requested that Russian forces at Qazvin advance on Tehran to be available if necessary; and the Persian Government began to draw money from the moratorium account. But the news of the advance of Russian troops from Qazvin, which the Russians began cautiously on November 7, caused a panic in the capital that affected even the Shah's nerve. The monarch began making noises about leaving Tehran for the south. His departure would have precipitated an even worse political crisis, opening up the alarming possibility that the titular head of state was fleeing the Allies and placing himself under the protection of the Germans and nationalists who had succeeded in making Isfahan the center of their activities. Only the timely intervention of the Minister of Foreign Affairs kept the Shah from bolting. But the panic was spreading – Moderates, Democrats, government officials, and people of no political complexion began holding meetings and collecting transport and baggage as rumors spread that the Prime Minister intended to transfer the entire Government to Isfahan.[123]

In this climate the Persian Government urged the Allies to recall their forces before public excitement made neutrality impossible. Marling and de Etter, who had requested the troops and who had in the past repeatedly urged their necessity, replied that the Russian Government alone could arrest the advance – which was prevarication – but the two representatives were not simply going to abandon a trump card that had taken so long to play. They did, however, assure the Cabinet that the advance was not a punitive action but one designed to protect Allied lives and property. This was little comfort to a Government facing near panic in a population that hated the Russians and that had fed for years on stories of Russia's real or imagined atrocities at Tabriz and Meshed in 1911. The Persian Government continued its appeal and promised to take affirmative steps to protect the Allied position.[124]

Pressing his advantage, Marling asked Muhtashim us-Saltana for Persian terms for the benevolent neutrality which he had suggested earlier, and the Minister for Foreign Affairs responded with a six-point proposal. In return for Persia's benevolent attitude the Government asked for: (1) settlement of outstanding differences with Russia over collection of revenues and the observation of the articles of the Treaty of Turkmanchai; (2) revision of the tariff; (3) arms; (4) Persia to be permitted to attend the peace conference if other neutrals were allowed; (5) undertaking by Russia to withdraw all troops from Persia; (6) cancellation of the 1907 Agreement and of other undertakings obtained by the 1911 ultimatum. These were rather bold terms for a Government faced with a Russian advance and shaky internal support; the fact that the Allies were willing to give the terms serious consideration was a measure of how seriously they — or the British at any rate — regarded the situation.

The Foreign Office raised no objections to points 1 and 2 (settling differences with Russia and tariff revision) and they were willing to discuss point 5 (Russian troop withdrawal), but they regarded point 3 (arms) as doubtful. Only Persian presence at the peace conference was rejected outright, the Foreign Office feeling, along with Marling, that the Germans had inspired it. On the whole they were willing to give sympathetic consideration to the proposals.[125]

The Persian Government continued to press for recall of the Russian troops along with their proposals and they tried to convince Marling that the advance had raised widespread fear which affected even the Shah, but Marling dismissed this idea and, although he did not discourage the discusssion of the proposals, was not willing to see the troops withdraw. Indeed, he regarded their advance as essential and he discounted any threat of the Shah's departure:

I am convinced that the Shah would not care to take a left seat in Prince Ruess's carriage and I knew that the Cabinet did not wish to see Persia involved in a war which could only have disastrous results for her.

Marling would soon have occasion to reconsider these remarks.[126]

The advance continued and so did rumors of a mass migration from the capital. Even the British Ambassador to Belgium reported the tremors. But the Russians were not prepared to back down after so many delays and they suggested informing Ahmad Shah that his departure might make his eventual return difficult. The Persian Government continued to press for recall and promised to check German intrigue, but Marling, like the Russians, was not for backing down; the Russians continued their advance.[127]

PANIC IN TEHRAN

The very slowness of the advance seemed to increase the peril, and public and private meetings spread a sense of desperation throughout the capital. In the Majlis deputies huddled in corners discussing possibilities and nationalists held secret meetings and began organizing to leave the capital. Finally on the night of November 11-12, word reached the Majlis that Mustaufi ul-Mamalik planned to move the Government to Isfahan. This news galvanized many of the undecided and by dawn Majlis deputies, government officials, nationalists and their armed supporters, along with many of the officers and rank and file of the gendarmes, and members of the German, Turkish and Austrian Legations crowded the road to Qom on the way south to Isfahan. Ironically, many of the Persians were able to finance their departure with money the Government had received only recently from the moratorium to pay arrears in salaries and stipends![128] The Allied Legations were not sorry to see them leave, and Marling even expressed the opinion that their absence would make relations easier, which may have been overly optimistic. Meanwhile, rumors of the Shah's imminent departure continued to circulate. Marling discounted these and on November 14 Buchanan passed along to Grey that Sazanov had heard from de Etter that not only was the Shah not leaving but was even talking of going out to meet the Russian troops.[129] Several Iranian sources of the period not only contradict this impression but make it clear that the Government was planning to leave as well.

Marling persisted in urging the advance although he did try to allay the Shah's fears of the Russians while also using the advance as leverage to good effect. In an interview on November 14 he reiterated that the advance was not a hostile move and took the opportunity to suggest certain additions to the Cabinet that would reinforce Allied confidence in Persian intentions of living up to the commitments implied by the moratorium, namely putting an end to German intrigue and declaring benevolent neutrality. But the Shah was not prepared to yield. He agreed to some changes, although insisting that the advance stop first. Marling said this was impossible and that if Persia did not act to stop the Germans, Russia would, and that if Persia was thus dragged into the war there might be dire consequences for Iran and the Shah.* The veiled threat failed to assuage the Shah's anxiety. His personal guards assembled in the courtyard of the Gulistan Palace and the royal carriage sat waiting amidst nervous courtiers for the Shah to finish preparing for the trip.

Only the timely intervention of several important Persian political figures (including Sa'd ud-Daula, Samsam us-Saltana, Farman-Farma, Ain ud-Daula, and Sipahsalar), who told the Shah he risked the dynasty if he left, plus veiled threats from de Etter about the return of Muhammad Ali Mirza, the young Shah's deposed father, prevented the nervous monarch from bolting.[130] Marling finally appreciated the degree of the Shah's alarm and the Russian Minister went to see Mustaufi ul-Mamalik to work out a settlement. In return for the inclusion of Ain ud-Daula and Farman-Farma in the Cabinet, Marling and de Etter agreed to allow the troops to advance no further than Karaj, about twenty-five miles west of the capital. In addition they agreed to withdraw these troops by stages as the new cabinet and the Allies held discussions to settle on a declaration of benevolent neutrality. On November 16 Marling urged the Foreign Office to agree to this and to consider the possibilities of offering some form of defensive alliance to secure Persian Government support. London reluctantly agreed to stop the advance that had taken so long to organize and this temporary easing of tensions persuaded the Shah not to leave, although Marling told the Foreign Office that he remained nervous and required constant management.[131]

* * *

The British had secured the Moratorium Agreement at last, after months of crisis, and once again had a Persian Cabinet they felt they

---

* Russia had already hinted at a reinterpretation of the 1907 Agreement and Grey answered a question in the House of Commons in mid-November on the subject, saying that the Persian Government could not make deals with the Germans 'without risking the position of Persia.' (11/16/15, FO 371/2435)

could work with. But what, after all, had they achieved in twenty months of deliberations? The Government was still shaky and the Germans and nationalists were by no means eliminated; in fact, much of the countryside was in their hands and they had succeeded in expelling the British communities in most of the cities in the south, south-central, south-west, and south-east of the country. The situation at Tehran, though, was more reassuring. All the enemy legations had evacuated and most of the troublesome nationalists had gone with them, in effect proroguing the Majlis. Thus the long-feared coup at the capital was an Allied one. Marling and de Etter were in a position to dictate to the government within certain bounds, and make sure, at last, that its composition was satisfactory. The Allies began trying to capitalize on this advantage and with the moratorium concluded, they turned to the idea of more formal ties that would bind Persia to the Allied cause.

CHAPTER FOUR

THE SEARCH FOR AN ACCOMMODATION: THE SIPAHSALAR AGREEMENT OF AUGUST, 1916

I confess I dread the oscillations of the Persian problem.

The financial leaven of the moratorium did nothing to alleviate Britain's security worries in Iran. The only positive benefit of the moratorium, a dubious one, was that it had helped to finance the *muhajirat*, or flight of the legations and troublesome nationalists, leaving the Allies in charge at Tehran. But control outside of Tehran was still disputed, and the value of control at Tehran was uncertain.

In the south British forces controlled the Gulf ports and protected the oilfields, and the Bakhtiari were vaguely loyal, but in almost every major city in the south — Isfahan, Yazd, Shiraz, Kerman, Hamadan, etc. — the nationalists and Germans had succeeded in driving out the British officials and communities. The gendarmes had defected virtually to a man to the nationalists; and at Qom the exiled nationalists, Majlis deputies, government officials and enemy legations began to organize a counter government, collecting taxes, calling for support from the countryside, and forming an army to dispute Russian control of the north. There was a threat that this force, augmented by the gendarmes, tribes and local brigands might link up with regular Ottoman forces and in combination drive the Allies out of the country, or so the British thought. And until the Russians proved they could handle this threat in the north, and the campaign in Mesopotamia had time to work its moral charms, British officials at the Foreign Office and in Iran began to consider more formal arrangements with the Persian Government to buttress the Allied position.

The basis for negotiating a more formal agreement began in early November 1915 with the Persian Government's attempts to stop the advance of Russian troops on Tehran by suggesting a change in the nature of Persia's neutrality. The Persians did not suggest joining the Allies but proposed benevolent neutrality whereby they would resist the influence of the Germans and nationalists and give facilities and approval to the Allies to protect their legitimate interests. This was attractive to the British because it would have removed the stigma of acting in Iran without the consent of the Government; but given the dubious political situation in Tehran, a cabinet the British did not really care for, and the open maneuverings of the Germans and nationalists to engineer a coup at the capital, the Persian Government proposals were not treated seriously. Russian forces were the answer and the negotiations were kept alive to buy time until they were in position.

But the advance precipitated a crisis made acute by the Shah's determination to quit the capital. Although a relatively weak and inconsequential man he was important as a symbol of state, and considerable machinations developed around his fears, the Germans and nationalists reminding him of the dreaded Russians, while the Allies tried to soothe him with veiled remarks about forfeiting his throne and Persian independence coupled with assurances that the advancing forces were friendly. Marling and de Etter did not really believe that the Shah was as disturbed about the Russian advance as Mustaufi ul-Mamalik and other cabinet ministers told them, but on November 15 the two representatives attended a *darbar*, a formal audience at the Gulistan palace along with many of the most influential men in the country. There it became clear that the Shah was on the verge of departing, his carriage and escort assembled and waiting, and only reassurances from Marling and de Etter that the troops would stop calmed the monarch's agitation. One is tempted to believe that there was a game of bluff in progress, with the Persians deliberately creating the impression that the Shah would leave as a last-ditch effort to stop the occupation of the capital. But this is only an impression; significantly, though, after the advance stopped at Karaj some twenty-five miles from Tehran, the Shah then began to insist that the Russians withdraw to Qazvin some 125 miles away or he would depart anyway. The two ministers accepted this as well, and the Shah agreed to stay.

A COOPERATIVE GOVERNMENT

With the Shah thus placated, Marling and de Etter set about making use of their advantages at the capital. The Germans and nationalists had failed to get the Shah or the Government to evacuate, but many of the junior level bureaucrats, most of the Majlis, the enemy legations and their supporters had moved to Qom in anticipation of the Shah's departure. With their removal from the scene Marling felt he would have less difficulty in representing Allied interests and with de Etter immediately set about the task of reconstituting the cabinet to reflect their improved position.

The Persian Government, faced with the choice of leaving Tehran and being the captive of the Germans and nationalists in exile, chased by Russian troops, or of remaining in the capital under the watchful eye of the British and Russians, shrewdly chose the latter alternative; after all, they had more experience in dealing with the Allies. Further-more most of the men who held responsible positions in the Government in Tehran would have been relegated to insignificance if they had submitted to the nationalists, who, though vocal, were not well-represented among the ruling elite; while if they remained in Tehran they continued to be the legitimate government, and could use that as a bargaining point to keep the Allies from partitioning Iran. The Germans and nationalists had public sympathy but the Russians and British had guns and battalions. With this in mind Mustaufi ul-Mamalik and his cabinet, plus other leading politicians and dignitaries such as Farman-Farma, Sipahsalar, and Ain ud-Daula, put themselves at the disposal of the British and Russian ministers, virtually offering them the privilege of naming the new cabinet. Mustaufi ul-Mamalik even went so far as to suggest his rival, Ain ud-Daula, as the best candidate for Prime Minister, a truly magnanimous gesture.

Marling and de Etter accepted the responsibility of selecting worthy candidates but they had to act within certain constraints. They could not actually dictate a cabinet because certain combinations would have broken up almost immediately and what both ministers wanted was a serviceable as well as an amenable cabinet. The two Allied represen-tatives preferred Farman-Farma as Prime Minister, a strong figure and a reasonably able administrator, if somewhat well known for financially making the most of his favors and abilities; but Farman-Farma had been closely identified with British and Russian interests and although the nationalists had left Tehran the Allies did not want to risk having so unpopular a figure as head of government. Besides, Ahmad Shah did not like Farman-Farma and neither Marling nor de Etter wanted to antagonize the monarch. Ain ud-Daula would have made a less suitable alternative, but the two ministers felt his name would add prestige to the government. He refused to cooperate, however, declining any post, and so Marling and de Etter decided to retain Mustaufi ul-Mamalik, whom the Shah liked and who, without the distractions of the Germans and nationalists, was not so unacceptable. So Mistaufi ul-Mamalik remained Prime Minister with Farman-Farma as Minister for the Interior, and Ain ud-Daula's obstinacy being overcome enough to become minister without portfolio, and on November 16 the new cabinet was settled.

With the new cabinet and a more favorable situation in Tehran, the tenor of the relations with the Persian cabinet underwent a subtle change. As noted above, throughout the crisis precipitated by the Russian advance, the British had considered Persian offers of benevolent neutrality only in so far as discussions bought time. The new cabinet and situation, though, suggested new possibilities and Marling, anxious to capitalize on these advantages, began to urge more serious consideration of the Persian offers, suggesting a defensive alliance as the means to secure Persia's benevolent neutrality, using the six points raised by Persia earlier in November as the opening basis for discussions. The Foreign Office was unenthusiastic about the idea since the only advantage, given Persia's negligible military value, would be to tie Persia openly to the Allies. Arthur Nicolson, the Permanent Under-Secretary of State, did not want to pursue the idea because of what the Persians might try to claim as their price and because it would have involved commitments of men and material that Britain would not back up.[1] But Marling persisted, backed up by circumstances and a new approach from the Persians.

On November 21 Marling reported that the Shah and the cabinet had expressed genuine concern over the state of affairs in Iran caused by German intrigues and they felt that Persia had to adopt a more definite attitude to avert disaster. The Persians were prepared to adopt benevolent neutrality but, as they pointed out, this left the door open to complaints from various parties and the very ambiguity of this type of relationship was a source of trouble. They proposed, therefore, siding with the Allies. Marling, anticipating the Persian demands for an alliance, passed this information on with his reasons for considering the idea:

His Majesty's Government are of course much better able than myself to gauge the consequences to ourselves if Persia entered the war against us, but I feel that they far outweigh any disadvantage of the present or the future attendant on the conclusion of a Persian Alliance.

If Persia joins Germany willingly or otherwise, German aims of immobilizing forces in India that are required elsewhere, of making our military position in Mesopotamia insecure, and of stirring up trouble in the Caucasus may well be realized.

If on the other hand Persia becomes our ally German plans here assuredly fail.[2]

Reacting to rumors that the Germans were offering monetary and territorial rewards for an alliance, Marling argued that an alliance would foreclose on any German promise to the Persians and undermine their attempts to use Persia against Britain at little expense. To secure this alliance Marling suggested meeting Persia's financial requirements, which would be less than the costs of fighting, and making certain political concessions, basically the six points put forward by Muhtashim us-Saltana in early November (see p. 114). To add weight to his argument he pointed out that if the Persians asked for too much the negotiations could be dropped, and he reminded his superiors that the Germans were making enticing offers to the Persians for an alliance, which even if they could not be fulfilled might attract the Persians. The Foreign Office instructed Marling to pursue negotiations, Grey adding a further reason: 'I am very much afraid that Shah and Persian Government may leave Tehran and join the gendarmerie. To prevent this it seems desirable to encourage their project of an alliance.' But the Foreign Office was still not enthusiastic. Marling persisted, however.[3]

On November 22 he reported that the Persian Government was waiting to see what the Allied attitude would be and added that if something were not done they would 'protest that their hand has been forced by the Gendarmerie and go over to the Germans.' This tack produced results and on November 23 the Foreign Office informed Marling, with a tone of reluctance, that, since he had already let the Persian Government know of a readiness to hold discussions, he could join de Etter and sound out the Persian position.[4] On November 24 the Foreign Office expanded on this, based on opinions expressed by the India Office, and instructed Marling that any talks should include a proposal 'directed against all *three* [Foreign Office emphasis] enemy powers [i.e., Germany, Austria and Turkey].'[5] The Foreign Office also wanted the removal of all enemy parties and the disarming and disbanding of the gendarmerie; the release of O'Connor, the consul at Shiraz; and the raising of the virtual siege of Bushire. In return the British Government was prepared in principle to accept an alliance and to supply munitions, to discuss further financial concessions, and to consider the six point program presented in early November. They were not prepared, however, to entertain any discussions that involved the holy places in Mesopotamia. The Foreign Office remained adamant on this point, but like Marling they had reconsidered their attitude and had become supporters of the alliance idea, especially after they received reliable information that the Germans were making expansive promises to the Persians to secure an alliance.[6] There was, however, considerable distance between this commitment and any satisfactory solutions, especially given the changeableness of circumstances and British opinion.

In October British officials had placed hopes in the Baghdad campaign as the best means of influencing the position in Persia and as late as November 4 the Viceroy still regarded Baghdad 'as the key to the situation in Persia.' But by the end of November General Nixon's campaign had encountered stiff resistance and for the first time since Force 'D' had entered Mesopotamia, British arms suffered a major check. The bubble of invincibility burst; and, although no one could be sure of the consequences, Marling and others believed the check would adversely affect the alliance negotiations[7] while simultaneously making an agreement with the Persians more necessary.

The Russians too, although not opposed to the alliance, were not quick to offer substantial support. Sazanov expressed a concern for accepting the agreement but indicated an inability to act outside Russia's sphere in Iran and he returned to the idea, repeatedly rejected by Britain, of offering Najaf and Karbala to Persia; the Russians felt that this would cause a complete revolution in public opinion favoring the Allies. But the Foreign Office had other considerations. They wanted a Persian solution but not one that would aggravate Arab or Sunni Muslim opinion or require too many concessions.* The Foreign Office was not convinced that an alliance would produce anything worthwhile or enduring. Under the circumstances — the reluctance

---

* The British were already involved in negotiations for Arab support and they wanted to avoid conflicting commitments that would aggravate them — an irony considering the conflicting commitments Britain eventually made.

to make any concessions and the feeling of having to negotiate under duress – it is difficult to believe that anyone could have seriously held the opinion that an alliance with a feeble government would really help, but stranger things have been known.

Marling, for one, believed in an alliance, or at least he argued as if he did. He either thought it would help or else one must conclude that his repeated urgings were mere meretricious posturings designed to make himself important in an unimportant backwater of the war – that is, when he was not urging the alliance to buy time. And although the Foreign Office did not favor an agreement, they had many other serious considerations to occupy their minds and were inclined, within certain bounds, to follow the instincts of the man on the scene, only reining him in when he got carried away. Thus when Marling uged a treaty for its moral value, bolstering his argument with the spectre of a German-Persian alliance, the Foreign Office decided to sound out the terms, but very cautiously. Once again the solution came down to a consideration of how much Britain was willing to pay, and it remained to see how much the Persian Government would seek. As it turned out, they wanted too much.

PERSIAN PROPOSALS

The Persian Government, perhaps waiting on events in Mesopotamia and still uncertain of the consequences of the flight of the nationalists, did not immediately reply to Marling's representations to present their proposals. Besides, there was more to be gained by negotiating under circumstances that worried the Allies than by appearing easily bought. But Marling did get a line on the general nature of what Persia would seek. According to his information on December 4, the Persian Government was considering asking for: (1) cession of holy places and Baghdad; (2) cancellation of debts; (3) arms and munitions for a force of 50,000 men; (4) large monthly subvention for the duration of the war; (5) cancellation of 1911 stipulations; (6) abrogation of 1907 convention; (7) large modifications in the Treaty of Turkmanchai; (8) arrangement of an £8,000,000 loan after the war through an international syndicate; (9) tariff revision; (10) limitations on the rights of foreigners to own real estate; (11) guarantees by Russia and Britain of Persian independence and integrity. In Marling's opinion Mustaufi ul-Mamalik, whom he had warned not to make exorbitant demands, was not strong enough to withstand pressures in the Cabinet and might, as a result, submit the whole list, much of which was far beyond any commitment Britain was willing to make. But Marling felt that if General Sir John Nixon's position was really bad, then only the immediate acceptance of the terms would offer any chance of securing the alliance; even this was not a rosy prospect if the pro-German elements, some of whom had not fled, used the opportunity to prolong negotiations.[8] The extent of the Persian demands, if indeed they were so broad, endangered the chances of concluding an alliance. The price was too high.

There was still no definite word from the Persian Government, but on December 6 Mustaufi ul-Mamalik confirmed Marling's information by presenting a new list of demands. It was time for the Allies to decide what they were going to do. Sazanov, for one, expressed reservations over the terms, even given the difficulties of the situation. Russia had no arms to spare for Persia and he worried that any arms given would reach enemy hands. He also made it clear that Russia would never consider cancellation of a 40 million ruble debt owed by Persia, nor grant a large monthly subvention or support a 50,000 man force. He counselled reminding Persia of the dire consequences of siding with the Germans — without using a threatening tone — and relying on Russian military operations in Iran to suppress dangerous situations.[9]

The Foreign Office also considered the Persian terms exorbitant. Although they passed along the Persian conditions to other departments for consideration they were already reconsidering the idea. Lord Crewe, who was acting as Foreign Secretary for an ailing Grey, and others felt that even the Persian Government was not anxious to raise the subject, and so they were willing to let the issue of an alliance rest.[10] There was some consideration, however, of a resort to further cash outlays in addition to the moratorium to keep Persia quiet.

The Army Council of the War Office, which the Foreign Office had informed of Persia's possible terms, regarded the Persian situation as serious from the military point of view, and felt that it was worth paying a 'very high price to ensure having Persia or part of it on our side under existing conditions.' They hoped a satisfactory solution could be reached without yielding to all Persian demands and they felt that 'a liberal attitude in respect to financial considerations [might] in the end prove a true economy.' This last point struck a responsive chord at the Foreign Office, or at least with Lord Crewe, who did not favor the alliance for the demands it would place on

Britain with little of material value in return.[11] He was prepared, though, for a free expenditure of money to keep Persia quiet.

This had not proved too effective in the past, but as the India Office noted, the objective in Persia was to avoid an open breach, and money held out the hope of keeping things quiet. The India Office did not completely rule out the alliance but, in keeping with the practice of imagining every conceivable obstacle, they worried that the alliance might force the nationalists into open revolt – although with most of them having fled to Qom and organizing a counter government, this objection seems strangely errant – and show up the cabinet as manifestly unable to fulfill its engagements, which would destroy any good effects of the alliance.[12] As a result of these considerations the Foreign Office decided to be conciliatory in manner and evasive in reply to the Persian Government proposals – in other words, to continue to play for time while hoping that this approach would allow Russian troops to take decisive action against sources of danger, which by early December were considerable.[13]

RENEWED CRISIS, NEW PROSPECTS

Reports from around the country showed high levels of anti-Allied activity, of efforts to organize a force to combat the Russians and to link up with the Turks. At Hamadan, in the west, nationalist irregulars bolstered by gendarmes attacked the local barracks of the Persian Cossack Brigade; and southwest of Tehran occurred the first armed clashes between the nationalist forces and a Russian column, while throughout the south nationalists looted the local branches of the Imperial Bank of Persia for funds. Even in Tehran there had been difficulties, with the pro-nationalist Minister of Posts and Telegraphs, who had remained in Tehran, using his position to prevent the central Government from sending its orders to the provinces while facilitating the nationalist efforts to excite the nation. Furthermore, the Mustaufi ul-Mamalik Government began to falter and the Shah, whose nervousness was already on record, had a new case of nerves and started talking about abdicating – at the same time, it should be noted, that Russian forces began serious operations against the nationalist elements in south-central Iran. These operations put the Persian Government and the Shah in the invidious position of being under the virtual control of the Allies and of having to watch and therefore seemingly condone foreign troops, in the country illegally, make war on Persian subjects, many of whom were Majlis deputies and Government officials – or relatives of government officials, including members of the Cabinet who had remained in Tehran. Having failed to convince the Allies to delay their operations it is not surprising that Mustaufi ul-Mamalik should talk of resigning or Ahmad Shah of abdicating. The Persian Government and the Shah had little leverage other than their usefulness as symbols and threatening to resign was the one sure way of attracting serious attention.

On December 10 Mustaufi ul-Mamalik began talking of resigning and on the same day Ahmad Shah sent his great-uncle, Kamran Mirza, to see the Russian Minister with the message that he considered the situation beyond one of his years and experience and that he would abdicate in favor of his father.[14] The Foreign Office was caught unawares. They did not like Mustaufi ul-Mamalik but were not sure of the results of letting another government collapse; they were not fond of the Shah either but losing him presented uncertain possibilities. It was unclear what the consequences would be and exactly who would benefit – the Germans or the Russians, who patronized the ex-Shah and saw this as an opportunity to have him back. The India Office did not favor the change, perhaps influenced by the idea that a 'Russian' Shah would adversely affect British interests. The Foreign Office was not exactly enthusiastic, but Grey raised the idea in another form.

He wondered about establishing a Council of Regency instead of the return of the ex-Shah.[15] The Russians completely opposed the idea – it was the ex-Shah or nothing. Sazanov rejected Grey's idea on the grounds that it would cause the Democrats to believe that it was an attempt to destroy the Majlis, although on what the Democrats were to make of the return of their *bête noire*, the ex-Shah, he was silent. Grey's idea received its final blow from Marling, who termed the suggestion a disaster. He favored keeping Ahmad Shah or returning Muhammad Ali. The issue was temporarily resolved when Farman-Farma managed to quieten the Shah's fears, but the monarch was shaken and he wanted more solid reassurances.[16] The activity of Russian troops in the direction of Qom and Hamadan worried him and although he was prepared not to abdicate he wanted certain guarantees. Specifically he wanted: (1) guarantees of the inviolability of his person and household; (2) freedom of movement in and out of Persia; (3) no interference with his correspondence; (4) a civil list of 30,000 tumans per month guaranteed by the Allies; (5) a suitable allowance in case he had to leave Persia; and (6) the crown jewels to be regarded as his personal property. In return he offered his wholehearted support and his willingness to nominate any Prime Minister the Allies named. Marling forwarded these proposals with a favorable recommendation for all but the final condition, since the crown jewels were national property, and the Foreign Office reacted similarly. Indeed, they informed Marling that they regarded such an arrangement as better than an alliance.[17]

The prospect of paying the Shah to secure cooperation was much more attractive than lugubrious negotiations for an alliance. Even the Russians responded favorably with some speed, and negotiations began; but there would be no quick resolution, for an agreement to subsidize the Shah was not settled until 1918. In the meantime the problem of Mustaufi ul-Mamalik's possible resignation remained.

Grey and Marling did not especially favor the Prime Minister but they wanted to keep a known quantity as long as possible and so wanted to bolster his position. The alliance as a means of supporting the Cabinet had already been discounted, if not rejected in London and Petrograd; and even Mustaufi ul-Mamalik had backed off from the proposal, admitting that he did not dare conclude one; but this did not resolve the problem of what to do. In an effort to find a solution, Marling held a four-hour meeting with the Prime Minister on December 11. The result was a compromise:

Persia is to adopt a policy of benevolent neutrality, and in order to have a force capable of putting down German agitation the Cossack Brigade is to be increased to 10,000 men with Russian officers. The two Powers to give or to assist Persia to obtain arms, etc., to agree to a small increase of import duties on sugar and cotton goods to provide for expenses, and to some of the six points ...

Marling hoped it would keep the Cabinet from resigning for a while; and, although Lord Crewe did not like the idea, the plan was to have far-reaching consequences in Anglo-Iranian relations, especially the terms concerning the augmentation of the Cossack Brigade. These negotiations, however, did not go very far immediately. Mustaufi ul-Mamalik's Government fell and its successor was more to the Allies' liking.[18]

Mustaufi ul-Mamalik was not a strong figure and the conditions of late December undermined what confidence he possessed. As long as he had the Shah's and Marling's support he could consider remaining, but when the Shah expressed a willingness to change governments for some financial consideration, the Prime Minister's position deteriorated rapidly and on December 24 his Government fell. Marling wasted no time mourning his passing and used his influence with the Shah to secure a Prime Minister the British could rely on. On December 25 Farman-Farma, who the British felt had pulled their chestnuts out of the fire, became Prime Minister and formed a cabinet acceptable to the Allies. The new Prime Minister, as Minister of the Interior in Ain ud-Daula's Government, had performed many services for the Allies, being the most effective holder of that office in combating German intrigues in the provinces. And although Marling and de Etter were not enthusiastic about his methods of choosing a cabinet (it was reported that Yamin ul-Mulk, for example, paid the Prime Minister 12,000 tumans, about £2,100, for the office of Minister of Finance), Marling believed Farman-Farma a capable administrator and credited his personal intervention with keeping many of the tribal leaders from openly joining the German-nationalists after they left Tehran.[19]

The succession of a more favorable cabinet, plus the fact that at the same time Russian troops had succeeded in driving the dissidents from Qom and Hamadan and appeared to be on the way to restoring a pro-Allied order, suggested that the situation was stable if not yet under control: the enemy had fled the capital, the Shah was amenable, a friendly cabinet was in power and the Russians were coping with the dissidents outside Tehran. With these advantages the Foreign Office concluded that any question of an alliance, which had hung about like a bad odor, could disappear without regret, especially if an agreement with the Shah could be arranged.

The deterioration of events in October-November 1915 and the proposals by the Persian Government for assistance had forced the Foreign Office to reconsider, in a desultory fashion, an alliance with Persia. The prospect of a separate arrangement with the Shah, however, offered more promising or acceptable possibilities and Grey informed Marling (who had requested instructions) that he was waiting to see what became of the talks with the Shah before pursuing alliance negotiations, unless Marling thought it essential to negotiate separately with the Persian Government.[20] Marling assured the Foreign Office that the Shah's appointment of Farman-Farma was a sign of his good faith and that the agreement with the monarch was personal and apart from any negotiations with the Persian Government. Thus he cleared the way for shelving the alliance, with Foreign

Office approval. Arthur Nicolson's minute to this telegram revealed much about the Government's attitude.

> I have made an addition to the Dep[artment] tel[egram] as we do not want
> – at least I understand the Gov[ernment] of India do not want – to hasten
> alliance negotiations which will be difficult to handle just now – we have,
> I think, squared the Shah and his principal min[is]t[er] [Farman-Farma]. I
> expect this will keep them straight better than any alliance.[21]

The Foreign Office did not want to pursue an alliance agreement. Its penchant for private arrangement to solve problems and the existence of a pro-Allied Cabinet seemed enough to protect British interests.

A NEW GOVERNMENT

The Persians had other ideas. Farman-Farma's Government had inherited the initial discussions for an alliance and wanted to pursue the matter. On January 13 Farman-Farma sent his son, Nusrat ud-Daula, to find out from Marling if Britain were still interested in an alliance. Marling replied non-committally, saying that the British Government might consider an arrangement if the Persians' asking price were not too high. Marling did not want to discourage a government he had helped to create and so he recommended that the Persian Government give an indication of their terms. The Prime Minister had prepared his son for this and Nusrat ud-Daula outlined Persia's position. The Government would undertake to make available all its resources – material and moral – and all its regular and irregular forces to the Allied cause in Persia. In return Persia asked for: assistance to equip a force of 50,000 (including the Persian Cossack Brigade); cancellation of all debts; a monthly subsidy of 500,000 tumans; a guarantee that Russia would evacuate the country; a revision of the tariff and the Treaty of Turkmanchai (see pp. 3-4 above); and a promise that discussions in a friendly spirit would be held after the war to settle the issue of foreign ownership of land. Farman-Farma was aware that these were virtually the proposals of the previous cabinet, but he did not feel he could ask for less, although he made it clear that the proposals were a bargaining position.[22]

Marling, who had just played down the necessity of an alliance, forwarded these new proposals with a favorable recommendation. He felt the alliance was worth having, the main value being that it would kill enemy hopes of an Islamic union and substitute for it positive action against the German cause. Marling's only reservation was that the increase in Persia's army would come through the Persian Cossack Brigade which was under Russian tutelage, and that tariff revision would be used to secure payment for this force in the future. But he was not opposed to the agreement in principle. The Foreign Office decided to investigate the possibilities; Grey instructed Buchanan to get Russian views, stressing that the proposals should be given serious considerations.[23] The circumstances for the alliance, it seems, were nothing if not changeable.

On January 16 the Persian Government formally presented its proposals for an alliance. Fifteen articles covered a broad spectrum of demands, but in essence they represented the position of various Persian Governments since the beginning of the war. The cabinets had changed but the Persian requests remained similar, in some cases escalating. Farman-Farma's Government's draft for an alliance included the following:

1. There shall be an alliance for fifteen years from date of signature on following terms.

2. Great Britain and Russia will within three months of signature furnish gratuitously to Persia modern rifles, ammunition, and guns sufficient in the judgment of Persian Government for 50,000 men, and will make good losses incurred in circumstances contemplated in article 4.

3. Should she request it, Great Britain and Russia will give Persia military assistance. Operations will be directed by a staff composed of Persian officers and officers of the Power sending troops. Commander-in-chief will be appointed by the Shah.

4. During continuance of the European War Persia will employ all her influence and all her forces, regular and irregular, to safeguard her interests and those of her allies in Persian territory. The two Powers will endeavor by all means to prevent an attack on Persia.

5. All troops of the two Powers will evacuate Persian territory as soon as need for their presence as provided in articles 3 and 4 has ceased. Persia will not be called upon to contribute to their expenses while in Persia, and will have the right to determine date of their departure.

6. From the date of signature Great Britain and Russia will abstain from all measures contrary to independence and territorial integrity of Persia, such as interference in her internal affairs, conclusion of public or private pact with tribal chiefs, &c., and any such existing conventions are hereby annulled.

7. Engagements of 24th December, 1911, and 20th March, 1912, taken by Persia in consequence of Russian ultimatum of 29th November, 1911, and of Anglo-Russian demands of 18th February, 1912, are cancelled.

Nor will the two Powers in future conclude any agreement with each other or with other Powers such as infringe Persian independence, and will oppose such an attempt on the part of any other Power.

8. Anglo-Russian monthly subvention until one month after conclusion of the great war of 500,000 tumans, as well as 750,000 tumans for upkeep of troops mentioned in article 2.

9. Persian debts of every kind whatever to be taken over by the two Powers.

10. Revision of Treaty of Turkmanchai and annexe concerning ceremonial.

11. Revision of customs tariff.

12. Persia will recognise rights of foreigners to hold landed estates on condition that such persons are subjected in all respects to Persian laws and customs. Immigration *en masse* to be prohibited unless immigrants are treated while in Persia as natives.

13. Persian sovereignty to be recognised over islands of Bahrein, Tomb, Sire, Abu Musa, Farur, and Ashouradi.

14. Persia to have the right to navigate the Caspian Sea and have men-of-war there.

15. Persia to be represented at Peace Conference.

Annexé.

Execution of treaty to be secured by signature thereof by France, Italy and Belgium.[24]

In effect the Persian Government were looking for an end to foreign interference in Iran's internal affairs, abrogation of arrangements that impaired the country's sovereignty, solid assurances to respect Persia's integrity, and help in establishing a uniform national force under the control of the central Government that would efface the patchwork of forces tied to one or other of the Powers, which by their nature reinforced the north-south division of Iran by the Russians and the British.

Even making allowances for pushing exaggerated demands to secure a better bargaining position, these proposals went beyond Mustaufi ul-Mamalik's tentative suggestions and articulated the Persian Government's position demonstrably. They contain many elements of earlier proposals and as such are very interesting. When presented with similar demands by unwelcome governments under strained circumstances, the British had regarded them as designed by the enemy, not a completely improbable possibility from the British point of view. But coming from a cabinet virtually called into being by Marling, the demands made by Farman-Farma put the Persian approaches in a different light. They were serious and they represented what Persia really wanted. The British were willing to discuss these proposals with a cabinet they approved of, but they discounted most of them and set about pruning them into acceptable shapes. Unfortunately they did not seem to realize that no Persian Government could accept the limited concessions the British and the Russians were prepared to offer.

Farman-Farma's cabinet, an Allied creature, was dealing with a less ambiguous political climate in Tehran, since many of the dissidents and Germans had left, but despite this Farman-Farma did not significantly alter the nature of the proposals except to make them more precise and, if anything, broader in scope. The overall internal situation still remained uncertain, while British reverses in Mesopotamia had embarrassed Allied prestige, and Farman-Farma traded on these difficulties to Persia's advantage.

In any event the situation in Mesopotamia plus the disaster at Gallipoli influenced the British to reconsider the Persian alliance. They had not forgotten the deal with the Shah, but the situation seemed to demand a more solid arrangement that could be used publicly to counter the adverse moral effects of military defeat in the East, and so the process of bringing together all the elements – India, the India Office, the Foreign Office, the men on the scene, and Russian opinion – necessary for realizing the alliance began.

Marling submitted his and de Etter's observations on the Persian draft on January 19. They were in favor of the agreement but proposed limiting the duration of the alliance to the period of the war, with perhaps additional guarantees that the two Powers would secure the throne to the Shah and his descendants. They also felt that it would be impossible for Persia to raise and equip a 50,000 man army in time to confront the Turks, believing the Persians had suggested the figure with an eye to the quantity of arms and ammunition and the corresponding subvention. As an alternative they recommended a 25,000 man force as the basis for realistic discussions.

They did not object to Article 3 concerning military assistance, feeling that even if the Shah's nominee were not agreeable to the Allies the Persian commander-in-chief would in any event be a mere cypher. With regard to Article 4, on Persia's willingness to supply aid to the Allies, they felt that the Persian obligation should be wider so as to include furnishing supplies at a reasonable price and that the Allies should agree to protect Persia and maintain the Qajar dynasty on the throne. They did not object to Article 5, concerning the withdrawal of British and Russian troops, but wanted to fix the date of evacuation by mutual consent. Marling and de Etter disagreed, however, over Article 6, which dealt with interference in Iran's internal affairs, particularly agreements with tribal leaders or influential men. The Russian Minister, in accordance with his Government's views, wanted to defer the question until after the war, while Marling, on the other hand, thought that this should not prove a stumbling block: 'I have so little belief in the value of agreements with tribal chiefs that I should see no objection to making concessions as regards future ...' But Marling's commitment was not irrevocable, and immediately after defending the Article he suggested the means for repudiating it:

I think it most unlikely that Persian Government will seriously press article, seeing that both Farman-Farma and Sipahdar enjoy foreign protection, and probably we could negative proposal if so desired.

In any case our arrangement with Sheikh of Mohammerah must be upheld.

Marling's reaction to article 7 (concerning Persia's recognition of the terms of the Russian demands at the time of the invasion in 1911 to force the Persians to dismiss the American financial adviser, Morgan Shuster, and the subsequent agreements that forced Persia to recognize the 1907 Agreement, which they had refused to do, and to agree to consult the two Powers before appointing any more foreign advisers) was somewhat different from his other remarks, concerned more with the state of Anglo-Russian than Anglo-Persian relations. Recalling in a modest way Townley's uncomfortable relations with his country's ally, a note of reservation about letting the requirements of the alliance with Russia obscure the protection of legitimate British interests crept into Marling's comments.

The British were largely dependent upon Russian forces for their main muscle in Iran and appreciated the importance of this – both for the possible price Russia would exact for their service, and for the service it definitely was in preserving British interests. And though Marling and de Etter worked well together, the Russian even taking up quarters at the British Legation during repairs to his own quarters, Marling began to detect a note of hectoring in the Russian attitude that was not wholly reserved for the Persians, which increased as Russian troops drove the dissident nationalist forces further and further away from Tehran and the north. As the Russians became more sure of themselves their willingness to negotiate with the Persians or to give due respect to British interests went into one of those periodic declines that seemed to accompany any improvement in Russia's position. This trend was not well-established when Farman-Farma presented his demands, but Marling had some observations and recommendations to make that reflect his determination to anticipate trouble.

ANGLO-RUSSIAN STRAINS, DEPARTMENTAL WRANGLING

The main area of concern was the augmentation of the Cossack Brigade, a Russian-controlled force. With the defection of the gendarmerie Britain had nothing to balance it with, and the prospect of seeing Russian influence expanded without some compensation frankly worried Marling – an anxiety that was to spread to, if it were not already shared by, the Foreign Office. With this in mind Marling wrote that he regarded the engagement requiring Persian recognition of the 1907 Convention as unimportant:

If His Majesty's Government intends, as I understand, to insist, if Cossack brigade is to be expanded as to provide adequately for maintenance of order in the north of Persia, similar force under British instructors shall be created in Southern Persia. Arrangement of this kind will be more practically effective in defining sphere of influence than any Persian recognition of 1907 Convention. It is clear that Russia regards question of alliance from different standpoint from ourselves. With their troops in North Persia in sufficient numbers, as they apparently believe, to make situation safe as regards their own interests, they attach far less importance to it than we do, and they are consequently inclined less to make concessions, even if apparent rather than real, than to exact them.

Regarding this last point, he outlined an example. The Russians wanted some measure of financial control over the subvention (a sum in addition to the moratorium that was intended to help equip Persia's national force), knowing that no Persian Government would accept such a measure except under compulsion. De Etter was aware of this but felt his Government would demand control of the military subvention, to make sure it was employed properly. In that event Marling felt Britain should take steps specifically to secure part of the subvention for a British-trained force. The Foreign Office concurred and instructed Buchanan, British Ambassador to Russia, to pursue the issue with Sazanov, while Marling was to see that it was included in any reply to the Persians. This determination to seek balancing concessions had been less obvious during the doubtful days before January 1916, but now that the main crisis seemed over the old bickering between the Russian and British Legations re-emerged and in various forms would dog every Allied effort in Iran down to the Russian Revolution, and after.

In regard to the size of the subvention, Article 8, Marling suggested 400,000 tumans instead of 750,000 for military purposes and that the extent of the general subvention should be left open to further negotiations. He felt Article 9, concerning Persian debts, had to be rejected outright but that Articles 10 and 11 (revision of Treaty of Turkmanchai and of tariffs) were acceptable but should be deferred until after the war. He also felt that Article 12 (ownership of land in Iran by foreigners) should be reserved for consideration later.

Marling regarded Article 13 (Persian sovereignty over Gulf islands) as inadmissible, since the British were not prepared to accept Persian claims in the Gulf, and Article 14 (Persian navigation and warships in the Caspian Sea) as Russia's concern alone. He felt Article 15, on Persian representation at the Peace Conference, should be resisted on the grounds that the proposed alliance was merely defensive. He described the article's insertion as an attempt by the Persian Government to appear as an independent Power and thought that the Persians would probably be prepared to guarantee that the representatives, if they were accepted, would take instructions from Britain. Finally, Marling presumed that the Persian annex, which dealt with securing the agreement of the other Allies, was unacceptable.[25] Although not making it explicit, Marling was voicing a generally held sentiment — no one wanted to introduce the interests of a meddlesome third Power. The Foreign Office accepted Marling's view and undertook to discuss these points with India, the India Office, and of course Russia.

Surprisingly, the Russians were not opposed to the agreement, although they considered the Persian proposals excessive. On January 21 Buchanan informed Grey that Sazanov was preparing counter-proposals, including plans to reduce the number of troops contemplated by Persia, and to make the development of this force an extension of the Persian Cossack Brigade, as well as a similar force in the south under the British.[26] On January 27 Marling was able to send the Foreign Office his and de Etter's counter-proposals, which were not official, since they were only the Russian Minister's ideas, but contained at least the outlines of Russian thinking.

This eleven-article draft pared down the Persian demands. Article 1 stipulated an alliance for the war's duration. Article 2 stipulated that the two Governments would facilitate the acquisition and transport to Persia of sufficient military supplies for a force of 25,000 to 30,000 men 'which is to include augmentation of Cossack brigade to 10,000 and a force of 10,000 men under British officers to operate in the south.' Marling and the Foreign Office had been busy. Articles 3 and 4 in de Etter's draft were in essence identical to the Persian proposals with the exception that Article 4 included a stipulation that the Persian Government facilitate Allied acquisition of supplies at current prices. Article 5 made the eventual withdrawal of troops the subject of agreement between the two Powers. Article 6 was an alternative to Article 9 of the Persian draft in which the two Powers promised to facilitate the liquidation of Persia's debts contracted before the present agreement. Article 7 corresponded to Article 8 of the Persian draft and fixed the monthly general subvention at £70,000 (or about 350,000 tumans) instead of 500,000 tumans, and the military subvention at £100,000 (about 550,000 tumans) instead of 750,000 tumans, £80,000 of which was to be earmarked in equal shares for the creation of a British force in the south and the expansion of the Cossack Brigade.

The Article also provided for the creation of a special mixed financial commission to control the expenditure of the military subsidy; and, finally, for the continuation of the moratorium, except that sums accruing from its retroactive character were to be applied to reduce Persian debts to the British and Russian banks. Article 8 corresponded to the Persian Article 6 and according to de Etter's terms the two Powers were to agree to refrain from future guarantees of protection to tribal groups and subjects while reserving the right to continue protecting those already under such care. Article 9 contained no definite terms but left it open for counter-proposals by the Russian Government to Article 7 of the Persian draft asking for the abrogation of various engagements. Article 10 was based on Article 10 of the Persian draft but deferred revision of treaties until the year after the war. It also provided for general discussions of rights of foreign ownership to land and the accountability of foreigners to Persian law only in respect to questions relating to land ownership. Article 11 deferred tariff revision until the year after the war.[27]

On the same day that the Foreign Office received these proposals (January 28), Austen Chamberlain, who had replaced Lord Crewe as Secretary of State for India, forwarded his department's views of the Persian draft and the opinion of the Viceroy, who felt that if concluded on moderate terms, the agreement would be 'distinctly favourable in conciliating Mohammedan opinion in India, and in strengthening hands of Ameer [of Afghanistan].' Chamberlain too believed that the alliance might improve conditions in India and Mesopotamia, where much of the population was Shi'a, and that every 'endeavour should be made to arrive at a speedy settlement ...'; but he also felt that certain of the proposals were highly controversial and others clearly inadmissable.

Chamberlain faced a quandary. He wanted to avoid commitments that would tie Britain's hands for a long period, but he recognized that even after the war the Germans might continue to seek influence in Persia. To resolve this dilemma, he proposed:

(a) That the treaty now to be concluded should contain a clause formally cancelling any agreement, or agreements, that may have been concluded with Germany, Austria-Hungary, Turkey, or Bulgaria since August 1914, and binding the Persian Government to conclude no such agreement during its currency.

(b) That the treaty should contain only those conditions which can be accepted without delay.

(c) That its currency should be until such time as the Two Powers are able to conclude a further treaty with Persia covering the remaining conditions and settling our future relations on a more permanent footing.

In addition, he wanted to scale down the alliance, and to include certain guarantees for Britain, reserving inconvenient items for discussions after the war.

Like Marling he believed that the two Powers should negotiate with Persia on the basis of a 25,000 man force, with the understanding that the contemplated force in the south would be organized and commanded by British officers, and he wanted some control over the military subsidy. In addition, he felt Article 2 of de Etter's proposals was not sufficient and he wanted the treaty to include stipulations for reparations for the indignities suffered by the British at Bushire, Shiraz, and elsewhere, and guarantees that the Persian Government would intern all enemy aliens as well as punish those Persian elements involved in anti-British attacks.

Concerning articles 6, 7, 10, 11, 12, 13, and 14 of the Persian draft, Chamberlain felt that they should be left for later consideration in another treaty, although he still had some observations about them. In regard to Article 6 (concerning treaties with local leaders) he felt Britain could not abstain from pacts with locals until such time as the Persian Government demonstrated that arrangements to provide local protection to British interests were no longer necessary; and that, even so, Britain would not give up its engagements with the Shaykh of Mohammarah. The Secretary of State for India was willing to ignore the 1907 Convention but he was not prepared to relieve the Persian Government from the obligation of consulting the two Powers on appointments of foreign advisors 'unless appointment of enemy subjects after the war can be precluded in some other way.' Chamberlain felt Article 13, regarding Persian sovereignty over certain Gulf islands, was inconvenient and for the most part inadmissible. He also found Article 9, concerning debts, Article 15, concerning Persian representation at a peace conference, and the annex as absolutely unacceptable.[28] Grey forwarded these views to Marling to be used as the basis for a counter-proposal.

Marling did not care for Chamberlain's views. In the past Marling had consistently opposed India or India Office suggestions, and in keeping with this tradition he considered, with justification, that Chamberlain's attempt to include punishment of the khans in south Persia was inappropriate to a treaty of alliance and that insistence on adequate financial controls would cause the Persian Government to lose interest in the treaty:

I fear that we must make up our minds that subvention for general purposes is rather a bribe than a means of introducing the thin end of the wedge for financial reform. Subvention is the price of Persian alliance, and I think this is not the time for us to look too closely into what is done with it.[29]

Yet at the same time that he denigrated Chamberlain's ideas for some form of control over the military subvention, he expressed the view to the Foreign Office that Article 7 of de Etter's draft would provide adequate control for Allied interests. He added, however, that the Persian Government might regard attempts at financial control as the first steps toward partition.[30] Favoring the Russian proposal over Chamberlain's mention of a similar approach was symptomatic of Marling's reactions to anyone else's ideas, especially anyone involved with Indian affairs. Marling was not alone in this position, since others at the Foreign Office had expressed highly unfavorable views of policies emanating from India or the India Office; and Oliphant minuted Chamberlain's current letter with some revealing remarks. He felt that it would not be a good idea to regard the India Office's desiderata as a *sine qua non*, and in some ways he preferred de Etter's counter-proposals. He also made a remark that suggested that Indian authorities had missed the point of the negotiations:

The amendments proposed by the India Office are moderate and much to the point. It must, however, be borne in mind that the proposed agreement is not required only by Persia; on the contrary, we shall, unless I am much mistaken, have great need of Persia's moral help in the next few months. (If matters were not to improve on the Tigris and Persia were to ally herself with Turkey, the effect throughout the East would be most serious from our point of view.)[31]

The Foreign Office preferred Marling's view and on February 5 informed the India Office, perhaps as a means of speeding up considerations, that 'the importance and urgency of securing the early cohesion of the Persian Government to the Allied cause can scarcely be over-estimated ...'[32] The Foreign Office expressed its agreement with Marling's estimation of the situation and with his tendency to approve Articles 2 and 7 of de Etter's counter-proposals (expanding Cossack Brigade and creating a British officered force in the south, and terms of the subventions). The India Office replied on February 8. It too was generally in favor of the counter-proposals and of Articles 2 and 7, but it still wanted guarantees that the khans would be punished, by Britain if Persia were unable to do so, suggesting a separate agreement if necessary to secure this right.[33] The India Office was also dissatisfied with the powers of the Mixed Financial Commission to give effect to Article 2 of de Etter's proposals (augmentation of Persian Cossack Brigade and establishment of British officered force). They suggested amending the article, giving the commission a controlling power over the constitution of the force, while Article 7 would give it the power to control the military subvention.[34]

The India Office was clearly not opposed to the agreement. It only remained for Sazanov to present his Government's official counter-proposals. But by mid-February he still had not responded and the British were left to construct their ideas on the basis of de Etter's draft. In the absence of more information, but faced with the necessity of action, Grey had to instruct Marling in a vacuum; on February 17 he sent his tentative observations, incorporating certain of the India Office's desiderata.

First, in accordance with Chamberlain's desires, he suggested that the duration of the treaty be for more than one year, and that the counter-proposals should contain the India Office's suggestions dealing with the duration of the treaty (i.e., that it should apply until the two Powers completed a new satisfactory agreement with Iran). Grey also passed along the India Office's desire for some arrangement concerning the punishment of the khans in south Persia and for some clearer specifications for the functioning of the Mixed Commission. Grey recognized that control of the general subsidy was impractical, but he felt military expenditure should be under British and Russian control; yet, given the absence of a Russian response, Grey was unable to go into detail on possible counter-proposals. Marling was left more or less on his own to concert with de Etter, in light of the British Government's expressed views, to make the best arrangements possible.[35]

In short, what Chamberlain, Marling, and the Foreign Office were willing to concede to Persia in return for an alliance was amazingly limited. In return for Persian commitment to the Allied cause, even though the contemplated instrument was conceived of as a defensive alliance, the Allies were willing to give: (1) more money; (2) an Anglo-Russian officered and financially controlled army; (3) vague promises that all the 'inconvenient' Persian demands would be considered in a friendly fashion, with no promises of commitment, after the war. There was not a great deal more in these concessions than in earlier Allied proposals, with the exception that they were now prepared to accept the creation of a Persian army which was not to have any real independent existence.

As Marling pointed out to the Foreign Office of February 2, the proposals contained in de Etter's draft providing for the expansion of the Cossack Brigade and the creation of a similar British force, which Britain considered a *sine qua non* along these lines, were fraught with difficulties because it would be ticklish to get the Persian Government to accept terms that could be regarded as the first steps towards partition.[36]

RUSSIAN SILENCE

The continued silence of the Russian Government, however, meant the alliance project could not proceed. Marling believed Farman-Farma, whose cabinet was in danger of falling — largely because de Etter had taken a personal dislike to the Prime Minister, disapproving of his financial peccadilloes — was willing to negotiate the alliance, the primary objective of which had now become to secure Persian consent to the creation of Anglo-Russian sponsored forces; but by mid-March the Russians still had not presented definite proposals. Although the Foreign Office was eager for some answer, Buchanan was able to get only vague information on Russian proposals, and what news there was was disturbing. Apparently the Russians were planning to limit the counter-draft to military and financial questions, ignoring completely all the Persian demands. Yet even this emaciated draft did not appear. Apparently Sazanov and the Russian Minister of War were unable to agree over the size of the force to be placed under Russian instructors and this dispute delayed the responses.[37]

These delays undermined the chances for an alliance, but the major blow to the treaty as proposed by Farman-Farma came in early March when his cabinet fell, according to Marling, through Russian-inspired opposition at Tehran designed to get a more pro-Russian candidate in as Prime Minister, while the Russians delayed any statement of their position on the alliance.[38] The fall of the cabinet and the failure of the negotiations seemed to be a replay of pre-war Anglo-Russian relations in Iran. Both sides remained committed to securing their respective interests even when this inhibited cooperative efforts. As a result the negotiations for an alliance advanced but little. For the Russians, who could fall back on substantial forces, this was not too worrying but for the British, who often had to rely on these same Russian forces, the situation was not reassuring. The British wanted an alternative to relying solely on the Russians, whose cooperation had helped to scuttle more than one approach designed to alleviate the Persian situation.

The battle of opinion in British Government circles and the recalcitrance of the Russians, whose military successes in Iran in early 1916 attenuated their willingness to buy Persian support, left Anglo-Iranian relations still unsettled. The alliance had fallen through; the Farman-Farma cabinet, from whom so much was hoped, had failed; and the Turks, who had blunted General Nixon's advance in Mesopotamia, were now threatening to capture a large British force there, threatening the whole British position in the Middle East. The only bright spots were Russian military successes against the German- and nationalist-inspired opposition. Even this was disturbing to some British authorities, because it meant Britain was forced to rely on Russian arms to protect its areas of influence. This was an embarrassment and some worried that the Russians might use this fact to intrude their claims into Mesopotamia.

GREAT EXPECTATIONS: THE SIPAHSALAR CABINET

The situation was not without prospects, however, for in Iran at least the alarms of 1915 had abated. Most of the enemy legations had left Tehran along with the most troublesome nationalists; and Farman-Farma's successor, Muhammad Vali Khan, Sipahsalar, seemed willing to cooperate with Britain and Russia. Marling was not altogether pleased with Sipahsalar's rise to power but could not ignore his willingness to hold discussions. Sipahsalar had been Minister of War under Farman-Farma and from the first had introduced difficulties into the cabinet. Marling had a very low opinion of Sipahsalar, whom he characterized variously as 'feather-brained,' 'vain,' 'hopelessly ignorant,' 'capricious, lazy and easily influenced.' Marling blamed him for many blunders that aggravated the internal situation, among them being the opposition to Farman-Farma. Marling also believed he was the center of a pro-Russian party led by a M. Kozminski, the Russian financial agent, who wanted to see Sipahsalar in power as a means of expanding Russian influence. Although the exigencies of 1915 had buried Anglo-Russian rivalry, the apparent tranquility of early 1916 had given it new life, or so Marling believed: 'no sooner was the common danger removed ... than the pro-Russian party set to work to oust "British" Farman-Farma and replace him by the Russian Sipahsalar.' According to Marling this group fomented quarrels between de Etter and Farman-Farma, whose avarice the Russian Minister despised, which began to undermine his position with the Russian. Farman-Farma was aware of the handicaps of such a loss of confidence, and when a group of women, reputedly paid by the Russian party, took *bast* (sanctuary) in the old Russian Legation to protest his continuance in office, he took the opportunity to resign. Marling was able to convince de Etter of Kozminski's role in this episode and thus briefly repair the rift in Anglo-Russian co-operation but the potential for discord remained. Farman-Farma departed, it would seem, at a convenient time. He had failed to reach a satisfactory settlement with the Allies and he may have decided to quit once he realized what the Allies, the Russians in particular, expected Persia to accept as the basis for an agreement.[39]

When Sipahsalar assumed office on March 2, although the alliance was at a standstill because of continued Russian silence, some of the issues in Anglo-Iranian relations had been settled. The Farman-Farma cabinet had been more forceful than its predecessors, and

Farman-Farma's efforts to restore the Government's authority in the provinces after the *muhajirat* had benefited Britain; but the alliance remained adrift, the payment of moratorium funds bogged down, and the Germans and nationalists were still potentially dangerous. With the exception of the salutary effect of strong Russian forces there was little to show for almost two years of attempts to resolve the Persian situation. Marling had a great deal to pursue with the new Persian cabinet.

Part of the ambiguity of the situation disappeared when the Russian Government finally stated its position on the alliance. It was not until mid-March and early April, almost two months after Buchanan told Grey that Sazanov was preparing counter-proposals, that the line of the Russian response began to emerge. On April 14 Marling informed the Foreign Office that the Russians were going to drop the alliance altogether in favor of a simpler agreement that would legitimize the expansion of the Cossack Brigade and the formation of a similar British force in the south.[40] On April 21 Buchanan confirmed this and said the Russians regarded the alliance as impracticable because of the Persian demands. Once again the Allies had not been able to concentrate decisively on a single plan and the prospects of an alliance withered, if they did not die.

On April 21 the Russians rejected the idea of the alliance in favor of a simpler agreement which proposed the creation of two forces and the establishment of a measure of financial control over the expenditure of funds for military purposes,[41] but which ignored all of Persia's other points. Marling had deprecated the idea that the Persians would accept any financial control, but Russia was insistent and Sipahsalar was willing to consider their demands.

Even before the Russians presented their alternative to the alliance de Etter had already taken some steps to introduce a measure of financial control. In March the Belgian head of the Persian Treasury resigned in a dispute with the Minister of Finance, and de Etter believed this could be exploited to broaden Allied control over Persian finances. He proposed to link the promise of Allied support and the proposed subvention in his counter-proposals as a means of getting the Persian Government to accept representatives from the Imperial Bank of Persia and the Banque d'Escompte (the major Russian financial institution in Iran) as advisors to report on expenditures and resources. This alone would not assure financial control, but with a change in Persian financial law to give the Treasury wider powers it could be the first step, and de Etter was determined to take it.[42]

Marling saw little advantage in it except that it would give the Allies some opportunity to supervise the retroactive sum of the moratorium.* On March 23 Grey, after consulting with officials of the Imperial Bank of Persia in London,[43] instructed Marling to join de Etter in insisting on representatives in the Treasury.[44] In addition Marling and de Etter still hoped to negotiate the creation of British- and Russian-controlled forces to secure military protection for Allied political security.

In the first instance the two ministries enjoyed success. On April 29 the Persian Government agreed to the idea of a Mixed Financial Commission to control the expenditure of funds provided under the terms of the moratorium.[45] The Commission (composed of a representative from the Imperial Bank of Persia and one from the Banque d'Escompte; two Persian notables, Amin ud-Daula and Sardar Mu'azzim; and a President, one of the Belgian advisors common in the Persian financial structure) was to run for the duration of the moratorium and was to have complete independence.[46] Thus by degrees an idea for establishing a commission to control a subvention for a national force, for which no agreement had been reached, had become a body for directing the expenditure of the moratorium, a fund established for the maintenance of the government. It was the introduction of the thin wedge of financial control that both Britain and Russian had been interested in since the late 1890s. But the attempts to reach a settlement based on Article 2 of the de Etter draft (expansion of the Cossack Brigade and establishment of a British-officered force) ran into difficulty when once again Russian procrastination delayed a settlement.

On May 27 the Persian Government broached the subject of an agreement and the terms they sought might well have been written in Petrograd. They wanted a decision for the policing forces and on the subsidy. They recommended: (1) an increase of the Persian Cossack Brigade by 10,000 plus thirty Russian officers − the expense of equiping the forces being borne by the Allies until a few months

---

* The Persian Government had requested these funds in February but Russian delays and worries over the potential misuse of the £220,000 involved left the issue undecided. The Russians did not agree to pay the accumulations until March 30, after the Allies had begun to press for Treasury representation. See pp. 56-60 above for a discussion of the moratorium.

after the war; (2) a grant of 200,000 tumans per month to be dispensed by the Mixed Commission to cover the whole financial administration for fifteen or twenty years.[47]

On June 2 Marling and de Etter met with Sipahsalar, who expanded on the Persian demands. In addition to wanting the policing force and the subsidy settled, he wanted a revision of the tariff structure and arrangements for foreigners to pay taxes as a means for getting the revenue necessary to pay for the two forces after the expiration of the Allied subsidy. The Foreign Office, the India Office and the Government of India were not opposed to the scheme; but after considerable delay the Russian Government once again introduced complications on June 24. They had consistently whittled down all Persian demands and now, with the best of terms, they still wanted to give up nothing. Not wishing to have their hands tied in any way, they refused to discuss the number of Russian officers and NCOs to be supplied or to guarantee any payments for the forces after the war. They wanted to defer any discussions of revisions of customs or tax arrangements, but wanted to investigate immediately the possibility of finding sources for financing the proposed forces.* In addition they wanted financial control without a time limit.[48]

In light of these changes Marling and de Etter composed new proposals on July 11 that would strengthen the Mixed Financial Commission, raise the forces in the north and south to 11,000 each with sufficient officers and NCOs, with the Allies bearing the cost until the end of the war, and promise the Persians that the Allies would listen sympathetically to Persian demands for tariff and tax revision. Still the Russian Government withheld a definite commitment, pursuing, as Buchanan believed, an interest in establishing a joint protectorate. The most that was forthcoming was an elaboration of their objections to revising the tax structure. Sazanov informed Buchanan that if this point were to be included he would have to

---

* The Russians were having considerable difficulties financing their own forces in Iran and financial worries bedeviled Anglo-Russian relations. The Russians refused to make payments to Persia because of financial difficulties and put obstacles in Britain's path. When the Imperial Bank of Persia had trouble securing enough silver bullion to mint coins and cover their paper issue, the Russians refused to move any of their silver reserves, even when promised reimbursement, and were somewhat reluctant to facilitate transfer of bullion from London via Archangel to Tehran or from China across Russia. Evidently the Russians were reluctant to see money circulating in Persia that they did not control, even if that money was supplied by an ally in circumstances threatening to Russian interests when Russia was having difficulties meeting its financial obligations.

consult with other departments for approval which would occasion serious delay. The only alternative was to offer vague assurances. Not wanting any delays, the Foreign Office agreed and Marling proceeded along the lines of his July 11 proposals.[49] The Russian Government might well have objected to giving up even this much (if it can be said it was giving up anything) but circumstances forced its hand. On April 29 British forces had surrendered their encircled position at Kut al-Amara in Mesopotamia to the beseiging Turkish army.[50] Besides rudely ending India's 'field day' in Mesopotamia, the disaster at Kut al-Amara freed numerous Turkish forces for operations in Iran and breathed new life into the menace of a Muslim *jihad*. By June this menace took definite shape.

Throughout the early months of 1916 Russian forces under General Baratoff had gradually been driving all enemy forces, either Persian irregulars or Turkish troops, from the country. By May the Russians had reached the western frontiers and seemed in control; but the effort of driving the German nationalist forces out, and of garrisoning and guarding all the vital points, coupled with losses through disease, had spread the Russians thin. Thus when Turkish forces freed from Kut al-Amara began to appear on Iran's border the Russian army was not prepared to meet the threat. By mid-summer the renewed Turkish offensive forced the Russians from Kermanshah and menaced Hamadan. Russian military authorities seemed unlikely to be able to find the necessary reinforcements to meet this new crisis – so an agreement with Persia suddenly seemed more attractive. As usual, a crisis had made the Russians willing to seek a necessary settlement. But even under the circumstances the Russians refused to grant substantive concessions. Marling was exasperated and characterized his role in the proceedings as little more than an observer:

Except for preparing the first draft of the joint note [January 1916] I have had myself little to do with the negotiations – if, indeed, such a term can be applied to proceedings which were really little more than a series of announcements by my Russian colleague to the Persian Government that this or that concession, which the two Powers had been earlier prepared to accord, was now to be struck out. There was nothing for me to do except to obtain for myself a repetition of the assurances given to my colleague that the Persian Government accepted these successive amputations without demur.[51]

The Foreign Office, too, was not altogether accommodating in the matter of the alliance. They wanted an agreement but they also had reservations, and the crisis of the Turkish advance only increased the feeling that Britain would have to make impossible concessions to secure Persian favor.

On July 5 Marling discussed the situation, which Russian reverses had turned topsy-turvy. According to Marling, the Persian Government was ready, despite the situation, to conclude an agreement on simple terms, such as a subsidy and a share in the holy places. Although Persian military support was insignificant, he felt Persia exerted a moral influence and that it was 'imperative to enlist that influence on our side by means of an alliance,' at least until Force 'D' could begin a new offensive. Not to do so would mean a Persia arrayed with the enemy – a complete debacle. After almost two years, British fears of Persia joining Turkey in the Central Powers were as great as at the outbreak of the War, and in many ways their efforts had only made the situation worse.

But the Foreign Office was not to be rushed; it felt than an agreement signed under duress could only be obtained by unfavorable concessions – meaning the holy places. On this point the Foreign Office remained adamant: no concessions. Instead it authorized Marling,

... to take such financial measures as you may at any moment think desirable for the purpose of securing action on the part of the Persian Government, the Bakhtiari, or any tribal force that you can utilise.[52]

This reluctance of both Russia and Britain to make concessions may have increased Marling's sense of being a mere spectator, and explain his readiness to go along with de Etter's proposals. It was these revised, much emaciated proposals that Marling and de Etter submitted to the Persian Government in late July. On August 2 he was able to report progress.

The Persian Government did not object to the new proposals but wanted assurances from the two Governments that they would facilitate the liquidation of Persia's debts.[53] The Foreign Office could see no objection to this, especially since 'liquidation' did not mean 'cancellation;' and the former word implied a new joint loan that could be used to expand Allied financial control.[54] With this point settled the Persian Government replied favorably to the agreement on August 5. They accepted creation of the military forces and asked for an additional force for Tehran; they also agreed to the extension of the powers of the Mixed Commission as long as it was not retroactive, and agreed to the subsidy, with the whole agreement being subject to Majlis approval.[55]

The ready acceptance of the treaty shocked Marling:

> I must confess that even after Saram ad-Dowleh [Persian Minister of Foreign Affairs] had brought me the Persian text of the proposed answer, I could scarcely bring myself to believe that the Cabinet would authorise its signature. The agreement itself is virtually one of the administrative partition of the country, and the consideration given for this tremendous concession is no more than a monthly subsidy of 200,000 tumans for the duration of the war. It seemed to me incredible that the Cabinet, with all its subservience, could find the courage to execute so unpopular an instrument, when the military position, which was its only real support, was fast crumbling away; and when the Ministers must recognise that when that support failed them they would be exposed to the resentment of the nation.

The incredible, however, had occurred and the exchange of notes took place. But as Marling suspected, the agreement enjoyed no firm base, and on August 12 the Shah sent for Sipahsalar and dismissed him as Prime Minister. As Marling noted, 'I have little doubt that the conclusion of this fateful agreement was one of the most potent arguments advanced to persuade the Shah to so unusual an assertion of his authority.'[56] With Sipahsalar's fall the agreement he signed went with him. Like quicksilver it had slipped unwittingly through the hand; and the effort to get a succession of Persian cabinets to honor it would keep Anglo-Iranian relations in turmoil for the remainder of the war.

CONCLUSION

The collapse of the Sipahsalar Agreement was attended by a peculiarly Persian bit of chicanery that illustrates the foolishness to which Anglo-Iranian relations so often aspired. After Sipahsalar's fall Marling succeeded in getting the Shah to appoint an acceptable Prime Minister, and he expected to get the new cabinet to give effect to the agreement just concluded. But Vusuq ud-Daula, the new Prime Minister, pretended that the agreement had never happened, or more precisely, that it had gone missing.

The new cabinet had begun office on shaky ground. After dismissing Sipahsalar, the Shah contemplated appointing Mustaufi ul-Mamalik, only giving up the plan when the Russian Minister threatened to leave the capital if he did. Finally the Shah agreed to appoint Vusuq ud-Daula, an acceptable candidate to Marling and de Etter but not one the Shah favored. Although Vusuq ud-Daula enjoyed Allied support, there was still considerable internal opposition and he had trouble forming a cabinet. Farman-Farma had fallen because of the maneuvering of Sipahsalar's party, and Farman-Farma's party had subsequently intrigued against Sipahsalar. Also, Ain ud-Daula and Ala us-Saltana had followers who played on rivalries. All were interested in protecting their own interests or returning to office, so that the life of any cabinet – birth or survival – was punctuated with the maneuverings of these groups. In addition, the pressure of the Turkish advance and the uncertainty it introduced into Britain's and Russia's ability to control the situation gave more independence to groups competing for influence. Thus, it was not until the end of August that Vusuq ud-Daula was able to form a more or less stable cabinet, and he was anxious lest public opinion undermine his tenuous grasp on power. The Sipahsalar Agreement was an issue that could incite indelicate opposition.

On September 1 Prince Firuz Mirza, Nusrat ud-Daula, Farman-Farma's eldest son, who was the new Minister of Justice, visited Marling to sound out his opinion on the expediency of immediately implementing the agreement. Nusrat ud-Daula wanted Marling to understand that the new Cabinet did not want to repudiate it, but that there was a general resentment against Sipahsalar's cabinet for having signed away Persian independence, and that since Vusuq ud-Daula's Cabinet was not established on the firmest ground it could not risk immediate fulfilment of the agreement without jeopardizing its position. After putting these cards on the table, Firuz Mirza outlined a further, practical difficulty. Evidently even after a thorough search of the archives of the offices of the President of the Council and of the Ministry of Foreign Affairs no trace of the notes could be found; and although members of Sipahsalar's cabinet had knowledge of the contents of the Allied joint note of August 3 they had never seen the reply nor had they been consulted in its preparation.

Marling regarded this as more than curious because it did not coincide with his information at all. Akhbar Mirza, the late Minister for Foreign Affairs, had mentioned that the reply had met with no opposition from the Cabinet and that they had unanimously approved it although the imminent fall of the Cabinet had lent some haste. What made the missing Agreement even more curious was the fact that on the day after Sipahsalar's dismissal the former Prime Minister had asked the Russian Minister to return the Persian identical note of August 5.

Marling felt that this bit of 'truly Persian trickery' was intended to relieve all the members of the late Cabinet except the Prime Minister, and particularly Akbar Mirza and Sardar Mansur, of the odium of having agreed to 'the surrender of Persian independence,' and very possibly, had destroyed the joint note and the draft of the Persian reply.[57]

But Vusuq ud-Daula was not able to squeeze out so easily. When Sipahsalar's cabinet fell Marling had urged that the first installment of the subsidy be paid in addition to the moratorium so that Vusuq ud-Daula would not assume that Britain did not support him, and the Foreign Office had agreed. Thus Britain felt that the Government had already accepted the agreement's existence. Vusuq ud-Daula wanted to safeguard his Cabinet from opprobrium and deny any knowledge of the compact, but the two Ministers pointed out that in that event their recourse would be to supply him with copies of the notes. The Persian Government was not to escape acknowledging the existence of the agreement. They had to content themselves with the right to take up the matter later. Thus the agreement began under a shadow and its fulfillment remained in doubt.[58]

The development and collapse of the Sipahsalar Agreement, plus the episode following it, were typical of the state of international relations in Iran during the war. British efforts to secure a favorable situation in Iran by financial measures, private agreements and semi-alliances had come to nothing. Nothing seemed to hold, an experience by no means confined to the British. Space does not permit a discussion of German efforts in the country but they were attended with similar confusion, one German agent committing suicide out of frustration; while another was almost thankful when a British party arrested him, sparing him the necessity of any more dealings with the Persians, for whom he had developed a healthy hatred – so strong, in fact, that the British published his diary as a propaganda measure! The efforts of the nationalists to organize a counter-government with German assistance fared no better, reading like a Gilbert and Sullivan production, plagued by petty bickering and rivalry.

But the Allies were able to rely on more material strength, even if limited, and given the smallness of the opposition this was generally enough. Despite their advantages, though, the British and Russians were consistently unable to reach a satisfactory settlement in Persia, either because they could not agree among themselves, or because they waited too long; or settlements failed as the result of a combination of these stumbling blocks and a unique Persian ability to avoid anything definitive.

Neither the British nor the Russians, however, limited themselves to arrangements with the Persian Government, which showed a realistic appreciation of the fragmented nature of Persian politics; but the variety of efforts pursued guaranteed even more difficulties and uncertainties to the whole affair, as will be seen later. The resulting confusion levied a tax on every British effort in Persia. The British only wanted the place to be quiet so they could go about the serious business of war, but like Penelope's tapestry, what was woven in the light came undone in the dark.

CHAPTER FIVE

THE SOUTH PERSIA RIFLES

We are not making much of a show in South Persia.

The genesis, development, and use or uselessness of the South Persia Rifles (SPR) typifies much of what went on in Anglo-Iranian relations during the war. The idea of a British-officered force, as noted earlier, coincided with the efforts to conclude an alliance once it became obvious that what the Russians expected was a way to expand the Cossack Brigade and thus their own influence.[1] Marling, India, the India Office and the Foreign Office all agreed – for once – that under those circumstances Britain needed a similar force in the south not only to restore order there during the war, but to have a force and a political instrument to secure British interests after the war. Actually, ideas of a British-officered force were older than the war, but they had never gone very far, partly because the Persians would not have accepted the idea and because the Russians would not have been pleased. The Swedish-officered gendarmerie, organized in 1911, had been as close as Britain could hope to come to a force in the south to maintain order; and that particular institution had proved an unmitigated disaster for Britain during the war when most of the force defected to the Germans, refusing even to obey instructions from the Persian Government.

The loss of the gendarmes, the activities of German agents in the south, the relatively small number of available regular British troops, and the weakness of the Persian Government meant that the south was prey to disorder, which during the war took on sinister overtones for British officials because, through the prism of war, every sign of disturbance, whether it had a long ancestry or not, became German-inspired disloyalty. And there were enough German-inspired incidents to convince anyone who might have been the least sceptical that the whole area seethed with potential disaster. Lack of men and material, though, limited the type of response, and so Marling, India, and the Foreign Office had to improvise.

One such virtuoso application was the recruitment of local tribesmen as irregulars. This took two forms, either making arrangements with some of the major tribal leaders – of such groups as the Bakhtiari, the Qashqa'i, the Khamsih Confederation, and Shaykh Khaz'al, leader of the Arabs of Khuzistan – who would use their tribal forces on Britain's behalf; or of recruiting individuals or small groups to act under the direction of British officers or NCOs, who formed the nucleus of a levy corps. By the end of the war forces based on the latter pattern were to be found in virtually every place where there was a British subject. There were levies at Ahwaz, Shushtar, Dizful, Mashad, Hamadan, in Sistan, Kerman, Kermanshah and elsewhere. Many of these might be generously considered as useless and most were makeshift, made up of unemployables, armed with whatever was to hand and of doubtful military capability. Sir Percy Cox's instructions to one of his youthful officers, C. J. Edmonds, who was bound for Dizful in southwestern Iran, is an example of the planning that went into some of these efforts: 'Good-bye, my boy,' Cox said, 'and do your best to keep the place quiet.'[2] But as symbols of Britain's presence and prestige, since they did not really face many threats, they were quite satisfactory.

Some of the local levy corps were more elaborate. The Eastern Cordon, for example, was fairly well organized, reasonably supplied and seasoned with quite a few Indian officers, NCOs and soldiers. The Eastern Cordon had developed in eastern Persia on the approaches to Afghanistan as an effort to stop the Germans from reaching Afghanistan. The force was slow to develop and it failed to keep some of the early German missions from getting into Afghanistan, but as it became better organized it was not only able to guard the frontier but also to extend its operations northward in 1917 to replace Russian forces in Khorasan, a province in northwestern Iran, as they began to disintegrate after the revolution. The Eastern Cordon forces were also an important link in the chain that forged a supply route for the abortive intervention against the Bolsheviks in Turkestan in 1918. But the most sophisticated of the levy corps was the South Persia Rifles, based on Shiraz in Fars province in southern Iran. No force was as large nor as controversial.

From the British viewpoint, the conception behind the force was simple: it was to replace the gendarmerie, restore order in the south, check enemy activities, balance the Cossack Brigade, and, since it was to have British officers, it would be thoroughly reliable. So simple was the idea that the British actually organized the force before the Persians agreed to recognize it. There the simplicity stopped. The South Persia Rifles became a subject of intense controversy not only between Britain and Iran but between British officials who squabbled with each other over the control, use and value of the force, whether it was military or political force, and over who was to command it, supply it and benefit from it. As with many of the approaches tried in Persia, the SPR created more problems than it resolved.

The alliance negotiations, first with Farman-Farma and then with Sipahsalar were mainly efforts to get the Persians to accept and thereby legitimize the South Persia Rifles. For Marling, the Foreign Office, the India Office and the Government of India, the Sipahsalar Agreement was more an enabling agreement than an alliance, which explains in part why the British gave up so little in trying to win Persia to the Allied cause. With an efficient British-controlled force in the south the British did not really need Persia as an ally, they only needed Persia to accept, quietly, the existence of the force. But the Persians proved reluctant, and as a result the South Persia Rifles took on a dual nature – as the point of conflict in Anglo-Iranian discontent, and as a functioning reality and symbol of British interest and prestige that required support.

This developed out of differences in interpretation over what was needed in Persia. The Persians wanted a uniform national army and Allied help to finance it. They wanted an all-Persian force or at least one officered by neutrals under Persian control and not another force on the lines of the Cossack Brigade. An army on that model meant no uniform force and its existence would be one more confirmation of the division of the country into north-south entities. The British, conversely, already accepted that division and were interested in securing order on a realistic basis, which in this case meant no more experiments with neutrals. As the British and the Persians tried to reconcile these differences of perspective the South Persia Rifles became something more than a military force. To the Persians it became another visible symbol of their humiliation and of the inexorable partition of the country. As such the Persians refused or resisted recognition. The British imbued the South Persia Rifles with their longings for a resolution in Iran, both for the troubles during the war and as a force for guaranteeing that the south would not continue in chaos after the war; and they convinced themselves that the South

Persia Rifles was the instrument of that peace. As such they were determined to have it recognized – exhorting, bullying, intimidating, or ignoring a succession of cabinets, while looking for one that would accept the force and still survive that recognition.

THE SOUTH PERSIA MILITARY POLICE

Throughout 1915 Britain and Russia faced the perennial difficulty of finding sufficient troops to protect Allied interests in Iran. Since neither power could send large numbers of troops, both became interested in alternatives. The Russians already had a locally-raised military force, the Persian Cossack Brigade, but it was largely a police force and personal bodyguard to the Shah and had not proved effective as a military force. Indeed, in the closing months of 1915 it had proved singularly unable to defend the Government's position in Hamadan in western Iran, where German-nationalist forces seized the city with little resistance from its reinforced guardians.

The British had initially countenanced the Swedish-officered gendarmerie as a foil to the Persian Cossack Brigade but the defection of large parts of that body to the Germans and nationalists left Britain without any comparable force to protect its interests. The British had experimented with securing the support of local tribal leaders, but that had not proved very satisfactory. The tribal leaders had either been reluctant to commit themselves, like the Bakhtiari, or had been unable to take effective action, like Qavam ul-Mulk of the Khamsih at Shiraz, who had been unable to protect the British establishment there. The British had also made minimal efforts to raise their own local supporters, most notably in the east, but this had not produced significant results; and so in 1916 the British and the Russians still lacked a diversity of military options.

The Germans, on the other hand, in the absence of regular units had managed to precipitate a crisis by the liberal use of money and a few trained men to act as a nucleus for the creation of irregular forces. Although they were also aided by tribal forces and trained gendarmes, it was the combined use of these resources that enabled the Germans and nationalists to achieve so much. And it was their success that encouraged the Allies to embark upon similar programs. Thus, parallel to the attempt to secure an alliance and the Shah's favor, the Allies endeavored to enlarge upon their military alternatives by creating locally enlisted forces under Allied officers, ostensibly to uphold the Persian Government's authority and maintain internal order. In reality these forces were designed to check German-nationalist intrigue and provide auxiliary support to Allied efforts to keep Persia neutral. In the process of creating these forces the Allies also revealed their determination to protect their respective interests.

The Persian Government had advanced several schemes since the beginning of the war for creating a national army. The Allies had repeatedly discouraged the idea, but their inability to resolve the Persian situation gradually made it more attractive. The creation of the Allied-inspired Farman-Farma cabinet seemed to give them the opportunity, and so in early January the idea took shape of expanding the Persian Cossack Brigade and of creating a countervailing British force.

According to Sir Charles Manning the main impetus came from Sipahsalar, the thoroughly pro-Russian Persian Minister for War. According to his plan, the Persian Government was to augment the Cossack Brigade by 10,000 men with funds from the moratorium and arms from the gendarmerie with the idea that the Allies would provide more permanent funding. When Marling heard of this scheme he intimated that the British would not countenance a Russian-officered force to police south Persia, and that any force employed there would have to have British officers, an eventuality he felt would mean a 'definition of [a] sphere of influence not far removed from partition.'³ Farman-Farma was aware of the difficulties involved in the proposal, but Sipahsalar, a military man and Minister of War with Russian backing, was determined to get funds for the military and even tried to bring pressure on Farman-Farma by refusing to attend cabinet meetings. Although de Etter did not approve of this tactic, at least publicly, he was nevertheless determined to increase the Cossack Brigade; and General Baratoff, the Commander of Russian forces in Iran, visited Tehran in early January to work out the details. After his visit the expansion of the Cossack Brigade became a certainty, which had a settling effect on Sipahsalar, and it only remained to work out the machinery for organizing, equipping and paying for this force.

Marling observed that Britain could not rightly object to a measure by Russia to protect her interests in the north, but he did not feel that Britain could allow this to speak for British interests. On January 9 and 10 he suggested that the Foreign Office consider taking advantage of the Russian proposal to press for a similar British arrangement in the south.⁴ He had already established a wedge for this proposal with the Persian Government and he was hoping to get the Foreign Office to capitalize on it. On January 12, 1916 he pushed the point again, mentioning that the Russians would have the Persian Cossack Brigade while Britain would have no force to protect its interests since the gendarmerie was out:

It is clear that our interests demand that some provision be made for dealing with South Persia and I suggest that in our discussions with the Persian Government we should inform the Persian Government that for the maintenance of order [in] Southern Persia where we have predominant interests we shall demand formation of corps under British officers or instructors as soon as we find it convenient to do so.⁵

Marling's opinions did not lack sympathy at the Foreign Office where Oliphant, the department's Persian expert, agreed completely. On his recommendation the Foreign Office consulted the India Office and the Director of Military Intelligence on January 13 about the possibility of seconding British officers to south Persia for the purpose. On January 14, Major-General Sir George MacDonogh, the Director of Military Intelligence (DMI) at the War Office, informed the Foreign Office that he thought the idea sound if India could furnish the officers.⁶

India also approved the idea. On January 19 the Viceroy, Lord Hardinge, wrote Chamberlain, 'We entirely agree as to the desirability of maintaining visible sign of British influence outside Russian sphere and have always advocated raising of a force under British officers for this purpose.' He recommended that Col. Sir Percy Sykes, an officer experienced in Persian affairs, undertake the task of organizing and commanding a force of military police in Sistan. Using local levies that had already been recruited as a nucleus, Sykes could form a local regiment and slowly extend his sphere of activity to Kerman and eventually to Bandar Abbas on the Gulf. In this way, the Viceroy believed, the frontiers of India would be guarded and the gradual expansion westward of British influence would reassert British prestige on a firm footing in south Persia. The Viceroy further recommended that the force be called 'military police' rather than gendarmerie because the latter term was 'discredited in Persia'⁷ — a reference to the defection of the Swedish gendarmerie.

Armed with this information the India Office informed the Foreign Office of their support for the idea. Indeed, on the 19th, the India Office felt that the measure was sufficiently important to be pressed regardless of the alliance negotiations then in progress. The India Office also recommended Sykes as an officer with considerable Persian experience who for years had travelled in Persia chronicling his discoveries and who had served as Consul-General in Mashad. He was on his way to India and the Viceroy was prepared to send him to begin organizing a British force in the south.* In order to disarm Persian Government opposition, the India Office recommended that Sykes' position could be explained ostensibly as part of a levy corps that India was organizing in Persian Sistan to check tribal and German instigated disturbances on the frontier of Baluchistan. Later, when the force in south Persia was actually organized and ready as an existing force at the disposal of the Persian Government, then perhaps use of the force elsewhere could be considered. It remained to settle the details.[8]

Settling the details, however, proved a thankless project. Not only did the effort create endless difficulties with the Persian Government, but it sparked wrangles among a variety of British officials as well, most particularly between Marling and the Viceroy. The main issue was the control and use of the proposed force, with both Marling and Hardinge claiming exclusive rights.

The Viceroy's position was clear: the force was a military one to be largely paid for and officered by the Indian Government in order to restore peace in eastern Persia and bring security to India's frontier. Hardinge naturally believed that he should control the force, though the Persians were expected to sanction its existence while accepting its independence.

Marling, on the other hand, saw the mission mainly as a political one aimed at restoring order and maintaining British prestige in south Persia. He recognized that India would have to supply the men and material, but he wanted to work through the Persian Government so the force would have a more Persian character – at least in appearance. In Marling's view this meant that he should have the deciding voice in the control of the force since it involved delicate relations with the Persians, who were touchy over the idea of an Indian-controlled force operating independently in Iran. Thus, from the beginning, the SPR became entangled in a demarcation dispute.

---

* Sykes travelled extensively throughout Iran as the titles of some of his articles and books suggest (see Bibliography) and was also the author of the now outdated *A History of Persia*, in two volumes.

Marling and India differed significantly over the nature of the effort to be made as well. The minister at Tehran wanted a mission to defend the British community there (see pp. 112-13), to restore order in Kerman, and prepare for a return to Shiraz. In addition, he wanted a force of 1600 regular troops sent from Egypt to Bandar Abbas to overawe the local population.[9] But Hardinge opposed this, apparently, though he did not say so directly, because the troops from Egypt would involve the War Office in an area regarded as an Indian sphere; and he opposed the mission to Qavam ul-Mulk because it would have been a political effort, and therefore would have been more difficult to keep under his authority. Hardinge proposed, instead, to send Sykes to Bandar Abbas with the title of Inspector-General of the South Persia Military Police to raise a local force, one that would be under his control.[10]
South Persia Military Police to raise a local force, one that would be under his control.[10]

The impasse created by these contradictory positions required the mediation of the War Cabinet who, on February 16, ordered the Foreign Office, the India Office, and the War Office to hold a joint meeting on Persia so that the General Staff could prepare an appreciation of the situation for the War Committee.[11]

On February 29 the War Committee considered the memorandum prepared by the Chief of the Imperial General Staff, which generally supported Marling's position; and on March 1 Grey informed Marling that the War Office would supply troops if necessary, but that they would not be allowed to operate in the hinterland. In addition, the War Office agreed to support Qavam ul-Mulk in every way possible (except with regular forces), including the loan of several British officers to raise a force under his authority, and instructed that Sykes hold discussions with him to discover his requirements.[12] Thus a compromise of sorts was reached, even though the disagreement was not resolved.

The War Committee had supported Marling's view of the type of force to be promoted in a decision that left open the ultimate control of that force – a point lost on neither Marling nor Hardinge. And initially India gained the advantage.

On March 6 the Viceroy informed the India Office that Sykes was to leave Karachi for Bandar Abbas on March 12, and that since this would delay Qavam ul-Mulk's imminent departure he should be encouraged with money and arms and not wait for Sykes.[13] This news came as a surprise to the Foreign Office, which had formed the impression that Sykes was already in Persia. Oliphant minuted:

Over a week ago the I.O. gave me the impression that Sir P. Sykes was in Persia and now we see he is not due for another week. With this dilatoriness it is scarcely possible for our local officials in Persia to make much headway ...

Lord Crewe, acting for the ailing Grey, capped this sense of exasperation by noting, 'We are not making much of a show in South Persia.'[14] It is doubtful that Hardinge deliberately misled the Foreign Office on Sykes' whereabouts, but the coincidence of his delay and the departure of Qavam ul-Mulk created the situation that India had wanted. Sykes was not to be attached to the Khamsih leader, and a case could still be made for his independence. The issues were far from resolved, and Hardinge had more surprises in store for the Foreign Office.

In the meantime, Sykes arrived in Bandar Abbas in mid-March and immediately began recruiting a force. But the nature of his force, its control, and its finances were yet to be settled.

Although finding the money for the force required another round of negotiating within the government, it proved to be fairly easy to arrange. A formula was worked out whereby India and the Home Government shared the cost. The Foreign Office stressed to the Treasury that the force was vital to the security of British interests and on March 30 they agreed to pay half. On May 5 they went even further. After Grey assured the Treasury that the scheme was 'dictated by vital Imperial interests,' the Lords of the Treasury accepted to pay half of any expenditures of the Sykes mission − a commitment that was to prove costly. This issue was settled, but it still remained to determine what Sykes was to do, who was to direct his activities, and whether or not the Persian Government would acknowledge his mission.[15]

THE SOUTH PERSIA RIFLES

The confused state of the Sipahsalar Agreement with the Persian Government left the status of Sykes' mission under a cloud. The Foreign Office had hoped that the Agreement would legitimize Sykes' activities, avoiding the impression of violating Persian neutrality, and give Britain a tool in the south to protect its interests without the commitment of scarce military resources and personnel. But the eccentricities of Persian politics and the vicissitudes of the military situation did not provide an altogether healthy climate for the idea, and the necessary cooperation within British administrative channels to smooth the path of this novel experiment was not all it might have been. The mission had begun life in controversy, its status debated and disputed, and this controversy continued.

Shortly after Sykes arrived in Bandar Abbas on March 16 he had begun to organize a Persian force as a support to Qavam ul-Mulk. However, the leader of the Khamsih Confederation needed nothing other than arms, and he had already begun to disperse German-nationalist parties and tribes, and to move on Shiraz. Sykes, therefore, determined in early April to go to Kerman, which German activities had forced the British colony to evacuate and where Sykes had once been consul, to drive out the Germans and to organize an additional (Kerman) brigade.[16] Marling and the Foreign Office had different ideas. They believed it was essential for Sykes to go directly to Shiraz.

Shiraz was the most important city in south Persia and the humiliating arrest of the British community there by nationalists in November, 1915, reinforced Marling's conviction that a clear demonstration of British resolve was needed to restore Britain's damaged reputation. The timing seemed excellent for just such an effort. Qavam ul-Mulk was beginning his campaign, Sulat ul-Daula, leader of the powerful Qashqa'i tribe of Fars, was offering his support, and Farman-Farma, ousted by Sipahsalar as Prime Minister, was expressing an interest in becomign Governor-General of Fars. The convergence of these forces persuaded Marling and the Foreign Office that it was essential to get Sykes to Shiraz without delay to support the three Persians, and to raise a local force that Britain could rely on.

The Viceroy, however, had other ideas. German activities had created disturbances on the Persian-Baluchistan border which he felt were of more immediate concern; there was already an effort underway to restore order to the frontier and Hardinge believed in a more gradual approach. Sykes would raise a force to contribute to this effort, and then slowly extend his area of operations westward from a secure base. The Viceroy did not want to send a mission into the Persian hinterland where it could be cut off by hostile tribes – requiring an expedition to rescue it – or by the minister at Tehran. Thus, India and Marling once again became locked in a struggle for the Sykes mission, with India fighting an infuriating rearguard action.

Even while Marling and the Foreign Office urged that Sykes

proceed to Shiraz he was on his way to Kerman,[17] so the Foreign Office had to content itself with wringing assurances from India that he would proceed to Shiraz from Kerman – an assurance long in the making. In the meantime, the Foreign Office, on May 16, urged India to send another officer to Shiraz to begin raising a force in preparation for Sykes' arrival. India demurred. On May 30 it expressed its objections. First, it could give the officer no escort, which exposed him to hostile tribes. Second, even if the officer were to arrive he could not start Sykes' scheme without Sykes' explicit instructions, and any precipitous action by such an embryonic force – were it started – would risk a reverse which could only lower British prestige further. This response sparked a debate.[18]

Marling, too, was aware that the crucial aspect of Britain's imperial survival was based on prestige and surgically-applied force. He disagreed with India, however, on how best to maintain prestige. In his own mind at least he had consistently urged strong action, deploring the 'raid and scuttle' policy of India which accomplished nothing locally and did nothing nationally to assist the Persian Government by creating an impression of British presence. Farman-Farma was prepared to go to Fars and restore order but he needed support, so that India's reluctance to send Sykes was frustrating. The Foreign Office communicated Marling's feelings to the India Office which did its best to get the needed cooperation, but India was not prepared to give up without a fight.[19]

On June 9 the Government of India again expressed its dislike of the proposal. 'We considered our policy in Persia should be quietly to reestablish our position with adequate force where possible and to avoid multiplying risks of further embarrassment.' The proposal was objectionable because it was a half-measure that would underscore Britain's military poverty and damage British prestige. In addition the new officer, without an escort, could not carry sufficient funds to pay for the scheme and there were no funds in Shiraz. And to make matters worse, Russian military reverses in western Iran in the face of the new Turkish offensive increased the risk that seditious elements would attack the officer. Instead, India recommended that after securing Kerman, Sykes should proceed to Shiraz via Yezd and Isfahan – in other words, gradual extension of influence. But if India could be persistent, Marling could be adamant.[20]

The Government of India, Marling fired back, was laboring under a misconception of the state of affairs in Kerman and at Shiraz. According to his information, Kerman was quiet and the German position had collapsed. A similar situation prevailed at Shiraz and an officer with a small escort could reach the city safely directly from Kerman. The Imperial Bank of Persia was going to reopen its branch in Shiraz and so the officer would have access to funds. In short, there were no serious obstacles and Farman-Farma was convinced he could restore order. The Foreign Office and the India Office agreed with Marling and on June 21 they again urged India to pursue with Sykes the possibility of going directly to Shiraz from Kerman. India did not reply until July 3, and if they were capitulating it was on their terms. Sykes was ordered to proceed to Shiraz – but via Yezd. The reason given was that locusts and supply difficulties made the direct route unfeasible.[21]

In the meantime, Sipahsalar, happy to oblige Marling and thereby remove his chief rival from the capital, appointed Farman-Farma as Governor-General to Fars. The former Prime Minister left on July 13. Marling wanted Sykes and the Prince to rendezvous in Shiraz, the idea being that their combined presence would simultaneously restore Persian Government authority and British prestige, but it was a long way to Shiraz. Still, Farman-Farma planned to reach Shiraz in late August and Sykes, who reached Yezd on August 14, was expected to follow.[22]

Sykes' destination may have been slowly worked out, but doubts remained about the status of his mission. He had been raising forces and his expedition to Shiraz was to continue this activity in conjunction with Farman-Farma's attempts to restore Government authority, with Sykes' force, the South Persia Military Police, replacing the discredited gendarmerie. Marling had hoped to secure official recognition of this force through the tripartite agreement with Sipahsalar by having the Persian Government accept Sykes into its service; but the dubious status of that arrangement after the fall of Sipahsalar left that recognition in doubt. In addition the Government of India was not eager to see Sykes' mission under the Persian Government except in a purely nominal sense; the attitude of the Government of India being that the force should be under their general control and direction since they were supplying everything. There was general agreement that Sykes' mission be kept under British control, but misunderstandings could still arise.[23]

One such misunderstanding illustrates how petty the squabbles could become. On August 7 the Viceroy informed the India Office that Sykes was unhappy with the appelation 'South Persia Military Police,' and he suggested 'South Persia Army.' According to Sykes the Persians disliked the title 'military police,' and he felt that the duties of the force deserved the title 'army.' The Viceroy deprecated 'army' because he believed the force should have a distinctive British name in order to emphasize the British character of the undertaking – on the order of 'Cossack.' India preferred 'militia' for this reason and because 'army' would give the false impression that the force was mainly a constabulary. The India Office and Foreign Office were consulted for their opinions.[24]

The Foreign Office was somewhat sceptical that such rectification of names was needed, Lancelot Oliphant remarking, 'I don't see change would effect opinion locally if they object to present title.'[25] But the India Office agreed with Sykes that 'South Persia Military Police' was bad and they, therefore, suggested 'Rifles' to replace the offending term. Oliphant still regarded this as petty but the Foreign Office could see no objections, and so on August 22 the India Office authorized the Viceroy to allow Sykes to call his proposed force the 'South Persia Rifles.' At this point Marling intruded an objection. He considered the choice unfortunate because the Persian word for 'rifles,' *tufangchi*, was the name commonly used for road guards, whose activities had given the term an unfavorable connotation. But the Viceroy and the India Office had already accepted the terminology. The chief result of this interlocution was to give Sykes' creation its well-known name. But this type of interdepartmental fustianism could have a more serious tone, as the dispute over Sykes' timetable and destination demonstrated.[26]

STRUGGLE FOR CONTROL OF THE SOUTH PERSIA RIFLES

The winter and spring of 1916 was a period of Allied military, if not political, success in Iran; but by the summer the picture began to change. The British defeat at Kut al-Amara in early April freed large numbers of Turkish forces for operations in Iran and by early summer these forces along with Iranian supporters began appearing in the west. The Russian forces that had cleared western Iran and had driven the Iranian nationalists to Ottoman territory were too overextended to handle this new pressure and were forced to give ground. The Russian authorities could not find adequate reinforcement and by

August, even though the Russian retreat was no rout, the Allied Ministers in Tehran were discussing evacuation and were exerting pressure on the Shah to accompany them if they did. This situation increased the importance of Sykes' mission, as well as similar endeavors in Sistan, the Sarhad and Makran on the Perso-Indian frontier. As a result the debate on Sykes' destination and timetable intensified.

Sykes' leisurely progress from Bandar Abbas to Kerman and then to Yezd had been a sore point with Marling and the Foreign Office, who had consistently urged haste. They were eager for Sykes to proceed to Shiraz where he could coordinate his efforts with Farman-Farma, the new Governor-General of Fars, to bring about a pro-Allied order. Their presence there plus the speedy development of a military force might also give Britain the necessary force to protect the south against the new Turkish-German-nationalist advances, even if the position in the north collapsed; but Marling and the Foreign Office had some difficulty in carrying this point with India. The Government of India were mindful of the dangers but were fearful of overextension and embarrassing reversals, perhaps more cautious after the disasters in Mesopotamia. They were also none too eager to relinquish control of Sykes' force.

India and Sykes decided that Isfahan should be the first target of the advance from Yezd, while Marling felt Shiraz was more important. The German-nationalist position there had collapsed and the enemy agents were prisoners; but a delay, especially with the mounting Turkish offensive, might allow them to escape and stage a new coup. He wanted Sykes to join Farman-Farma at Isfahan and proceed jointly to Shiraz, to which the Foreign Secretary agreed and informed the India Office. But the Viceroy replied that Farman-Farma should proceed to Shiraz, while Sykes went to Isfahan, where his presence would influence the situation at Shiraz and put Isfahan under firm control.[27]

Marling, though, continued to urge the necessity of Sykes' presence at Shiraz. Farman-Farma left Isfahan for Shiraz on August 24 and Marling wanted Sykes to follow without delay. The Foreign Office supported Marling and authorized him to order Sykes to proceed. At the same time, India ordered Sykes to sit tight until he received explicit orders, for they did not believe his delay was important. But Marling had his way and on August 27 India ordered Sykes to proceed to Shiraz. However, on August 30, the Viceroy informed the India Office that Sykes was already on his way to Isfahan because of a shortage of supplies at Yezd and that his return would cause difficulties.* The Foreign Office had no choice but to agree to allow him to proceed. In the meantime the controversy around Sykes grew, while the question of who controlled the mission remained unresolved.[28]

Marling, who believed Sykes' mission was subject to Foreign Office influence, complained that Sykes was acting entirely on his own without consideration for the Government's opinion; while Sykes, who thought Marling's opinion should be considered, complained of Marling's ordering him about, and expressed his belief that his orders should come from India. This feuding, of course, spread to India, the India Office and the Foreign Office. India and the India Office wanted Sykes to have more discretion, regarding his mission as a military operation and feeling that Marling might not know all the facts about the situation. The Foreign Office did not welcome this controversy, but they felt confusion would result if Sykes were permitted to disregard Marling's views unless explicit military conditions would not allow him to obey. This dispute opened the whole question of the channel for communicating with Sykes.[29]

The India Office suggested a solution. Marling should keep India and the India Office informed of his views and they would try to conform to them; but in the event of conflict they would refer the question to the Government. Sykes would act when there was agreement and wait when there was not. In any event orders were to go through India. The Foreign Office did not like the proposal, since Sykes' departure for Kerman had resulted from just such a confusion. They wanted to avoid a repetition of this muddle and insisted that Sykes should take orders from Marling.[30]

Foreign Office determination in the matter stemmed from several sources. First, the declining situation in Iran underscored the necessity for strong action, for which the Foreign Office believed India was unprepared. They felt India placed too much reliance on Russian forces, placing Britain at the mercy of Russia, and did not give adequate importance to Sykes' mission. G. P. Clerk, a senior official at the Foreign Office, put this apprehension succinctly: 'If we continually call on Russia to defend us in Persia we weaken our power

---

* Sykes' departure for Isfahan began before he received news of India's concession to the Foreign Office desires. But India's delays gave Sykes the opportunity to advance on Isfahan even though he knew that Marling was pushing for Shiraz.

of resisting her copious appetite for subsequent rewards there.' The Foreign Office, therefore, wanted measures to ease this reliance. This meant pushing for a new advance by Force 'D' in Mesopotamia, a subject they took up with the War Committee, and using Sykes in a more determined manner to bolster Britain's position, not only in terms of security but as a counter-weight to Russia.

Second, as a consequence of these feelings, the Foreign Office did not see Sykes' mission as a purely military one. They regarded his force as a policing one and a political instrument; hence their efforts to have the Persian Government sanction its existence and their determination to let Marling exercise control over it.[31]

The Foreign Office viewpoint prevailed and on September 20 the India Office notified the Viceroy that Sykes should take his orders from Marling. India agreed to this but were not prepared to concede control over the South Persia Rifles — Marling could order Sykes about but India intended to retain control of his command. The Foreign Office did not object to this as long as India did not take action without first consulting them. This should have resolved the matter, although it is difficult to see what the solution was, but India had one more bolt.[32]

On October 9 the India Office agreed with the Foreign Office that Marling should control political matters in Iran; but they pointed out on behalf of the Viceroy that this meant control of a semi-military force and that as a consequence the India Office wanted to put on record that the authority claimed and given to Marling 'absolves the Government of India of responsibility for the safety of Sir Percy Sykes, and his force and the other officers and irregular forces stationed in South Persia.' On behalf of the Government of India, Sir Thomas Holderness, the Permanent Under-Secretary of State for India, wanted it understood that if Marling was to direct the force then 'the Government of India must be definitely relieved of responsibility for movements which they will no longer direct.'[33]

The Foreign Office regarded this opinion askance; in Lancelot Oliphant's words, 'there is an absence of logic in this letter.' First, the Foreign Office had already agreed that India should control the other forces in Persia; they regarded it as somewhat strange that India should expect Marling to be responsible for other forces in Iran because it was essential that he should direct the one on the borders of the Russian sphere. India also controlled the potential reinforcements for Sykes' British contingent and if they were giving up all responsibility that meant Marling should control them, which was absurd. The Foreign Office was making a clear distinction – Sykes' mission was political and different from all the others and therefore required a different status and method of control. The Foreign Office decided not to respond in writing to India's letter but to settle the issue on a personal, amicable level. As a result, Oliphant met with Arthur Hirtzel, the Political Secretary in the India Office, and they worked out a solution recognizing the Foreign Office's view.[34]

The resolution of who was to control Sykes' mission did not, however, end the difficulties; rather the complication surrounding it only increased.

The Sykes mission remained complicated, and the affair was muddled further by Sykes himself, who succeeded in upsetting everybody, but most of all the Government of India, which was perhaps taking out its frustrations on its agent. India complained of his incompetence, complained that he spent too much money without submitting a detailed budget or a program for creating a realistic force; and most seriously, accused him of lacking a sense of humor!

Marling too complained of Sykes, saying that he was entirely too independent and inclined to ignore instructions. The combination of this calumny and the fact that in late 1916 Austen Chamberlain (who replaced Lord Crewe as Secretary of State for India) thought the situation in south Persia required a man with regular military experience, encouraged the Foreign Office and the India Office to replace Sykes. But then Marling changed his mind, discovering that Sykes was more tractable than he had thought.

In February 1917 Marling, not prepared to give up his hard-fought control of the South Persia Rifles, resisted Sykes' replacement on the grounds that a regular officer would convince the Persian Government, who were not being very cooperative, that the South Persia Rifles was in fact a British military mission. Marling suggested Sykes remain in charge with a regular officer to advise him on military matters. This idea won out and left Marling in control over the direction of the mission, much to the annoyance of India. This spirit persisted, dogging the entire life of the force. India was never reconciled to Sykes and even Marling began to reconsider his support. Throughout 1918 he complained that Sykes was not following his instructions nor keeping the Legation in Tehran fully informed. In addition Marling claimed Sykes was acting beyond his instructions, a claim supported by the British Consul-General at Shiraz who had been assigned to work closely with Sykes. The Consul complained that Sykes ignored his advice, censored his mail and had all but accused him of treason. He also said that Sykes and Farman-Farma were constantly at odds. In short, there was no cooperation, and dissension plagued the force at Shiraz as well as everywhere else.

If that were not enough, the South Persia Rifles was not even very reliable, and its presence excited the hostility of local tribal leaders who saw the force as a potential threat to their interests. In the summer of 1918 tribal forces attacked Shiraz and much of the South Persia Rifles deserted; Sykes and the British mission had to rely on the small Indian escort he had brought with him for protection. Even after Sykes left Iran in October 1918, the force remained a farce, yet the British adamantly refused to consider giving it up. Only the Government of India, deprived of any role in the force except as supplier, had the temerity to suggest that it be surrendered as a gesture to the Persians to win their goodwill, a suggestion treated by the Foreign Office and the India Office as if the Viceroy and his staff had taken leave of their senses. By the end of the war, maintaining the South Persia Rifles had become one of the cardinal features in British policy in Iran, creating the anomaly of affirming to the Persian Government that the South Persia Rifles was a Persian force while denying the Persian Government a role in it.

NEGOTIATING TO KEEP THE SOUTH PERSIA RIFLES

Although the British had difficulty in settling among themselves the nature of the South Persia Rifles, they remained determined to sustain it as an instrument of policy. Negotiations to keep the South Persia Rifles had begun with the Vusuq ud-Daula Government immediately after it had established itself, when the fall of the Sipahsalar Government threw the treaty that established the South Persia Rifles into doubt. It became clear, after Vusuq ud-Daula's little subterfuge over the treaty, that the Persians were going to be fastidious about the agreement, not abrogating it outright, but simply refusing to act as if it had any force.

Throughout late August and early September 1916, Marling tried various approaches to get the Persian Government to acknowledge that treaty, but the Turkish offensive complicated the effort. The Russians were unable to halt the advance and General Baratoff, the Russian commanding officer, went so far as to suggest that the

Legations and the Government evacuate Tehran. This climate made it unlikely that a new government would risk acknowledging an agreement that had undone its predecessor. By late September, though, the Russians were able to halt the Turkish offensive, which had over-extended itself, and by November had restored the situation to the *status quo ante*. With this improvement Marling hoped to get something positive from Vusuq ud-Daula. On November 23 the Prime Minister made a proposal and Marling, hoping to use this as a starting point to get official recognition of the South Persia Rifles, expressed a willingness to consider the proposals.

Vusuq ud-Daula's proposals were nothing less than an attempt to revise the Sipahsalar Agreement completely, recalling the set of desiderata that had figured in every Persian approach since the beginning of the war. The Prime Minister sought to limit the powers of the Mixed Financial Commission, excluding it from a role in shaping the budget, and then went on to outline eight points that would enable his government to give effect to the August Agreement.[35]

The Prime Minister proposed: (1) substitution after the war of officers of a third power for British officers in the South Persia Rifles and Russian officers in the Cossack Brigade; (2) monthly installments under the Moratorium Agreement to be 200,000 tumans instead of £50,000;* (3) revision of customs tariff; (4) withdrawal of all foreign troops at the end of the war; (5) engagement by the Allies to abstain from acts of interference in Persia's domestic arrangements such as giving protection to Persian subjects and agreements with tribal chiefs; (6) engagement by Allies not to conclude in the future any convention between themselves or with other powers whether friendly or enemy which would infringe Persian independence or would aim at the annexation or provisional occupation of Persian territory or would give ground for compensation; and to oppose similar designs by other powers; (7) Persia to have representatives with only deliberative power at the peace conference; (8) non-indemnification of British subjects for losses suffered in Persia during the war.

Marling forwarded the proposals with his qualified endorsement. In his opinion only points seven and eight were totally unacceptable

---

* Since the original agreement the pound had dropped in value in relation to the tuman and the Persian Government, needing the money, wanted this arrangement to make up for the disparity. In effect it was an increase in the sums being paid to the Persians.

and even the Persian Government, he explained, realized that Britain would not concede the first point. He said it 'would be satisfied with affirmative reply qualified by some condition, fulfilment of which would depend on ourselves, e.g., that neutral officers must be selected by common agreement between the three powers.' Marling felt that the Allies had already intimated a readiness to discuss the issues of point three, and de Etter was confident that his Government would respond favorably to withdrawal if based on the condition that internal security permitted it. The Russians had also given verbal assurances regarding point five and Marling hoped Britain would follow. On point six, Marling believed that the 1907 Convention covered the point – and that Britain could merely offer its 'good offices' in relation to any agreement by other powers. In short, he favored the proposals.[36]

The Foreign Office was inclined to accept Marling's evaluation, but as usual not without some careful pruning of the Persian demands. The nature of the objections reveal an unstated but underlying theme in the thinking about Persia. Well before the war the British had begun to accept the idea that their interests in the Middle East and Persian Gulf required a more thorough-going settlement than the Persians as an independent state could be expected to give. This plus Russian pressure convinced Grey's Foreign Office that some more satisfactory arrangement was required. The demands of the war, however, temporarily suspended the realization of that intention. Nevertheless, the British conducted their relations in Persia with that idea in mind and studiously avoided making commitments that would embarrass their intentions after the war.

Thus, the Foreign Office objected in particular to point five, about giving protection to various individuals; and to point six that would have kept them from making agreements of the 1907 variety. George Clerk, a senior Foreign Office official, noted, expressing the sentiments of his superiors, that,

after all our experience in Persia I do not see how we can avoid some system of ensuring decent and orderly government. The system may leave the nominal independence of Persia, but it is bound to contain measures of control which could be cited as infringing Persian independence. Any assurance on this point will require careful qualification.[37]

Lord Curzon put his oar in on the subject as well. Although he was not in the Foreign Office his expertise on Persia made his views cogent, at least to himself. In light of later events, Curzon's comments on the Persian proposals are interesting. In a letter to the Foreign Office he expressed his nervousness about the contemplated assurances, and in Curzon fashion he elaborated on his anxiety. First, he did not believe that either Russia or Britain would withdraw their officers from the Persian Cossack Brigade or the South Persia Rifles and he did not see why Britain should be a party to 'a make believe or tie our hands in any way.' And on point five he made himself quite clear. Curzon appreciated the vagaries of the Persian political scene and did not want to make concessions that would inhibit British policy. Arrangements with local khans to provide order were essential, especially since Curzon saw continued Persian disintegration and the expansion of British responsibility.[38]

The Foreign Office shared these sentiments but they were prepared to accept an arrangement, but the India Office had strong reservations. They accepted points two and three (amount of payments and revision of customs tariffs), rejected points seven and eight (representation at peace conference and non-indemnification), and would have preferred rejecting the rest unless Grey felt that concessions were necessary. They deprecated point one (substitution of British and Russian officers) as beneath British dignity. They did not want to tie their hands over point five (making local agreements) because they felt this would limit Britain's ability to avoid a situation that would make it impossible for Britain 'to conclude local agreements and arrangements which might well be the sole means of maintaining public order, in the absence of an effective central Government ...' The India Office concluded their arguments with an interesting display:

If the four requests are rejected [1, 6, 7, and 8] Mr Chamberlain would suggest with regard to them, the Two Powers might declare their sympathy with the underlying motive, while pointing out that the state of things of which they are the victims and the present Persian Government the heirs, is entirely due to the incapacity, corruption, and bad faith of the latter's predecessors; and intimating that until strong evidence is furnished of improvement in all branches of the administration and of public life in Persia, they are not prepared to relinquish any of the means which they possess of palliating evils which only the Persians themselves can eradicate.[39]

Based on this the Foreign Office, on December 2, informed Marling that if he saw no other alternatives he should give the Persians assurances on points two, three, and four (amount of moratorium payments, revision of tariffs, and troop withdrawal after war), while rejecting points seven and eight (representation at peace conference and non-indemnification). It wanted point one (substitution of British and Russian officers) reserved until after the war and to settle the issues of point five (local agreements) with general assurances that Britain would endeavor not to interfere unduly in Persian domestic arrangements. It felt the 1907 Convention covered point six (conventions by the Powers), but wanted Marling to keep in mind that Britain and Russia would probably revise it after the war. As in former arrangements the British were prepared to meet Persia's demands for money, but avoided commitments that would limit Britain's ability to protect or pursue its strategic interests.[40]

These proposals were presented to the Persian Government, which did not reject them as a basis for discussion, but progress in reaching any agreement was slow. On December 21 Marling informed the Foreign Office that he was near an agreement for a decree establishing the Mixed Financial Commission — which would give effect to the August Agreement by setting up the machinery for its administration — but on December 24 he could report no further progress and suggested threatening to withhold the retroactive subsidy of the moratorium, which was still being paid to finance the Persian Government, if no action were taken by January 15.[41]

Meanwhile the cabinet in Britain changed, the Government of Lloyd George replacing the Liberals. The new Foreign Secretary, A. J. Balfour, did not, however, introduce any major changes in policy toward Persia. His interests were directed elsewhere and Persian policy tended to remain in the hands of the permanent officials and the representative in Tehran. In the months to follow, though, as the new Government began to streamline the operations of the cabinet and to extend the powers of coordinating committees responsible to the cabinet, a subtle shift began and the control of foreign policy drifted towards various powerful committees and their chairmen, most notably Lord Curzon. But that was in the future; for the immediate present, there was little change in British efforts in Iran.

The Sipahsalar Agreement remained in limbo and with it the fate of the South Persia Rifles, nor had Vusuq ud-Daula's Government gone very far towards recognizing the agreement concluded by the former cabinet. These negotiations had dragged on since August 1916 and no final solution had been reached. As a result the Allies, while agreeing to increase the moratorium payments, decided to turn to a policy of pressure. The Foreign Office and the India Office agreed to withhold further subsidy payments unless the Persian Government accepted the financial and military arrangements and the Sipahsalar Agreement — namely, recognize the South Persia Rifles. This pressure seemed to have an effect and on January 13, 1917, Marling was able to report progress. The Persian Cabinet passed a decree more or less accepting the modified terms of the Agreement. But the Shah had already dismissed one cabinet for conducting a similar arrangement and his attitude now complicated the settlement.[42] He opposed the terms and he was hostile to Vusuq ud-Daula.

Exactly why the Shah opposed the settlement is unclear. He disliked Vusuq ud-Daula and may, therefore, have been trying to embarrass him; and he had dismissed Sipahsalar for concluding the agreement in the first place, which indicated a degree of hostility to the agreement. Whether this was based on patriotism is hard to say. The Shah may have felt the agreement was contrary to his country's interests, or he may have been raising difficulties because no one paid him the necessary attention. The negotiations with him in late 1915 and early 1916 over a personal subsidy had been suspended when the alliance negotiations began in earnest, and the monarch may have been reminding everyone that he could be difficult. Interestingly, Marling proposed at this time that one month of the moratorium subsidy be paid without the control of the Mixed Financial Commission as a means of expediting the agreement with Vusuq ud-Daula — the idea being that this money would find its way to the Shah who would then relax his opposition.

The original suggestion for this maneuver may have come from Vusuq ud-Daula, who did suggest to Marling that the British threaten to cancel the moratorium if there was no satisfactory reply from the Persian Government to British efforts to give effect to the August Agreement. A somewhat unusual approach for the Prime Minister to take, but it must be remembered that he was not firmly in possession of his office and was, therefore, not averse to using what influence he could to bring pressure on the Shah, who did not like him. Also his Government needed the money to survive and he may have been willing to resort to this device to convince Marling that his Government was really accommodating but that it needed help, while knowing that he could then use this show of support to keep negotiations alive without actually reaching a settlement.

Marling prepared a note that incorporated the threat to cancel funds, delivering it on January 23, 1917. It called the Persian

Government's attention to the long delay in giving effect to the August Agreement, which provided for the extension of the powers of the Mixed Financial Commission and contained the threat of cancelling the agreement — and thereby the subsidy — if the Persian Government did not act by February 1.[43]

On January 31, Marling received a 'friendly' reply from the Persian Government to the effect that they would, in consultation with Britain and Russia, hire foreign advisors to control financial reorganization. In effect, Persia was proposing reform and not financial control. Marling saw the reply as an advance. It was not, after all, a definite refusal, and it virtually admitted the validity of the August Agreement. The note also did not mention the South Persia Rifles or the Persian Cossack Brigade, which Marling interpreted as tacit recognition of their status. This seems unduly optimistic, but given the frustrations in settling with the Persian Government perhaps Marling saw these negative gains in a more favorable light. His enthusiasm was not wholly without a touch of cynicism, however. He knew that the Foreign Office would oppose reform over control, but he felt that the delay in insisting on the reorganized Commission would give Vusuq ud-Daula time to select a suitable president for the Mixed Financial Commission so that when it did begin it would do so on the right lines, meaning in keeping with British expectations. Marling also believed that the Persian Government's financial embarrassment would force them to settle in Britain's favor; but he did not want to see the cabinet fall either.[44] Neither did the Russians. In fact, they were even willing to delay insisting that the Persian Government immediately arrange the Mixed Financial Commission, as they were increasing their troop commitments and did not want to alienate the Persian Government. The Turks were still a threat and the Russians wanted to wait until a military victory strengthened their hand. But the Russians were no more willing than the British to countenance changes in financial control.

Marling informed the Persian Government that his Government would consider the reform idea. At the same time he took the opportunity to inform the Persians officially that the British Government had selected Sir Percy Sykes, an officer in the Indian army with years of consular experience in Persia, to reorganize the public forces in the south, and requested that Sykes receive an official appointment from the Persian Government at once. The Persian Government responded to this with very deliberate speed — it was not until March

13, almost two months later, that it agreed to recognize Sykes; and even this required further prompting from Marling.[45]

The Persian reply recognized Sykes, without commitment to the August Agreement, but it did not define his powers, and expressed the desire to have a third Power supply instructors for the South Persia Rifles after the war. The note also returned to the theme of tariff revision as a means of financing Sykes' force after the war. Marling felt that these conditions were included to disarm domestic criticism − another idea he may have received from Vusuq ud-Daula − and he suggested that the Foreign Office authorize him to agree verbally to tariff revision on condition that British instructors were retained. Arthur Balfour, who had replaced Sir Edward Grey as Foreign Secretary in December 1916 with the change of government, accepted the idea, but he wanted Marling to be sure that this in no way compromised the retention of British instructors for the Persian force, a subject the Government considered non-negotiable.[46]

FRUSTRATION AND CONFUSION

With Vusuq ud-Daula in power, the Turks checked, and the chaos of 1915-1916 survived and somewhat eased, there was reason for optimism that outstanding difficulties in Persia could be settled. The Sipahsalar Agreement was still in limbo, but by March 1917 Sykes had received some acknowledgement, which could be taken as a positive sign; and even if the August Agreement remained in doubt, the Mixed Financial Commission was operating anyway, giving the Allies a measure of financial control which could be used to see that the money was spent wisely. Persia's financial need also gave Britain a weapon to resort to in dealing with difficult obstructions. By threatening to cut off funds the British could induce the Persians to be more reasonable or pliable. To add to this positive climate, most of the nationalist forces in Iran had collapsed into ignominious confusion and obscurity; the expeditionary force in Mesopotamia had expunged its disgrace of the year before and at the beginning of March finally captured Baghdad. With these advantages Marling and others believed a completely satisfactory attitude in Persia would soon follow. But their optimism was a bit premature.

Almost as British forces moved into Baghdad, revolution began in Russia. Although not immediately apparent, Russia was beginning its long decline into chaos and civil war, a collapse with serious implications for the entire Allied cause. In Iran it meant a reverse in an otherwise improving situation. The position there had largely depended on Russian troops, and with the collapse of authority at the center the extremities of Russian influence went progressively numb. Everything changed.

Between late 1916 and March 1917 the efforts of the nationalists to organize a counter-government had collapsed, torn apart by internal dissension and then driven from the country by Russian troops. Many of the nationalists fled to Turkey to wait for a chance to return, but others had slowly worked their way back to Tehran so that by the spring of 1917 many of them were in the capital. They were joined by others who resented the overbearing attitude of the Allies and despised their own government for its weakness. With the Russian Revolution these elements took heart and began appearing in public once again. They began pressing for new elections for the Majlis and they began trying to undermine the Vusuq ud-Daula Government. All the advantages that the British had visualized suddenly evaporated and with them went the effort to legitimize the South Persia Rifles.

Uncertainty continued throughout the Spring of 1917 and Marling, without Russian support, had few resources. Early in the year he had hoped to use the subsidy as a lever to get the Persian Government to accept Sykes and the August Agreement, but now even that hold was severely undermined, for if Britain withdrew the moratorium, the only hold left, Vusuq ud-Daula would most surely fall and a hostile cabinet would assume office, undoing all the previous gains. The moratorium had to be paid. As Marling put it, the Shah's fears of losing his civil list that was supplied through the moratorium made its continued payment important in keeping a hostile cabinet from office.[47]

Yet even this leverage could not rescue the situation, for the Prime Minister had too many enemies. The revived Democrats and nationalists wanted him out, and Ain ud-Daula and Sa'd ud-Daula, two former prime ministers, schemed against his Government for the chance of gaining power. He received support from some religious leaders and from such moderates as Mushir ud-Daula and Mustaufi ul-Mamalik, but his Government could not withstand the increasingly virulent attacks that demanded new Majlis elections.

Vusuq ud-Daula tried to stall these attacks by proposing electoral reforms, but the Shah refused to decide the issue and referred it to a council of ex-ministers, clergy, merchants, etc. This was a device for dodging or spreading responsibility, and in this instance the council too avoided the issue by referring the matter to an assembly of everyone in Tehran who had ever sat in Parliament. Vusuq ud-Daula's ability to influence political affairs was declining and in addition to everything else he faced growing hostility from the Shah. The crisis reached a climax in late May when a group of radicals in Tehran calling themselves the Committee of Punishment assassinated the editor of a pro-British newspaper, the *Asr-i Jadid*.* When Vusuq ud-Daula asked the Shah for powers to handle this situation, he refused and, faced with this plus orders for fresh elections, Vusuq ud-Daula resigned on 27 May.[48]

On June 6 Ala us-Saltana formed a new cabinet. Marling was not pleased with the new Government. Although Ala us-Saltana was a Moderate, his cabinet included five individuals who had supported the Germans in 1915 and had been active in bringing down Vusuq ud-Daula.[49]

The formation of the new cabinet was a blow to Britain's efforts in Iran, for there had not been many successes in dealing with Vusuq ud-Daula and the new cabinet rendered even those null and void. The decline in Russian ability to support the Allied effort in Tehran had not been replaced by a corresponding rise in Britain's power to force issues on its behalf and so the Democrats and nationalists managed to make Marling's position uncomfortable.

In the meantime the new Persian Government refused to recognize the increase of the Persian Cossack Brigade under the terms of the August Agreement, and they intimated to Marling that they hoped

---

* Several Persian sources mention this group, the Committee of Punishment, as being a group of former native Persian Cossack officers and radicals who decided to exact punishment from supporters of foreigners. They assassinated several minor officials and Matin us-Saltana, the editor of *Asr-i Jadid*, and published several flysheets denouncing traitors and those who had relations with foreign powers. After the fall of Vusuq ud-Daula the new cabinet impeded police efforts to investigate the murders, but eventually the members of the Committee were arrested. At the time everyone, including Marling, believed that the assassinations were politically motivated, but later police investigations showed that in most cases personal revenge or a desire to get someone else's job was involved. The Democrats used the events to make anti-British propaganda and, in some instances, to extort money from Vusuq ud-Daula, but even these Democrats were in no way implicated with the Committee itself. (Marling-Balfour, 9/11/17, FO 371/2982; Abdalla Bahrami, *Tarikh-i Ijtima'i va Siyasi-yi Iran az Ziman-i Nasir ud-Din Shah ta Akhar-i Silsila-yi Qajariya* [Tehran: Sina'i Press, 1344 Shamsi], p. 487; Ali Asghar Shamim, *Iran dar Daura-yi Saltanat-i Qajar* [Tehran: Ibn Sina, 1342 Shamsi], pp. 464-465.)

to replace the British in the South Persia Rifles with neutral officers. British authorities regarded this as a nuisance, and Lord Curzon, who, with the changes brought in by the Lloyd George Government, had begun to be consulted on Persian affairs, wrote, 'Whatever is done, neutrals must not be readmitted ... They are an unmitigated nuisance and as a rule anti-British.' Opinion developed that the only thing to do was wait until the Persian Government ran short of money and needed British aid, though the Persian Government seemed bent on its course and even refused to make use of moratorium funds as if to emphasize this.[50]

The British position suffered a further shock when the new Russian Government began expressing sympathy for Persian nationalists and disavowed any aggressive intentions or desire to interfere in internal affairs. This meant that Britain was left alone to bear the hostility of the nationalists. As a result Marling proposed a new policy to regain Persia's friendship while at the same time preserving Britain's position:

I believe a spontaneous offer to tear up the 1907 Convention as far as it concerns Persia and to discuss again provisions of [the] August Agreement would go far to regain for us esteem forfeited by them and by placing us again in the position of friendly advisers, afford the chance of persuading Persia to accept foreign help in setting her house in order. If as may be anticipated Russia no longer desires to insist on August Agreement as far as it concerns her and the increase of the Cossack Brigade and *joint* [Marling's emphasis] financial control thus disappeared, we shall find ourselves in the position of having to impose British financial control and the South Persia Rifles on Persia's acceptance. Just as the signature of Agreement was brought about by the presence of Russian troops, so troops will be necessary to enforce its execution. I can scarcely imagine, even if troops are available, His Majesty's Government would contemplate a measure which appears to me repugnant to our national sentiment and incompatible with [the] principle for which we are now fighting.

Persia is moving fast to anarchy and while I have no belief whatever in her self-regeneration I urge that our better course to save her is to give support to the few native elements that desire better state of things rather than to alienate them by trying to impose reform.

Marling, therefore, suggested retreating on cooperation with Russia, whose value as an ally was dubious at best, and shaping a policy in Iran that reflected the changed internal conditions. In its way it was a rather bold departure, for in most of his previous efforts Marling had not been interested in developing relations with Iran based on mutual grounds but in forcing Iran to accept a status dictated by Russia and Britain. But a spirit of change was in the air. Lord Curzon, a member of Lloyd George's cabinet and a known Persian expert, agreed that it might be necessary to tear up the 1907 Convention (which Curzon, a Russophobe, disliked anyway). Curzon, however, felt that to do so during the war would jeopardize Britain's position and claims in south Persia. But events in Persia demanded some new approach, especially since it appeared likely that a purely Democrat cabinet, with its supposed pro-German leanings, would assume office.[51]

SEARCHING FOR AN APPROACH

The Government of India suggested a new line that went even further than Marling. On June 25 the Viceroy expressed India's grave concern about the anarchy in Persia and the formation of a Democratic government definitely hostile to Britain, 'especially as present wave of democratic feeling appears infinitely more genuine and widespread than any before.' The Viceroy felt that the result of a Democratic victory would involve the disintegration of the South Persia Rifles, upon which Britain based her military position in Persia; the evacuation of Shiraz; special measures to protect the Gulf ports; an open road for the Turks to Afghanistan with all its consequent dangers, plus a menace to the oilfields and to General Maude's position in Mesopotamia.[52]

To obviate these consequences the Viceroy recommended conciliating the de facto leaders of Iran – the Democrats – with financial assistance if necessary, 'and if this be possible money should not be spared.' The Viceroy had further suggestions for conciliation:

To this end we should not hesitate to scrap [the] 1907 Convention or to reconsider [the] August Agreement. As regards the South Persia Rifles, we should be prepared to discuss the greater measure of Persian control in the future to retention of British officers so long as we pay – but not having neutral officers if Persia assumes responsibility of payments after the war.

The Viceroy also wanted to drop joint financial control and went so far as to suggest bringing back Morgan Shuster, the American forced out by the Russian invasion of 1911, as a financial advisor. Finally, in a self-recriminatory statement, the Viceroy wrote, 'It is obvious that any attempt to continue old reactionary policy is doomed to failure in Persia and can only discredit us elsewhere.' The Viceroy believed that the best way to forestall a new Turkish advance was to have Persia solidly on Britain's side and this could not be achieved in the old way.[53]

India's suggestion once again exposed the lack of agreement within official circles, and Marling, who had opened the doors to this area of thought, carried the lance against India's position. The main feature of this disagreement revolved around conflicting interpretations of the importance of the Democrats and other nationalist elements in Iran. In India's opinion the nationalists were a serious force to be dealt with directly, a view that would become the central feature in India's estimations of what to do in Iran down to the end of the war and after. To Marling, and with him the Foreign Office and the India Office, however, the Democrats were a noisy, noisome minority whose influence was limited and who could not be trusted to give proper consideration to British interests. Marling and his superiors rejected the idea of conciliating this group and instead concentrated on keeping more acceptable figures in office while working to undermine Democratic influence – a policy that increased domestic antagonism.

In the short term, Marling's evaluation was correct. The Democrats were an isolated minority, and after the confusion of 1915-1916 they were scattered and disorganized. This plus the fact that the Democrats were professedly hostile to British interests did not encourage Marling or the Foreign Office to treat them seriously. But in rejecting the Democrats, the British rejected Iranian nationalist sentiments as legitimate claimants for attention. Before 1907 the British had, whether sincerely or not, supported these feelings openly as an element in Persian society that looked to the West, and Britain, for ideas of modernization and reform. But the agreement with Russia soured this affiliation. The Persian nationalists rejected the British as false friends; and the British, intent on protecting their position, at first ignored and then viewed this element hostilely, dismissing them as inconsequential.

Unfortunately this policy missed a crucial point in Iranian political life. Disorganized and factious the nationalist movement may have been, but it still had disruptive influence and it articulated a growing sentiment in Iran that could only be ignored at great cost, further isolating Britain's role from the spirit of the time. Marling could bring pressure on the Shah or the Persian Government to keep the Democrats from power, but he could not keep them from threatening or frustrating British attempts to pursue their interest without hindrance.

As more than one Persian Prime Minister tried to point out to Marling or the Foreign Office, no government could survive the kind of concessions the British expected. Despite confirmation of this in the endless cabinet crises, Marling and the Foreign Office insisted on their view, with disastrous effects. In the long term India was right, but in maintaining their view they increasingly swam against the current and consequently rendered their influence on policy impotent. But that was in the future. At the present the issue was just beginning and Marling, who seemed determined to take any view so long as it was opposite that of India, stressed the dangers of having the Democrats in power while dismissing their potential.

He painted a picture of anarchy and the threat of Democratic rule, while he felt that India exaggerated the ill results of hostile Democratic influence. The anti-British sentiments were not pro-German, but rather a wish to get rid of foreign interference and the South Persia Rifles. Persia was willing to use the Germans but had no intention of reciprocity. Marling felt Persia would pursue the neutrality of 1915 – i.e., official passivity with unofficial aid to the enemy – and that as long as General Maude was secure in Baghdad, and there were no risings in India or separate Russian peace on terms unfavorable to Britain, the most that would happen would be anti-British propaganda spread among the rank and file of the South Persia Rifles.[54]

These arguments did not exactly meet the issues raised by India, a fact India was quick to point out. In India's opinion Marling had misunderstood its views, and found it difficult to understand his. It felt that Marling painted a sufficiently uncomfortable picture of a Democratic cabinet in power, especially when local Democratic circles were boasting of a renewed Turkish advance. Based on this information India had tried to suggest a constructive policy which it felt offered more rewards than the alternative of the 'Persian neutrality of 1915.' India believed that Persian anarchy would give the Turks an opportunity to flank Britain's position in Mesopotamia and thus threaten the oil fields and Maude's communications to such an extent as to endanger Britain's whole position. India believed that the only way to check this dangerous situation was 'to conciliate really strong democrats and help them establish a working government and that adherence to reactionary policy may lead to very serious consequence.' The Foreign Office, which felt that the dangers feared by India were real ones and that Britain should have a plan for 'conciliating or frustrating' the nationalists, asked Marling for his views on July 7.[55]

Marling reported the same day. He regretted the misunderstanding and said he was only speaking of the Persian threat, not of what the Turks might do. He agreed with India as to the need for a policy, but he had different goals: 'I wish to weaken [the] party that calls itself democrat by removing its only political capital, viz: – Hostility to Foreigners i.e. Britain (as Russia is counted out) ...' Marling then elaborated on his views, which showed little agreement with India. In his opinion India's belief that anarchy could be avoided by strengthening the Democrats was dangerous:

This is to credit the 'Democrats' with a desire to bring about improvement in Persia whereas their only object is to acquire power to be used for their personal advantage. Democrats in Iran are very much what Committee for Union and Progress was in Turkey.

By raising this point Marling damned India's position with the stigma of being similar to pre-war British policy that allowed the Germans to maneuver Turkey into the war. Marling also belittled India's idea that the South Persia Rifles was a military asset: 'I trust that no calculations will be based on such an assumption.'[56]

After demolishing India's view of the situation, Marling turned to recommending his own constructive policy. He began by deprecating a policy of reform:

In Persia politics are a matter of money making and such advocates of reform as exist are too few and too feeble for us to work through them against vested interests of corruption. Moreover, endeavour to encourage reform would be represented by hostile elements as further evidence of interference.

Instead, Marling suggested that Britain confine itself to securing benevolent neutrality and the acquiescence of Persia to the South Persia Rifles. He wanted to reopen discussions on the August Agreement and to drop completely the proposal for financial control. He also reversed his opinion on the 1907 Convention. He now believed that scrapping it would see a return in Persia of the practice of playing one power off against another; 'by maintaining it we can at least to a certain extent prevent Russian agents from lending themselves to such tricks.' Instead he suggested letting Persia cancel their recognition of the Convention.[57]

This last issue lost some of its importance, however, when in late July the Russian Government showed signs of recovering its former determination. Therefore no immediate steps were taken along either Marling's or India's line, but Marling felt sufficiently sure of the situation to reject further Persian proposals for settling outstanding problems in Anglo-Persian relations.[58]

On July 31 the Persian Prime Minister proposed: (1) the creation of a 15,000 man force for guarding roads paid for by revision in the customs tariff; and (2) engagement of foreign advisers for the financial administration. Marling did not favor these proposals. He informed Ala us-Saltana that revision was a long, drawn-out process and what Britain wanted to know about immediately was his Government's view on the status of the South Persia Rifles. The Prime Minister replied that Britain's acceptance of his proposals (which were not greatly different from others that had come from more acceptable Governments) would simplify arrangements over the South Persia Rifles. This smacked of blackmail and Marling retorted that it 'was unreasonable for Persia to address to a Power a note offensive in form and inspired by mistrust ...' Marling said the Persian note stood in the way of negotiations and Marling feared 'that until an answer was received as to Persia's attitude towards Sir Percy Sykes' mission the British Government would decline to bind themselves in way desired.'[59]

Anglo-Iranian relations had reached an impasse and throughout the summer and fall there was little progress. There were further assassinations of pro-British supporters, and the Democrats in the cabinet hampered efforts to investigate the incidents. Every day the Democratic press carried virulent attacks against the British and against Ala us-Saltana's Government, which contained some moderate elements. The Persian Government continued to press for some decision on its proposals but declined to recognize the South Persia Rifles; and on September 11 it sent a note asking for the end of the Mixed Financial Commission. Furthermore the Turks were showing signs of renewed activity. The situation had features of *déjà vu*. In this instance, however, Russian troops were not available to rescue the situation, and in fact they had become a major problem.[60]

The collapse of Russian central authority meant the disintegration of Russian forces in Iran and elsewhere. In a few instances the British were able to supply Russian officers with money to keep at least fragments of their commands in the field, but discipline and organization evaporated. Russian soldiers took to looting and brigandage and to drunken brawls, which further compromised the Allied position in Persian eyes and left the north open to Turkish incursions and internal disorder. The absence of Russian forces also emboldened the Persian Government and hardened its stand on the South Persia Rifles and relations in general.

At one point Marling even considered giving up on the South Persia Rifles, outlining his ideas in a private letter to Hardinge, who was now Permanent Under-Secretary at the Foreign Office, on September 10. He felt that since Britain contemplated turning over the South Persia Rifles to Persia after the war they might as well do it now. Britain was spending over £100,000 per week on the force and was receiving little in return. The South Persia Rifles originally were to balance the Persian Cossack Brigade, stop the Germans and maintain security, but there was no longer a necessity to balance the Persian Cossack Brigade and the German menace was spent, while the sum paid for the maintenance of the South Persia Rifles was considerably more than the value of trade in south Persia. He knew that withdrawal would mean a loss of prestige but he felt Mesopotamia made up for it. Marling also gave voice to an opinion that illustrated his view of Persia's value: 'To my mind Persia is no longer a possible factor in the war, and therefore we should not waste money and efforts there.'[61]

These thoughts did not find a welcome audience in London, where a new spirit of leadership, or at least of organization, was beginning to make itself felt. Among the many changes that the Lloyd George Government made was to try to coordinate the activities of diverse decision-making bodies, subordinating them to committees with the cabinet as the ultimate arbitrator. Asquith's Government had persisted in running the war largely without modifying the cumbersome pre-war deliberation processes, and there was limited coordination between departments, a fact that weakened the war effort and contributed to Asquith's fall. Lloyd George began to reverse that tendency by introducing a change in cabinet organization.

The particulars need not be detailed here, but one consequence of these changes was to weaken the former independence of the Foreign Office, subordinating it to coordinating committees charged with formulating policy for specific areas. One such committee was the Persia Committee, chaired by Lord George Curzon, set up to supervise and end the muddle in British policy in Persia. Curzon was an opinionated man who aroused strong reactions in others – people either disliked him or despised him. But as an acknowledged expert on Persia who had long been an advocate of a forward policy in the Middle East, Curzon gradually made his views on Persia felt. The

Foreign Office, the India Office and the Government of India resented the increasing interference with their independence and they especially disliked Curzon's imperious manner, but the confusion in British policy and the muddle in Iran meant their position was weak and they had to accept the new guiding spirit. A new crispness and determination began to develop in British policy, and Marling's continued wavering and self-contradiction, and India'a defection over the issue of the South Persia Rifles, did not receive a tender welcome.

Lord Curzon's Persia Committee rejected Marling's idea of turning over the South Persia Rifles to Persia as being neither practicable nor desirable. Instead it suggested that Marling should try to promote the return of Vusuq ud-Daula and give him assurances of a willingness to negotiate revised arrangements after the war – something the British were unwilling to do with Ala us-Saltana's unreliable government. They also instructed Marling not to make any substantial sacrifices in the present circumstances because of the doubtful value of Persian goodwill. Marling was also asked to comment on the feasibility of extending British forces into the Russian areas of the Eastern Cordon if the Russians should collapse, and of paying subsidies to the khans of the Bushire hinterland to keep them quiet. In other words, Britain was not prepared to make concessions and was considering steps that would further aggravate the situation.

This position was not without its opponents, though. Major General Macdonogh, the Director of Military Intelligence who represented the War Office on the Persia Committee, did not consider Persia of doubtful value. He believed everything should be done to keep Persia from throwing in with the enemy and suggested sacrifices to accomplish this. He wanted Britain to: (1) agree to help in the formation of a national army; (2) change the name of the South Persia Rifles as a means of defusing hostility (as if names were the problem!); (3) give Persia assurances that Indian troops would withdraw as soon as the Persian army was capable of maintaining order; and (4) agree that the Persian army should be under the command, nominally at any rate, of a Persian officer. This was a minority opinion, however, and Curzon felt this was over-reacting to the situation. He did not believe the time was opportune to entertain any of the Director of Military Intelligence's suggestions.[62]

The Persian Government too could follow a hard line. On October 12 it informed Marling of its intention to establish a uniform force under neutral officers. The Persian Government went further. They insisted that: (1) British officers and men withdraw from the South Persia Rifles immediately, turning it over to the Governor-General until the arrival of neutral officers; (2) arms of the old gendarmerie be returned and new ones purchased by the Persian Government; (3) the cost of the force be paid by a revision of the customs; (4) the Persian Government should find neutral officers; and (5) financial experts should be introduced as soon as an appropriate neutral was found. Marling was at a loss to explain this note and felt that it was intended to embarrass any successors of the cabinet with uncompromising proposals.[63]

In fact the cabinet was shaky. The Democratic press attacked it continually and the Shah seemed prepared to withdraw his support. In late October he sent Qavam us-Saltana, Vusuq ud-Daula's brother, to see Marling about the possibility of a new cabinet. The Shah was interested in learning if Marling could ensure the conditions that would enable such a cabinet to work. Specifically Ahmad Shah asked for a monthly subvention of 200,000 tumans; payment of the moratorium in Persian krans at the rate of at least 55 krans to the pound (the original exchange rate before the pound declined) without the control of the Mixed Financial Commission, which was to be dissolved; and a supply of arms.

Marling told Qavam us-Saltana that it seemed the Shah expected Britain to pay to get rid of an incompetent cabinet. Marling said Britain might be willing to give six months' arrears of the moratorium to a new and friendly cabinet and meet the exchange rate, but would not agree to the abolition of the Mixed Financial Commission or give arms. He also wanted to know what a new cabinet would do in return. Would it recognize Sykes? Qavam us-Saltana, however, could not guarantee that his brother would be in the new cabinet. Marling felt that by their actions the Persians were virtually cancelling the Sipahsalar Agreement and that Britain should therefore consider it preposterous to give any guarantees without Vusuq ud-Daula in office. He counselled a cool reply and a wait-and-see attitude in case the cabinet should fall on its own.[64]

Meanwhile the Persia Committee met on November 10 to develop a statement of policy to guide Marling, describing three main objects. First, it attached importance to the appointment of a friendly government, one actuated by friendliness to British interests, preferably under Vusuq ud-Daula. It wanted no concesssion until such a cabinet was assured. Second, it wanted to secure Persia from Turkish and

German intrigues and particularly it wanted to stop roving bands that menaced internal security. Britain was prepared to provide a fleet of armored cars to a friendly Persian Government to undertake this task. Finally, the Committee wanted recognition of the South Persia Rifles until the end of the war, after which the Government 'will be prepared to discuss the matter in a *friendly* spirit with a *friendly* Persian Government' (Committee's emphasis).

In return Britain was prepared to: (1) pay the arrears of the British share of the moratorium calculated at the revised rate so long as Persia met the above stipulations; and (2) pay a monthly subsidy, subject to the same conditions. The fulfilment of this policy, though, depended on a new friendly cabinet.[65]

The British did not have to wait long for the opportunity. On the 24th of November Ala us-Saltana's Government fell and Ain ud-Daula became Prime Minister for the second time since the beginning of the war, with Vusuq ud-Daula as Minister of Education. Marling had a hand in frustrating an earlier attempt to save the cabinet; and he felt that the new one was the result of the Shah's aversion to any abrupt changes, but that it paved the way for Vusuq ud-Daula's eventual return.[66]

This was not an unrealistic evaluation. Ain ud-Daula's cabinet began to disintegrate almost immediately and on December 9 the Shah let Marling know that he was willing to appoint Vusuq ud-Daula in return for certain promises. He wanted Britain to ensure his safe departure from Iran and to guarantee him a pension and his estates if appointing Vusuq ud-Daula cost him his throne. This was encouraging and Vusuq ud-Daula was ready to serve, although he suggested letting Sipahsalar form a cabinet to see if his imperious nature could not control the dissidents better (and, perhaps, attract some of the heat and make his own return easier). As a result Marling suggested Britain pay the Shah a pension of 75,000 tumans per month during the war if he did his best to secure a friendly cabinet.[67]

Shortly after this Vusuq ud-Daula submitted his proposals as to how Britain could make his return feasible.* He asked for: (1) genuine assistance for regenerating Persia; (2) creation of a uniform force under neutral officers; (3) cancellation of the 1907 Convention and cognate agreements; (4) representation at the Peace Conference;

* It was common practice for a prospective Prime Minister to secure advance support of this type to use in convincing others to join the cabinet.

(5) subvention of 250,000 tumans a month; (6) payment of 125,000 tumans per month for the Persian Cossack Brigade; (7) arms or one million tumans to buy them; and (8) credit of one million tumans for possible operations against internal dissident groups such as the Jangalis (see note, p. 198). In return he promised to crush the Democrats and form a government that would cooperate with Britain. Marling passed these along to the Foreign Office with favorable comments and urged that assurances be given to the Shah and money found for a friendly cabinet. These proposals bore a remarkable resemblance to earlier Persian proposals that Britain had rejected, but coming from Vusuq ud-Daula, especially under the different circumstances of late 1917, they seemed more palatable, at least if discussing them seemed likely to get him into office.[68]

Immediately after submission of these proposals, events in Tehran took a turn for the worse, or at least the pressure seems to have finally worn Marling down. Marling learned that the Committee for Punishment had assassinated the head of the Detective Service of the police. He urgently informed the Foreign Office that this would have a profound effect upon the Shah, who might throw himself into the arms of the Democrats and appoint an extreme cabinet. Marling urged the Foreign Office to grant the assurances asked by Vusuq ud-Daula so that a friendly cabinet would be able to assume office. This reaction seemed out of proportion to the crisis and Curzon made a scathing evaluation of Marling's nerve:

I am a good deal concerned at Marling's climb down. We put forward a scheme the policy of November 10 which was the maximum of generosity and concession. He accepted it. Now he proposes a complete surrender to all that Persia has ever asked ... all this to get in power for a few months a man who had not the qualities requisite to carry out the programme.[69]

But the Foreign Office still appreciated the need for a favorable cabinet and on December 20 authorized Marling to offer Vusuq ud-Daula certain assurances. He could promise him support if he formed a cooperative cabinet, and that Britain would be willing to look favorably on a uniform force after the war, but British officers would have to remain until at least six months after the war. Britain was also willing to agree to suspend – not cancel – the 1907 Convention and to allow Persia to attend the Peace Conference if other non-belligerents came. In addition Britain promised to pay 100,000 tumans on the moratorium (the Russians were no longer able to pay their share), to grant a subsidy of 100,000 tumans and to pay 50,000 tumans

of the arrears of the moratorium. The Foreign Office also sanctioned
the support of the Cossack Brigade.* In return Britain expected the
Government to maintain order and to allow the South Persia Rifles
to continue until the end of the war. They also agreed to pay the Shah.
Although this response scaled down Vusuq ud-Daula's demands, they
were an attempt to meet him at least half-way. But Marling could not
seem to profit even from these concessions, that would have been
unthinkable to the British earlier in the war. He once again urged that
Britain accept the Persian Government's proposals. In the interim,
Ain ud-Daula's Government fell and the Shah, who now insisted on
a pension of 100,000 tumans plus an additioal 15,000 tumans per
month if Vusuq ud-Daula were in office and a lump sum of 100,000
tumans, waited to appoint a new government to see if Britain would
meet his terms. Marling not only had to get his Government to agree
to the Shah's demands, but to accept Vusuq ud-Daula's proposals
before he could bring the elements together; and he urged the Foreign
Office to at least accept points one and two of the demands (genuine
assistance in regenerating Persia and a uniform force under neutral
officers) to expedite the possibility.[70]

The Foreign Office was disappointed. Oliphant thought the terms
should be accepted, but Lord Hardinge, who had replaced Nicolson
as Permanent Under-Secretary, felt that Marling had lost his nerve
and had not even pressed for the conditions outlined by the Foreign
Office on December 20. They were not prepared to give ground, and
they determined to do nothing further but strengthen the South Persia
Rifles and the Persian Cossack Brigade, which was now being
financed by Britain. On December 23 Marling explained that he had
done his best to beat down the demands but that Vusuq ud-Daula
felt the situation was too risky to fortune and life (he had received
threats from the Committee of Punishment) unless Britain were
willing to support him wholeheartedly. However, the Foreign Office
was not prepared to go further than their comments of December 20.
In any event the Shah's courage failed, or as Marling put it, the
situation went beyond his capability, and he declined to appoint
Vusuq ud-Daula. The cabinet crisis continued, and Anglo-Iranian
relations reached a new low.[71]

---

* On December 2, the Russians had suspended all hostilities with the Central Powers.
This meant the final collapse of all Russian assistance in the war and the British searching
for means of securing their position. There were also plans to send various British missions – e.g., Dunsterville – to Iran to take the place of the disappearing Russian army.

The cabinet crises, however, did not result in the disaster Marling had feared. The Democrats did not seize control of the Government, but neither Marling nor the Foreign Office could have been pleased with the outcome. The Shah, who had not received visible proof of Britain's support, accepted Mustaufi ul-Mamalik as the new Prime Minister. Mustaufi ul-Mamalik began forming a new government in January 1918, his fourth term of office as Prime Minister, and the eleventh cabinet since August 1914.

RENEWED PRESSURE

On January 8 Mutamin ul-Mulk, a confidant of Mustaufi ul-Mamalik, called on Marling to discuss relations and the working out of a formula for settling Anglo-Iranian differences. Marling emphasized that Britain wanted recognition of the South Persia Rifles and benevolent neutrality. Mutamin ul-Mulk did not believe that this was impossible and suggested *pourparlers* between the two Governments with the object of settling the subject of the South Persia Rifles in conformity with the principles of neutrality. He said the Persian Government desired that the South Persia Rifles would eventually form part of a uniform force under European officers chosen by mutual consent. They also desired a revision of the tariff, the right to send delegates to the Peace Conference if other non-belligerents attended, and money. These were modest proposals and not out of key with what the Foreign Office had been prepared to give Vusuq ud-Daula in December.[72] Marling passed the proposals along to the Foreign Office and the Persia Committee deliberated them on January 12.

The Committee had much to consider. In addition to the Persian proposals there were the problems of the differences of opinion between the Home Government and India and new advances by the French Government to share in the burden in Iran. The French had suggested in December that they use their moral influence in Iran to help check enemy activities. They proposed that Britain and France offer Persia guarantees of integrity, recompense for wartime losses, a fund for organizing an all-Persian force under French and British control, an organization for financial reform (the Persian Government had approached France on the subject of advisors), a large advance without security, and an Anglo-French agreement granting these terms that would in no way alter the Anglo-Russian Convention of 1907.[73]

The Persia Committee was not enthusiastic about French concern. Curzon, who through the Committee was more and more shaping British policy in Persia, deprecated their involvement. Lord Robert Cecil, Secretary of State for India, agreed, feeling that to accept the French offer was to introduce another vested interest. And for once India and Marling agreed on something – they both disliked the idea of a French complication. The only recommendation for French involvement was that it would spread the odium of unpopularity, but this was not enough to compensate for the potential aggravation. The Persia Committee, therefore, decided politely to refuse the French.[74]

The problems between the Home Government and the Government of India, though, were more tedious. India had consistently played a dissident role in Persian policy and continued to advocate a major change. It also mounted an attack against Marling (whose stock had fallen with Curzon and the Foreign Office, which began to deprecate his constant wavering), calling him a reactionary and urging his recall. The Persia Committee was not overly enthusiastic for India's proposals. The policy of conciliation advocated by India would have been compromised by efforts to replace the Russians and to check the Turks by unilateral force, and so they decided on accommodation. Instead of a major change of policy the Committee determined, reluctantly, to encourage moderate Democrats, such as Mustaufi ul-Mamalik, and to insist on British officers in the South Persia Rifles until the conclusion of the war and the right to veto the choice of neutral officers. This was not truly a compromise, it was more an attempt to secure a favorable government that would remain silent, thus giving a good front to British activities.[75]

Marling was not able to act on these guidelines immediately because Mustaufi ul-Mamalik encountered difficulties in forming a cabinet. The Democrats kept up their agitation and Marling did not think that he would be able to form a government without including some of the more radical elements. The only ray of hope was that no one believed such a cabinet could survive. There was a great deal of talk about a coup, either by Germanophiles or Anglophiles; the latter element approached Marling on at least two occasions about the possibilities. Marling did not commit himself to these overtures but he did encourage moderate elements with assurances of Britain's goodwill and willingness to discuss the 1907 Convention, the South Persia Rifles, tariffs, and the peace conference. Given the uncertainty of the situation, however, no one was willing to commit themselves, and it was not until January 19 that Mustaufi ul-Mamalik was finally able to put a government together. In Marling's opinion this cabinet was too timid to reply to Britain's representations.[76]

But on February 3 the Persian Government presented a list of proposals. Its note began with a declaration of Persia's determination to create a uniform force under neutral officers and then outlined five additional demands. First, the Persian Government wanted assistance in the evacuation of all foreign troops and the transfer of the South Persia Rifles to Persian control. Second, it wanted the abrogation of the 1907 Convention and the effects of the 1911 ultimatum. Third, it desired participation at the Peace Conference. Fourth, it reiterated Persia's long-standing interest in the revision of the customs tariff. Finally, it wanted the payment of the whole surplus of the customs revenues as well as past and future installments of the moratorium without conditions. These were steep demands, but the Persian Government also indicated that it was willing to negotiate along the lines suggested by Marling.[77]

In a private conversation with Marling the Foreign Minister said that his Government would not object to the retention of consular guards or to the levies holding down the Eastern Cordon. He also said that his Government intended to use the Cossack Brigade to check enemy activities. Marling doubted the efficacy of this, since Russians officered the Brigade and their status and loyalty to the Persian Government was doubtful, despite the fact that Britain was now paying for their maintenance; but he passed the information along and the Persia Committee decided to consider the Persian Government's position.[78]

The British Government was anxious to avoid complications in Iran. Various projects for checking the Turks and for operating in southern Russia to keep that country in the war depended upon Persia's cooperation or acquiescence. The British did not have large numbers of troops for these enterprises and they hoped to secure Persia's favor and to use the levy corps and the Persian Cossack Brigade in lieu of regular troops to guard lines of communication. The question of an alliance surfaced again. There was, however, considerable distance between the interests of the two countries; this plus the weakness of the Persians kept any agreement in a constant state of doubt. Therefore the Persia Committee considered it desirable to placate the Persian Government by gradually withdrawing the British troops sent with Sykes to work with the South Persia Rifles.

However, they were determined not to relax any of the financial arrangements previously made. In other words they offered little more than a token withdrawal that would allow the Persian Government to save face.[79]

The British decided to withdraw the small number of British troops with Sykes but not the troops in the Gulf ports, with the Eastern Cordon, in the oilfields, or operating in western Iran. They counted on the South Persia Rifles and the other levy corps to protect their interests when the regular forces left. In addition they decided to replace the Russian officers of the Cossack Brigade with British officers, thus adding another string to their bow. Despite this rather stingy withdrawal, India believed it was a step in the right direction. It had not retreated from the idea of conciliating nationalist sentiments and saw the gradual withdrawal as a demonstration of good intention from which Britain could secure the maximum political benefit. To add strength to this India suggested reducing the troops in the ports to normal size when there were no further threats and to turn over the Eastern Cordon to local Persian forces when they were efficiently able to protect the approaches to Afghanistan. Even India, though, did not wish to impede Dunsterville's mission (see below, p. 199) or proceed with the withdrawal from central Persia in great haste.[80]

The Persian Government was in no hurry either. While it professed a desire to come to terms, Marling could detect a tendency to procrastinate. In the meantime, the Russians, who still provided some forces − financed by Britain − for protecting the lines of communication in northwestern Iran, continued their evacuation. And while negotiations were in progress the Persian Government did little to arrange for the security of the area. Marling doubted whether they could anyway. The only real force available to the Government was the Cossack Brigade and it was spread all over the north already guarding vital interests. Marling concluded that only British forces could accomplish the task, whatever arrangements were made with the Persian Government.[81]

Marling was once again ready to take the offensive. Just a few months previously, when there was a chance of putting Vusuq ud-Daula into office, he had argued that major concessions were the only hope for preventing a radical victory. Now he returned to the theme of vigorous action. He proposed that Britain employ its forces directly in western Iran to protect vital communications and suggested that it make a declaration to the Persian Government of the points that it was willing to discuss, prefaced by a statement that Britain was acting out of necessity. He felt that this would cause some protest, but that if Britain acted with vigor, not stopping at half-measures (a favorite theme with Marling), then the protest would not be any worse; and a show of force might even end Persia's vacillation.

In his opinion the situation was ambiguous, for Britain found itself in the position of claiming to protect Persia's independence and integrity while acting contrary to it. He felt that negotiations only entailed pointless delay and the necessity of making increased concessions. He also deprecated India's ideas as being obvious procrastination which would give extremists the opportunity to accuse Britain of insincerity. In Marling's opinion negotiations were a waste of time; Britain's only safe policy was swift action without reference to the Persian Government — the blow to be softened by the declaration of concessions.[82]

As might be expected, India found Marling's zeal excessive. It still advocated a more liberal policy. India expressed the strongest political objections to the use of force which would, without definite provocation, discredit Britain with Persia and raise the anger of Muslims throughout the region. It urged conciliation. But these arguments did not persuade Marling. The South Persia Rifles and the Persian Cossack Brigade were useless to protect British interests — the South Persia Rifles could not leave the south and the Persian Government could not be counted on to employ the Cossack Brigade. In Marling's opinion previous efforts at conciliation had brought nothing but further demands. Once again Marling and India met head on.[83]

The Foreign Office was startled by Marling's show of pluck. It was afraid that his proposals would lead to a military occupation, which was out of the question on material and moral grounds. Instead it asked for any alternative proposals in return for gradual withdrawal that would have a chance of success. Britain was prepared to offer the Persian Government fifty armored cars if it would employ them to protect western Iran, but Britain and India felt even the commitment of a small British force would lead to an escalation.[84]

Marling's pluck collapsed. He could suggest no alternative. Persia had no forces to stop enemy agents and his Government was opposed to a military policy. The only recourse was conciliation. Marling asked if he should say that Britain agreed to withdraw and to enter into *pourparlers* on a uniform force with the South Persia Rifles under British officers until the end of the war; and he asked whether Britain agreed to points two, three, and four of the latest Persian note (abrogation of 1907 Convention and 1911 ultimatum, representation at peace conference, and revision of customs tariffs) and to financial assistance. Marling said this approval would only encourage extremists and increase demands. He did point out that the cabinet was shaky and that liberal use of secret service funds and the despatch of troops to Tehran might smash the extremists and put a favorable cabinet in office. This at least was better than concession.[85]

If Marling could not suggest alternatives, India could. It felt that Britain should do its best to strengthen the hand of the Persian Government so that it could withstand extremist pressure and cooperate with Britain. India once again outlined a policy of conciliation. It wanted to assure the Persian Government of Britain's respect for Persia's independence and integrity and to reinforce this by a gradual withdrawal of troops. Furthermore, it suggested scrapping the 1907 Convention, admitting Persia to the peace conference on the same basis as other non-belligerents, agreeing to tariff revision and a promise of money. In return India asked that the South Persia Rifles should remain unchanged for the war's duration and for an agreement in principle to the formation of a uniform force under neutral officers. It also expected the Persian Government to take actions against enemy agents, using the armored cars and personnel that Britain was prepared to put at Persia's disposal. If this policy failed, Britain could still resort to force but then would have 'a clear case before the world.'[86]

The Foreign Office were perplexed by Marling's *volte face* and they were divided over what to do. The decision, however, was up to the Persia Committee. They discussed Marling's sudden reversal on February 25 and decided to explain to him that Britain's disinclination to use force did not mean that they were pursuing a policy of unlimited conciliation.[87]

On February 27, the Foreign Office, acting on this basis, and largely on a draft by Curzon, set out in detail British policy in Persia: (1) maintenance of genuine neutrality of Persia through the war and the prevention of enemy parties from subversion or mission to Afghanistan; (2) protection of British interests in Persia, Afghanistan, and neighboring areas; (3) support of a friendly Persian cabinet. For these Britain was willing to pursue a policy of limited conciliation. They would withdraw regular troops from central and south Persia, but they insisted upon British officers in the South Persia Rifles and in the Cossack Brigade, or (since Marling ruled out this possibility) the offer of fifty armored cars, which, they pointed out, Marling had failed to mention to the Persian Government.

The Foreign Office wanted it clearly understood that Britain was determined to maintain the Persian Cossack Brigade and the South Persia Rifles; and if it appeared that the enemy were likely to regain their former sway then Britain might consider it necessary to send troops to northwestern Iran and to Tehran. The Foreign Office instructed Marling to tell the Persian Government that they wanted the Persians to take care of the matter but that Britain would if Persia did not. The Foreign Office also decided that it was pointless to discuss further aid until a stronger cabinet assumed office.[88]

While these instructions were on their way to Marling, the situation at Tehran deteriorated. On February 26 Mustaufi ul-Mamalik resigned because of the pressures and his inability to secure a settlement with Britain. The extremists, many of them members of the *muhajirat* who had slowly returned to the capital after the collapse of the counter-government, worked to effect a rupture. They tried to organize a national force to use against British interests and they planned anti-British demonstrations in Tehran. Provincial unrest continued and the British vice-consul in Resht burned his cyphers and prepared for his arrest by the Jangalis, a Persian nationalist movement with considerable armed support in Gilan and Mazanderan, two provinces bordering the Caspian Sea. Pro-British sympathizers were afraid to speak out, the editors of various Tehran newspapers subsidized by Marling prepared to leave town, and one Moderate politician who might have been a candidate to replace Mustaufi ul-Mamalik asked Marling not to communicate with him lest it ruin his chances.

As if these problems were not enough, Bolshevik agents and troops began appearing in the north and the Jangalis menaced British communications with the Caucasus and held out the threat of a coup aimed at Tehran. In Marling's opinion the situation approached that of November 1915, only this time there were no Russian forces. Marling saw the only remedy as direct force – the despatch of 10,000 men to occupy western Iran. The alternative was the long-dreaded rupture with Iran that would have untold adverse consequences.[89]

On March 1 the Persia Committee met to discuss this crisis. In view of the situation they decided unanimously to send a British force from Mesopotamia to northwest Persia, provided it could be supplied. The objective of this force was to get in touch with Major-General L. C. Dunsterville (who was leading a mission to Baku to try to keep the war effort alive in Russia) at Hamadan and then to occupy the road from Hamadan to Qazvin and to be prepared to move to Resht and then Enzeli, the Persian port on the Caspian vital for communications with Baku. This move and the enterprises in the Caucasus, however, the Committee considered secondary to the emergency in Iran. They authorized Marling to inform the Persian Government of British intentions in the northwest. They also considered sending British troops from Shiraz to Isfahan and beyond, and the possibilities of raising Kurdish or other levies simultaneously with the occupation of the northwest roads.[90]

UNBLUSHING BLACKMAIL

Disaster seemed imminent in March of 1918. The collapse of the Government in February, after less than two months in office, and the political activities of extremists, threatened to destroy the whole structure of Britain's efforts in Iran. And even though the Persia Committee had decided to send troops to northwest Persia, organizational difficulties and inclement weather caused delays. It was not a time for procrastination.

Marling passed along rumors of a revolutionary coup, aided by the Bolsheviks, to depose the Shah and establish a republic. The Russian commander of the Cossack Brigade informed Marling that the Shah had asked for an escort to Qom. Although Mustaufi ul-Mamalik returned to power on March 11, there still seemed no end to the worries. On March 15 terrorists assassinated one of Marling's subsidized journalists and extremists inhibited the Government from investigating the matter.[91]

The only reassuring aspect was that a political opposition existed in Tehran that was prepared to retaliate against an extremist coup, but Marling declined to assist this group when they approached him, because in his opinion they lacked leadership, planning and power. Furthermore, the Cossack Brigade could not act, and Marling vetoed the despatch of British forces and the South Persia Rifles from Shiraz on the grounds that it would aggravate Russian opinion (it still not being clear if Russia would ever be a force in Iran again) and encourage more local hostility. There seemed to be no solution but waiting for the inevitable.[92]

On March 18 the Persian Government added to this atmosphere in their response to Marling's notification on March 11 of Britain's intention of sending more troops to Persia. In responding, the Government took the opportunity to expand on the issues raised by its note of February 3. They objected to military actions now as in the past, and regarded Dunsterville's actions in the northwest as a violation of neutrality and Britain's promise to respect Persia's independence. The Government expressed gratification over Britain's willingness to revise the tariff and to abrogate the 1907 Convention, but objected to the condition that the selection of neutral officers for the uniform force be determined by agreement between the two Governments. They demanded unconditional representation at the peace conference on the grounds that unlike other non-belligerents, Persia had suffered from invasion. They also renewed financial demands and concluded by saying that they would succeed in maintaining neutrality and order. This was hardly a moderate presentation and confirmed Marling's contention that offers of conciliation only escalated demands.[93]

The Persia Committee (soon to be reconstituted as the Eastern Committee, a body designed to coordinate all British policy in the Middle East) convened on March 22 to discuss the situation. At this meeting General Sir George MacDonogh, the Director of Military Intelligence, stressed the War Office's concern. It had urged the movement of Sykes from Shiraz to Isfahan that Marling had vetoed, and still pushed for it. When Balfour asked the Director of Military Intelligence what threat animated the military's concern he received the rather startling reply that General Haig, the Commander-in-Chief of British forces in Europe, had himself expressed concern for the Persian situation. He felt that every town in Persia should be occupied to render Britain's position absolutely secure or 'failing which we must be prepared for the whole defence of the Khyber to be jeopardized, with the subsequent loss of India.' This seemed to be intruding on a traditional Indian concern but the war and the dangers of chaos in Iran had broken down many traditions. The fact that a Cabinet committee, not the Foreign Office, was listening to these opinions to determine British policy was only one such change. And even the War Office, long a bastion of Westerners, could not escape the fact that Britain's world position demanded a broader-based policy.

The Persia Committee decided to consult Marling on the possibility of raising a Bakhtiari force to meet the situation, since both he and

India deprecated the despatch of British forces from Shiraz.* Although Marling did not object to the plan – only the despatch of some of Dunsterville's men to form the training nucleus – it would be months before such a force could influence events in Tehran. The only choice still seemed one of waiting on events.[94]

Yet there were some signs of change. In late March several Moderate politicians resigned from the cabinet. This weakened the cabinet and Mustaufi ul-Mamalik had considerable difficulty in finding replacements. For no apparent reason there was also a decline in anti-British agitation, but the situation was still unstable. In these circumstances Marling busied himself in securing a more stable government. He still had hopes of replacing Mustaufi ul-Mamalik with Ain ud-Daula, at least for a few weeks, until British troops were in a position to force a more favorable cabinet. Marling received encouragement for this project when the Shah expressed his willingness to dismiss the cabinet, but Mustaufi ul-Mamalik was tenacious and the Shah was timid. The Prime Minister's resources, however, could not survive the shock of resignations in his cabinet and Samsam us-Saltana, a Bakhtiari Khan, formed a new Government on May 3.[95] This cabinet was no stronger than Mustaufi ul-Mamalik's and in Marling's view little better, but he had uses for it:

I have done my best to keep afloat the last two Cabinets, unfriendly as they were, so that Vossuq, who is almost the only string to our bow should not go into office until the arrival of our troops at Hamadan and approach of new harvests about the end of this month should clear the situation here.[96]

This last reference, to the harvest, deals with shortages in grain because of bad weather and the war in Azerbaijan that destroyed the harvests of 1916 and 1917. Much of the country suffered from famine and the major cities such as Tabriz, Shiraz, Hamadan and Tehran faced serious shortages of foodstuffs. In Iran this meant scarcity of flour and high prices for bread – the staple food of much of the

---

* The Bakhtiari Levy Corps proposed in 1916 remained only a plan. The seriousness of the situation, however, made the idea's revitalization attractive and the War Office took action. They informed the Commanding Officer of Force 'D' that the Government had decided to raise a Bakhtiari levy corps to protect Britain's position in Persia (War Office-G.O.C. Force 'D', 3/23/18, FO 371/3259). Curzon, as chairman of the Eastern Committee, was shocked by this initiative. His committee had not authorized such a telegram or such a policy and he objected strongly (Curzon-CIGS, 3/23/18, FO 371/3259). The issues in Persia were as much political as miliary and Curzon was determined to have the final, if not the only, say.

population. In the past this condition had always been a breeding ground for riots and demonstrations. The population was easily aroused and the British feared that this condition could be turned against them. In Shiraz and Hamadan the British subsidized the price of bread and imported flour to keep the prices down and the population quiet. In Tehran the situation was slightly different. As in other cities government officials and wealthy individuals speculated in grain and kept supplies off the market to run the prices up. (One Persian source even implicated Ahmad Shah in this business.) But Marling did not favor relief; or at least not the funds the United States offered the Persians at this time for relief.

Marling's and the Home Government's opinions are very revealing of attitudes current in British thought. Both were interested in maintaining the exclusiveness of British interests in Iran and this extended to trying to prevent an American relief organization from dispensing funds in Persia. Marling did not want the money reaching the cabinet. He felt that the money would ease the financial embarrassment of the Persian Government; and if it were used honestly, which he doubted, that it would go to famine relief in Tehran which would tend to remove one of the main causes of popular complaint against the government, which Marling hoped to replace with Vusuq ud-Daula. The Foreign Office, too, tried to head off the relief effort and it was not until the American Relief Commission came to London and made clear its determination to work through the British Minister in Tehran that the Foreign Office reversed themselves, suddenly welcoming the financial support once they were sure the money would not be used to intrude American interests into Iran or support an unwanted Persian Government.[97]

In the meantime no cabinet seemed able to hold itself together. In part British hostility or indifference to any cabinet but one headed by Vusuq ud-Daula inhibited the formation of a stable government. The Persians needed money and the British could supply it, but no government could make deals with the British without offending large sections of political opinion which could challenge any government. The leading politicians had to form coalition cabinets and if policy then went too far in one direction or another the offended elements of the cabinet would then resign. Samsam us-Saltana's Government fell victim to these pressures in mid-May, before Britain was in a position to back up Vusuq ud-Daula with force. To Marling this meant if Vusuq ud-Daula were to be able to form a government, Britain would have to resort to money.

Marling suggested offering resumption of moratorium payments at £30,000 a month, payment of the unpaid installments (the Persian Government, in a show of independence, had stopped requesting payments a year earlier in April 1917) of the moratorium in £15,000 increments over twelve months, plus a subsidy of 100,000 tumans. The last sum would be discontinued after a few months, but the other payments would give Vusuq ud-Daula the funds needed to operate his Government. In return he would recognize the South Persia Rifles as before, cease protesting over the activities of British troops, and instruct Persian authorities to show friendly attitudes.[98]

The return of Vusuq ud-Daula was growing more important. The Turks were increasing their activities in western Iran and, with troubles throughout the country, the British desperately wanted someone in power they could rely on. On May 20 Marling openly worried about the potential of Iran siding with the Turks, who were enjoying military successes in the Caucasus. This anxiety influenced Marling to reopen an old idea: 'Under the circumstances I submit that we should endeavour to make sure of Mussulman Persia before that position [Persia joining the enemy] is reached, and this by making an alliance with her.'[99] Vusuq ud-Daula was ready to go along, possibly for territorial concession in Turkish Kurdistan. The Foreign Office was not enthusiastic about an idea that had produced so little in the past, and Persia had little to offer but moral weight. If the choice was alliance or Persia joining the Turks, however, then the alliance became something to consider and the Foreign Office was willing to pursue the idea.[100]

Marling thought that a Muslim ally would have far-reaching effects. So did India. They could see real advantages in such an alliance but they wondered if a Persian cabinet could make an alliance without popular support. India had not given up hope of conciliation, expressing the idea, one they would repeat in coming months, that an alliance now would be still-born. They felt the Democrats would repudiate it and that the Cabinet would fall, leaving the alliance to share the fate of the Sipahsalar Agreement. An alliance also opened the possibility of further military commitments and new obligations. India urged another choice. But the Eastern Committee, meeting on May 21, approved the idea.[101]

Getting Vusuq ud-Daula into office, though, was another matter. The situation was uncertain and he was closely identified with British interests, and before the Shah would appoint him he raised the old question of a subsidy, which had never been settled. The Shah wanted

20,000 tumans a month while Vusuq ud-Daula was in office and a guaranteed pension in the event he had to go into exile. Marling considered this 'unblushing blackmail' but he felt it might be necessary, given the importance attached to Vusuq ud-Daula's return; however, he felt he could get the Shah to accept 15,000 tumans and no subsidy if the Foreign Office approved. The Eastern Committee considered it and authorized Marling to use his discretion.[102]

Meanwhile Vusuq ud-Daula made plans to organize a demonstration in Tehran to force the Shah's hand. He also assured Marling that the cornerstone of his policy would be close relations with Britain and an attitude towards the Turks that would lead to a rupture of relations. In return he suggested territorial concessions and neutral officers for the South Persia Rifles.[103]

Samsam us-Saltana, reacting to the pressure from all sides, resigned on May 31, and Vusuq ud-Daula seemed the likely successor. But there were other contenders. Sipahsalar wanted the post and offered the Shah large sums of money for it, and Ala us-Saltana also exerted pressure to secure the position. Vusuq ud-Daula too could use pressure and he planned to have the bazaars closed, a long-standing tradition for exerting pressure on the Shah or the Government, and he urged the British not to pay the Shah. Vusuq ud-Daula was confident of being able to force the Shah's hand. But on June 12 the Shah invited Samsam us-Saltana to form another cabinet.

The British had not met the Shah's demands for protection and money and so he was prepared to wait to appoint Vusuq ud-Daula until he had more positive proof of Britain's support. Marling urged Vusuq ud-Daula to exert what pressure he could on the Shah, but in Marling's opinion the delay in sending troops to Hamadan and German successes in Europe undermined chances of success. He had hopes of getting Vusuq ud-Daula in, but the Shah appeared determined to apoint anyone but him.[104]

Marling continued his pressure – on the Shah and on officials in Britain. This pressure finally had an effect – the Eastern Committee decided to replace Marling, who had lost their confidence, with Sir Percy Cox. Marling, meanwhile, still urged more troops and with the new disturbances at Shiraz, a stubborn monarch, a hostile cabinet and unreliable levies, force seemed the only answer. He still held to the view that Britain's enemies in Iran believed that his announcement of more troops in March was a bluff and that without some visible signs of force the Turks and the Germans would be able to capture the situation. To make matters worse, the long-awaited demonstrations by Vusuq ud-Daula's party, which began on July 4, completely fizzled out.[105]

The bazaar closed and demonstrations were to start. According to the plan, the bazaars were to close on Thursday. The organizers had promises of police support and the neutrality of the Cossack Brigade. They also had unofficial British support and Colonel Stokes, the military attaché, worked with the Persian organizers as Marling's intermediary. On Thursday armed men (Colonel Staroselski, the commandant of the Cossack Brigade, supplied the arms) seized the mosque in the bazaar. The move was poorly coordinated and had no support from other parts of the bazaar. This gave the move the complexion of a coup aimed at the Government and not a popular movement.[106]

The Shah ordered the Cossack Brigade to stop these activities, which they did. Marling was not pleased, either with the failure or the Cossack Brigade's role in it. In particular Marling blamed Colonel Stokes for planning a movement along lines he and Vusuq ud-Daula would never have approved. Marling had contributed large sums of money to encourage the movement, but he felt that Stokes had compromised the Legation by sending arms to the bazaar in a van Stokes owned.* The whole affair was a fiasco.

On July 9 the Persian Government declared a state of siege and began calling in Bakhtiari *suwars* (tribal cavalry – the Prime Minister was a Bakhtiari Khan). Marling felt this was an attempt to keep the cabinet in power by force. The Persian Government also complained to the Foreign Office of Marling's unsympathetic attitude towards them and his role in the Tehran riots. The Persian Government also had a few surprises.[107]

In early August the Persian Government, without warning, cancelled all treaties and concessions on the grounds that they had been obtained by fraud or force. They also expressed interest in friendly relations with all nations and decided to enter into treaties of friendship and commerce with any country that would meet Persia's present needs and safeguard common interests. Then the Persian Government

---

* There was no love lost between Marling and Stokes. In March Colonel Stokes wrote a memorandum that attacked the idea of using force in Iran. He urged conciliation and the removal of people associated with the former policy – namely Marling (Marling-Balfour, 3/1/18, FO 371/3259). Now Stokes had disgraced himself and Marling urged his replacement (Marling-Balfour, 6/16/18, FO 371/3261).

abolished all Foreign Office Tribunals and Karguzar Courts (courts designed to handle case involving foreigners) and said that in the future all disputes involving foreigners would be held in ordinary courts. These moves were an assault on the entire structure of European-Iranian relations developed since the nineteenth century.[108]

This departure angered Britain; the Shah told the Cabinet that they were following a dangerous course and on August 4 he dismissed them verbally. The Cabinet, however, refused to accept this, wanting the order in writing. Eventually the Shah had his way, and on August 5 Vusuq ud-Daula received a summons to form a new cabinet. He had already reassured Marling that the previous cabinet's last-minute declarations, which many believed were an attempt to embarrass any potential successors with a patriotic display, could be treated as dead letters. For his part Marling wanted to give Vusuq ud-Daula assurances along the lines of the proposals of December and the Foreign Office approved the idea. They had their man back and were determined to do everything within reason to support him. Interestingly, shortly after Vusuq ud-Daula assumed office Marling made the first payment of 15,000 tumans (which Marling had arranged in May and finally got the Shah to accept) to the Shah for his support of Vusuq ud-Daula.[109]

With Vusuq ud-Daula finally in office and the war running to a successful conclusion in Mesopotamia the question of an alliance began to recede. Never possible with the weak and unwelcome governments before Vusuq ud-Daula, it became less necessary once he was in office. Instead the British gradually returned to the idea of using money to meet the needs of the Persian Government, renewing the moratorium and dropping the Mixed Financial Commission, which was largely moribund.

MOVING AWAY FROM ACCOMMODATION

With Vusuq ud-Daula back in office with British support there was finally reason to expect that outstanding issues could be resolved. There had been almost a year's inactivity since his fall in June 1917, and the British had put great store in his return as the only way of reaching a settlement. Vusuq ud-Daula, too, was anxious for a settlement but he was not prepared, or could not afford, to give in on the South Persia Rifles.

On August 10 he informed Marling that he could see no other course but to nominate neutral officers for the South Persia Rifles. He suggested the Swedes and the possibility of retaining a few British officers, but he maintained that it was essential for Britain to remove the source of so much trouble. Marling pointed out that Britain could scarcely be expected to support a neutral force or to consider their appointment as a guarantee of the situation in south Persia.

Vusuq ud-Daula admitted that Britain could scarcely be expected to pay for such a force, but he argued that if it had not been for the South Persia Rifles under British officers the military situation in the south would never have developed. He further maintained that the recent events in Fars (see pp. 170, 253-4) had prohibited him from recognizing the South Persia Rifles for a long time. This was not a very cooperative attitude from a Government supported closely by Britain, but Marling did not believe that he was stalling. In June, before Vusuq ud-Daula assumed office, Marling had labelled the South Persia Rifles a military and political liability whose recognition, if ever obtained, would only be temporary, pending arrangements for neutral officers. Vusuq ud-Daula's comments were merely a statement of the obvious.[110]

British officials in London, however, were determined not to surrender control of the South Persia Rifles, although they also realized the importance of keeping Vusuq ud-Daula. In late June the Eastern Committee had expressed a willingness to see the title 'South Persia Rifles' abolished and to consider the force the first unit in a Persian uniform force, but it still wanted British officers to remain for the war. The positions of the two Governments, even with Vusuq ud-Daula's return, were still no closer. They even had trouble agreeing on an appropriate neutral to take over the South Persia Rifles.[111]

The British opposed the Swedes, who had been in charge of the old gendarmerie and whom the Persians still favored; and the Persians rejected the British suggestion that Americans might replace the British. But the positions were not irreconcilable. Vusuq ud-Daula pointed out that the selection of acceptable Swedish officers could take months and that in the interim the South Persia Rifles, still with British officers, could be ostensibly under the control of the Governor-General of Fars. The British hoped to postpone a decision and they opposed the Swedes in any event, but at this stage they were willing to accept Norwegian or Roman Swiss officers.[112]

Vusuq ud-Daula accepted the Swiss idea and the British accepted the idea of having them if Britain controlled the choice, and of turning nominal control of the South Persia Rifles over to Farman-Farma. Before Marling left Iran he also settled the issue of money. He arranged for the Prime Minister to receive 350,000 tumans a month as the minimum to meet expenses, mainly arrears in government salaries. By supplying this money the British gave effect to their determination to support the new government, one they had worked hard to get in office and one they expected to do a great deal to justify their confidence. The sum went a considerable way in making up for the losses in revenue the Government suffered as a result of the confusion of the internal situation. It amounted to 4,200,000 tumans annually or about a third of what the Government budget had been before the war. When considering that the services on Iran's various debts, which amounted to about 3,000,000 tumans, were suspended during the war – or cancelled because of the Russian revolution – the sum was even larger.[113]

At last it seemed that the issue of the South Persia Rifles was settled. Vusuq ud-Daula had made it abundantly clear that his Government could not recognize them and survive and London had reluctantly agreed to Swiss officers. But to British officials in London who wanted to keep Vusuq ud-Daula *and* the South Persia Rifles, British successes in Palestine and the anticipation of an Ottoman collapse seemed more likely to guarantee Vusuq ud-Daula's survival than a communique on the neutral officers of the South Persia Rifles.

Renewed determination not to give in over the South Persia Rifles emerged slowly. Except in India, there had always been a reluctance to remove the British officers, but as the war in the Middle East improved for Britain in the late summer and early fall of 1918 authorities in London became more determined not to rush into any commitments until they clearly understood their options. Victory in the Middle East, especially one that did not involve Russia or any other ally, had certain implications that required unhurried consideration. In this light even Vusuq ud-Daula, for whom much effort had been exerted, became a less valuable commodity.

The lineaments of this new thoughtfulness began over an old question – an alliance with Persia. After his return to office Vusuq ud-Daula again raised the issue and the Foreign Office did not oppose the suggestion. There seemed to be no major objections and the alliance promised to regularize Britain's position. Moreover the Turks were still moving ahead in the Caucasus and Sir Percy Cox, who replaced Marling on September 16* (see p. 204), could not guarantee that the pro-German and Turkish elements in the capital could be controlled. Cox discussed the situation with Vusuq ud-Daula and he believed that he could push through an alliance if Britain were prepared to make certain concessions. He suggested Britain categorically reiterate its determination to respect Persia's independence; press with a recognizable Russian Government for abrogation of the 1907 Convention; and consent to Persia having direct control of the South Persia Rifles and the immediate employment of neutral officers. This last point would be cushioned by turning the South Persia Rifles over to the Governor-General of Fars who would keep a sufficient number of British personnel to administer the force. Cox believed that, to maintain Vusuq ud-Daula in office, a communique accepting these terms was essential. But events elsewhere obviated the need for a concession.[114]

When the terms for the Persian alliance reached London, General Edmund Allenby had begun his final campaign in Palestine. The Foreign Office viewed Persia's terms for an alliance from the perspective of an imminent victory in the East, which made a concession to secure Persian support less valuable. The terms were not rejected outright but point three (control of the South Persia Rifles) caused considerable hesitation. The War Office favored the idea, which could be carried out slowly, but Eyre Crowe in the Foreign Office was adamantly against the idea. One of the most intellectual and informed of the Foreign Office permanent officials, Crowe had finally escaped the obscurity of the commerce section where his inability to get along with Grey had exiled him; with his return to influence he became a strong voice in urging the maintenance of Britain's position in Iran. His comments reveal his beliefs and the sense of change in British policy away from dilatory conciliation to a more openly determined position:

On several occasions during this war His Majesty's Government were face to face with a general situation which appeared to impose on them the necessity of committing themselves to a course of future policy which we felt not in reality to be in our true interests, but which, nevertheless, had to be adopted because only on that condition did it seem possible to secure a particular thing which at that moment seemed of transcending importance.

---

* Cox came as Special Commissioner and not as the Minister.

Continuing in this convoluted style, Crowe mentioned another instance of embarrassment – i.e., securing French and Italian support of the Arabs involved those countries in the issue and would raise difficult post-war considerations. Now he felt that Britain was being asked to make far-reaching concessions. He was not opposed to all of Persia's demands but he felt that any concession over the South Persia Rifles was a mistake. The use of neutral officers had not worked in the past, and if Britain accepted it now they would be committing themselves to a principle in the stress of the moment and later 'we shall feel the embarrassment of what we had reluctantly done, and shall be casting about for some means of getting out of our engagement.' He, like others, felt that Allenby's progress would change the situation in the Middle East and Britain could get by without giving in. He suggested temporizing. On September 27 the Foreign Office instructed Cox to stall the issue if possible. This sentiment gained momentum.[115]

On October 1 Cox suggested the line for stalling the transfer. He proposed tying it to the opening of and returning of security to the Bushire-Shiraz trade route, which, he said, would give Britain time. But the Persian Government still urged a communique on the subject to disarm local critics. They suggested a semi-official exchange of notes over the 'leisurely steps' of transfer that could also stipulate that no neutral officers would arrive until the end of the war. This was a retreat by the Persian Government, but London's line was hardening and a new stage in the relationship was beginning to develop. Or rather an incipient feature was making itself felt. In the past the British had only made concessions under pressure and when that declined they tended to retrench. A general retrenchment now began.[116]

The news from Palestine was very encouraging and the need to make a declaration on neutral officers just to support Vusuq ud-Daula seemed less urgent. In fact the Foreign Office did not send a reply on the subject for almost a month and in the interim the lines hardened further. It became increasingly obvious that Britain would triumph in the Middle East and the question of what to do after the war began impinging increasingly on considerations of what to do during the war. What to do about Persia became more important than an arrangement with Persia.

While authorities in London debated the virtues of accommodating Persia, political conditions in Tehran reverted to a familiar pattern.

Pressure groups started undermining the Government and the Shah began to waver in his support. There was also mounting pressure against Farman-Farma's position at Shiraz. On October 14 Cox again urged the Foreign Office to expedite a friendly announcement that would strengthen Vusuq ud-Daula's position and to inform him of whether or not to insist on the retention of Farman-Farma in Fars. But the Foreign Office was not as moved by these concerns as before. Oliphant wanted to strengthen Vusuq ud-Daula but Crowe, who, along with Curzon, was increasingly becoming the spokesman for the new outlook, opposed the idea. Imperial interests were involved and he did not want to make any rash commitments:

I very much dislike the policy of making commitments in one field without any certainty that decisions in other fields may not result in a general situation in which we may be brought to regret bitterly having made such commitments which tie our hands whilst everything else remains fluid and undecided.

We ought to take a long view of the Persian Question, which is inseparable from the general question of our position in the Persian Gulf.

Sooner or later it will become clear that Persia running on lines antagonistic to this country would be a permanent menace which we simply cannot afford to tolerate. We must have and retain political influence, in some form or other.

Crowe went on to disparage the employment of neutrals, and agreed that Persia was not likely to join the enemy on the eve of their defeat.

If Persia is by force of circumstance compelled to follow a pro Brit [sic] policy, there cannot be the same pressing need for our support of Vossuq in particular as there was so long as any alternative to Vossuq implied hostility and danger to us.[117]

Crowe carried these thoughts further in another minute concerning Persia's representation at the Peace Conference:

Sir Percy Cox should be in a position by now to make it clear to Vossuq and to the Shah that we are top-dog and that in our own interests they must come out into the open as the supporters and workers of a pro-British policy.[118]

The need for accommodation was lessening.

The weight of these arguments had their effect. On October 25 the Foreign Office informed Cox of the new directions: the guiding principle of British policy was to be the permanent maintenance of British influence and not temporary expedients to meet sudden and pressing emergencies. While Britain was still anxious to maintain a friendly cabinet, Vusuq ud-Daula was no longer essential:

In these circumstances His Majesty's Government are not convinced that there is any justification for entering into Agreement such as that proposed in respect of the South Persia Rifles which might eventually turn out not to be in the best interests either of Persia or this country.

London now saw no reason to support the idea of neutral officers at a moment when it did not seem necessary, but the Foreign Office was prepared to ease the blow. It authorized Cox to categorically reiterate Britain's respect for Persia's independence and to promise that Britain would push for the abrogation of the 1907 Convention with a Russian Government they could recognize. It also did not oppose the transfer of the South Persia Rifles to Farman-Farma, if his position could be guaranteed or if Britain were given the right to veto the appointment of future Governors-General of Fars who might jeopardize the arrangements.[119]

Once more India, whose opinions on policy in the Middle East were becoming inert, dissented. They agreed that Britain should maintain its influence but they felt that this could be achieved more effectively by regaining the confidence and friendliness of the Persian people 'than by measures construed by them as interference with their independence.' India thought that the tide of war gave Britain a golden opportunity to regain this confidence by a liberal policy − which meant giving up the South Persia Rifles and accommodating Persian nationalist sympathies. The mood in London, however, was growing increasingly away from accommodation.[120]

There had never been much of a spirit of accommodation, except when circumstances seemed to demand conciliatory gestures, and with the collapse of Ottoman resistance (an armistice was reached on October 30) the necessity of an arrangement receded. In part this resulted from the decline in pressure on Britain, but it also developed from a realization that Britain had won the war in the Middle East. The only possible competitor, Russia, had eliminated itself, or at least its potential to interfere was unknown, and Britain had a unique opportunity to settle the whole Eastern Question, not just the Persian Question, in its interests. As the British became more aware of the potentials of victory they also found themselves committed to a conflicting array of contradictory wartime treaties and pledges which seemed to compromise the benefits of a victory won by British effort. This was true for the rest of the Middle East, but not in Iran. There Britain's position was unemcumbered by embarrassing promises to outside powers, and there were no other foreign powers, as in the past, to counter-balance Britain's influence. This was the first time this had happened and it took British authorities a little time to adjust to the prospects. When the men concerned with British policy began to realize the potential, however, they became increasingly determined to exploit the new advantage. The issue of the South Persia Rifles was one example of this new awakening, but it was by no means the only one. Britain was attracted by the possibilities in Iran and determined to guard against poachers.

CHAPTER SIX

A TRUE AND LASTING ORDER: SEARCH FOR A POST-WAR POLICY

In the closing months of 1918 the major British concern in Iran was no longer enemy columns and agents but the issue of how to preserve the gains made during the war. This came down to two related questions: what to do in Persia to secure British influence, and what to do to guarantee the exclusiveness of Britain's position. There were no apparent answers for the first question, but increasingly the answer to the second question came down to isolating Iran diplomatically. This meant forestalling such issues as the employment of foreigners in Iran, and of trying to guarantee that the Peace Conference would not produce decisions detrimental to British interests.

Before the war the opinion at the Foreign Office had been turning away from regarding Persia as an independent state. Foreign Office officials had recognized that Persian weakness, the demands of the Russian entente, and the need to safeguard British interests had reached a state incompatible with Iran's independence, however much that was desirable in and of itself. The war, however, intervened and temporarily shelved the logical outcome of such an attitude; and during the war a major change occurred in Britain's position in Persia. As a result of the war all Britain's rivals were eliminated and British money, advisers and troops were all that stood between Persia and anarchy. These advantages, when viewed through the prism of pre-war thinking, loomed large in the British imagination at the close of the war, and the temptation to follow the line suggested by these advantages and thereby secure a permanent, unchallenged position in Persia was overpowering. The strategy was simple: keep everyone else out and force the Persians to talk only to Britain.

This tendency towards exclusiveness is illustrated by Britain's reaction to Persia's decision to employ a financial adviser. In early November Vusuq ud-Daula thanked Cox for Britain's financial assistance and took the opportunity of informing him of his Government's intention to hire an expert financial adviser to put some order into Iran's finances. Cox naturally suggested that the position go to an Englishman and Vusuq ud-Daula naturally told him that this would not be acceptable to public opinion. But he did want Britain's advice on a suitable neutral source for an adviser. This news caused a stir in the Foreign Office. The British had had enough unhappy experiences of foreigners in Iran without wanting to encourage their return; and the Iranians agreed, but there the consensus stopped, for the British themselves had begun to consider their position in Iran as peremptory, over-riding Iranian wishes.

Once again Eyre Crowe, who had emerged as a strong spokesman for maintaining Britain's exclusive position, led the attack on any idea of giving up Britain's new position in Iran:

The situation is an extraordinary one. Not only are British interests in Persia absolutely predominant but we actually finance her government. There would be no Persia except for the fact that the Persian Government lives on subsidies and on British loans which are never repaid ...

He felt that the Persians were asking a great deal: '... especially if regard be had to the fact that none but a British financial adviser can in practice be counted upon to deal honestly and clearly with Persian financial problems.' He thought Cox should hold out for a British adviser. Robert Cecil, the Secretary of State for India, was disposed to agree, although he felt that this was 'a long step towards a British protectorate of Persia.' He thought it best, however, to refer the matter to Balfour, who, along with the rest of the cabinet, was in Paris for the preliminary arrangements for the coming peace conference.[1]

Balfour's reply agreed with Crowe and Cecil. The reply expressed disappointment at Persia's attitude and virtually repeated Crowe's sentiments:

Not only are British interests in Persia absolutely predominant but it must be remembered that the whole structure of Persia's finance, such as it is, is based on British subsidies and loans and that we are vitally interested in seeing that some order is introduced into the method of spending the money which we supply ... And we consider that none but a British adviser can be counted upon to deal impartially, honestly and clearly with Persia's financial problems in the satisfactory solution of which British and Persian interests are equally and exclusively involved.

The reply stressed that no impairment of Persia's sovereignty was intended. The adviser would be an employee of the Persian

Government and removable by them. If public opinion would not allow an immediate settlement, then Cox, in Tehran, was to let the matter rest until general peace and the disappearance of the Turkish menace might produce a radical change in the orientation of Persian policy and make the Persian Government understand:

... that the presence of a British financial adviser, far from threatening their sovereignty would tend to consolidate it in the only manner in which it can be consolidated ... and would effect reforms both countries desire and produce mutual goodwill and confidence.[2]

When Cox presented the essence of this position to the Persian Prime Minister, Vusuq ud-Daula could only reply that public opinion would not tolerate a British adviser, at least for the present. But the Foreign Office was adamant: they wanted an English adviser or nothing. The only solution seemed to be to shelve the issue, which Cox suggested and the Foreign Office approved.[3]

The sidetracking of Persia's intention of hiring foreigners to reorganize the finances was only one of Britain's efforts to safeguard its position in Iran. Earlier in 1918 the Foreign Office had rejected a French offer of loans and advisers to keep that influence out of Iran. On a similar tack India and the Home Government had rejected trying to involve the Americans in Iran and had vetoed suggestions that Japanese forces might be employed in India and the Middle East to relieve British troops for use in Europe. This latter proposal disappeared under concern that began to see Japan as the new menace to empire, replacing Germany. By excluding the introduction of French, American or Japanese influence into India, Iran or Mesopotamia, the British hoped to guarantee the exclusiveness of their position, won with so much sacrifice. The major concern for Britain in Iran was what policy to pursue to guarantee this exclusiveness, especially since the approaching Peace Conference threatened to provide Iran with a platform.

The Persians were making the settlement of this question difficult. They were obstinate over the issue of British advisers and they seemed determined to seek representation at the Peace Conference. As the lines of possible Persian claims at the Conference began to emerge the British became more and more apprehensive that outside influences might become involved. This the British wanted to avert and so keeping Persia from the Conference or, failing that, neutralizing its appearance, became one of the cardinal features of Anglo-Iranian relations in late 1918 and early 1919.

On October 31, the day after the armistice with Turkey, Nusrat ud-Daula, Farman-Farma's eldest son and the Minister of Justice, called on Cox to inform him of his Government's intention to form a representative committee composed of various shades of political opinion to deliberate on Persia's desiderata at the Peace Conference.[4] It was apparently the Persian Government's intention to claim the right of direct representation since Iran had been a theatre of war between four of the belligerents – a fact they claimed set them apart from other neutrals. Several times during the war Britain had told Persia that it would support Persian presence at the Peace Conference on the same terms as other non-belligerents, if other Powers agreed, but when confronted with the prospect the British had occasion to pause.

Cox wanted to know if Britain should support Persia's claims for representation. He knew that Persian politicians had an exaggerated idea of what Persia could reasonably expect to gain and he wondered if it would not be better to allow the Persians to make their claims and have the Conference turn them down. In this way Britain could avoid incurring Persia's resentment. On the other hand it was possible that Persia might put forward embarrassing claims against the British; Cox wanted to know what line to follow.[5]

The Foreign Office decided to make a neutral reply. Britain was not making the decision on representation of non-belligerents, this would have to be made by the assembled Allies. The most that Britain could say was that they would welcome Persia at the place of meeting of the Conference and that their representatives could be consulted if and when the occasion developed. This was not a very satisfying answer for Persia, but even giving this much became a source of anxiety for the British.[6]

On November 17 Cox had an audience with the Shah on the subject of Persia's representation at the Conference. The Shah urged Persia's participation and asked for Britain's help in arranging it. He suggested admitting Persia as an honorary member – not for its views as to terms to be imposed but to secure definite representation at subsequent deliberations. Failing this he hoped Persia would be admitted to discussions concerning compensation for neutrals. The Shah hoped Britain would help convince the other Allies to admit Persia and that Cox would see that it would be advantageous for Britain's popularity in Persia to take the initiative on the subject.[7] The Foreign Office, however, merely reiterated its stand that only the assembled Allies could make the decision. This was an evasion. Persia was not asking for the British to make a decision, but just to support its application with other powers, which the British were not prepared to do. They did not want to arouse anti-British sentiments in Iran by openly opposing Persian representation but they were certainly not prepared to facilitate it. What Britain was prepared to do, however, was not clear. In an effort to get some idea of his Government's policy, Cox raised the question of what Britain planned to do to maintain its influence in Persia.

Cox suggested that Britain hold frank discussions with the United States before the Peace Conference and get the Americans to recognize the Persians as:

one of the outstanding ulcers of chaos in [the] civilized world and give us an Inter-Allied or International mandate to carry out its reformation within a period of a year with full guarantees for its integrity and independence.

In his opinion the Peace Conference, a Congress, or the League of Nations could say something to the effect that: 'You [Persia] have demonstrated in the last ten years your inability to govern yourselves and walk alone. The result is that your country is a prey to chaos and famine and is threatened by Bolshevism.' Consequently it was necessary to reform Persia in the interest of humanity and civilization and, the Cox argument ran, Great Britain was the country most competent to do it. While Cox was suggesting that Britain shoulder this burden he also pointed out one of the dilemmas facing British policy. Russia was gone and Iran was a free field for British labors, but a vicious circle existed. Persia required, before Britain could withdraw its troops and subsidies, an armed force and administrative reform; '... but our interests require assistance to her should be delayed in the hope of avoiding introduction of other nationalities.' If Britain were simply to withdraw, chaos (or worse, the Bolsheviks) would follow. Something needed to be done and Cox urged a decision.[8]

The Foreign Office liked Cox's suggestions and decided to work up a memorandum for the War Cabinet that would lead up to the conclusions he recommended. India, on the other hand, despite its respect for Cox's experience and ability, emphatically dissented from the suggestion. In its opinion it was a flagrant departure from the numerous statements on respecting Persia's integrity and independence and, furthermore, one that would involve military commitments on a large scale – these troops would have to come from India and this would be an unwarranted drain on the military resources as well as being prohibitively expensive. India also doubted the availability of qualified staff and was worried that the plan would further emasculate Persia and make withdrawal more impossible. India was particularly concerned that the principle suggested by Cox, whereby a large Power intervened in neighboring countries when there was administrative chaos, involved far-reaching consequences and might increase Britain's commitments throughout Asia. India wanted a policy of conciliation to win Persia's confidence and not to replace a Russian dominance with a British one. Cox was not convinced by these arguments, however.[9]

Cox admitted that before his arrival in Tehran he had shared India's view but he felt that conditions now were different. First, Britain was completely victorious, and second, there was the threat of the spread of Bolshevism and revolutionary ideas.* Cox also raised the spectre of other powers taking an interest in Persia:

I cannot but feel convinced that whether it suits us or not the powers who have been fighting beside us for world principles and, who are now about to assemble, literally to 'reconstruct the world' and see justice established therein will interest themselves collectively in the future of Persia were owning to the inveterate corruption, extortion and injustice on the part of the ruling class, from the Shah downwards ... At present Persia is only saved from bankruptcy by our financial help and from active disorder by presence of our troops. Were these safeguards to be withdrawn ... North Persia must become prey to complete chaos if not to violent revolution ... In our interests we cannot contemplate such a disquieting prospect in a border state.

It was Cox's contention that only a few ignorant demagogues thought that Persia could do without foreign assistance and he felt that if the Assembled Powers decided to take Persia in hand, with full guarantees of future independence and safeguards against unscrupulous exploitation, public opinion would acquiesce. Cox further maintained that Britain was the most likely choice for Persia's protector, but if Britain was not prepared to undertake the task directly, then a decision on who should undertake it – pliant power like Belgium, for example – needed to be made.[10]

---

* For an account of this bugbear to British and Allies concerns, consult the considerable literature on Allied intervention in Russia, especially Ullman's three volumes. Also of particular interest on the Allied preoccupation with the spread of Bolshevism is Arno J. Mayer's *Politics and Diplomacy of Peacemaking; Containment and Counter-revolution at Versailles, 1918-1919.*

The Foreign Office sided with Cox. Oliphant thought India's opinion unproductive and he felt that Britain should exert what influence it could to avoid the subject of Persia at the Peace Conference. Hardinge agreed and felt that India had completely misunderstood the Persian mentality. 'The Persian Gov[ernmen]t do not want "a real chance" for Persia since it would be incompatible with making money.' The Foreign Office decided that if Persia could not be excluded from the Conference, the best course was to prepare its case so that Britain could secure a mandate or determine who did.[11]

Part of Britain's determination to exclude Persia from the Conference which had only gradually developed, stemmed from the composition of Persia's delegation and from the indications of what Persia expected to ask from the Conference. The British had hoped that Vusuq ud-Daula would be included, but the Shah, claiming that he could not do without him, insisted that Mushavar ul-Mamalik, the Minister for Foreign Affairs, Mu'in ul-Vuzara, the second son of Ala us-Saltana and a figure the British regarded as an extreme nationalist, and Zika ul-Mulk, the Shah's former tutor and a Moderate, compose Persia's mission.

The Foreign Office was not pleased with these choices. They considered Mushavar ul-Mamalik untrustworthy and that the inclusion of Mu'in ul-Vuzara was a sure sign that Persia intended to raise every embarrassing question possible.[12] The Shah was determined on this choice, however, and not even mention of his British-supplied pension could divert him. This fact hardened Britain's determination to keep Persia from the Conference. But its disapproval of the Shah's choice was not the decisive factor in wanting to isolate Persia, for this decision had been made before the final selection of the delegation. The major reason for excluding Persia stemmed from Britain's desire to stave off foreign interests and from the realization that the Persians intended to make broad claims at the Conference.[13]

Cox outlined the scope of possible Persian desiderata in late November. Many of the demands had appeared in various Persian proposals during the war, but some were disturbing departures. The Persian Government desired: (1) representation at the Peace Conference; (2) abrogation of Treaties and Concessions prejudicial to independence and integrity and undertakings from the signators of the Treaty of Peace ensuring Persia's status; (3) compensation for losses suffered during the war; (4) economic liberty − or in other words, no foreign control over Persia's finances, and liberty to set tarrifs; (5) revision of treaties still in effect and extension of the annulment of capitulations to all powers (applied only to Russia); (6) new commercial treaties and customs tariffs within the principle of commercial liberty; (7) support for revision of existing concessions in conformity with the foregoing; (8) readjustment of frontiers and compensation for encroachment.[14]

The tone of these proposals suggested that Persia was seeking a major readjustment of its position and was planning to appeal to an international body for support. If successful, such a move would have altered Britain's status in Iran and would have attracted outside interests into an area the British hoped to keep inviolate. Under these circumstances it became imperative to head Persia off.

In anticipation of this the Foreign Office prepared a lengthy memorandum setting forth in detail the policy Britain proposed for Persia. It covered most of the points raised by Persia and outlined British counter-claims or plans for combating the Persian desiderata. The main hope, however, was that Britain could smother Persia's chance of speaking at the Conference and so keep the lid on any discussions of Persia's fate. The Foreign Office was aware of the uniqueness of the new order in Iran and they were determined not to miss their chance of solving a worrisome business. According to the memorandum:

The policy of His Majesty's Government at the Peace Conference is understood to aim, as far as possible, at excluding Persia as a non-belligerent from all discussions, with a view to keeping our hands free to settle our post-war policy directly with the Persian Government without the necessity, as heretofore, of framing our policy to meet Russian views. Apart from the merits of this policy ... and apart from the legal and moral merits of Persia's case for participation at the Conference, it appears necessary to be prepared with alternatives in case events have gone too far to permit such a policy being successfully pursued ...

It is clear [since Britain could not control the choice of delegates or confine Persian proposals within acceptable limits before the Conference] that His Majesty's Government must be prepared for the eventuality of the question of Persia arising directly or indirectly at the Conference; and once it does so it may be difficult to limit the discussion. Indeed, the inclusion by the Persian Government in the vague desiderata of every question from political independence and frontiers to economic concessions and capitulations, indicate how discussion, once started, may be extended.

In view of these possibilities the memorandum outlined three major areas for policy consideration and brought together the material data for decisions on the specific questions that involved British interests. The main areas covered political, economic and general questions.

The economic section dealt with possible Persian claims for reparations, changes in extra-territoriality, railway construction, and customs and financial reform. Basically the British hoped to settle these issues directly with Persia. Britain was particularly concerned to protect the Anglo-Persian Oil Company concession and to prohibit a trans-Iranian railway, that might be used by an invading army, from approaching the borders of India, although other schemes were considered. The memorandum also stressed the determination to insist on capitulatory rights until the Persian Government could offer reliable guarantees for order and justice not provided by Persia's judiciary system. The memorandum, echoing Eyre Crowe's sentiments, also proposed to examine Persia's claims for reparations closely with a view to silencing them with Britain's counter-claims for compensation for lives and property lost as a result of Iran's inability to check tribal disorders or German nationalist agitation.

The general questions dealt with the status of the Shaykh of Mohammarah and Persian claims to islands in the Persian Gulf. Again the memorandum stressed avoiding the question at the Conference, if possible, but in the event that they were discussed, Britain proposed to maintain the status quo and to oppose the extension of Persian sovereignty to the Gulf islands.

The most interesting part of the memorandum is the section dealing with British political interests in Iran, and it is worth quoting it in some detail. Much of it is the result of comments by Lancelot Oliphant, Harold Nicolson, Eyre Crowe, Charles Hardinge, Cox and A. J. Toynbee. It reiterates the need to isolate Iran if Britain were unable to exclude Persia from the Conference. The political section begins with a reaffirmation of Britain's concern for Persia's independence and integrity. There is an important difference to be noted, however, between a concern for and a guarantee of integrity:

The independence and integrity of Persia have always in theory been cardinal principles of His Majesty's Government's policy. Two factors, the aggressive policy of other powers and internal disorder in Persia have, however, modified these principles in practice and led to more or less direct interference by His Majesty's Government in Persian affairs. While the first of these factors may for the present be held to have disappeared with the temporary dissolution of Russia, Turkey and Germany, the second factor remains, and has indeed assumed greater importance through the substitution of the danger of Bolshevik contagion ...

The question of Persian independence and integrity at the Peace Conference seems therefore to resolve itself into the question of whether or not anarchy in Persia is to be allowed to continue.

The British, obviously, answered this question in the negative, but they believed, as expressed by Hardinge and Cox, that the ruling classes of Persia were not concerned with the problem and were not to be trusted with the solution. This fact endangered Britain's interests.

British policy in Persia must primarily be governed by considerations as to the security of India [it should be remembered that India, supposedly concerned with this issue, had already expressed opposition to the ideas expressed by this memorandum] ... and probably also in the future considerations arising from the contiguity to Persia of a Mesopotamia under some form of British protection.[15]

The memorandum then points out that no other power had the direct interest in Persia's internal condition that Great Britain had, but that the spirit of the Peace Conference was affected by humanitarian ideas and that the assembled powers would therefore not overlook Persia's anarchy. In view of these considerations it was obvious that Persia needed foreign assistance to rehabilitate itself. Britain's concern, then, was to control the selection of Persia's benefactor. There were five possibilities: (1) induce the Conference to shelve the whole Persia question and allow Britain to rehabilitate Persia; (2) urge a mandate for a power chosen by Persia; (3) endeavor to secure a mandate for some other power; (4) endeavor to secure a mandate for Britain; (5) if the Peace Conference were opposed to a British mandate, try to secure the selection of a mandatory power that would accept British assistance.

All of these possibilities had difficulties or objections. The Conference was not likely to shelve the issue and if it did the result would be that Britain, and not an international body or another power, would have to bear the onus of Persian unpopularity and would have done nothing 'to meet international criticism of a continuance of our predominant position in Persia.' Point two was objectionable because the Persians would be difficult and it would mean the introduction of another great Power's influence. Point three had the same objections, but like point five, if Britain could make the choice, a pliant power might be found that would treat British interests 'most sympathetically.' Point four was Britain's real objective, but it was not obvious that the Conference would appoint Britain as the mandatory power. Point five was little different from point two and its somewhat pointless repetition may be 'Freudian' evidence of what Britain really expected at the Conference:

> In light of the above considerations, the policy of His Majesty's Government at the Peace Conference should be in the first place to press for a direct mandate ... for Great Britain to give Persia financial, military, and administrative assistance, and that if this policy be found impracticable, His Majesty's Government should aim at securing such a mandate for Belgium (or Norway) to be secured (either through the intermediary of the Conference or by direct and private arrangement with His Majesty's Government) to the co-operation of His Majesty's Government in Belgium's or Norway's task.[16]

India protested against this policy to the end, but to no avail. Britain had an opportunity to settle the Persian Question, if not the whole Middle Eastern Question. India's concern for reconciling 'demagogues' and 'corrupt politicians' could not stand up to this potential or to the momentum of the downhill run to the Peace Conference.

It is clear from this general statement of British policy plus the views expressed by a variety of British officials, excluding India's opinion, that there was little diversion into the humanitarian concerns that accompanied British claims for a mandate in Palestine and Iraq. The main difference, of course, being that world opinion – especially that of France – was focused on the fate of Palestine and Iraq, as parts of the Ottoman Empire, as possible new, struggling states, and as a national home for the Jews. Persia, however, was not in the limelight and the British hoped to keep it that way and derive maximum benefit from this fact. In 1919 Curzon would advance humanitarian claims and altruistic motives to justify his policy in Persia, but in 1918 the motives were more clearly utilitarian and grew out of the belief that the Persians were hopeless at self-government and that Britain could not afford to miss the opportunity to settle its interests in Persia on solid imperial soil. The Foreign Office recognized the premium that post-war attitudes placed on self-determination and the constraints on crude self-aggrandizement, but this did not prevent the British from pursuing a policy toward Persia that would give Britain paramount control behind a local façade of independence.

THE ANGLO-PERSIAN AGREEMENT OF 1919

The British had determined in 1918 to exclude Persia from the Peace Conference if possible and, if not, to secure a mandate for Britain or some pliant second power. Britain wanted to settle its interests in Iran without foreign meddling, a factor that had interfered in Anglo-Iranian relations for a hundred years. If Iran made a successful bid for attention at the Conference then the whole problem would re-emerge. Consequently Britain decided to oppose Persia's represen-tation at the Conference on the grounds that Persia had not been a belligerent. Curzon, acting Foreign Secretary while Balfour was in Paris, hoped that by isolating the Persian Delegation and holding out promises to Persia of British assistance the whole issue could be avoided and the Delegation would settle for frank discussions with Britain. Curzon believed, and Sir Charles Marling (in London as an adviser) concurred, that Persia needed British support and that only a few radical elements really opposed Britain's sincere interest in rehabilitating Iran. As Marling put it, 'In his heart the Persian, even the rabid "Democrats" – where Democracy is about as genuine as that of the Committee of Union and Progress in Turkey – know perfectly well that we are really Persia's friend.'[17]

It only required waiting until the Persians came to their senses. The Persian Delegation to the Conference was not to Britain's liking, especially since it appeared determined to pursue an independent course outside Vusuq ud-Daula's control. In this light Curzon decided to have no intercourse with the Persian Delegation to the Peace Con-ference until it had no choice but to turn to Britain.[18]

The only voice that continued to urge caution and careful consider-ation before applying the solutions in Iran that new circumstances seemed to allow, was India. The Government of India realized that a genuine nationalistic spirit was alive in Iran, despite its seeming confusion, and they felt that this force should be recognized and conciliated.

India did not argue that Britain should abandon the position won in Iran, but objected that British policy failed to consider legitimate Persian sympathies. Sir Hamilton Grant, the Secretary of the Foreign Department of the Government of India during the war, who was in London as an adviser for the peace, put forward at a mid-December meeting of the Eastern Committee what he thought were the essential views of India. Grant took exception to Curzon's view that Britain had done everything to reassure Persia of Britain's concern for its integrity. He felt that public opinion in Iran could be influenced in Britain's favor and although he had no illusions as to the 'general meanness or futility of the Persian character,' he felt that there was still a 'curious kind of patriotism and nationalism which is neither to be bought or overawed.' In Grant's opinion Britain might have done everything to reassure Persia but he felt that the manner in which 'our various announcements and guarantees have been made has not been of a very convincing or ingratiating kind.' He continued:

There has been a want, if I may say so, of real frankness and kindliness about the tone of our communications to the Persian Government: in the words of the old song, 'It's not exactly what we say but the nasty way we say it.'

In this light he outlined what India expected. India opposed a mandate for Britain as too expensive, politically and economically. India also opposed a mandate for other powers because it would mean footing the bill to secure the interference of another power. But it did not favor abandoning Iran to chaos, proposing instead to assist Persia on a limited scale. India felt it essential to regain the confidence of the Persian people by abolishing the South Persia Rifles, withdrawing British troops from Fars, the Bushire-Shiraz road and other areas as soon as conditions allowed, abolishing the 1907 Convention, and agreeing to revise customs laws. In return India would have Britain ask only that Persia accept British financial advisers in the regulation of Persia's finances, coupled with a subvention and lenient terms on repayment of debts. Grant believed that a declaration along these lines (a draft of which he had prepared) would reassure Persian opinion and go a long way towards achieving the amiable agreement both Britain and Persia needed.[19]

Officials in London, however, did not share India's concern for Persian nationalistic feelings and regarded its spirit as a German inspiration at worst and a self-seeking political gambit at best. Even Cox, on the scene, with his eyes focused on securing British interest, believed that only a few demagogues thought that Persia could forego foreign assistance, which rightly should only come from Britain.[20] Curzon agreed with Cox and he determined to ignore or discount Persian nationalism and India's opinion and to proceed with a settlement that satisfied his goals.

Victory had left Britain with a unique opportunity in Iran and Curzon, a long-time advocate of a definitive settlement, was determined to be the architect of a new order in Iran and the Middle East that would once and for all establish Britain's position beyond dispute or anxiety. In some respects Anglo-Iranian relations in 1919 were Curzon-Iranian relations. And in 1919, as *interim* Secretary of State for Foreign Affairs, Curzon, the Persian expert, had an opportunity finally to put Britain's position on a firm basis. He could argue from a position of relative strength – British money supported the Persian Government, British troops or levies provided internal security and the main rivals, Germany and Russia, had ceased to be a menace. With these advantages Curzon's arguments, at least to himself, sounded convincing.

Guided by this personal vision, Curzon set out to settle the issues that had troubled Anglo-Iranian relations during the war and before. He wanted a secure, stable, pro-British Iran that would recognize and protect British interests in the Gulf and provide a buffer to foreign interests and advances on India. Curzon came from that group of 'Persophiles' that favored Persian regeneration along British lines.

Curzon's conviction was supported by the fact that Sir Percy Cox, the long-time Resident on the Persian Gulf and another noted Middle East expert, was Britain's acting minister in Iran; and that the Persian Government of Vusuq ud-Daula was pro-British. Vusuq ud-Daula had come to power in 1918 with Britain's active support and the money for meeting his Government's expenses was largely provided by a British subsidy. In addition the internal Persian opposition to Britain, led by the so-called Democratic Party, which had offered considerable resistance during the war, was in disarray. Thus the whole weight of circumstance seemed to indicate that the time was ripe for a final settlement.

Two main problems faced the British in their attempt to arrange matters in Iran; first was the perennial problem of how best to secure British interests in Iran, second was the issue of Persia's representation at the Peace Conference and the attendant worry that this would attract unwelcome foreign interests. The British wanted the Persians to appreciate that only Britain would aid them and until the Persian Delegation to the Peace Conference came to realize this Britain avoided contact with and support of Persia's mission.

On January 11, 1919 Curzon telegraphed his views to Cox, informing him of the Eastern Committee's decision to avoid the subject of Persia at the Peace Conference. At the same time he expressed a willingness, once it was obvious that Persia would not receive a hearing, to meet with the Persian Delegation to the Peace Conference to discuss questions of future relations. Curzon outlined for Cox the general features of what he had in mind: (1) unqualified renewal of assurances of Britain's respect of Persia's independence and integrity;

(2) abrogation of the 1907 Convention, which Britain already considered in abeyance; (3) creation of a uniform force with South Persia Rifles as the nucleus in the south and the Persian Cossack Brigade as the northern focus; (4) appointment of a British financial adviser; (5) withdrawal of British troops at the earliest possible moment justified by the situation.

Curzon regarded these proposals as extremely generous and he made them to assuage Persian doubts as to Britain's good faith. He hoped that Persia would respond in the same spirit and if it did not and if it insisted on unacceptable proposals then Britain might have to consider withdrawing help altogether. Curzon did not want Cox to communicate his proposed terms immediately but first wanted him to 'try to induce atmosphere' suggested above, namely that Persia needed Britain's help.[21]

Cox was able to communicate encouraging news. He reported that Persian public opinion was less hostile than it had been for some time and more inclined to realize that Persia had to depend on Britain. He also had several conversations with Prime Minister Vusuq ud-Daula, Akhbar Mirza, the Minister of Finance, and Firuz Mirza, the Minister of Justice, concerning advisers and support, and they had expressed confidence in Britain. The latter two individuals had been helpful in the past, as had their fathers, the Zill us-Sultan and Farman-Farma, respectively. The British came to call these men 'the Triumvirate' and to put great faith in their judgment. Cox said they broached the subject of British financial aid timidly for fear that if their proposals were rejected they would suffer odium for nothing. On the other hand, if they could receive assurance of Britain's readiness to give effective help to Persia and if a preliminary understanding could be reached, then they could undertake the necessary propaganda to carry an agreement through. The Triumvirate was anxious for negotiations to begin lest the Persian Delegation at the Conference, the Shah's appointees, should 'queer the pitch' by talking with others in Europe.[22]*

---

* This hint of rivalry between the Cabinet, or at least the Triumvirate, and the Peace Delegation grew into full-fledged competition before the negotiations were concluded. The reasons are not exactly clear from presently available sources but Vusuq ud-Daula obviously resented the rival source of influence. The Shah encouraged the delegation idea and forbade Vusuq ud-Daula to join it. Mere personal jealousies may have motivated the animosity. But more likely, the Prime Minister seriously believed that Persia had no choice but Britain and he hoped to get the best terms possible and feared that the Peace Delegation would undermine the chances.

The Triumvirate also accepted the idea, opposed late in the war, that any financial adviser employed by Persia should come from Britain.[23] Thus Persia was acknowledging the need for British assistance and removing one of the stumbling blocks that had aggravated British officials, who had felt Britain's considerable financial support of Persia entitled them to name a financial adviser, in late 1918. On this basis Cox urged that Britain adopt some moderate scheme that would capitalize on Persia's willingness to negotiate.[24]

The Foreign Office appreciated the information and the fact that the three most influential members of the Persian cabinet were aware of 'realities' and ready to adopt a position similar to Britain's; but there was a problem. They felt that the fact that the Persian Government had sent representatives to Paris who seemed to have different opinions from the Government made it difficult to enter into negotiations until it was clear that Persia intended to follow only one policy. The most the Foreign Office, i.e., Curzon, was prepared to permit was to continue to explore the possibilities of an agreement while Curzon consulted with Balfour about convincing the Persian Delegation to give up at Paris and come to London.[25] Presenting this opinion to the Persian Government was an attempt to squelch the Persian Delegation from the Persian end while Curzon endeavored to bury the issue at the Conference.

In the meantime, during early 1919, India had an opportunity to respond to Cox's idea of a moderate scheme for Persia. They agreed that financial reform under British officers was important but were taken aback by the extent of control suggested. Cox had suggested not only a financial adviser for the Treasury and the Ministries of the Interior, Public Works, Agriculture, Law and Education, but also advisers for each major province. He had also suggested that the British Commander of the uniform force be given virtual administrative independence. In short, he was proposing tight control.

India felt that this full program of reform might prove too strong meat even for the ultra pro-British Triumvirate. There was another worry:

... as we know from experience pro-British optimism of men so bound up with us as Vossuk and the sons of Zill and Farman-Farma are a very uncertain barometer of public opinion. In a matter of such moment we cannot afford a repetition on a large scale of our experience over the South Persia Rifles where recognition of the South Persia Rifles by Vossuk was closely followed by his downfall, and the repudiation of his recognition by successive cabinets contributed directly to our troubles in South Persia.

In India's opinion it was not enough that the cabinet accepted the idea. In their view the proposed reforms had to run so little counter to public opinion that any cabinet could carry them into effect as a matter of course. India doubted that Cox's scheme, which smacked of the Egyptian model, could meet this criterion and so they argued for a minimal agreement. They favored financial control through an adviser introduced into departments where his presence would produce the best results, rather than an elaborate network of advisers. They also favored the idea of letting a neutral organize Persia's uniform force. Only in this way, India believed, could Britain help Persia and guarantee the chances of successful reform.[26]

Curzon, however, was not sympathetic to India's view. He wanted an agreement with Persia and had confidence in Cox; his objection to proceeding being the problem presented by the Persian Delegation. Two factors made this problem less pressing. First, the Peace Conference decided against non-belligerents' representation, thereby reducing the threat that Persia could claim a hearing. Second, the Shah, who had supported the Delegation at Paris, became more tractable.

Although Ahmad Shah was receiving a British subsidy, negotiated during the war, threats to curtail the subsidy had not appreciably altered his stand over the Delegation and he was a source of trouble. But in February 1919 the Shah conceived a desire to go to Europe, which required money and that meant British support. Cox tried to discourage him but the Shah was determined to go and he expected British help to arrange the trip. As a result he became willing to support British-sponsored reform, though he did feel that there would be little public support for the idea while the Peace Conference was still in session. He suggested, as an interim measure, that the cabinet begin with propaganda to win support for the idea while he went to Europe; then in five or six weeks he could wire his approval and with the proper groundwork laid the scheme would have every chance of success. The Triumvirate felt that the Shah was being sincere and so Cox sought Curzon's view.[27]

Curzon opposed the Shah's visit. He felt that the Shah's presence in Europe would give him the opportunity to link up with the Peace Delegation and add considerably to Britain's difficulties at Paris. Curzon suggested that Cox delay the issue and have Vusuq ud-Daula say that his cabinet could not function without the Shah's presence.[28] But the Shah would not be put off. He developed the conviction that Britain was being unfriendly, which opened the possibility that he would revert to his former intrigues and troublemaking that had caused difficulties for Britain during the war. Therefore, it became worth considering whether it might not be better to get the Shah out of the country in exchange for his approval of an agreement.

Meanwhile the Persian cabinet continued to express interest in an agreement. In late February 1919 they asked Britain to give them some grounds on which to build popular support. They suggested permission: (1) to employ or encourage Persian capital for necessary railway construction; (2) to create a transportation company; (3) to establish a public works company; (4) to announce the British readiness to discuss specifically and sympathetically the possibility of meeting the Persian Government half-way on some of the desiderata which they had proposed to seek at the Peace Conference. In this connection they asked that the Allies (a) guarantee Persia's independence; (b) support efforts to secure war damages from Turkey and Russia; (c) agree in principle to a revision of the tariff; and (d) assist in the possible recovery of some lost territories.[29]

The Foreign Office, in a reply drafted largely by Lancelot Oliphant, still felt unable to pursue the matter officially so long as the Persian Delegation was in Paris. But this did not prohibit comment. These comments are interesting for what they indicate about British thinking towards Iran.

Not only did the end of the war leave Britain with a unique political position in Persia, but it also opened the field to the advancement of British economic interests, especially in the north where the Russians had tried to exclude all interests but their own. With this prospect in mind, Curzon (whose book on Persia in the late 1800s examined, among other things, economic potential in Iran) wanted to see British interests promoted. It was not his idea to exclude altogether other interests or investments, but he was interested in exploiting Britain's unique position in Iran to see that Britain had a coordinated policy of investment that would give his country a headstart in those areas of special concern to Britain, especially in the transport industries. Nor was it the intention of this attitude to exclude the Persians from investing in the development of their own country, but Curzon, based on past observations, did not have a very high opinion of Persia's abilities to promote internal development on its own, and he was not prepared to see railway or other transport development pass from British control. Thus, the Foreign

Office made a vague reply to the Persian Government's exploratory efforts.

The Foreign Office felt that Persian capital would naturally be encouraged to invest in railways but Britain could give no guarantees in advance that this would be the case. They also thought a purely Persian transport company would fail and that it was premature to discuss public works projects. As to point four, the Foreign Office had the gravest objections to inviting others to guarantee Persia's independence but no objections to items (b) or (c). The Foreign Office was unwilling to comment on item (d) lest this be used as a lever by Persia to force their way into the Conference.[30]* Discussions over an agreement and the Shah's trip all hinged on the fate of the Delegation in Paris. The Shah continued to press for permission to leave and Curzon continued to stall.[31] But in mid-March Cox began to urge that Britain find some way of circumventing the stalemate.

On March 20 Cox informed Curzon that the Shah's attitude was more than satisfactory. He was keeping his promises, avoiding intrigues and discouraging the practice in others. He was friendly, amiable and supportive of the cabinet. Consequently, Cox felt that if something were not done to reassure him he would have reason to believe that his cooperative attitude went for nothing. Cox reported that the atmosphere in Tehran and elsewhere was less hostile than it had been in years, but he felt nonetheless that the Shah's acquiescence and goodwill were essential to a settlement. Cox urged a reply that would not discourage the Shah, even if it did not promise immediate compliance with his wishes.[32] Curzon decided to waive his objections to the Shah's journey but on the conditions that the monarch promised to abstain from all intrigues or associations with 'undesirable persons' and not to visit Paris during the Peace Conference. He also had to give the Prime Minister full authority before he left to conclude an agreement and he had to promise not to leave until the agreement was reached (Curzon was afraid that Vusuq ud-Daula would use the Shah's absence to renege on negotiations). In any event the situation in Paris no longer looked so threatening and by winning over the Shah it became easier to box in the Delegation.[33]

The improvement in conditions in Tehran and the growing

---

* In fact, the British hesitated to comment specifically to the cabinet for they had indications that information passed to the Persian Cabinet found its way to Mushavar ul-Mamalik, the head of the Persian Delegation in Paris.

likelihood that the Persian Delegation in Paris was hopelessly isolated meant that negotiations could move ahead. Britain could put an end to the anomalous position of exerting every pressure on Persia to seek only British assistance while delaying negotiations until the Paris Delegation was no longer a threat. Reaching this resolution quickly became more important because of growing post-war pressure in Britain to cut back on obligations in the East, particularly military ones.

In late December, 1918 J. M. Keynes, acting for the Treasury and as the vanguard of a trend to cut expenditures, informed the Eastern Committee that the Vote of Credit, passed by Parliament at the beginning of the war, would expire in March, 1919 and all new demands on the Treasury would require a Parliamentary vote. Keynes pointed out that the level of expenditures in Iran, about £2,550,000 per month, not counting the military stores brought in, were out of proportion to the results obtained and that every economy would have to be employed to cut future expenditures.[34] Since most of these funds went to the various military missions, the Treasury was, in effect, serving notice on the British military presence in Iran. To Curzon and Cox this meant withdrawing the only reliable forces in Iran capable of defending the country from internal chaos and worse, the Bolsheviks. The most that these architects of the Persian settlement could hope for was a delay in withdrawal and thus there was an urgent timetable for securing the agreement.

Curzon opposed this post-war policy of cut and run. In the Eastern Committee meeting of December 30, 1918 he characterized this policy and the India Office's tendency to support it as 'immoral, feeble and disastrous.'[35] It threatened to undo all the gains of the war, to abandon Britain's traditional position in Persia and to desert Iran in the face of the Bolshevik menace. But the most that Curzon could win — or assume, since no definite decisions but Curzon's were reached — was a delay in the proposed evacuations. In the meantime Curzon outlined to Cox his proposals for negotiating with Persia (see p. 227 above). Curzon intended to push ahead.

But Curzon's policy was challenged by Edwin Montagu, the Secretary of State for India. Montagu had not been present at the meeting in December and in early January, 1919 he wrote to Curzon protesting the manner in which the affair was being handled.

I notice in the draft minutes [of the Eastern Committee's meeting] a statement that the Committee agreed with the Chairman. Surely you will not allow this to stand? For the situation was this: Mr Balfour was away. I was away: I do not see it recorded that C.I.G.S. was present: Lord Robert Cecil (I don't know whether he is a member of the Committee or not now) had left before he had heard either Sir Hamilton Grant or Sir Arthur Hirtzel. And therefore the Committee consisted of the Chairman: and the Chairman, of course, not unnaturally, agreed with the Chairman.[36]

Montagu did not favor Curzon's plans and refused to commit India to paying half the expenses. Under attack from the Treasury and 'betrayed' by the India Office, it seemed Curzon's policy was doomed. But Curzon was able to convince Montagu of the need for resolution of the Persian situation and he had reason to believe that his plan, an eventual economy, could be got past the Treasury.

The problem of evacuation remained, however. Curzon disliked it and Cox argued that a too rapid withdrawal would deprive the Persian Government of the means to maintain order and leave the country open to renewed disorder. He urged a slowdown.[37] With the improving conditions in Tehran, the successful isolation of the Persian Delegation at Paris, and the winning over, ignoring or silencing of opposition, all obstacles to a settlement were disappearing. It only remained to conclude the negotiations.

In early April, 1919 Cox reported that the Persian Government was still interested in an agreement and was fully prepared to rely solely on Britain. Even the Shah was urging that something definite be done. The Triumvirate favored an agreement but they felt that quick action was necessary while all the factors were favorable.[38] They urged that negotiations begin on the general terms of an agreement and, since they had already given thought to this, passed along a draft for an agreement plus a confidential subsidiary agreement. They further proposed that when these instruments were concluded the Persian Government would then inform Mushavar ul-Mamalik, head of the Persian Delegation, that his mission to Paris was finished, thus presenting him with a *fait accompli*. Cox passed the Persian proposals to Curzon and in the ensuing weeks a preliminary agreement emerged.

The text of the Persian proposal runs as follows:

In virtue of the close ties of friendship which have existed between the two Governments in the past and in the conviction that it is in essential and mutual interests of both in future that these ties should be cemented and progress and prosperity of Persia should be promoted to utmost, it is hereby agreed between the Persian Government on the one hand and His Britannic Majesty's Minister, acting on behalf of his Government, on the other as follows: –

1. British Government reiterates in the most categorical manner the understanding which they have repeatedly given in the past to respect the independence and integrity of Persia.
2. British Government will supply at the cost of Persian Government the services of such expert advisers as may be necessary for the several Departments of the Persian administration.

   These advisers shall be engaged on contracts and endowed with adequate powers, the nature of which should be a matter of agreement more or less between the Persian Government and advisers.
3. British Government will [group omitted] provide at the cost of Persian Government such officers and munitions and equipment of modern type as may be adjudged necessary by a Joint Commission of military experts, British and Persian, which shall assemble forthwith for the purpose of estimating the needs of Persia in the direction of a uniform force which the Persian Government proposes to create for the establishment and preservation of order in the country and on its frontiers.
4. British Government in consultation with Persian Government shall seek in customs revenue or other sources of income at the disposal of the Persian Government adequate security for a substantial loan to be provided or arranged by British Government for Government of Persia for the purpose of financing the reforms indicated in clauses 2 and 3 of this agreement, and pending the completion of negotiations for such a loan, British Government shall advance such funds as may be necessary to provide personnel and equipment for initiating the said reforms.
5. British Government, fully recognising the urgent need which exists for the improvement of communications in Persia, both with a view to the extension of trade and prevention of famine, are prepared to co-operate with Persian Government for encouragement of Anglo-Persian enterprise in this direction both by means of railway construction and other forms of transport, subject always to examination of the problems by experts, and to agreement between the two Governments as to particular projects which may be most necessary, practicable, and profitable.
6. British Government agree in principle, in so far as they are concerned, to the examination of existing treaties with a view to their revision in conformity with the present-day requirements, and will be prepared to enter into special negotiations for the purpose as soon as, in the opinion of the two Governments, a suitable moment has arrived.
7. The two Governments agree to appointment forthwith of a joint committee of experts for examination and revision of the existing customs tariff with a view to its reconstruction on a basis calculated to accord with the legitimate interests of the country and to promote its prosperity.
8. British Government will lend their full support to Persian Government for the establishment of her position as a member of the League of Nations.[39]

In addition to this draft the Persian Government also included the outlines of a subsidiary agreement. It included the following:

In continuation of the agreement come to and executed this day between the two Governments on the subject of the provisional advisers, &c., a confidential agreement is hereby entered into by parties on following two further subjects. It shall, for the present, remain secret: −

(a) It being hereby mutually agreed and decided between the parties that British and Persian Governments will make no claims against one another for losses incurred by one Government from the other resulting from recent World War, the British Government undertakes to support the claims of Persia to obtain compensation for material damage suffered by Persia from action of other belligerents.

(b) It being understood that Persian Government is anxious to obtain a rectification of the frontier of Persia in certain localities, the British Government accordingly agree to receive confidentially the detailed explanations of the desires of the Persian Government and to examine them with an open mind; furthermore, in case of any particular item the justice or expediency of which [is] in the interest of the people concerned they may become convinced the British Government will endeavour to the best of their power to assist the Persian Government to attain their object in such manner and by such means as may be decided between the parties to be possible and expedient.[40]

These terms were remarkably similar to proposals put forward by a variety of Persian Governments, some of which the British regarded as distinctly unfriendly, in the course of negotiations during the war to resolve British security worries. There had been sixteen cabinet changes between 1914 and 1919, reflecting the strains and fluctuations of war and internal politics; but, despite the supposed differences in sympathies of these cabinets for various of the belligerents, they had all sought similar concessions. They tried to limit the degree of foreign interference in internal Persian affairs, to cancel the 1907 Convention, to end extra-territoriality, to secure financial independence, to recover lost territory, to develop a national army and to win foreign guarantees for Iran's independence. The British balked at these terms when presented by a supposedly unfriendly cabinet but were prepared to consider them favorably when presented by one that appeared cooperative and that owed its life to British support. Thus, when the Triumvirate outlined their desiderata they received sympathetic consideration.

Cox received the Persian proposals favorably. He had no comment to make on articles 1, 3, 4, and 5. He felt article 6 was worded innocuously and vaguely enough but that Britain might want to make some changes. Article 7 was mainly interested in securing more revenue and the Persian Government included article 8 in order to captivate public sentiment. The article that most concerned Cox was article 2 of the main draft and articles (a) and (b) of the subsidiary agreement.

Cox said in regard to article 2 that the power of the adviser should be a matter for agreement between the two Governments but the Triumvirate felt that this might cause difficulties if stated explicitly. They argued that since Britain would not allow advisers to accept terms Britain did not approve the result would be the same. Cox also wanted to include a clause that would prohibit Persia from looking elsewhere for advisers and loans. Again the Triumvirate objected that this would cause trouble because it sounded very similar to an ultimatum. Instead the Triumvirate argued that this did not need explication since Britain would be supplying advisers and controlling the finances.[41]

The Triumvirate made the inclusion of the proposals of the subsidiary draft an essential point of their position. Cox was aware that these subjects were sensitive to officials in London but he felt obligated to pass them along. He also expressed the hope that Britain could accommodate some of these proposals, especially since some concessions would make the acceptance of the agreement more palatable to public opinion. He suggested something in the Caucasus, Central Asia or along the Turco-Persian border that would not violate self-determination and at the same time compensate Persia for the damage caused by Turkey and Russia.[42]

In addition to the formal terms the Triumvirate and the Shah had additional requirements. The Shah expected something in return for his support – personal assurances of support, support for the dynasty, and 20,000 tumans a month for life.[43] The Triumvirate, on the other hand, wanted guarantees of personal support and considerable sums of money to help overcome potential opposition.

The Triumvirate, according to Cox, were convinced that the policy under consideration was the best one but they were also aware that a good many persons or elements, acting for selfish reasons they mistook for patriotism, would oppose the agreement. This opposition had to be overcome either by coercion or persuasion. The Triumvirate were prepared, with British support, to do both but a policy of persuasion would require a great deal of secret service funds in order to 'square' the rest of the cabinet, the newspapers, and the Majlis. They asked for 500,000 tumans paid down with no questions asked. The Triumvirate also asked for guarantees of asylum and assurances

of an income in the event that things went wrong and they had to leave
the country. With these preliminaries out of the way, it was possible
to get down to serious haggling over conditions and wording.[44]

Curzon approved Cox's efforts and he found the draft proposals
generally acceptable. The only immediate change he suggested was
the insertion of '*all* such expert advisers' in article 2 and the inclusion
of a stipulation that would put the financial adviser in the service of
Britain and not of the Persian Government. Although it was too soon
to comment in detail on the main proposals, he had some observations
concerning the subsidiary agreement and the desiderata of the Shah
and the Triumvirate. In fact the majority of the correspondence
between Curzon and Cox dealt with these private arrangements. But
Curzon basically approved Cox's efforts; he did, however, object to
secret agreements because of the prevailing feelings against them and
he did not want to bind Britain to maintain the Qajar dynasty or to
subsidize the Shah in perpetuity. He also felt that payment of 500,000
tumans, if approved, would have to be a part of the general advance.

I desire to express my appreciation of the manner in which you have conducted
the negotiations ...

In view of strong feeling against secret agreements, it would appear
desirable, if anything is to be done on these points [subsidiary agreements],
to embody it in subsequent letter to Minister. His Majesty's Government
would like further time to consider (a) and (b). It would need addition of
such words as 'if and when opportunity offers.'

Colonel Wilson is being consulted about the frontier.

His Majesty's Government could not commit themselves to maintenance
in perpetuity of Kajar dynasty, or to subsidy to Shah, which would amount
at present rate to 120,000 1. a year.

If Persian finances are properly administered rise in revenue would
beneficially affect civil list of Sovereign.

Further payment of 500,000 tomans would, if ever approved, have to be
merely an advance out of any prospective loan.[45]

Cox proceeded to deal with these comments. He pointed out that
it was not the Persian Government who desired secret arrangements,
for they were willing to see their inclusion in the principal agreement.
Cox added, however, that if the

... compact between ourselves and Persian Government in first clause of (a)
would be considered 'unholy' if published, perhaps the understanding could
be arranged by exchange of letters and only last clause, beginning with 'British
Government' come unto agreement.

After dealing with these problems Cox turned to the remarks on the expectations of the Shah and the Triumvirate. Cox was aware that these subjects were uncomfortable but he believed in their necessity and he had some rather cynical suggestions to match the Persian requests. He pointed out that the life of the present Shah was not likely to be a long one because of his increasing obesity. In regard to the dynasty he wondered if it would not be possible to say ' "Shah and his successors will have our friendly support [? as long as]." etc., or that "we will not support any change of dynasty as long as"?' Cox also felt that some settlement was necessary over the 500,000 tumans.

If advanced out of a loan it would be less palatable, because item would have to appear in Government accounts, which would be inconvenient to parties whose palms were greased.

Cox urged at least a diluted form rather than a complete rejection and suggested that the Anglo-Persian Oil Company might be persuaded to share the cost.[46]

Curzon and the Foreign Office appreciated the ins-and-outs of negotiating in Persia and had some cynical observations of their own. Oliphant minuted:

I am very doubtful whether we s[houl]d be justified in gambling on the Shah's life. It is true that he is so stout as to be almost deformed; but even if his life be precarious one must not forget 'creaking hinges.'

He also objected to 'oiling the wheels,' especially since the Treasury would cause trouble and the Foreign Office did not want to involve the A.P.O.C.[47]* Cox was informed that the most that Britain was prepared to do was to continue the subsidy already paid to the Shah so long as he supported Vusuq ud-Daula and to agree to offer the Qajar dynasty Britain's friendly support. In view of the difficulties in finding a source of funds for the 500,000 tumans, the Foreign Office wondered whether, if the funds were forthcoming in the near future, 'might it not be possible for the Persian Government to accept it, even though only as an advance before their Ministry of Finance is reorganized.' They did not suggest how to explain the missing funds to a reorganized Ministry of Finance.[48]

---

* The A.P.O.C. was making far-reaching demands for oil and railway concessions in the Middle East and the Foreign Office had not made up its mind to approve these claims. In fact they eventually rejected them, but at this point they did not want to compromise themselves by asking the A.P.O.C. for financial support.

Cox asked for clarification. He had not held further talks with the Triumvirate since he presented their proposals and he wanted a clear understanding of Britain's position before he resumed the negotiations and he was still unsure of Britain's position on the subsidiary agreement — whether it was to be treated separately. His main interest, however, was in settling the private arrangements.

He agreed on the suggestion of 'support' for the dynasty but he tried once again to see if something could not be done about the Shah's subsidy. Vusuq ud-Daula's incumbency was uncertain and presumably the Shah's support would still be necessary if Vusuq ud-Daula left. Cox wanted to know if it would not be possible to continue the subsidy for ten years with the following reservation: 'until such time as improved administration has increased total revenue by double amount of subsidy' (which was running about £70,000 a year).

The payment of the 500,000 tuman gratuity also remained in doubt. Cox felt that as a last resort the 500,000 tuman payment could be made as an advance — presuming that the item was not probed in the future (Cox saw the flaw in the Foreign Office's suggestion). In any event, Cox believed some arrangement was necessary and if the above scheme proved difficult he wanted to know if he could offer half the amount; or if a system could be devised whereby Britain would pay an extra month of the monthly subsidy of 350,000 tumans being paid to the Persian Government. Cox could suggest no method, or at least none that would not come under scrutiny, and he still had nothing definite to say to the Persians on the personal assurances asked for by the Triumvirate.[49]

On April 30, while Cox waited for answers to his inquiries, the Government of India entered into the debate. India appreciated Cox's success with the Shah and Triumvirate; because of this and their earlier opinion against relying on such a small base they regretted even more that their views had been ignored. The very fact that the Shah and the Triumvirate were asking for guarantees and money confirmed India's misgivings about placing faith in them. They remained chary of Cox's financial, military and political commitments. Particularly India worried that the scope of Cox's plan would 'insensibly decrease to zero' Britain's chances of ever being able to withdraw from Persia. There were other serious worries:

On the other hand, chances of our having sooner or later to use force based on India to maintain our position in Persia against wave of nationalism would arise sooner rather than later. Existence of anti-British feeling among Moslems in Egypt and India and threat of it in Kurdistan, coupled with unsettled condition of Afghanistan, renders the present a highly dangerous moment for initiation of so hazardous an experiment.[50]

Cox was prepared to defend his position. He regretted that India had misgivings about the negotiations but he believed that the position they felt obliged to take up inclined them to see phantoms. Cox tried to minimize the differences of opinion, or to point out that the differences were more apparent than real. India too wanted to offer financial assistance and to provide an instruction mission for the uniform force if Persia desired it. In Cox's view this was not appreciably at variance with his own suggestions except that he wanted to avoid a hodge-podge of foreign advisers and neutral officers who would be a source of friction and delay.

Cox could not help but feel that the time was ripe for an agreement, especially since Britain could still provide protection in the north with its own forces, and he took exception to the tenor of India's comments on his negotiations. It was not, as India would have it, 'Cox's latest scheme,' but the policy of the British Government and in Britain's imperial interests; and contrary to India's military worries the situation was opportune for a settlement that would strengthen Persia, whereas if the opportunity were lost, Persia would relapse into anarchy, necessitating large-scale intervention.[51]

Cox was not prepared to see much value in India's opinion. Cox, the former servant of the Government of India, shared the views of another old India hand – Curzon. Together they were ready to override all opposition that interfered with their vision for a Persian settlement. Cox and Curzon had long been critics of the bungling of relations with Iran and now they were determined to prove the worth of their convictions.

On May 9, 1919 Curzon informed Cox that the Eastern Committee* had been able to review carefully the text of the proposed agreement, which they were anxious to conclude. The Interdepartmental Conference, held on May 7, discussed the situation in Iran and the best means of securing the stability of Britain's future position there.

* In January, 1919 the Eastern Committee had recommended its own demise to the Cabinet, who approved it. An Interdepartmental Conference, to be called from time to time as Curzon felt necessary, was to replace it. The term, however, survived and Curzon refers to it in this telegram to Cox. For demise of Eastern Committee, see PRO-CAB 23/6/512/2, 1/10/19.

Curzon termed the negotiations, if successful, a notable act of State policy. The question that worried him was whether or not the negotiations would be successful. He realized that an agreement would require further financial commitments and given the climate for economy in Britain it was not obvious that such a step would be sanctioned. The Treasury was urging thrift and India's objections to paying half the expenses of a new cabinet jeopardized the chances. The most the Treasury was willing to do was briefly continue the subsidies currently paid.[52] Curzon hoped to reverse this, since he had succeeded in convincing Montagu of the importance of the agreement, and now he turned to winning over the Treasury.

In the Conference Curzon carefully detailed his reasoning and the need for haste. He wanted to avoid the issue of Persia at the Paris Conference and the longer it remained unsettled the greater were the chances of Persia attracting foreign attention. Curzon had no faith in the Paris Conference's ability to settle matters in the Middle East. He had asked himself what the duty of a British politician should be and had replied that it was to build up the bastions of India, 'which had always been and must be the pivot and focus of British interests in the East.' In his opinion the war had changed the position of Persia from the point of view of British interests.

She [Persia] now lay between India and Mesopotamia, and a tranquil Persia was of vital importance to the prosperity of both countries. He [Curzon] looked on the present opportunity of establishing Persian stability as one which ought not to be lost ... He wished to make it clear that these negotiations, which involved large questions of statesmanship, ought not, in his opinion, to be handled in any narrow or small-minded spirit.

Montagu agreed with Curzon. The Treasury still had to decide whether or not to sanction any further payments but Curzon was marshalling his forces. Only India remained recalcitrant and Curzon had already isolated their position by winning over Montagu. It remained to settle the outlines of the agreement and the Conference turned to considering the Persian proposals.[53]

They had only minor changes to suggest in the wording of the principal agreement and preferred to dispense with references to renegotiation of treaties (clause 6) and territorial compensation, which might involve the attentions of other nations, unless differently worded and included in a separate letter. They wanted specifics on the security Persia was prepared to offer for the proposed loan and they expressed a desire that its payment would be in sterling, which was easier to remit. In regard to the private arrangements, they were unprepared to go beyond general assurances of friendly support for the Qajar dynasty and doubted that Parliament would consent to paying the Shah a subsidy. They were also unimpressed by the Triumvirate's request for additional money, remarking: 'If Ministers are so frightened of proposed agreement as to fear expulsion, agreement itself would not rest on very secure foundation.'[54]

Cox discussed these suggestions with the Triumvirate, who agreed to the various changes and to the idea of transferring clause 6 to a separate letter. They were willing to have a separate letter dealing with tariff revision, compensation for war-damages, and rectification of frontiers but they stressed that these points were indispensible in helping to check public opinion and to ensure the success of the agreement. They too did not want the issues raised at the Peace Conference and Cox suggested that the separate letter contain vague promises along these lines that would have the matter wait on the conclusion and dispersal of the Conference. The Delegation in Paris still haunted negotiations.

In regard to the Shah, Cox felt he would be disappointed but that he could be controlled. The Triumvirate were also willing to forego personal assurances and made it clear that they had no apprehensions about the success of the policy. They were willing to extend the security of the proposed loan to include the customs of Sistan, Kermanshah and Azerbaijan. They were also willing to have the loan paid in sterling, but they still needed the secret service money which could be paid as an advance on account of the loan.[55]

The agreement was moving towards a conclusion but certain perplexities still remained. Curzon wanted to avoid delays but he also did not want to rush into accepting terms that would later cause trouble. Specifically he wanted clarification of the terms to be covered in the proposed separate letter. He did not want to commit Britain to embarrassing tariff revisions, compensation schemes or territorial readjustments that would involve other countries. He was also concerned about the 500,000 tumans requested by the Triumvirate. Curzon had never been pleased with what he considered a bribe and he worried that if it ever became public it would effectively damn the career of the Triumvirate and excite severe criticism in Britain. Curzon was ready to conclude the agreement at once if he could receive reassurance on these points.[56] Cox was prepared to give it.

Cox argued that something along the lines of the separate letter was necessary to give the Cabinet the ability to show that they had obtained by other means what had been expected from the Peace Conference. The Cabinet, however, did not expect Britain to commit itself to modifications of treaties or abandonment of privileges. As far as the money was concerned, it was possible to reduce the amount but some substantial secret service payments were necessary to give the Cabinet the ability to stay in power at least long enough to assure that the new policy was firmly established. Cox suggested a more euphonious definition of the 'bribe' such as ' "education of public opinion" ' or ' "costly initiation of reforms" ' in order to avoid the contingency Curzon feared.[57]

It is difficult to believe that Curzon could have found too much solace in this reply but the momentum for settling was mounting. On May 30 Curzon informed Cox that the Chancellor of the Exchequer had agreed to a loan of £2,000,000 to Persia secured on the customs of the south and of Sistan, Kermanshah and Azerbaijan, provided that India paid half. Curzon could already count on India Office support and so the last hurdle had been passed.[58] India admitted its defeat, but not without a Parthian shot: 'In view of our misgivings with regard to present scheme we trust liability now accepted by you will not be further extended.'[59] It only remained to settle the fine points.

The negotiations in June settled the issue of interest rates and payment schedules. The Persian Government wanted to repay the loan at seven per cent per annum over a twenty year period with the right to pay off the loan at any time from any future advances from Great Britain. The British wanted an interest rate of eight per cent over a fifteen year period but they accepted the Persian terms.[60] In early June the negotiations entered the final phases.

On July 7 Cox informed the Foreign Office that the French text of the principal agreement was ready. He wanted to know if he needed special authorization to sign, since he was a minister *ad interim*, and what assurances were to be given the Shah.[61] Curzon authorized him to sign the agreement and told him to promise the Shah, who was still receiving a subsidy, Britain's friendly support as long as he acted in accordance with the policy and advice of the British Government. He also informed him that Britain was prepared to extend asylum to the Triumvirate if the occasion developed.[62]

With these personal matters out of the way, Curzon tried to scale down the Triumvirate's request for 500,000 tumans (about £200,000 or ten per cent of the total loan). He suggested £20,000. However, the Triumvirate felt that such a sum would do more harm than good, as it would only stimulate the appetites of numerous people who could cause difficulties if not satisfied. They saw two alternatives: (1) pay nothing and fight out the agreement on its merits; or (2) pay liberally and establish the policy without a fight. Cox believed that the Triumvirate would have to pay freely to get things moving and he urged accommodating them so things would go smoothly. Cox did not want to fight out the agreement on its merits.

Curzon did not want to pay – not £200,000 at any rate.

We have offered £20,000. They ask for £200,000. *This is not merely exorbitant it is corrupt* [my emphasis].

I thought I had said this to Cox a dozen times over but I cannot get it into his head.[63]

And Curzon did not want £200,000 worth of corruption. He tried to get the message across:

Advance of 10% of entire loan for suggested purposes cannot possibly be considered small advance. You know my intense dislike of this phase of the transaction and with this expression of my opinion I must leave you to make the most suitable terms you can.[64]

This sounded vaguely like Pilate washing his hands; and the Triumvirate would not respect Curzon's scruples. The most suitable terms remained £200,000.*

On July 27 Cox began sending to the Foreign Office the final drafts of the principal agreement, the loan agreement, the letter of assurance to the Shah, and the separate letters on tariff revision, etc., for the Triumvirate. These required only minor changes. On August 4 the India Office approved the texts and the Treasury followed suit. The last obstacle disappeared.

On August 9, 1919 the long delayed agreement settling Anglo-Iranian relations was signed. Curzon had succeeded in putting these relations on a firm basis. He had assured the glacis of empire. In one stroke he had concluded an issue that had evaded resolution throughout the war and throughout the nineteenth century and had given form to his dreams. In the euphoria of success he could hardly be expected to realize that he had built his foundation, his policy, his dreams on Persian sand.

---

* The sum actually paid was £131,000.

There were inherent flaws in Curzon's policy that undermined its chances of success from the beginning. First, according to the Persian Constitution, the Agreement needed the approval of the Majlis. Elections were a lengthy business in Iran and as the elections dragged on, aided by the procrastination of the Cabinet, the opponents of the Agreement had time to marshal their forces. They began using the Agreement, which they characterized as a sell-out of Persia, to arouse Persian nationalism and to shake the Government's position. The momentum of this movement eventually stalled the Agreement beyond hope. Second, Curzon had not counted on the vehemence of the foreign reaction. Both America and France reacted as if Britain were trying to establish an Egypt in Iran. Curzon could deny this but no one believed him. America would soon have the example of oil and Britain's attempt to lock up all sources of it outside America, to excite the imagination.* The French, on the other hand, had a long memory, not forgetting Egypt. Third, the hostility expressed by these powers gave encouragement to Iranian nationalists, who could point to outraged foreign opinion as a sign of what the Agreement really meant. Once again a comprehensive agreement had run foul of nascent Persian nationalism; after another half-century of development, a revolution and a war, that nationalism had a new cause. In the atmosphere created by the nationalists it became increasingly difficult for the Persian Government to uphold the Agreement. Before the end of 1919 they were seeking modifications and by the end of 1920 the issue was dead.

It also became increasingly difficult for Curzon to withstand pressures at home that wanted to cut commitments in Iran. Curzon had intended the 1919 Agreement to do exactly that, but before it could have an effect Persia needed stability, and without adequate armed force the central government was virtually powerless. Only the various British missions and troops gave the Government any real armed force; a fact that undermined the Government even further with the nationalists. The country remained sharply divided, with separatist movements in Kurdistan, Azerbaijan and in the Caspian provinces. In addition, British involvement in Russia had aggravated the Soviets,

---

* For American fears, see 'Multinational Oil Corporations and U.S. Foreign Policy,' Report by the Senate Subcommittee on Multinational Corporations of the Committee on Foreign Relations, 1/2/75. U.S.G.P.O., Washington, D.C., 1975. For the development of British oil policy in the Middle East in this period, see Marian Kent, *Oil and Empire: British Policy and Mesopotamian Oil, 1900-1920*, Macmillan, 1976.

who were sending agents and troops to Iran to challenge the British. In the face of these mounting pressures Persia needed British troops – a fact that India had predicted. Unfortunately for Curzon's policy, officials in London were determined to reduce those very forces.[65]

As Britain lost the conviction to pursue the anti-Bolshevik campaign in Russia, the military presence in Iran lost much of its rationale to an economy-minded Government. Curzon could not halt this process at home and he could not force the pace in Iran, despite biting telegrams to the new Minister, Herman Norman, to see that the Agreement did not fade away. Even Montagu would not support Curzon, who resorted to the spectre of Persian anarchy and rampant Bolshevism to save his masterstroke. It was of no avail. British troops continued to evacuate, their position in the north assumed almost before they left by Soviet forces. Ironically India came to Curzon's defense and argued that withdrawal would open Britain up to the charge of breach of faith, having agreed to aid Persia and then abandoning it; India worried that this would increase difficulties with Afghanistan.[66] Even this support, however, could not halt the pace of withdrawal. This was the final flaw in Curzon's policy, for as India had feared, it needed British troops in large numbers 'sooner rather than later.'

In the meantime the Persian Government came under increasing criticism from the nationalist press. In addition the Jangali movement in the Caspian provinces, thought to have withered away, re-emerged with Soviet support and began exercising control over much of the area. There were also separatist movements in Azerbaijan and Khorasan and social unrest throughout the country. These factors, plus the British withdrawal in the face of Soviet advances, influenced the Persian Government to seek an agreement with Russia. Curzon objected to this course, worrying that it might firmly establish the Bolsheviks between Mesopotamia and India, but Curzon's wishes and imperious orders to Norman, Cox's replacement, could not halt the collapse.[67] Vusuq ud-Daula's Government fell in July, 1920 under intense pressure, and the Persian Government continued its efforts to negotiate with the Russians in the hopes that an agreement would halt the menace.[68] Although in the late days of 1918 and in 1919 the British had come to believe they could do without Vusuq ud-Daula, he had been in power well over a year and his presence had given a certain sense of continuity to relations. His departure under fire only weakened the Agreement more, and the succeeding cabinet of Mushir ud-Daula had to worry about the menacing internal crisis created in part by the 1919 Agreement.

Norman, who had replaced Cox so that he could return to Mesopotamia, tried all the old methods for overcoming Persian resistance. He threatened the Shah with the loss of the subsidy paid by Britain, and he urged the Foreign Office to give him more money to help him defray certain expenses.[69] Curzon also instructed Norman to impress on the Persian Government that Britain's continued support depended on the loyalty of the Government to the Agreement.[70] Money was of no avail, for the Shah was not impressed and Britain's support only contributed to Persia's worries. The pressure did not have its old effect. By late 1920 Curzon was admitting the obvious – the 1919 Agreement was in abeyance, if not dead. It went to its grave on February 21, 1921 when a *coup d'état*, led by a newspaper editor and politician, Sayyid Zia ad-Din Tabataba'i, and an Iranian military officer in the Cossack Brigade, Riza Khan, replaced the wobbling central government, and the ratification of the Agreement ceased to be a possibility. Within the week this new regime concluded a treaty of friendship with Russia and began to reorganize the country's armed forces to restore internal order. The 'noble act of state policy' was a shambles and Curzon was bitter:

Personally I will never propose another Agreement with the Persians. Not unless they came on their knees would I even consider any application from them, and possibly not then. In future we will look after our own interests in Persia not hers.[71]

Even Curzon, the Persian expert, had been unable to secure the position in Iran. He had succeeded in making an agreement but he was no more successful in making it stick than other Foreign Secretaries who had tried to settle the Persian situation under less advantageous conditions.

In his determination to secure the Agreement, Curzon had overpowered all opposition. He knew the answers and he turned a deaf ear to voices that raised inconvenient objections. India had urged a new policy, one of reconciliation based on the realization that Persian nationalism was not just the occupation of a few extremists. But Curzon had not been interested in dealing with Iran, but had seen Iran as a means to an end, not as a legitimate end in itself. He saw the opportunity to secure India's frontiers and was determined to do this in a manner he saw fit. He convinced himself that he spoke for Persia and then found the men who would listen.

This tendency, to rely on the right men in office, on winning influence, had characterized British practice throughout the war. In part this was a rationalization of political practice in Persia; nevertheless it blinded the British to change, and it tended to base Anglo-Iranian relations on personalities not on policies.

Both Cox and Curzon were aware of political opposition to their efforts but they believed that most of this was trumped-up, inconsequential, and easily won over and subdued. It might have been better if they had checked more closely into numbers when the Triumvirate told them that a good many persons and elements might oppose the Agreement. Instead Curzon relied on his brand of personal diplomacy, and rather than working out a policy in resonance with Persian realities, he thrust his ideas upon a Government he had created for the purpose. In forcing the Agreement he excited the elements he despised and put a weapon in their hands to bring down the whole structure.

India had been right. The new nationalism of such re-emerging nations as Turkey, Iran, Egypt and the lands of Arabia and Mesopotamia and even India could not be ignored. In the post-war era they came into direct conflict with European imperialism; but on new terms, for the emerging nationalistic sentiments were much less willing to deal with the Europeans.

The British emerged victorious from the First World War but it was not a happy triumph. Britain, as all the countries of Europe, had spilled much blood and treasure to make a peace that settled none of the problems that had made the war. In addition the war let the genie of nationalism and revolution out of the bottle. To win a European war the British had to turn to outsiders. They had to make promises to peoples that their power had held in thrall; they had also to mortgage their policy to the ideas of yet another outsider, Woodrow Wilson. In doing so they made more promises than they could keep. British policy in the inter-war years was much concerned with dealing with the problems raised by these conflicting promises. It had been a wearying war; it would be a trying peace.

CONCLUSION

In a review of volume XII of *Documents in British Foreign Policy: The Near and Middle East*, Bernadotte Schmitt observed of British policy in the immediate post-war years that, 'This is a most extraordinary collection of documents the reviewer has ever read, for it is one long record of frustration.' There were troubles in Egypt, Palestine, Mesopotamia/Iraq; lurking Bolsheviks; difficulties with the French over Syria; and, of course, the vexing complications caused by Turkey. In Iran, too, Curzon's 'noble act of statesmanship' foundered and Iran seemed destined to resume its role as Dulcinea to Britain's Don Quixote.

Yet, these were the troubles born of victory. It is a tale of an embarrassment of riches. Britain emerged from the war not only with the empire intact but with a strapping collection of additions. The frustration came from trying to devise a scheme to hold on to these spoils at a time when world opinion and local, obstreperous nationalism began to frown on imperial domination; at a time when imperial sinews had reached the limits of endurance and could no longer sustain a forward policy. Frustration grew out of opposition and exhaustion.

British interests in Iran survived the war, yet not a single policy employed between 1914 and 1919 worked as expected, few worked at all, and some made matters worse. While it is fairly easy to detail why and how these various policies stumbled along, an equally tantalizing question is difficult to answer: why, if nothing worked, did British interests survive more or less intact, or significantly improve? How was it possible for so many approaches to fail so ignominiously and yet still avoid disaster?

Chance? Certainly the convergence of various forces had a fortuitous effect, but chance, as Pasteur shrewly observed, favors the prepared individual. And yet, Britain seemed so unprepared for the events in Persia, so completely at a loss. Why, then, did British interests survive?

The simple answer is that nothing that happened in Persia was of sufficient consequence to deprive Britain of its position. None of the challenges were able to overcome the inertia of the situation, to organize the disparate elements into a cohesive force able to challenge Britain's position. Then, why all the fuss? Why did officials in London and India concern themselves at all with events in Iran? The answer must lie in the fact that they could not know that the challenges were insubstantial; nor is it possible even now to show that doing nothing would have been better, that it would not have given the opposing forces just the opportunity they needed to create a dangerous situation.

Marling, the Foreign Office, and the Viceroy all appreciated that Persia was a negligible military factor. What concerned them was the unpredictable moral and propaganda effect of having yet another Muslim power join the war against the Allies. The encouragement given by Britain to the Arabs to revolt against their Turkish rulers was in part an attempt to defuse that uncertain threat; and the success of the revolt, though modest, was a lesson in subversion – what Britain could do, others could do to Britain. Thus, it was a 'might be' that motivated concerned officials. In a war people are not inclined to take the long view, the optimistic view that things left to themselves will not get out of hand. The tendency is to act, if only to forestall an eventuality. However unlikely the consequences may seem in the calm of hindsight, in a war the unlikely is commonplace, the stakes are high, and the penalties for failure ignoble. When individuals become involved in situations where everything is a gamble, and they are unwilling to lose, the temptation is to stack the deck.

It should also be remembered that governments act because their agents act. Governments are composed of individuals, each with their own ideas of necessity. In a situation such as the one in Persia it was impossible to restrain local agents from taking actions, and since London and India were dependent on their local representatives for information, those local agents, who did not want to be left out of the excitement, were in a position to stampede their governments into action in the sincere belief that they were being objective. This was a pattern that plagued more than one of the Great Powers before the war, and one for which there was no sure remedy, especially given the consequences of ignoring local representations.

Thus, officials in London and India acted, and despite the clumsiness of those actions British interests survived and prospered, at least in the short term. Another reason this was so was because, however feeble British efforts were, the problems that dogged those efforts, that made shambles of every attempt, also blighted the efforts of Britain's opponents. The diffuseness of power, the lack of regional consensus, and petty, personal rivalry were as much handicaps for the Germans and the Persian nationalists as they were for Marling and the Foreign Office. The British, however, started with a firmer power base. They had Russian support, a strong presence in India, and many years' experience in local politics. This gave them a crucial edge that enabled them to weather the challenges despite the clumsiness of the responses.

This leaves the question of why British policy in Persia was so ineffectual. The chief reason was that Britain had no policy for Persia, or more accurately, it was a negative, reactive policy. In order to have a policy a nation must have a clear idea of its goals and the challenges threatening those goals. It must be able to decide what can and must be done to promote and protect those goals, and it must have a positive idea of its purpose so that it can choose rationally between alternatives and not simply react. This does not mean a nation can know in advance every threat to its interests and have a canned response; but neither can a nation make sound assessments of threats without knowing what is threatened and having some idea of why. This is precisely what Britain did not do or have in Persia, and is one reason why British approaches were so fitful.

The explanation for this has been mentioned earlier, namely, that Britain was not really interested in Persia. Iran was a factor, not a welcome one, in other concerns; and this bifocal vision obscured the need for a direct policy for Persia. The main reason for this, of course, was Persian weaknesses, Persian inability to make the British take them seriously; but even so, events in Persia could and did have an effect on British interests that British policy makers, concentrating on larger issues, were ill prepared and little disposed to handle, a situation complicated by the diffuseness of the British policy-making structure and the rivalry that existed between various elements of the bureaucracy. Too much may be made of this, but the confusion wrought by interdepartmental rivalry cannot be overlooked as a source of Britain's troubles in Persia.

Paradoxically, many of the problems in Anglo-Iranian relations were intimately connected with the very pursuit of British interests in the area. Britain was not directly to blame for Persia's weakness and political factiousness, but efforts to promote British interests, along with the actions of Russia and other powers, exacerbated

Persia's problems. The Persians were ill prepared for forced initiation into the world economy or international relations, and the process had deleterious effects on both Persia's economy and political stability. These were the result of profound processes over which Britain could exercise little control, even though the pursuit of specific interests could compound the overall negative effect. Thus, British policies, even those designed to help Persia, worked against British interests and helped to create a situation requiring more effort which produced more negative results. It was one of many vicious circles that characterized Anglo-Iranian relations.

Nothing illustrates this better than the effort during the war to restore order in south Persia, the area of interest Britain regarded as most legitimately its own. The south had been prone to disorder for some years before the war, a fact that disturbed Anglo-Iranian relations even though British officials appreciated that the Persian Government was weak and the local tribes virtually autonomous. This fact had led to several small expeditions by British forces, attempts to negotiate with local tribal leaders – over the objections of the Persian Government – interference in intra- and inter-tribal affairs, and finally the creation of Swedish-officered gendarmerie. Despite these efforts there was little improvement in the south, and the war only made matters worse, opening up the additional prospect of a German-inspired revolt.

To cope with this situation Marling, the Viceroy, and the Foreign Office all devised a plan of action. First, they tried to get redress through the Persian Government. It had limited effect, initially because the Persian Government refused to remove the Governor-General in Fars during the early years of the war simply because the British insisted he was anti-British; and subsequently because many of the problems of disorder were quite beyond the Government's resources to stop, a fact that Marling and others appreciated, but one they held the Persians responsible for nevertheless. The failure to get the Persian Government to take effective action led to limited direct involvement, with military demonstrations in the Gulf. This, however, did nothing to intimidate the interior and may have made matters worse by antagonizing local sentiments. Next, the British resorted to a tribal policy. They endeavored to secure the cooperation of the two largest tribal groups, the Khamsih and the Qashqa'i. This policy too had limited results for the Khamsih and the Qashqa'i were rivals and it was virtually impossible to harness them together. In addition,

British actions alienated the leader of the Qashqa'i, whom they had humiliated in 1911, and he turned against them. One of the reasons for this was a consequence of the effort to create the South Persia Rifles and to get Farman-Farma as Governor-General of Fars.

Marling and the Foreign Office did not want to rely solely on tribal support and so attempted to add more flexibly to their efforts to secure order in south Persia. This revolved on sending a British mission to Shiraz to create a local levy corps, and on the presence of Farman-Farma, whom the British saw as a strong figure. The problem was that the tribal leaders in Fars saw Farman-Farma as a strong man too, and they did not want him in Shiraz. Though Marling was able to effect a compromise, Sulat al-Daula of the Qashqa'i was not reconciled to having his influence diminished by a representative of the Persian Government and at the same time to standing by while the British organized a constabulary that would reduce his influence even further. He reacted by attacking the South Persia Rifles, many of whose recruits deserted, not having joined the force to fight. Sulat al-Daula's adventure collapsed, but not before disconcerting British policy and requiring a more organized, direct commitment of regular forces to relieve the pressure in the south.

This particular embroglio combined every aspect of British policy in Persia during the war. It included attempts to work through the government, to employ tribal support, to create local levy corps, and the resort to direct force. Singly or in combination, the efforts achieved none of the objectives. Attempts to work through the government failed because the Persian Government counted for little. It was divided and its authority much diminished. The Germans and the nationalists paid it little heed in pursuing their goals, and neither Britain or Russia went very far to support the Persian Government, even though they expected it to act while limiting its ability and scope of action. Furthermore, the other policies pursued by Britain served to undermine further the government's feeble authority and thus the policies worked against each other.

The creation of local levy corps was not a success because too much was expected of them. The various tribal and civilian elements recruited for the various levy corps, such as the South Persia Rifles, were more interested in money than in Britain's reasons for the forces, and did not sell loyalty along with their bodies. In addition, it takes time to raise and train a body of men to perform efficiently. Forces such as the South Persia Rifles also ran counter to local sentiments, and many private citizens as well as tribal leaders resented the interference in Iran's internal affairs. Thus, the force lacked a supportive body of public opinion that could have contributed to the force's morale. Furthermore, there was no political consensus in Persia, and so the fragmentation that made it difficult for the Persian Government to exercise influence, afflicted British efforts as well, and meant that local levies often exacerbated local tensions and rivalries to the detriment of public order.

Efforts to employ tribal support suffered from the same disabilities. There was no unity or political consensus among or within the tribes, and no sense of loyalty to Britain, or anyone else. Many tribal leaders disliked the British, while others liked German gold. And all the tribal leaders used the various competing interests to enhance their own independence and wealth. A policy based on the tribes undermined the Persian Government's ability to influence them, which increased the domestic problems; and it involved British policy in the trickery and endless ins-and-outs of government-tribal relations.

The resort to direct force produced the only guaranteed results, but the forces available for operation in Persia were very limited, and neither the Government of India nor the War Office were prepared to countenance operations in the Persian hinterland. This severely limited the use of direct force until the collapse of Russia forced a reassessment and occasioned a more forward military policy. Until then, Britain had to rely on Russian forces and on the moral effects of its own campaigns in Europe, Gallipoli and Mesopotamia. But reliance on Russian forces brought with it certain disadvantages, chiefly the threat of extending the Russian sphere of influence southward, something the Foreign Office were determined to avoid. It was searching for some alternative to that that gave life to many of the efforts to secure tribal support and to raise the South Persia Rifles.

Finally, British efforts were debilitated by their dependence on personalities. In the fragmented political atmosphere of Persia, in a political system based largely on personalities, this was unavoidable, but it also made it impossible to maintain a consistent approach. As long as relations were based on dealing only with those individuals regarded as trustworthy and loyal, relations were at the mercy of rapidly changing circumstances; and such an approach, by favoring one individual, alienated others and thereby increased the inherent insecurity by aggravating rivalries.

This was demonstrated in the events surrounding the Moratorium, the Sipahsalar Agreement, and the 1919 Agreement. In the last instance, Curzon, like his predecessors, believed that the Persian political system was based on personalities and that the best, the only way, to achieve one's purpose was to work through sympathetic individuals. This, of course, was true; but what Curzon failed to realize was that the underpinnings of that system were changing and with those changes the influence of individuals who derived their power and status from the old system was declining. However much a system may be based on personal politics, that system draws its rationale from a set of accepted ideas and customs; and when those change, the bases for personal authority change. In Persia, personalities remained important, but the social realities giving them power changed and that meant a change in personnel. Curzon and others were not quick enough or were unwilling to accept a diminution of influence and insisted on pinning their approaches on personalities tolerated in office for how accommodating to British interests they could be. The main goal of British policy remained the management of the international situation. But World War I was the breakdown of the international system; and while it brought the destruction of Britain's chief rival, Germany, and removed Russia as a competitor in Persia, it unleashed a variety of local ambitions. In Persia it also destroyed the old system of Great Power checks and balances. This presented British officials with a unique opportunity to resolve the Persian question, but it also gave the Persians an opportunity to escape from the influence of the Great Powers. However much trouble the Russians had given British policy makers, they had at least upheld a particular system of relations. With the collapse of Czarist Russia that support disappeared and with it the old system. That left Curzon and those who sought to secure Britain's position in Persia to deal directly with the Persian situation for the first time.

Curzon's response was to isolate Persia diplomatically and force the Persians to accept an agreement designed to reform Persia in such a way as to contribute to Britain's imperial defense. But the new forces at work in Persia, that Curzon was ill-equipped to appreciate, repudiated the idea and Curzon who had no means to enforce his will, was reduced to fulminating.

NOTES

CHAPTER 1

1. R. L. Greaves' *Britain, Persia and the Defense of India, 1854-92* (London: Athlone Press, 1959) is still the best account of the evolution of Britain's concern for the defense of India and Iran's place in those considerations. Also see her 'British Policy in Persia, 1892-1903,' *Bulletin of the School of Oriental and African Studies* 28 (1965): 34-60 (part I) and 284-307 (part II). A less authoritative study is 'British Policy in Persia, 1858-1890,' *English Historical Review 69* (1954): 554-79 (part I) and 70 (1955): 55-71 (part II), and 'The Reopening of the Central Asian Question, 1864-1869,' *History* 41 (1956): 122-36, by A. P. Thornton. Also see S. F. Shadman, 'A Review of Anglo-Persian Relations, 1789-1815,' *Journal of the Royal Central Asian Society* 31 (1944): 23-39; also R. M. Savory, 'British Policy and French Diplomacy in Persia, 1800-1810, *Iran* 10 (1972): 31-44, for a slightly different perspective on the same period. On other aspects of the question see G. J. Alder, 'Britain and the Defense of India – the Origins of the Problem, 1798-1815,' *Journal of Asian History* 4 (1972): 15-44. A somewhat previous study is Edward Ingram's 'An Aspiring Buffer State: Anglo-Persian Relations in the Third Coalition, 1804-1807,' *Historical Journal* 16 (1973): 509-33; the Persians may have been surprised to know, even at this early date, that they were trying to make themselves a buffer rather than endeavoring to secure an alliance to help defend their frontiers. On Persian foreign policy, see R. K. Ramazani, *The Foreign Policy of Iran, 1500-1914* (Charlottesville: University of Virginia Press, 1966); and the somewhat tendentious *Tarikh-i Ravabat-i Siyasi-yi Iran va Inglis dar Qarn-i Nuzdahom*, 8 vols. (Tehran: Iqbal, n.d.) by Mahmud Mahmud. For an example of the debate on frontier policy, see Ira Klein, 'Who made the Second Afghan War?' *Journal of Asian History* 8 (1974): 97-121.

2. Viscount Sir Edward Grey, *Twenty-five Years, 1892-1916*, 2 vols. (New York: Stokes, 1925), Vol. I: 169. Grey expressed his feelings to Count Benckendorff, Russian Ambassador to London (1903-19), over difficulties in Anglo-Russian relations caused by high-handed Russian measures in Iran to force the Persian Government to dismiss an American financial adviser, Morgan Shuster, who was in Iran at the request of the Persians to reorder the financial administration of the country. For details see Grey's memoirs, cited herein, I: 152-71; Morgan Shuster, *The Strangling of Persia* (New York: Century Co., 1912); Robert McDaniel, *The Shuster Mission and the Persian Constitutional Revolution* (Minneapolis: Bibliotheca Islamica, 1974); Keith Robbins, Sir Edward Grey: *A Biography of Lord Grey of Falloden* (London: Cassell, 1971). Firuz Kazemzadeh, 'Russia vs Morgan Shuster,' *Magazine of the Yale Graduate School* 4 (Fall, 1964): 41-48, is an interesting summary.

3. Viscount Morley, *Recollections*, 2 vols (London: Macmillan, 1929), 2:179. Also quoted in Greaves, 'British Policy,' cited above, I:35.

4. See Greaves, *Britain*, cited above, p. 192ff; also see her other works in the bibliography.

5. See Sir John Malcolm, *A History of Persia*, 2 vols. (London, 1815), II; and Sir Harford Jones Brydges, *An Account of the Transactions of His Majesty's Mission to the Court of Persia in the Years 1807-11*, 2 vols. (London: John Bohn, 1834).

6. See note 1 above for article by Ingrams for some observations of the motives for Britain's interest in Persia.
7. The Russians-are-Coming School gained strength during the latter half of the 19th century and produced a long list of books on the menace. See J. H. Gleason, *The Genesis of Russophobia in Great Britain* (Cambridge: Harvard University Press, 1950); and G. J. Alder's *British India's Northern Frontier, 1865-1895: A Study in Imperial Rivalry* (London: Longmans, 1963). One of the most influential contemporary works was Sir Henry Rawlinson's *England and Russia in the East: A Series of Papers on the Political and Geographical Condition of Central Asia* (London: John Murray, 1875); and in the same vein, George Curzon's *Russia in Central Asia in 1889 and the Anglo-Russian Question* (London: Longmans, Green, 1889) and his *Persia and the Persian Question*, 2 vols. (New York: Barnes & Noble, 1966; first edition, 1892), II. For the military preparations in India, see Adrian Preston, 'Sir Charles MacGregor and the Defence of India, 1857-1887,' *Historical Journal* 12 (1969):58-77; James Allen, 'British Policy toward Persia in 1879,' *Journal of the Royal Central Asian Society* 22 (1935):601-16. The clash of Anglo-Russian interests in Central Asia was often referred to as the 'Great Game'; on this see Edward Ingram, *The Beginning of the Great Game in Asia, 1828-1834* (Oxford: Clarendon Press, 1978), and, *idem*, 'A Preview of the Great Game in Asia – I: The British Occupation of Perim and Aden in 1799,' *Middle Eastern Studies* 9 (1973):3-18; 'II: The Proposal of an Alliance with Afghanistan, 1798-1800,' 157-74; 'III: The Origins of the British Expedition to Egypt in 1801,' 296-314; 'IV: British Agents in the Near East in the War of the Second Coalition, 1798-1801,' 10 (1974):15-35; also, *idem*, 'The Rules of the Game: A Commentary on the Defense of British India, 1798-1829,' *Journal of Imperial and Commonwealth History* 3 (1975):257-79; in addition, see the Raleigh Lectures in History for 1926, 1936, and 1940, H. W. C. Davis, *The Great Game in Asia, 1800-1844*, J. L. Morison, *From Alexander Burnes to Frederick Roberts*, and B. H. Sumner, *Tsardom and Imperialism in the Far East and Middle East, 1880-1914*, respectively Gerald Morgan, 'Myth and Reality in the Great Game,' *Asian Affairs*, New Series, 4 (1975):55-65, is a useful study of military intelligence; Michael Edwardes, *Playing the Great Game: A Victorian Cold War* (London: Hamish Hamilton, 1975); Pierce Fredericks, *The Sepoy and the Cossack* (London: W. H. Allen, 1972) is a popular account but useful; David Gillard, *The Struggle for Asia, 1828-1914: A Study in British and Russian Imperialism* (London: Methuen, 1977). On Russian conquest and policy in Central Asia, see: Edward Allworth (ed.), *Central Asia: A Century of Russian Rule* (New York: Columbia University Press, 1967); Seymour Becker, *Russia's Protectorates in Central Asia: Bukhara and Khiva 1865-1924* (Cambridge: Harvard University Press, 1968); Wayne Vucinich (ed.), *Russia and Asia: Essays on the Influence of Russia on the Asian Peoples* (Standford: Hoover Institute Press, 1972); and the excellent *Russian Central Asia, 1867-1917: A Study in Colonial Rule* (Berkeley: University of California Press, 1960) by Richard Pierce.
8. See G. J. Alder, 'The Key to India?: Britain and the Herat Problem, 1830-1863,' *Middle Eastern Studies* 10 (1974):186-209 (part I) and 287-311 (part II).
9. On British investments, potential and real, and their fate, see Curzon's *Persia*, cited above; Thomas Brockway, 'Britain and the Persian Bubble, 1889-1892,' *Journal of Modern History* 13 (1941):36-47; G. R. G. Hambly, 'An Introduction to the Economic Organization of Early Qajar Iran,' *Iran* 2 (1964):69-82; Charles Issawi, *The Economic History of Iran, 1800-1914* (Chicago: University of Chicago Press, 1971). On Iran's economic problems, Robert McDaniel, 'Economic Change and Economic Resiliency in 19th Century Persia,' *Iranian Studies* 4 (1971):36-49; P. W. Avery and J. P. Simmons, 'Persia on a Cross of Silver, 1880-1890,' *Middle Eastern Studies* 10 (1974):259-86. On reform, see Shaul Bakhash's solid *Iran:*

Monarch, Bureaucracy and Reform under the Qajars: 1858-1896 (London: Ithaca Press for St. Antony's College, Oxford, Middle East Monograph No. 8, 1958). On a Persian development project, see my article 'The Mazanderan Development Project and Hajji Muhammad Hasan: A Study in Persian Entrepreneurship, 1884-1896,' *Iran: Toward Modernity: Studies in Thought, Politics and Society*, ed. by Elie Kedourie and Sylvia Haim (London: Frank Cass, 1980).

10. On the loans, see Firuz Kazemzadeh, *Russia and Britain in Persia, 1864-1914: A Study in Imperialism* (New Haven: Yale University Press, 1968): 302-85; Greaves, 'British Policy, II', cited above, pp. 297ff.

11. The gradual evolution of British policy towards more formal commitment to other powers is a subject of growing interest and is an element in the Eurocentric-exocentric debate. The 'end of isolation' was a pleasant historical fiction, but it does indicate a period of increasing British angst and concern for Empire. On the diplomatic revolution, see George Monger, *The End of Isolation: British Foreign Policy, 1900-1907* (London: Athlone Press, 1964); see Michael Howard's interesting and stimulating *Continental Commitment* (London: Temple Smith, 1972) for a study on various aspects of Britain's growing sense of danger and the need to take a role in European affairs; for an examination of this change of direction and its overall context see Max Beloff, *Imperial Sunset*, Vol. I: *Britain's Liberal Empire, 1897-1921* (London: Methuen, 1969), especially pp. 86-119; see Christopher Howard for a study of the origins of the term 'splendid isolation' in *Splendid Isolation* (London: Macmillan, 1967), as well as his 'The Policy of Isolation,' *Historical Journal* 10 (1967):77-88; Ronald Hyam and Ged Martin, *Reappraisals in British Imperial History* (London: Macmillan, 1976), is good on empire and its place in British thinking; also see L. N. Penson, 'The New Course in British Foreign Policy, 1892-02,' *Royal Historical Society, Transactions* 25 (1943):121-38. For a brief but interesting survey with useful documents, see Kenneth Bourne's *The Foreign Policy of Victorian England, 1830-1902* (Oxford: Clarendon Press, 1970); also see, *The New Cambridge Modern History*, Vol. 12 in both the 1960 edition (*The Era of Violence, 1898-1945*, ed. by David Thomson) and in the 1968 edition (*The Shifting Balance of World Forces, 1898-1945*, ed. by C. L. Mowatt); and the *Cambridge History of British Foreign Policy, 1783-1919*, ed. by A. W. Ward and G. P. Gooch (London: Cambridge University Press, 1922). On the internal developments that affected or reflected British imperial thinking or re-organization, see Bernard Semmell, *Imperialism and Social Reform: English Social-Imperial Thought, 1895-1914* (London: Allen & Unwin, 1960); G. R. Searle, *The Quest for National Efficiency: A Study in British Politics and Political Thought, 1899-1914* (Oxford: Blackwell, 1971); Julian Amery, *Joseph Chamberlain and the Tariff Reform Campaign*, 2 vols. (London: Macmillan, 1969). There are also a variety of studies on changes in British institutions that reflect the need for a new imperial system of priorities. See J. Ehrman, *Cabinet Government and War, 1890-1940* (London: Cambridge University Press, 1958); Zara Steiner, *The Foreign Office and Foreign Policy, 1898-1914* (London: Cambridge University Press, 1970), as well as the other works by Steiner on the Foreign Office and reform in the bibliography. One of the institutional changes of significance was the development of the Committee of Imperial Defense; on its origins and development, see Franklyn Johnson, *Defence by Committee: The British Committee of Imperial Defence, 1885-1959* (London: Oxford University Press, 1960); John MacKintosh, 'The Role of the CID before 1914,' *English Historical Review* 77 (1962):490-503; John Gooch, 'Sir George Clarke's Career at the Committee of Imperial Defense, 1904-1907,' *Historical Journal* 18 (1975): 555-70, reprinted in John Gooch, *The Prospect of War: Studies in British Defence Policy, 1847-1942* (London: Frank Cass, 1981). On the most important figures in

the development of the CID and in later administrative changes, see S. Roskill's excellent study, *Hankey, Man of Secrets*, 3 vols. (London: Collins, 1970-73); Nicholas D'Ombrain, *War Machinery and High Policy: Defence Administration in Peacetime Britain, 1902-1914* (London: Oxford University Press, 1973). There were also attempts to reform the army and navy and to devise a list of priorities for imperial defense. There was also an attempt to involve the colonies more directly in imperial defense, although Britain tried to retain control over imperial power. On army and navy reforms, see Leslie Gardiner, *The British Admiralty* (Annapolis, Md.: U.S. Navy Institute, 1968); Richard Hough, *Admiral of the Fleet: The Life of Sir John Fisher* (New York: Macmillan, 1970); P. M. Kennedy, *The Rise and Fall of British Naval Mastery* (London: Allen Lane, 1976); R. L. MacKay, *Fisher of Kilverstone* (Oxford: Clarendon Press, 1973): D. M. Schurman, *The Education of a Navy: The Development of British Naval Strategic Thought, 1867-1914* (London: Cassell, 1965); the various studies by A. J. Marder and Stephen Roskill on British naval policy and development are among the most essential studies; see Marder's *The Anatomy of British Sea Power: A History of British Naval Policy in the Pre-Dreadnought Era, 1880-1905* (London: Frank Cass, 1964); *idem*, (ed.), *Fear God and Dread Nought*, Vol. II: *Years of Power, 1904-1914* (London: J. Cape, 1952); *idem, From the Dreadnought to Scapa Flow: The Royal Navy in the Fisher Era, 1904-1919* (London: Oxford University Press, 1961), an expanding study that has reached its fifth volume; see Roskill's *Churchill and the Admirals* (London: Collins, 1977); *idem, The Strategy of Sea Power, Its Development and Application* (London: Collins, 1962). On army reforms, see John Dunlop, *Development of the British Army, 1899-1914* (London: Methuen, 1938); John Gooch, *The Plans of War: The General Staff and British Military Strategy c. 1900-1916* (London: Routledge & Kegan Paul, 1974); W. S. Hamer, *The British Army: Civil-Military Relations, 1885-1905* (London: Oxford University Press, 1970); Brian Bond, *The Victorian Army and the Staff College, 1854-1914* (London: Methuen, 1972); A. J. A. Morris, 'Haldane's Army Reforms, 1906-1908: The Deception of the Radicals,' *History* 56 (1971):17-34; Lowell Satre, 'St. John Brodrick and Army Reform, 1901-1903,' *Journal of British Studies* 15 (1976):117-39; Albert Tucker, 'The Issue of Army Reform in the Unionist Government, 1903-5,' *Historical Journal* 9 (1966):90-100. On the development of the Commonwealth and colonial participation in imperial policy formation, see D. C. Gordon, *The Dominion Partnership in Imperial Defence, 1870-1914* (Baltimore: Johns Hopkins Press, 1965); also see his 'The Admiralty and Dominion Navies, 1902-1914,' *Journal of Modern History* 33 (1961):407-22; Richard Preston, *Canada and Imperial Defense: A Study of the Origins of the British Commonwealth's Defense Organization, 1867-1919* (Durham, N.C.: Duke University Press, 1967): John Kendle, *The Colonial and Imperial Conferences, 1887-1911* (London: Longman, 1967); for a general introduction, see Nicholas Mansergh, *The Commonwealth Experience* (London: Weidenfeld and Nicolson, 1969); R. Hyam, *Elgin and Churchill at the Colonial Office, 1905-1908: The Watershed of the Empire-Commonwealth* (London: Macmillan, 1968); Paul Knaplund, *Britain, Commonwealth and Empire, 1901-1955* (New York: Harper, 1957); W. David McIntyre, *The Commonwealth of Nations: Origins and Impact, 1869-1971* (Minneapolis: University of Minnesota Press, 1977); Gwendolin Carter, *The British Commonwealth and International Security: The Role of the Dominions, 1919-1939* (Toronto: Ryerson Press, 1947); Luke Trainor, 'The British Government and Imperial Economic Unity, 1890-1895,' *Historical Journal* 13 (1970):68-84.

12. The Anglo-Japanese alliance, the Anglo-French entente and the Anglo-Russian entente reflected Britain's re-organization of imperial defense and attempts to develop limited international commitments to relieve the strain on Britain and

to check Germany. There is a growing body of literature on this subject. On the Anglo-Japanese alliance, see the essential studies by Ian Nish, *The Anglo-Japanese Alliance: the Diplomacy of Two Island Empires* (London: Athlone Press, 1966), and *Alliance in Decline: A Study in Anglo-Japanese Relations, 1908-23* (London: Athlone Press, 1972); also see the works by Monger and Gleason cited in note 11 above; Peter Lowe, 'The British Empire and the Anglo-Japanese Alliance, 1911-1915,' *History* 54 (1969):212-225; idem, *Great Britain and Japan, 1911-1915* (London: Macmillan, 1969); E. W. Edwards, 'The Japanese Alliance and the Anglo-French Agreement of 1904,' *History* 42 (1957):19-27; Zara Steiner, 'Great Britain and the Creation of the Anglo-Japanese Alliance,' *Journal of Modern History* 31 (1959):27-36. On the Anglo-French entente, see P. J. V. Rolo, *Entente Cordiale: The Origins and Negotiations of the Anglo-French Agreement of 8 April 1904* (London: Macmillan, 1969), a useful short summary but suffers because it uses no unpublished documents; J. D. Hargreaves, 'The Origin of the Anglo-French Military Conversations in 1905,' *History* 36 (1951):244-48; Christopher Andrew, 'France and the Making of the Entente Cordiale,' *Historical Journal* 10 (1967):89-105, as well as his chapter 'The Entente Cordiale from its Origins to 1914' in Neville Waites (ed.), *Troubled Neighbours: Franco-British Relations in the Twentieth Century* (London: Weidenfeld and Nicolson, 1971); S. R. Williamson, *The Politics of Grand Strategy: Britain and France prepare for War, 1904-1914* (Cambridge: Harvard University Press, 1969). On Anglo-Russian relations, see the works cited in note 14 below. On the developing Anglo-German antagonism that induced Britain to pursue closer ties with France and Russia, see E. L. Woodward, *Great Britain and the German Navy* (London: Frank Cass, 1964); R. J. S. Hoffman, *Great Britain and the German Trade Rivalry, 1875-1911* (New York: Russel & Russel, 1964); H. W. Koch, 'The Anglo-German Alliance Negotiations: Missed Opportunity or Myth?' *History* 54 (1969):378-92; M. Langhorne, 'The Naval Question in Anglo-German Relations, 1912-1914,' *Historical Journal* 14 (1971):359-70. For general studies of these issues, see Monger, Gleason, the *New Cambridge Modern History*, all cited above; C. J. Lowe and M. L. Dockrill, *The Mirage of Power*, 3 vols (London: Routledge & Kegan Paul, 1972); idem, *The Reluctant Imperialists: British Foreign Policy under Sir Edward Grey* (London: Cambridge University Press, 1977).

13. Much of the work on this particular subject of European-Asian relations remains to be done, especially for the Middle East. East Asia, Southeast Asia, India, even the African countries, have fared better. There are troubles with comparative examinations but the Iranian experience shares many similarities with the Chinese experience, and as long as one realizes that the differences are important, that there was no single response to the West in either country or that there was no uniform Western impact, a comparison is useful, especially since much preceptive work has been done on China. India, though closer in many ways and sharing many features of the Iranian experience, is less useful because India was actually converted into a subject state while Iran and China remained nominally independent but caught between the rivalries of several powers. For an introduction to China and the West, see J. B. Crowley (ed.), *Modern East Asia; Essays in Interpretation* (New York: Harcourt, Brace & World, 1970), especially the chapters by Paul Cohen, 'Ch'ing China: Confrontation with the West, 1850-1900,' pp. 29-61; and Akira Iriye, 'Imperialism in East Asia,' pp. 122-150. The perceptive intellectual history – the response of intellectuals to the West and change – of Joseph Levinson, *Confucian China and its Modern Fate*, 3 vols. (Berkeley: University of California Press, 1964), and *Liang Chi'i Ch'ao and the Mind of Modern China* (Cambridge: Harvard University Press, 1959) are other important studies. And Mary Wright's *The Last Stand of Chinese Conservatism: The*

T'ung-chih Restoration, 1862-1874 (Stanford: Stanford University Press, 1957) is still a major source on the reaction of traditional societies to change and their methods of coping with it. For the Middle East, see Bernard Lewis' *Middle East and the West* (London: Weidenfeld & Nicolson, 1963); also Norman Daniel, *Islam, Europe and Empire* (Edinburgh: Edinburgh University Press, 1966); P. J. Vatikiotis (ed.), *Revolution in the Middle East and Other Case Studies* (London: Allen & Unwin, 1972); W. R. Polk and R. Chambers (ed.), *The Beginnings of Modernization in the Middle East: The Nineteenth Century* (Chicago: University of Chicago Press, 1968). On Turkish modernization, which has general similarities with Iranian modernization as a result of contact with the West, see Bernard Lewis, *The Emergence of Modern Turkey* (New York: Oxford University Press, 1961); Nivazi Berkes, *The Development of Secularization in Turkey* (Montreal: McGill University Press, 1964); Roderick Davison, *Reform in the Ottoman Empire, 1856-1876* (Princeton: Princeton University Press, 1963); Stanford Shaw and E. Shaw, *History of the Ottoman Empire and Modern Turkey* II: *Reform, Revolution and Republic, 1808-1975* (London: Cambridge University Press, 1977). Kemal Karpat's 'The Transformation of the Ottoman State, 1789-1908,' *International Journal of Middle East Studies* 3 (1972):248-81, is also worth attention. For more detailed studies on Iran, see Hamid Algar's unsympathetic biography of one of Iran's best known modernizers, *Mirza Malkum Khan: A Study in the History of Iranian Modernism* (Los Angeles: University of California Press, 1973); Ann Lambton's 'The Breakdown of Persian Society' in *The Cambridge History of Islam*, Vol. I: *The Central Islamic Lands*, ed. by P. M. Holt, *et al.* (London: Cambridge University Press, 1970):430-67; her 'The Impact of the West on Persia,' *Iranian Affairs* 33 (1957):12-25; and her 'Persian Society Under the Qajars,' *Journal of the Royal Central Asian Society* 48 (1961):123-39. Also see Colin Meridith, 'Early Qajar Administration: An Analysis of Its Development and Function,' *Iranian Studies* 5 (1971):59-84; William Millward, 'Traditional Values and Social Change in Iran,' *Iranian Studies* 4 (1971):2-35; A. Reza Sheikholeslami, 'The Role of the Sale of Offices in Qajar Iran, 1858-1896,' *Iranian Studies* 4 (1971):104-15. Nikki Keddie, 'The Iranian Power Structure and Social Change, 1800-1969: An Overview,' *International Journal of Middle East Studies* 2 (1971):3-20, is a useful summary. On the issue of society and change, see James A. Bill, *The Politics of Iran: Groups, Classes and Modernization* (Columbus: Charles Merrill, 1972); Leonard Binder, *Iran: Political Development in a Changing Society* (Berkeley: University of California Press, 1964); S. N. Eisenstadt, 'Convergence and Divergence of Modern and Modernizing Societies: Indications from the Analysis of the Structuring of Social Hierarchies in Middle Eastern Societies,' *International Journal of Middle East Studies* 8 (1977):1-27; Manfred Halpern, *The Politics of Social Change in the Middle East and North Africa* (Princeton: Princeton University Press, 1963); Daniel Lerner, *The Passing of Traditional Society: Modernizing the Middle East* (New York: The Free Press, 1958); Robert Nisbet, *Tradition and Revolt: Historical and Sociological Essays* (New York: Vintage Books, 1968); Richard Pfaff, 'Disengagement from Traditionalism in Turkey and Iran,' *Western Political Quarterly* 16 (1963):79-98; Benjamin Rivlin and Joseph Szyliowicz (eds.), *The Contemporary Middle East: Tradition and Innovation* (New York: Random House, 1965).

14. The Anglo-Russian entente developed out of the changing international picture after the 1880s and most particularly after the embarrassments of the Boer War. For a review of some of the literature on that shift, see note 12 above. In addition to Grey's memoirs and the other works cited on the Anglo-Russian convention in note 3 above, see R. P. Churchill, *The Anglo-Russian Convention of 1907* (Cedar Rapids, Iowa: Torch Press, 1939); Rose Greaves, 'Some Workings,' cited

above; the articles in Hinsley's *British Foreign Policy,* cited above; and those by
Lowe and Dockrill, *Mirage,* I, cited above; also consult David MacLean, 'Finance
and "Informal Empire" Before the First World War,' *Economic History Review,*
Second Series, 29 (1976):291-305; *idem,* 'English Radicals, Russia and the Fate of
Persia, 1907-1913,' *English Historical Review* 93 (1978):338-52; Beryl Williams,
'The Strategic Background to the Anglo-Russian Convention of August 1907,'
Historical Journal 9 (1966):360-73. Briton Busch, *Britain and the Persian Gulf,
1894-1914* (Los Angeles: University of California Press, 1967), especially pp.
348-83, is of use on Britain's overall interest in the area and on the development
of British policy. For the official diplomatic background, see G. P. Gooch and
Harold Temperley, *British Documents on the Origins of the War, 1898-1914,*
Vol. IV: *The Anglo-Russian Rapprochement, 1903-7* (London: H.M.S.O., 1929).
On British discontent with the Convention and the fact that it needed revision,
see Ira Klein, 'The Anglo-Russian Convention and the Problem of Central Asia,
1907-1914,' *Journal of British Studies* 11 (1971):126-47; Greaves, 'Some
Workings,' Part II, cited earlier; and Vol. 10, Part II, *The Last Years of Peace,*
of *British Documents on the Origins of the War.* On the difficulties for Iran caused
by the convention, see McDaniels, *Shuster Mission,* cited earlier.

15. For the complete text, see J. C. Hurewitz, *Diplomacy in the Near and Middle
East: A Documentary Survey* (New York: Van Nostrand, 1958), Vol. I, pp. 265-7.
16. Grey, *Twenty-Five Years,* cited above, vol. I, p. 166.
17. On Nicolson's position, see Stuart Cohen, 'Sir Arthur Nicolson and Russia: The
Case of the Baghdad Railway,' *Historical Journal* 18 (1975):863-72.
18. The Agreement made a gesture in this direction but Grey made claims to Britain's
special position in the Gulf explicit in a separate declaration made when the two
Powers signed the Convention. See *British Documents,* cited earlier, IV, No. 455,
pp. 501-2.

CHAPTER II

1. Howard Sachar, *The Emergence of the Middle East, 1914-1924* (New York: Knopf,
1969), pp. 1-31, deals with the Ottoman Empire's entrance into the war.
2. For more information on the overall issues of the war in the Middle East, consult
Elizabeth Monroe's valuable *Britain's Moment in the Middle East, 1914-1956*
(London: University Paperbacks, 1965); Fritz Fischer, *Germany's Aims in the
First World War* (New York: W. W. Norton & Co., 1967 [in Germany, 1961]);
Howard Sachar, *ibid.*; Briton Busch, *Britain, India and the Arabs, 1914-1921*
(Berkeley: University of California, 1971); Arnold Wilson, *Loyalties:
Mesopotamia 1914-1917* (London: Oxford University Press, 1930). For a look
at Germany's successful relations with the Ottomans, see Ulrich Trumpener's
revisionist work, *Germany and the Ottoman Empire, 1914-1918* (Princeton:
Princeton University Press, 1968); Frank Weber, *Eagles on the Crescent: Germany,
Austria and the Diplomacy of the Turkish Alliance, 1914-1918* (Ithaca: Cornell
University Press, 1970), which takes a revisionist look at the inter-relationships
that shaped the Central Power alliance. On the war between the Ottomans and
the Russians, see W. E. D. Allen and Paul Muratoff, *Caucasian Battlefields: A
History of the Wars on the Turco-Caucasian Border, 1828-1921* (London:
Cambridge University Press, 1953).
3. On the development of India's role in the war in Mesopotamia, consult Briton
Busch, *ibid.* Also see Stuart Cohen, *British Policy in Mesopotamia, 1903-1914*
(London: Ithaca Press, 1976) for general British interest in Mesopotamia.
4. In recent years considerable new work has been done on Sir Edward Grey's years
at the Foreign Office. The man, however, remains an enigma. For some of the most

recent material, see the varied articles in F. H. Hinsley (ed.), *British Foreign Policy under Sir Edward Grey* (Cambridge: Cambridge University Press, 1977), plus the works by Zara Steiner mentioned in the bibliography. Also consult the notes to Chapter I above, especially numbers 2, 11, and 12. In addition, see Roberta Warman, 'The Erosion of Foreign Office Influence in the Making of Foreign Policy, 1916-1918,' *Historical Journal* 15 (1972):133-59; Howard Weinroth, 'The British Radicals and the Balance of Power, 1902-1914,' *Historical Journal* 13 (1970):653-82; Alan Sharp, 'The Foreign Office in Eclipse, 1919-22,' *History* 61 (1976):198-218; John Murray, 'Foreign Policy Debated: Sir Edward Grey and His Critics, 1911-1912' in *Power, Public Opinion, and Diplomacy: Essays in Honor of Eber Malcolm Carroll by His Former Students*, ed. by Lillian Parker Wallace and William Askew (Durham, N.C.: Duke University Press, 1959); Helmut Mejcher, 'British Middle Eastern Policy 1917-21: The Inter-departmental Level,' *Journal of Contemporary History* 8 (1973):81-101; Edward Corp, 'Sir Eyre Crowe and the Administration of the Foreign Office, 1906-1914,' *Historical Journal* 22 (1979):443-54.

5. Muvarikh ad-Daula Sipihr, *Iran dar Jang-i Buzurg, 1914-1918* (Tehran: no publisher, 1336 Shamsi), pp. 18-19.

6. On the development of British policy in Mesopotamia, see Busch, *op. cit.*; Stuart Cohen, *op. cit.*; also see Cohen's 'Mesopotamia in British Strategy, 1903-1914,' *International Journal of Middle East Studies* 9 (1978):171-81, for a summary of pre-war British thinking. On British policy and Ottoman involvement, see Joseph Heller, 'Sir Louis Mallet and the Ottoman Empire: The Road to War,' *Middle Eastern Studies* 12 (1976):3-44; Allan Cunningham, 'The Wrong Horse? – A Study of Anglo-Turkish Relations before the First World War,' *St. Antony's Papers No. 17, Middle Eastern Affairs No. 4* (London, 1965):56-76; Howard Sachar, *op. cit.*, which, despite its title, deals with the Ottoman Empire and the war. On aspects of German involvement in the Middle East, see Ulrich Trumpener, *Germany and the Ottoman Empire*, cited above, as well as his other works mentioned in the bibliography. Cf., Weber, *Eagles on the Crescent*, cited above, who, along with Trumpener, gives a revisionist account of the relations among the Central Powers.

7. For information on the background and history of the Mesopotamian campaign, consult Brigadier-General F. J. Moberly's exhaustive, *History of the Great War Based on Official Documents, The Campaign in Mesopotamia, 1914-1918*, 4 vols. (London: H.M.S.O., 1927); A. J. Barker, *The Neglected War: Mesopotamia, 1914-1918* (London: Faber & Faber, 1967); S. A. Cohen, 'The Genesis of the British Campaign in Mesopotamia, 1914,' *Middle Eastern Studies* 12 (May 1976):119-32; V. H. Rothwell, 'Mesopotamia in British War Aims, 1914-1918,' *Historical Journal* 13 (1970):273-94; Douglas Goold, 'Lord Hardinge and the Mesopotamia Expedition and Inquiry, 1914-1917,' *Historical Journal* 19 (1976):919-45; Aaron Klieman, 'Britain's War Aims in the Middle East in 1915,' *Journal of Contemporary History* 3 (1968):237-51; Helmut Melcher, *Imperial Quest for Oil: Iraq, 1910-1928* (London: Ithaca Press, 1976) – this book, like the works by Stuart Cohen and Marian Kent mentioned in the bibliography, place too much emphasis on oil in British policy formation before 1919. Also consult the Government of India's *Precis of Correspondence Regarding the Mesopotamian Expedition – Its Genesis and Development*, WO 106/52; for other information on the campaign see CAB 24/2/12 G Series, which contains views of Lord Kitchener; CAB 37/123 for a memorandum by General E. G. Barrow, Military Secretary to the India Office on the importance of the Middle East; and CAB 37/162/32 for a Memorandum by Arthur Hardinge on the Mesopotamian campaign. This memorandum reviews British strategic commitments and military

plans in the area before the war and then discusses the development of the campaign itself. Two works by Arnold Wilson, *Loyalties: Mesopotamia 1914-1917*, cited above, and *Mesopotamia, 1917-1920: A Clash of Loyalties: A Personal and Historical Record* (London: Oxford University Press, 1931), also provide details on the origins of the campaign and its development. In addition to other standard histories there are also numerous memoirs, too extensive to list here, of the campaign by the soldiers who fought in it and the politicians who opposed or promoted it.

8. Viceroy-Grey, 9/10/14, FO 371/2080. On other aspects of tension in the Anglo-Russian alliance, especially in relation to the Straits Question, see: Rothwell, *op. cit.*; Michael Ekstein, 'Russia, Constantinople and the Straits, 1914-1915,' in F. H. Hinsley, *op. cit.*, 423-35; Robert Kerner, 'Russia, the Straits, and Constantinople, 1914-1915,' *Journal of Modern History* 1 (1929):400-15; C. J. Smith, Jr., 'Great Britain and the 1914-1915 Straits Agreement with Russia: The British Promise of November 1914,' *American Historical Review* 70 (1965):1015-34; William Renzi, 'Great Britain, Russia and the Straits, 1914-1915,' *Journal of Modern History* 42 (1970):1-20. For background information, see Barbara Jelavich, *The Ottoman Empire, the Great Powers, and the Straits Question, 1870-1887* (Bloomington, Ind.: Indiana University Press, 1973); William Langer, 'Russia, the Straits Question and the European Powers, 1904-1918,' *English Historical Review* 44 (1929):59-85; George Zotiades, 'Russia and the Question of Constantinople and the Turkish Straits during the Balkan Wars,' *Journal of Balkan Studies* 11 (1970):281-98.

9. Moberly, *Mesopotamian Campaign*, I, pp. 78-79.

10. Townley-Grey, 11/2/14, FO 371/2080.

11. Townley-Grey, 9/5/14, FO 371/2080.

12. Townely-Grey, 9/24/14 and 10/1/14, FO 371/2080; Townley-Grey 10/14/14 and 10/16/14 and 10/14/14, FO 371/2080; Buchanan-Grey, 10/3/14 and Townley-Grey, 10/8/14, FO 371/2080.

13. Townley-Grey, 11/2/14, FO 371/2080; see note 10.

14. Minute by Lancelot Oliphant to Buchanan-Grey, 10/6/14, FO 371/2080.

15. Persian Minister of Foreign Affairs – Vice-Governor of Azerbaijan, 10/16/14, No. 21, p. 11 and MFA – Persian Ambassador Constantinople, 10/17/14, No. 24, pp. 13-14 and MFA – Sublime Porte, 10/24/14, No. 27, p. 15, *Neutralité Persane: Documents Diplomatiques* (Ministères Des Affaires Etrangères Empire de Perse, no date). In subsequent references, this work will be abbreviated to '*N.P.*' MFA – Persian Ambassador London, 10/27/14, No. 29, p. 16 and MFA – Turkish Ambassador to Iran, 10/29/14, No. 34, pp. 19-20, *N.P.*, cited above.

16. Russian Minister of Foreign Affairs-Persian Minister of Foreign Affairs, No. 88, p. 50, *N.P.*, *ibid.*

17. Grey-Russian MFA, 11/10/14, FO 371/2080.

18. Note from Benckendorff-FO, 11/12/14, FO 371/2080.

19. Grey-Buchanan, 11/12/14, FO 371/2080.

20. Buchanan-Grey, 11/14/14, FO 371/2080.

21. For information on the see-saw campaigns in Azerbaijan and the Caucasus, consult Allen and Muratoff, *Caucasian Battlefields*, cited above; Ahmad Kasravi, *Tarikh-i Hizhda Sala-yi Azirbaijan* (Tehran: Amir-i Kabir Press, 1350 Shamsi), pp. 592-602.

22. Turkish Ambassador – Persian MFA, No. 104, pp. 57-58; Persian MFA – Turkish Ambassador, No. 105, pp. 58-59, *N.P.*, cited above.

23. Townley-Grey, 11/21/14, FO 371/2080; Grey-Buchanan, 11/23/14, FO 371/2080.

24. Townley-Grey, 11/18/14, FO 371/2080.

25. Townley-Grey, 11/24/14; Townley-Grey, 11/18/14 (see note 24 above); Townley-Grey, 11/20/14, FO 371/2080; Buchanan-Grey, 12/4/14, FO 371/2080.

26. Brig.-Gen. F. J. Moberly, *Operations in Persia, 1914-1919: History of the Great War Based on Official Documents* (CAB 44/37), p. 60. Like his work on Mesopotamia this is an exhaustive review of British activities in Persia during the war. Unlike the history of the Mesopotamian campaign this work was deemed too sensitive politically and was never published. Townley-Grey, 12/28/14 and minute by George R. Clerk, FO 370/2080.

27. Persian MFA – Russian Minister, 12/19/14, No. 131, p. 73, and Persian MFA – Russian Minister, 12/23/14, No. 148, pp. 88-89, *N.P.*, cited above; Townley-Grey, 12/30/14, FO 371/2080.

28. Townley-Grey, 1/29/15, FO 371/2427.

29. Letter from Townley-Grey, 1/18/15, Grey Papers FO 800/70.

30. Letter from Townley-Grey, 1/18/15, *ibid.*

31. Persian MFA – Persian Ambassadors, London and Petrograd, 1/16/15, No. 155, p. 94; and Persian MFA – Persian Ambassador, Constantinople, 1/17/15, No. 156, pp. 94-95, *N.P.*, cited above.

32. Townley-Grey, 1/7/15, FO 371/2427; and Letter from Townley-Grey, 1/18/15, *op. cit.*

33. Persian Ambassador, London-MFA, 1/13/15, No. 168, p. 102; Karguzar of Qazvin-MFA, 1/14/15, No. 70, p. 102; Persian Ambassador, Constantinople-MFA, 1/14/15, No. 171, p. 103, *N.P.*, cited above.

34. Letter from Townley-Grey, 1/18/15, cited above.

35. Translation of a Persian circular enclosed in Townley-Grey, 12/30/14, FO 371/2431.

36. For information on party organization and activities, see Malik ash-Shu'ara Bahar, *Tarikh-i Mukhtisar-i Ihzab-i Siyasi: Inqiraz-i Qajariya* (NP: n.p., 1323 Shamsi); Ali Ashgar Shamim, *Iran dar Daura-yi Saltanat-i Qajar* (Tehran: Ibn Sina, 1342 Shamsi); Hasan 'Izam Qudsi, *Khatirat-i Man ya Rushan Shudan-i Tarikh-i Sad Sala*, 2 vols. (Tehran: Abu Raihan Press, n.d.); and Sipihr, *Jang-i Buzurg*, cited above.

CHAPTER III

1. Townley-Nicolson, 10/29/14, FO 800/376, Nicolson Papers.
2. Buchanan-Grey, 1/11/15, FO 371/2427.
3. Grey-Buchanan, 1/18/15, FO 371/2427.
4. India Office-FO, 2/15/15, FO 371/2428.
5. Townley-Grey, 2/9/15, FO 371/2427.
6. Nicolson-Buchanan, 3/15/15, FO 800/377, Nicolson Papers.
7. Grey-Townley, 2/18/15, FO 371/2427.
8. Townley-Grey, 2/21/15, with a minute by Grey, FO 371/2427.
9. Townley-Nicolson, 10/29/14, FO 800/376, Nicolson Papers.
10. *Ibid.*
11. Marling-Grey, 3/15/15, FO 371/2429.
12. Muvarikh ad-Daula Sipihr, *Iran dar Jang-i Buzurg, 1914-1918* (Tehran: no publisher, 1336 Shamsi), pp. 140-1.
13. *Ibid.*, p. 142.
14. *Ibid.*
15. Despatch from Townley to Grey, 1/18/15, FO 371/2431.
16. Townley-Grey, 2/2/15, FO 371/2427.
17. Sipihr, *Jang-i Buzurg*, cited above, p. 151.
18. *Ibid.*
19. Townley-Grey, 3/16/15, FO 371/2429.

20. Townley-Grey, 3/20/15; Same-Same, 3/21/15, FO 371/2429.
21. Townley-Grey, 3/21/15, FO 371/2429.
22. Townley-Grey, 3/24/15, FO 371/2429.
23. Townley-Grey, 4/3/15, FO 371/2429.
24. Moberly, *Operations in Persia, 1914-1919: History of the Great War Based on Official Documents*, CAB 44/37, p. 61.
25. Townley-Grey, 4/5/15, FO 371/2429.
26. Cox-Secretary General for India (hereafter referred to as SGI), 3/27/15, FO 371/2429.
27. Minutes by L. Oliphant and G. Clerk to Grey-Townley, 4/12/15, FO 371/2429; Townley-Grey, 4/14/15, FO 371/2429.
28. Marling-Grey, 4/23/15, FO 371/2430.
29. Sipihr, *Jang-i Buzurg*, cited above, p. 160; despatch from Marling-Grey, 5/18/15, FO 371/2430.
30. Viceroy-IO, 3/11/15, FO 371/2427; Viceroy-IO, 4/8/15, FO 371/2427; Records of a meeting with Persian Ambassador, 4/9/15 and 4/10/15, FO 371/2429.
31. Grey-Townley, 5/16/15, FO 371/2429.
32. Cox-SGI, 4/19/15, FO 371/2429.
33. Siphir, *Jang-i Buzurg*, cited above, p. 161.
34. Marling-Grey, 4/23/15, FO 371/2427.
35. Minute by A. Nicolson to Marling-Grey, 4/23/15, FO 371/2427; Moberly, *Operations*, cited above, p. 63.
36. Sipihr, *Jang-i Buzurg*, cited above, p. 163.
37. Marling-Grey, 4/27/15, FO 371/2427.
38. Sipihr, *Jang-i Buzurg*, cited above, pp. 168-70.
39. Marling-Grey, 4/28/15, FO 371/2427.
40. Marling-Grey, 5/1/15, FO 371/2427.
41. Grey-Marling, 5/4/15, FO 371/2427.
42. Hardinge-Nicolson, 7/8/15, FO 800/376, Nicolson Papers.
43. Marling-Grey, 5/12/15, FO 371/2427; Grey-Buchanan, 5/14/15, FO 371/2427.
44. Marling-Grey, 7/1/15, FO 371/2428; Marling-Grey, 7/7/15, FO 371/2428; Moberly, *Operations*, cited above, p. 68.
45. Marling-Grey, 5/16/15; Marling-Grey, 5/16/15; Grey-Marling, 5/16/15, FO 371/2427; Marling-Grey, 5/18/15, FO 371/2430.
46. Report by A. P. Trevor, Persian Gulf Resident, 7/3/15, FO 371/2432.
47. Marling-SGI, 5/20/15, FO 371/2430.
48. Marling-Grey, 6/16/15, FO 371/2428.
49. Marling-Grey, 7/7/15, FO 371/2428.
50. Viceroy-IO, 5/15/15, FO 371/2432.
51. Viceroy-IO, 5/29/15, FO 371/2430.
52. Minute by G. R. Clerk to note from Russian Ambassador, 5/25/15, FO 371/2432; Marling-Grey, 5/30/15; Grey-Marling, 6/1/15, FO 371/2430.
53. Marling-Grey, 6/10/15, FO 371/2428.
54. *Ibid.*
55. Grey-Marling, 6/12/15, FO 371/2428.
56. Marling-Grey, 6/21/15, FO 2428.
57. FO-IO, 6/24/15, FO 371/2428.
58. FO-IO, 7/2/15, FO 371/2428.
59. Cox-SGI, 5/22/15; Same-Same, 6/13/15, FO 371/2430; A. P. Trevor, Resident Report No. 4, 7/3/15, FO 371/2432.
60. *Ibid.*
61. Viceroy-Consuls of Mashad, Bushire, Sistan, 7/2/15, FO 371/2430.
62. Viceroy-Consul, Sistan, 7/6/15, FO 371/2430.

63. Marling-SGI, 7/4/15, FO 2430.
64. IO-Viceroy, 7/7/15; Grey-Marling, 7/9/15, FO 371/2433.
65. IO-FO, 7/13/15, FO 371/2433.
66. IO-Viceroy, 7/7/15, FO 371/2430.
67. Viceroy-IO, 7/8/15, FO 371/2430.
68. Hasan Izam Qudsi, *Khatirat-i Man ya Rushan Shudan-i Tarikh-i Sad Sala*, 2 vols. (Tehran: Abu Raihan Press, n.d.), I, p. 280; Sipihr, *ibid.*, p. 180.
69. Sipihr, *ibid.*, pp. 182-3.
70. Qudsi, *Khatirat-i Man*, I, cited above, p. 280; Sipihr, *ibid.*, p. 180.
71. Marling-Grey, 6/7/15, FO 371/2428; Marling-Grey, 9/1/15, FO 371/2433.
72. FO-Marling, 7/6/15, FO 371/2428.
73. Marling-Grey, 7/10/15, FO 371/2428.
74. Sipihr, *Jang-i Buzurg*, cited above, p. 184; Marling-SGI, 7/12/15, FO 371/2428.
75. For the background to Wassmuss' activities, see Christopher Sykes, *Wassmuss: The German Lawrence* (New York: Longmans, Green & Co., 1936), pp. 97-99.
76. Moberly, *Operations*, p. 87.
77. Marling-Grey, 7/13/15, FO 371/2430.
78. Marling-Grey, 7/15/15, FO 371/2433.
79. Viceroy-IO, 7/17/15, FO 371/2430.
80. Marling-Grey, 7/18/15; Same-Same, 7/19/15, FO 371/2433; Cox-SGI, 7/17/15, FO 371/2433; SGI-Cox, 7/24/15, FO 371/2431; Admiralty-FO, 7/17/15, FO 371/2431.
81. Letter from Marling-A. Nicolson, 7/21/15, Grey Papers FO 800/70.
82. *Ibid.*
83. Cox-SGI, 7/16/15, FO 371/2431; Viceroy-IO, 8/11/15, FO 371/2433; Marling-Grey, 8/19/15, FO 371/2433.
84. Sipihr, *Jang-i Buzurg*, cited above, pp. 186-8.
85. *Ibid.*, pp. 188-9; Kasravi, *Tarikh-i Hizhda Sala*, p. 625.
86. *Ibid.*, Sipihr, cited above, pp. 194-5.
87. *Ibid.*, p. 197.
88. *Ibid.*, p. 198.
89. Marling-Grey, 8/29/15, FO 371/2431.
90. Consul, Sistan-SGI, 8/2/15, FO 371/2431.
91. Marling-Grey, 9/1/15, FO 371/2433.
92. Marling-Grey, 8/31/15, FO 371/2433; Marling-Grey, 9/2/15; FO 371/2433; Marling-SGI, 9/2/15, FO 371/2431.
93. Marling-Grey, 9/4/15, FO 371/2434.
94. *Ibid.*
95. Viceroy-IO, 9/6/15, FO 371/2434.
96. Marling-Grey, 9/7/15, FO 371/2434.
97. Grey-Marling, 9/9/15, FO 371/2434.
98. Persian MFA-Marling, 9/2/15; Marling-Persian MFA, 9/5/15, FO 371/2436; Marling-Grey, 9/9/15, FO 371/2434.
99. *Ibid.*
100. Marling-Grey, 9/12/15 and FO-Treasury, 9/12/15, FO 371/2434.
101. Marling-Grey, 9/13/15, FO 371/2435.
102. Treasury-FO, 9/16/15, FO 371/2434.
103. IO-FO, 9/24/15, FO 371/2434.
104. Marling-Grey, 9/22/15; Marling-Grey, 9/19/15; Grey-Marling, 9/26/15, FO 371/2434.
105. Cox-SGI repeating telegram from Marling-FO, 9/17/15, FO 371/2434; Marling-Grey, 9/18/15, FO 371/2436.
106. Despatch from Marling-Grey, 11/22/15; Marling-Grey, 9/26/15, FO 371/2434.

107. Grey-Marling, 9/30/15, FO 371/2435.
108. Grey-Buchanan, 10/2/15, FO 371/2435.
109. Marling-Grey, 10/13/15, FO 371/2435.
110. Despatch from Marling-Grey, 11/22/15, FO 371/2435.
111. *Ibid.*
112. FO-Marling, 10/13/15, FO 371/2435.
113. Marling-Oliphant, 10/13/15, FO 371/2435.
114. Marling-Grey, 10/21/15, FO 371/2435.
115. *Ibid.*
116. Marling-Grey, 10/21/15, FO 371/2436.
117. Marling-Grey, 10/27/15, FO 371/2435; Marling-Grey, 10/28/15, FO 371/2435.
118. Buchanan-Grey, 10/29/15, FO 371/2435.
119. Marling-Grey, 11/1/15; Same-Same, 11/2/15, FO 371/2435.
120. Marling-Grey, 11/3/15, FO 371/2435.
121. Viceroy-IO, 10/21/15, FO 371/2436.
122. Lt. Col. Sir Frederick O'Connor, *On the Frontiers and Beyond: A Record of Thirty Years Service* (London: John Murray, 1931), pp. 231-4.
123. Grey-Marling, 11/3/15, FO 371/2436; Sipihr, *Jang-i Buzurg*, cited above, pp. 219-224; Marling-Grey, 11/5/15 and 11/6/15 and 11/8/15, FO 371/2435. See Sipihr, *Jang-i Buzurg*, cited above, for more information on the episode. Also see Qudsi, *Khatarat-i Man*, cited above, and Amanallah Ardilan and Hosayn Sami'i, *Avvalin Qiyam-i Muqdis-i Mili dar Jang-i Bayn al Milali-yi Avval ya Khataratha-yi Aqa-yi Husayn Sami'i (Adib as-Saltana) va Aqa-yi Amanallah Ardilan (Haj Az al-Mamlik)* (Tehran: Ibn Sina, 1324 Shamsi).
124. Marling-Grey, 11/9/15, FO 371/2435.
125. Grey-Marling, 11/10/15, FO 371/2435.
126. Marling-Grey, 11/10/15, FO 371/2435.
127. Sir F. Vithier-Grey, 11/11/15; Buchanan-Grey, 11/11/15; Marling-Grey, 11/12/15, FO 371/2435.
128. Sami'i, *Avvalin Qiyam*, cited above, pp. 16-17.
129. Buchanan-Grey, 11/13/15, FO 371/2435.
130. Sipihr, *Jang-i Buzurg*, p. 237.
131. Marling-SGI, 12/22/15, FO 371/2435; Marling-Grey, 11/16/15, FO 371/2437.

CHAPTER IV

1. Minutes by L. Oliphant and A. Nicolson to Buchanan-Grey, 11/18/15, FO 371/2437.
2. Marling-Grey, 11/23/15, FO 371/2437.
3. Minute by E. Grey to Marling-Grey, 11/21/15, FO 371/2436.
4. Grey-Marling, 11/23/15, FO 371/2437.
5. Grey-Marling, 11/24/15, FO 371/2437.
6. FO-Buchanan, 12/1/15, FO 371/2436.
7. Viceroy-IO, 11/15/15, FO 371/2436; Marling-Grey, 11/26/15, FO 371/2437.
8. Marling-Grey, 12/5/15, FO 371/2438.
9. Buchanan-Grey, 12/8/15, FO 371/2438.
10. Minutes by Lord Crewe (Acting for Grey), G. R. Clerk, and H. Nicolson, *ibid.*
11. War Office Army Council-FO, 12/9/15, FO 371/2438.
12. IO-FO, 12/9/15, FO 371/2438.
13. FO-Buchanan, 12/15/15, FO 371/2438.
14. Marling-Grey, 12/13/15, FO 371/2438, with minutes by H. Nicolson and G. R. Clerk on financing the Shah.

15. IO-FO, 12/17/15; Grey-Marling, 12/15/15, FO 371/2438.
16. Buchanan-Grey, 12/18/15; Marling-Grey, 12/18/15; Buchanan-Grey, 12/15/15; Marling-Grey, 12/17/15, FO 371/2438.
17. Marling-Grey, 12/22/15; Grey-Marling, 12/23/15, FO 371/2438.
18. Marling-Grey, 12/11/15; Same-Same, 12/12/15 and minute by Lord Crewe, FO 371/2438; Hasan Izam Qudsi, *Khatirat-i Man ya Rushan Shudan-i Tarikh-i Sad Sala*, 2 vols. (Tehran: Abu Raihan Press, n.d.), pp. 295-7.
19. Marling-Grey, 3/24/16, FO 371/2733.
20. Grey-Marling, 1/4/16, FO 371/2731.
21. Marling-Grey, 1/12/16, with a minute by A. Nicolson, FO 371/2731.
22. Marling-Grey, 1/14/16, FO 371/2731.
23. Marling-Grey, 1/13/16; a minute by L. Oliphant to Marling-Grey, 1/14/16, FO 371/2731.
24. Marling-Grey, 1/16/16, FO 371/2731.
25. Marling-Grey, 1/19/16, FO 371/2731.
26. Buchanan-Grey, 1/22/16, FO 371/2731.
27. Marling-Grey, 1/28/16, FO 371/2731.
28. IO-FO, 1/29/16, FO 371/2731.
29. Marling-Grey, 2/4/16; FO 371/2731.
30. Marling-Grey, 2/3/16; FO 371/2731.
31. Minute by L. Oliphant to letter from IO, 1/29/16 (see note 28), FO 371/2731.
32. FO-IO, 2/4/16, FO 371/2731.
33. IO-FO, 2/8/16, FO 371/2731.
34. IO-FO, 2/9/16, FO 371/2731.
35. Grey-Marling, 2/17/16, FO 371/2731.
36. Marling-Grey, 2/3/16, FO 371/2731.
37. Marling-Grey, 3/12/16; Buchanan-Grey, 3/16/16; Same-Same, 3/27/16, FO 371/2731.
38. Marling-Grey, despatch 105, 8/26/16, FO 371/2733.
39. Marling-Grey, despatch 36, 3/24/16, FO 371/2733.
40. Marling-Grey, 4/9/16, FO 371/2731.
41. Buchanan-Grey, 4/21/16, FO 371/2731.
42. Marling-Grey, 3/15/16, FO 371/2731.
43. Minute by Grey to Marling-Grey, 3/15/16, FO 371/2735.
44. Marling-Grey, 3/23/16, FO 371/2735.
45. Marling-Grey, 8/26/16, FO 371/2733.
46. Copy of the dossier of the Persian Cabinet fixing the powers of the Mixed Financial Commission, FO 371/2730.
47. Marling-Grey, 5/27/16, FO 371/2736.
48. Marling-Grey, 6/24/16, FO 371/2736.
49. Marling-Grey, 7/11/16; Buchanan-Grey, 7/21/16; Buchanan-Grey, 7/26/16; Grey-Marling, 7/28/16, FO 371/2731.
50. For a discussion of this episode, see Briton Busch, *Britain, India and the Arabs, 1914-1921* (Berkeley: University of California Press, 1971); Brig.-Gen. F. J. Moberly, *History of the Great War Based on Official Documents: The Campaign in Mesopotamia, 1914-1918*, 4 vols. (London: H.M.S.O., 1927); Arnold Wilson, *Loyalties: Mesopotamia 1914-1918* (London: Oxford University Press, 1930); and Sir Charles Townsend, *My Campaign in Mesopotamia* (London: Thornton Butterworth, 1920), the memoirs of the British commander at Kut.
51. Marling-Grey, despatch 105, *op. cit.*
52. Marling-Grey, 7/15/16, FO 371/2737.
53. Marling-Grey, 8/2/16, FO 371/2736.
54. Minute by Harold Nicolson, *ibid.*; Marling-Grey, 8/14/16, FO 371/2736.

55. Marling-Grey, 8/7/16, FO 371/2736.
56. Marling-Grey, despatch 105, *op. cit.*
57. Marling-Grey, unnumbered despatch, 9/16/16, FO 371/2736.
58. Marling-Grey, 8/13/16, FO 371/2736; *ibid.*

CHAPTER V

1. See Floreda Safiri, 'A History of the South Persia Rifles: 1918-1921,' (D. Phil., University of Edinburgh, April 1976), for the most detailed account. Sir Percy Sykes' own account in Vol. II of his *History of Persia* leaves much to be desired.
2. Based on a personal interview with C. J. Edmonds, July, 1976.
3. Marling-Grey, 1/9/16, FO 371/2732.
4. Marling-Grey, 1/9/16 and 1/10/16, FO 371/2732.
5. Marling-Grey, 1/12/16, FO 371/2732.
6. Minute by L. Oliphant to Marling-Grey, 1/9/16; DMI-FO, 1/14/16, FO 371/2732.
7. Viceroy-Secretary of State for India (hereafter, SSI), 1/19/16, FO 371/2732.
8. IO-FO, 1/19/16, FO 371/2732.
9. Marling-Grey, 1/23/16, FO 371/2732.
10. Viceroy-SSI, 1/28/16, FO 371/2732.
11. Moberly, *Operations in Persia, 1914-1919: History of the Great War Based on Official Documents* (CAB 44/37), p. 142; minutes of Interdepartmental Conference, 2/21/16, FO 371/2732.
12. Grey-Marling, 3/1/16, FO 371/2725; Moberly, *ibid.*, p. 151.
13. Viceroy-SSI, 3/16/16, FO 371/2725.
14. Minutes by L. Oliphant and Lord Crewe, *ibid.*
15. Sykes-Secretary to the Government of India (hereafter, SGI), 3/17/16, FO 371/2732; Treasury-Grey, 3/30/16; Grey-Treasury, 4/30/16 and 5/5/16, FO 371/2732.
16. Sykes-SGI, 4/9/16, FO 371/2726.
17. IO-FO, 5/16/16, FO 371/2725.
18. Viceroy-SSI, 5/30/16, FO 371/2726.
19. Marling-Grey, 5/31/16, FO 371/2726.
20. Viceroy-SSI, 6/9/16, FO 371/2726.
21. Marling-Grey, 6/11/16; SSI-Viceroy, 6/21/16; Viceroy-SSI, 6/3/16, FO 371/2726.
22. Marling-Grey, 8/14/16, FO 371/2726.
23. Viceroy-SSI, 8/13/16, FO 371/2726.
24. Viceroy-SSI, 8/7/16, FO 371/2726.
25. Minute by L. Oliphant to IO-FO, 8/10/16, FO 371/2726.
26. SSI-Viceroy, 8/22/16; Marling-Grey, 8/28/16, FO 371/2726.
27. Marling-Grey, 8/16/16; FO-IO, 8/18/16; Viceroy-SSI, 8/21/16, FO 371/2726.
28. Marling-Grey, 8/25/16; Grey-Marling, 8/26/16; Viceroy-SSI, 8/23/16; Same-Same, 8/27/16 and 8/20/16, FO 371/2726.
29. Marling-Grey, 8/30/16, FO 371/2726; Sykes-SGI, 9/3/16, FO 371/2727; IO-FO, 9/5/16; FO-IO, 9/9/16, Fo 371/2726.
30. IO-FO, 9/13/16; FO-IO, 9/19/16, FO 371/2726.
31. Minutes by H. Nicolson and G. R. Clerk to Marling-Grey, 7/1/16, FO 371/2724.
32. SSI-Viceroy, 9/20/16; Viceroy-SSI, 9/26/16; FO-IO, 10/4/16, FO 371/2726.
33. IO-FO, 10/9/16, FO 371/2726.
34. IO-FO, 10/9/16 with minute by L. Oliphant, FO 371/2726.
35. Marling-Grey, 11/22/16, FO 371/2736.
36. Marling-Grey, 11/23/16, FO 371/2736.
37. Minute by G. R. Clerk to Marling-Grey, 11/23/16, FO 371/2736.

38. Letter from Lord Curzon, 11/25/16, FO 371/2736.
39. IO-FO, 11/29/16, FO 371/2736.
40. Grey-Marling, 12/2/16, FO 371/2736.
41. Marling-Grey, 12/21/16 and 12/24/16, FO 371/2736.
42. Marling-Balfour, 1/13/17, FO 371/2983.
43. Marling-Balfour, 1/23/17, FO 371/2983.
44. *Ibid.*
45. Marling-Balfour, 3/13/17, FO 371/2983.
46. Marling-Balfour, 3/20/17; Balfour-Marling, 3/23/17, FO 371/2983.
47. Marling-Balfour, 5/11/17, FO 371/2988.
48. Marling-Balfour, letter No. 75, 6/11/17, FO 371/2983.
49. Marling-Balfour, 6/6/17, FO 371/2988.
50. Marling-Balfour, 6/14/17 with minutes by H. Nicolson and Lord Curzon, FO 371/2983.
51. Marling-Balfour, 6/17/17 with a minute by Lord Curzon, FO 371/2983.
52. Viceroy-SSI, 6/25/17, FO 371/2983; also in L/P&S/10/712.
53. Marling-Balfour, 7/3/17, FO 371/2983.
54. Viceroy-SSI, 7/5/17, FO 371/2983.
55. Balfour-Marling, 7/7/17; Marling-Balfour, 7/7/17, FO 371/2983.
56. Marling-Balfour, 7/9/17, FO 371/2983.
57. Marling-Balfour, 7/9/17, FO 371/2983.
58. Moberly, *Operations*, cited above, p. 244.
59. Marling-Balfour, 7/31/17, FO 371/2983.
60. Marling-Balfour, 9/11/17, FO 371/2982.
61. Marling-Hardinge, 9/10/17, FO 371/2981.
62. Minutes of meeting of the Persia Committee, 10/20/17, FO 371/2981. On Curzon's personality and ideas about the defense of empire and Persia's place in that effort, see Harold Nicolson, *Curzon: The Last Phase, 1919-1925* (New York: Harcourt, Brace & Co., 1939); David Dilks, *Curzon in India*, 2 vols. (London: Rupert Hart-Davis, 1969-70); and Kenneth Rose, *Superior Person* (London: Weidenfeld & Nicolson, 1969).
63. Marling-Balfour, 10/12/17, FO 371/2981.
64. Marling-SGI, 10/27/17, FO 371/2981.
65. Minutes of Meeting of Persia Committee, 11/10/17, FO 371/2988.
66. Marling-Balfour, 11/24/17, FO 371/2988.
67. Marling-Balfour, 12/9/17, FO 371/2988.
68. Marling-Balfour, 12/17/17, FO 371/2988.
69. Minute by Curzon, *ibid.*
70. Balfour-Marling, 12/20/17, FO 371/3259; Marling-Balfour, 12/20/17; Same-Same, 12/22/17, FO 371/2988.
71. Minutes by Oliphant, Hardinge, Robert Cecil to Marling-Balfour, 12/22/17, *ibid.*; Marling-Balfour, 12/24/17, FO 371/2988.
72. Marling-Balfour, 1/8/18, FO 371/3258.
73. French Ambassador-FO, London, 12/26/17, FO 371/2982.
74. Marling-Balfour, 1/5/18; IO-FO, 1/10/18, FO 371/3258.
75. Minutes of meeting of Persia Committee, 1/12/18, FO 371/3258.
76. Marling-Balfour, 1/16/18; Same-Same, 1/19/18; Same-Same, 1/25/18, FO 371/3258.
77. Marling-Balfour, 2/3/18, FO 371/3258.
78. Marling-Balfour, 2/4/18, FO 371/3258.
79. Minutes of meeting of Persia Committee, 2/9/18, FO 371/3258.
80. SSI-Viceroy, 2/9/18; Viceroy-SSI, 2/12/18, FO 371/3258.
81. Marling-Balfour, 2/12/18, FO 371/3258.

82. Marling-Balfour, 2/12/18 and 2/14/18, FO 371/3258.
83. Viceroy-SSI, 2/18/18; Marling-Balfour, 2/18/18, FO 371/3258.
84. Balfour-Marling, 2/21/18, FO 371/3258.
85. Marling-Balfour, 2/23/18, FO 371/3258.
86. Viceroy-SSI, 2/16/18, FO 371/3258.
87. Minutes of meeting of Persia Committee, 2/25/18, FO 371/3259.
88. Balfour-Marling, 2/27/18, FO 371/3259.
89. Marling-Balfour, 2/26/18, FO 371/3259.
90. Minutes of meeting of Persia Committee, 3/1/18, FO 371/3259.
91. Marling-Balfour, 3/15/18; Same-Same, 3/9/18 and 3/11/18, FO 371/3259.
92. Marling-Balfour, 3/15/18; Same-Same, 3/20/18, FO 371/3259.
93. Marling-Balfour, 3/21/18, FO 371/3259.
94. Minutes of meeting of Persia Committee, 3/22/18, FO 371/3259.
95. Marling-Balfour, 4/2/18, 4/23/18 and 5/3/18, FO 371/3259.
96. Marling-Balfour, 5/18/18, FO 371/3260.
97. Marling-Balfour, 5/5/18 and 4/17/18, FO 371/3272.
98. Marling-Balfour, 5/18/18, FO 371/3260.
99. Marling-Balfour, 5/20/18, FO 371/3260.
100. Balfour-Marling, 5/23/18, FO 371/3260.
101. Marling-Balfour, 3/24/18; Viceroy-SSI, 5/24/18; Balfour-Marling, 5/22/18, FO 371/3260.
102. Marling-Balfour, 5/26/18; Balfour-Marling, 5/27/18, FO 371/3260.
103. Marling-Balfour, 5/30/18, FO 371/3260.
104. Marling-Balfour, 6/12/18 and 6/29/18, FO 371/3260.
105. See Briton Busch, *Mudros to Lausanne: Britain's Frontier in Western Asia, 1918-1923* (Albany: State University Press of New York, 1976), p. 39; Marling-Balfour, 7/1/18, FO 371/3261.
106. Marling-Balfour, 6/16/18, FO 371/3261.
107. Marling-Balfour, 6/7/18 and 6/9/18; Minutes of a conversation with the Persian ambassador to London, 6/9/18, FO 371/3261.
108. Marling-Balfour, 8/2/18 and 8/3/18, FO 371/3261.
109. Marling-Balfour, 8/4/18, 8/2/18 and 8/5/18; Balfour-Marling, 8/7/18, FO 371/3261.
110. Marling-Balfour, 8/10/18, FO 371/3261; Same-Same, 6/7/18, FO 371/3260.
111. Minutes of meeting of Eastern Committee, 6/29/18, FO 371/3260.
112. Marling-Balfour, 8/19/18; Balfour-Marling, 8/22/18, FO 371/3261.
113. Marling-Balfour, 8/27/18; Director of Military Intelligence (hereafter referred to as DMI)-FO, 8/2/18, FO 371/3262; Marling-Balfour, 8/22/18, FO 371/3261; Same-Same, 9/8/18; Percy Cox-Balfour, 10/27/18, FO 371/3262.
114. Marling-Balfour, 9/9/18 with minutes by E. Crowe and R. Cecil; Cox-Balfour, 9/27/18, FO 371/3262. On Cox's career, see P. P. Graves, *The Life of Sir Percy Cox* (London: Hutchinson, 1941).
115. Minute by E. Crowe to Cox-Balfour, 9/27/18; Balfour-Cox, 9/27/18, FO 371/3262.
116. Cox-Balfour, 10/1/18, FO 371/3262.
117. Cox-Balfour, 10/14/18 with minutes by Oliphant and Crowe, FO 371/3262.
118. Minute by Crowe to Cox-Balfour, 1/15/18, FO 371/3261.
119. Balfour-Cox, 10/25/18, FO 371/3262.
120. Viceroy-SSI, 11/1/18, FO 371/3263.

CHAPTER VI

1. Cox-Balfour, 11/3/18 with minutes by Crewe and Cecil, FO 371/3262. Substantial portions of this chapter have appeared in *Towards a Modern Iran: Studies in Thought, Politics and Society*, ed. by Elie Kedourie and Sylvia Haim (London: Frank Cass, 1980).
2. Balfour-Cox, 11/11/18, FO 371/3262.
3. Cox-Balfour, 11/21/18; Balfour-Cox, 11/24/18, FO 371/3263.
4. Cox-Balfour, 10/31/18, FO 371/3262.
5. Cox-Balfour, 11/3/18, FO 371/3262.
6. Balfour-Cox, 11/7/18, FO 371/3262.
7. Cox-Balfour, 11/18/18, FO 371/3263.
8. Cox-Balfour, 11/14/18, FO 371/3263.
9. Viceroy-SSI, 11/26/18, FO 371/3263.
10. Cox-Balfour, 11/27/18, FO 371/3263.
11. Minutes by Oliphant and Hardinge, *ibid.*
12. Cox-Balfour, 12/6/18 with a minute by Oliphant, FO 371/3263.
13. Balfour-Cox, 12/10/18, FO 371/3263.
14. Cox-Balfour, 11/26/18, FO 371/3263.
15. 'Memorandum Regarding the Policy of His Majesty's Government Towards Persia at the Peace Conference,' 12/17/18, I.O.R. L/P&S/20/C193.
16. *Ibid.*
17. Memorandum by Charles Marling, 12/28/18, FO 371/3263.
18. Curzon-Balfour, 3/1/19, FO 371/3859.
19. Memorandum by Sir Hamilton Grant, 12/10/18, FO 371/3858. On the debate on a change of policy, see Frederick Stanwood, 'Revolution and the "Old Reactionary Policy": Britain in Persia, 1917,' *Journal of Imperial and Commonwealth History* 7 (1978):144-65.
20. Cox-Balfour, 11/27/18, FO 371/3263.
21. Curzon-Cox, 1/11/19, FO 371/3858.
22. Cox-Curzon, 1/13/19, FO 371/3858.
23. Cox-Curzon, 1/14/19, FO 371/3858.
24. Cox-Curzon, 1/22/19, FO 371/3858.
25. Curzon-Cox, 1/23/19, FO 371/3858.
26. Viceroy, SSI, 1/28/19, FO 371/3858.
27. Cox-Curzon, 2/6/19, FO 371/3858.
28. Curzon-Cox, 2/13/19, FO 371/3858.
29. Cox-Curzon, 2/25/19, FO 371/3858.
30. Curzon-Cox, 3/5/19, FO 371/3859.
31. Curzon-Cox, 3/17/19, FO 371/3859.
32. Cox-Curzon, 3/20/19, FO 371/3859.
33. Curzon-Cox, 3/28/19, FO 371/3859.
34. Memorandum by J. M. Keynes, 12/31/18, FO 371/3863.
35. Quoted in Harold Nicolson, *Curzon: The Last Phase, 1919-1925. A Study in Post-War Diplomacy* (New York: Harcourt, Brace & Co., 1939), p. 132; and Briton Busch, *Mudros to Lausanne: Britain's Frontier in Western Asia, 1918-1923* (Albany: State University Press of New York, 1976), p. 135.
36. Quoted in Nicolson, *ibid.*, p. 133.
37. Cox-Curzon, 1/19/19, FO 371/3858; Cox-Curzon, 3/14/19, FO 371/3859.
38. Cox-Curzon, 4/9/19, FO 371/3860.
39. Cox-Curzon, 4/10/19, FO 371/3860.
40. Cox-Curzon, 4/10/19, FO 371/3860.
41. Cox-Curzon, 4/10/19, FO 371/3860.

42. *Ibid.*
43. Cox-Curzon, 4/11/19, FO 371/3860.
44. *Ibid.*
45. Cox-Curzon, 4/17/19, FO 371/3860.
46. Cox-Curzon, 4/19/19, FO 371/3860.
47. Minute by Oliphant, *ibid.*
48. Curzon-Cox, 4/23/19, FO 371/3860.
49. Cox-Curzon, 4/25/19, FO 371/3860.
50. Viceroy-Secretary of State for India (hereafter referred to as SSI), 4/20/19, FO 371/3860.
51. Cox-Curzon, 4/30/19, FO 371/3860.
52. Treasury-FO, 4/21/19, FO 371/3860.
53. Minutes of Inter-Departmental Conference on Middle Eastern Affairs, 5/7/19, FO 371/3860.
54. Curzon-Cox, 5/9/19, FO 371/3860.
55. Cox-Curzon, 5/13/19, FO 371/3860.
56. Curzon-Cox, 5/17/19, FO 371/3860.
57. Curzon-Cox, 5/21/19, FO 371/3861.
58. Curzon-Cox, 5/30/19, FO 371/3861.
59. Viceroy-SSI, 6/13/19, FO 371/3861.
60. Cox-Curzon, 6/5/19; Curzon-Cox, 6/10/19, FO 371/3861.
61. Cox-Curzon, 7/7/19, FO 371/3861.
62. Curzon-Cox, 7/11/19, FO 371/3861.
63. Cox-Curzon, 7/17/19 with a minute by Curzon, FO 371/3861.
64. Curzon-Cox, 7/30/19, FO 371/3861.
65. On the arguments against Curzon, see Keith Jeffrey, 'Sir Henry Wilson and the Defence of the British Empire, 1918-22,' *Journal of Imperial and Commonwealth History* 3 (1977):270-93. Also see, Paul Guinn *British Strategy and Politics, 1914-1918* (Oxford: Clarendon Press, 1965); Elizabeth Monroe, *Britain's Moment in the Middle East, 1914-1956* (London: Chatto & Windus, 1963); and Briton Cooper Busch, *Mudros to Lausanne.*
66. Richard Ullman, *The Anglo-Soviet Accord* (Princeton: Princeton University Press, 1972), fn. p. 367.
67. Curzon-Norman, *Documents on British Foreign Policy, 1919-1939*, ed. by Rohan Butler, J. P. T. Burry, and M. E. Lambert, Series I, (London: H.M.S.O., 1963), Vol. 13, Nos. 406 and 407. (Hereafter referred to as *DBFP.*)
68. Norman-Curzon, *DBFP, ibid.*, Nos. 500, 503, 521.
69. Norman-Curzon, *DBFP*, ibid., No. 463.
70. Curzon-Norman, *DBFP*, ibid., No. 487.
71. Minute by Curzon to a note from Montagu, 2/23/21, FO 371/6409, quoted in Briton Cooper Busch, *Mudros to Lausanne*, p. 286.

BIBLIOGRAPHY*

OFFICIAL PAPERS

Great Britain

Public Record Office, London
　　Cabinet files, series 23 (Minutes of the Imperial War Cabinet, 1917-1919);
　　24 (G. & G. T. series papers: Memoranda for War Cabinet, War
　　Council, War Committee and Dardenelles Committee, 1915-1920);
　　27/24-40 (Memorandum of Eastern Committee); 37 (Cabinet papers
　　for the Committee of Imperial Defense); 42 (Papers of the War
　　Council, Dardenelles Committee and War Committee); 44 (Official
　　Histories).
　　Foreign Office files, series 371 (post-1905 correspondence), 800 (Grey
　　Papers); 800 (Curzon Papers); 60 (pre-1905 correspondence).
　　War Office files, series 106 (Directorate of Military Operations and
　　Intelligence papers) 1914-1921.
India Office Records, London
　　Political Department, Political and Secret Subjects files, (L/P&S/18);
　　(L/P&S/20).
Imperial War Museum, London
　　The Papers of Field Marshall Sir Henry Wilson.
British Museum, London
　　Arthur Balfour Papers, Field Marshall Robertson Papers, Arnold Wilson
　　Papers.

United States

National Archives, Washington, D.C.
　　Microfilm 715 (Records of the Department of State Relating to Internal
　　Affairs of Persia, 1910-1920), files 891 (Political Affairs); 891.4
　　(Social Affairs); 891.5 (Economic Matters); 891.6 (Industrial
　　Matters); microfilm 820 (General Record of the American Com-
　　mission to Negotiate Peace); microfilm 582 (Records of the Depart-
　　ment of State Relating to Political Relations between Great Britain
　　and Other States, 1910-1929); microfilm 367 (Records of the Depart-
　　ment of State Relating to World War I and its Termination, 1914-
　　1929); (8f Consulat Papers, Tehran); C37 (Consular Papers, Tabriz).

---

* In the interests of economy, not all works mentioned in the notes are listed in the
bibliography, and the diacritical marks in the Persian titles have been omitted.

PUBLISHED DOCUMENTS AND PAPERS

Great Britain

British Documents on the Origin of the War, 1898-1914. Edited by G. P. Gooch and H. W. V. Temperley. London: HM Stationery Office, 1938.

Documents on British Foreign Policy, 1919-1939. Edited by Rohan Butler, J. P. T. Bury and M. E. Lambert. Series I, Vols. 4 and 13. London: HM Stationery Office, 1963.

Foundations of British Foreign Policy from Pitt (1792) to Salisbury (1902) or Documents, Old and New. Cambridge: Cambridge University Press, 1938.

Parliamentary Debates (House of Commons). Fifth Series. London: HM Stationery Office.

U.S.S.R.

Soviet Documents on Foreign Policy. Jane Degras, editor. London: Oxford University Press, 1951.

Germany

German Diplomatic Documents, 1871-1914. Selected and translated by E. T. S. Dugdale. London: Methuen & Co., 1930.

Persia

Neutralité Persane: Documents Diplomatiques. Ministère des Affaires Etrangères Empire de Perse. No date.

United States

Committee on Foreign Relations, United States Senate. 'Multinational Oil Corporations and U.S. Foreign Policy.' January 2, 1975. Washington, D.C.: G.P.O., 1975.

Papers Relating to the Foreign Relations of the United States, 1919. Washington, D.C.: G.P.O. U.S.D.S., 1946.

Middle East

Hurewitz, J. C. *Diplomacy in the Near and Middle East: A Documentary Survey*. New York: D. Van Nostrand Co., 1958.

_____. *The Middle East and North Africa in World Politics: A Documentary Record*. New Haven: Yale University Press, 1975.

Peace Conference

Papers Relating to the Foreign Relations of the United States, The Paris Peace Conference. Washington, D.C.: G.P.O. U.S.D.S., 1946.
Temperley, H. W. V., editor. *A History of the Peace Conference.* London: Froude & Hodder & Stoughton, 1920-1924.

MEMOIRS

Arfa, Hassan. *Under Five Shahs.* London: John Murray, 1964.
Asquith, H. H. *Memories and Reflections, 1852-1927.* 2 vols. Edited by Alexander Mackintosh. London: Cassell, 1928.
Blacker, L. V. S. *On Secret Patrol in High Asia.* London: John Murray, 1922.
Bradley-Birt, F. B. *Persia: Through Persia from the Gulf to the Caspian.* Oriental Series, Vol. XX. Boston: J. B. Millet Co., 1910.
Brydges, Sir Harford Jones. *An Account of the Transactions of His Majesty's Mission to the Court of Persia in the Years 1807-11.* 2 vols. London: James Bohn, 1834.
Buchanan, Sir George. *My Mission to Russia and Other Diplomatic Memoirs.* 2 vols. Boston: Little, Brown & Co., 1923.
Bulow, Prince von. *Memoirs of Prince von Bulow: From the Morocco Crisis to Resignation, 1903-1909.* 2 vols. Boston: Little, Brown & Co., 1931.
Dickson, Maj.-Gen. W. E. R. *East Persia: A Backwater to the Great War.* London: Edward Arnold, 1924.
Donohoe, Maj. M. H. *With the Persian Expedition.* London: Edward Arnold, 1919.
Dunsterville, Maj.-Gen. L. C. *The Adventures of Dunsterforce.* London: Edward Arnold, 1920.
Dyer, Brig.-Gen. R. E. H. *The Raiders of the Sarhad: Being the Account of a Campaign of Arms and Bluff Against the Brigands of the Persian-Baluchi Border During the Great War.* London: H. F. & G. Witherby, 1921.
Forbes-Leith, F. A. C. *Checkmate: Fighting Tradition in Central Persia.* New York: R. M. McBride, 1927.
Gould, B. J. *The Jewel in the Lotus: Recollections of an Indian Political.* London: Chatto & Windus, 1957.
Grey, Viscount Sir Edward, *Twenty-Five Years, 1892-1916.* New York: Stokes, 1925.
Hale, F. *From Persian Uplands.* New York: E. P. Dutton & Co., n.d.
Hankey, Lord Maurice Pascal. *Government Control in War.* Lees Knowles Lectures. Cambridge: Cambridge University Press, 1945.
_____. *The Supreme Command, 1914-1918.* 2 vols. London: G. Allen & Unwin, 1961.
Hardinge, R. Hon. Sir Arthur H. *A Diplomatist in the East.* London: J. Cape, 1928.
Ironside, Maj.-Gen. Sir Edmund. *High Road to Command: The Diaries of Maj.-Gen. Sir Edmund Ironside, 1920-1922.* Edited by Lord Ironside. London: Leo Cooper, 1972.

Kalmykow, Andrew. *Memoirs of a Russian Diplomat: Outposts of the Empire, 1893-1917.* Edited by Alexandra Kalmykow. New Haven: Yale University Press, 1971.

Lansing, Robert. *The Peace Negotiations: A Personal Narrative.* New York: Houghton Mifflin, 1921.

Malcolm, Sir John. *Sketches from Persia: From the Journals of a Traveller in the East.* Philadelphia: Carey, Lea & Carey, 1928.

Morley, Viscount. *Recollections.* 2 vols. London: Macmillan & Co., 1929.

O'Connor, Lt. Col. Sir Frederick, *On the Frontiers and Beyond: A Record of Thirty Years Service.* London: John Murray, 1931.

Robertson, Sir William. *Soldiers and Statesmen, 1914-1918.* 2 vols. New York: Charles Scribner's Sons, 1926.

Shuster, Morgan. *The Strangling of Persia.* New York: The Century Co., 1912.

Sazanov, Sergei. *Fateful Years, 1906-1916: The Reminiscences of Sergei Sazanov.* London: J. Cape, 1928.

Skrine, Clarmont. *World War in Iran.* London: Constable & Co., 1962.

Townsend, Sir Charles V. F. *My Campaign in Mesopotamia.* London: Thornton Butterworth, Ltd., 1920.

Tuohy, Ferdinand. *The Crater of Mars.* London: William Heinemann, Ltd., 1929.

_____. *The Secret Corps: A Tale of 'Intelligence' on All Fronts.* London: John Murray, 1920.

Wilson, Arnold. *Loyalties: Mesopotamia 1914-1918.* London: Oxford University Press, 1930.

_____. *Mesopotamia, 1917-1920: A Clash of Loyalties: A Personal and Historical Record.* London: Oxford University Press, 1931.

_____. *S.W. Persia: Letters and Diary of a Young Political Officer, 1907-1914.* N.P.: Readers Union Ltd., 1942.

PERSIAN LANGUAGE SOURCES

Adamiyat, Firidun. *Amir-i Kabir va Iran.* Tehran: Khwarizmi Press, 1348 Shamsi.

Adamiyat, Muhammad Husayn Ruknzada. *Diliran-i Tangistan.* Tehran: Iqbal, n.d.

_____. *Fars dar Jang-i Bayn al-Milali.* Tehran: Iqbal, 1349 Shamsi.

Afsar, Parviz. *Tarikh-i Gendarmerie-yi Iran.* Qom: Qom Press, 1334 Shamsi.

Afshar, Riza. 'Gusha'i az Tarikh-i Mu'asir,' *Publication of the Faculty of Literature of the University of Tehran,* VI, 4 (1333 Shamsi), pp. 435-447.

Alva'i, Nur'allah Darishvan (Majahid as-Saltana). *Tarikh-i Mashruta-yi Iran va Mumbish-i Vatanparastan-i Isfahan va Bakhtiari.* Tehran: Danesh, 1335 Shamsi.

Ardillan, Amanallah and Sami'i, Husayn. *Avvalin Qiyam-i Muqdis-i Mili dar Jang-i Bayn al-Milali-yi Avval ya Khataratha-yi Aqa-yi Hosayn Sami'i (Adib as-Sultana) va Aqa-yi Amanallah Ardilan (Hajji Az al-Mamalik).* Tehran: Ibn Sina, 1332 Hejra Qamari.

Arzanpur, Yahya. *Az Saba ta Nima: Tarikh-i Sad u Panja Sal-i Adab-i Farsi.*
2 vols. Tehran: n.p., 1351 Shamsi.

Azari, Ali. *Qiyam-i Kulunil Muhammad Taqi Khan Pisyan dar Khurasan.*
Tehran: Sipahr Press, 1349 Shamsi.

Bahar, Muhammad Taqi 'Malik ash-Shu'ara.' *Tarikh-i Mukhtisir-i Ihzab-i
Siyasi:- Inqiraz-i Qajariya.* N.P.: n.p., 1323 Shamsi.

Bahrami, Abdallah. *Tarikh-i Ijtimai va Siyasi-yi Iran az Ziman-i Nasir ad-Din
Shah ta Akhar-i Silsila.* Tehran: Sena'i Press, 1344 Shamsi.

Bamdad, Mihdi. *Shar'i Hal-i Rijal-i Iran dar Qarn-i Davazdahhum, Sizdah-
hum, Chahardahhum Hijra.* 5 vols. Tehran: Zovar Press, n.d.

Bihzad, Muhandis Karim Tahirzada. *Qiyam-i Azirbayjan: Inqilabi-yi
Mashrutiyat-i Iran.* With a foreword by Seyyid Hasan Taqizadeh.
Tehran: Iqbal Press, n.d.

D'Allemagne, Henri-René. *Safar Nama az Khorasan ta Bakhtiari.* Translated
by Fereh Vashi. Tehran: Gilan Press, n.d.

Dastgirdi, Vahid. *Rah-Avard-i Vahid.* Tehran: Firdowsi Press, 1929.

Dihgan, Ali. *Sarzamin-i Zardusht.* Tehran: Ibn Sina, 1348 Shamsi.

Divanbigi, Riza Ali. *Safar-i Muhajirat dar Nukhustin Jang-i Jihani.* Tehran:
Chapkhanah-yi Bank-i Meli-yi Iran, 1351 Shamsi.

Daulatabadi, Yahya. *Hiyat-i Yahya.* 4 vols. Tehran: Ibn Sena 1331 Shamsi.

Fakhra'i, Ibrahim. *Sardar-i Jangal.* Tehran: Javidan Press, 1351 Shamsi.

Ibrahami, Hushang. *Satar Khan Sardar-i Mili.* Tehran: Tus Press, 1352
Shamsi.

Kasravi, Ahmad. *Tarikh-i Hizhda Sala-yi Azirbaijan.* Tehran: Amir-i Kabir
Press, 1350 Shamsi.

———. *Tarikh-i Mashruta-yi Iran.* Tehran: Amir-i Kabir Press, 1351 Shamsi.

Kavianpur, Ahmad. *Tarikh-i Rizaiya.* Tehran: Asia Press, n.d.

Kavih. First Series. 1916-1918.

Kirmani, Ahmad Majd al-Islam. *Tarikh-i Ingilab-i Mashrutiyat-i Iran.* 3 vols.
Isfahan: University of Isfahan Press, n.d.

Kirmani, Nazim al-Islam. *Tarikh-i Bidari-yi Iranian.* 3 vols. Tehran: Bunyad-i
Farhang Press, n.d.

Khatirat-i Siyasi-yi Mirza Ali Khan Amin ad-Daula. Compiled and edited by
H. F. Farmayan. Tehran: Iran Press, 1962.

Mahmud, Mahmud. *Tarikh-i Ravabat-i Siyasi-yi Iran va Inglis dar Qarn-i
Nuzdahum-i Miladi.* 8 vols. Tehran: Iqbal Press, n.d.

Maki, Husayn. *Mukhtisiri az zindignai-yi Siyasi-yi Sultan Ahmad Shah Qajar.*
Tehran: Chapkhana-yi Shirkat-i Tazamani Alami, 1323 Shamsi.

Malikzahda, Mihdi. *Tarikh-i Inqilab-i Mashrutiyat.* 7 vols. Tehran: Saghmat
Library, 1948.

Mihdavi, Abd ar-Riza Hushang. *Tarikh-i Ravabat-i Khariji-yi Iran.* Tehran:
Amir Kabir Press, 1349 Shamsi.

Muhammad Hasan Khan, I'timad as-Saltana. *Al-Ma'asir va al-Asar.* Tehran:
Sina'i Press (reprint), n.d.

———. *Ruznama-yi Khatirat-i I'timad as Saltana.* Edited and with an Introduction by Iraj Afshar. Tehran: Amir Kabir Press, 1350 Shamsi.

Mukhtari, Habib Alla (Mukhtar as-Saltana). *Tarikh-i Bidari-yi Iran.* Tehran:
Tehran University Press, 1947.

Mustaufi, Abdullah. *Sharh-i Zindigani-yi Man ya Tarikh-i Ijtima'i va Idari Doura-yi Qajariya.* 3 vols.

Nafisi, S. *Tarikh-i va Siyasi-yi Iran dar Daura-yi Mu'asir.* Vol. I. Tehran: Publication Foundations of the East, 1335 Shamsi.

Nikitin, B. *Iran ki Man Shinakhtam.* Translated by Humayun Sabiq. Tehran: Morafat, n.d.

Nura'i, Firishta. *Tahqiq dar Ifkar-i Mirza Malkum Khan Nazim ad-Daula.* Tehran: Franklin Press, 1352 Shamsi.

Parizi, Bastani. *Muhit-i Siyasi va Zindigani-yi Mushir ad-Daula.* Tehran: Ibn Sina, 1341 Shamsi.

Qudsi, Hasan Izam. *Khatirat-i Man ya Rushan Shudan-i Tarikh-i Sad Sala.* 2 vols. Tehran: Abu Raihan Press, n.d.

Quzanlu, Jamil. *Tarikh-i Nizami-yi Iran.* Tehran: Firdousi, 1315 Shamsi.

Ra'in, Isma'il. *Haydar Khan Amu Ugli.* Tehran: Javidan Press, n.d.

Sadiq, Issa. *Yadgar-i Umr: Khatirati az Sar Guzasht.* Tehran: Dihkhudah Press, 1352 Shamsi.

Sasani, Khan Malik. *Siyasatgiran-i Daura-yi Qajar.* 2 vols. Tehran: Firdausi, 1346 Shamsi.

_____. *Yadbudha-yi Sifarat-i Istambul.* Tehran: Firdousi, 1345 Shamsi.

Sipihr, Muvarrikh ad-Daula. *Iran dar Jan-i Buzurg.* N.P.: 1336 Shamsi.

Shaji'i, Zahra. *Namayandigan-i Majlis-i Shaura-yi Milli dar Bist-o-yik Daura-yi Qanunguzari.* Tehran: Danishgah-i 1344 Shamsi.

Shahidi, Col. Yahya. 'Guzarishi az Uza-i Gumruk-i Iran dar Ziman Qajar,' *Barrasiha-yi Tarikhi,* No. 5 (Azar-Dai 1351 Shamsi), pp. 153-186.

Shamim, Ali Asghar. *Iran dar Daura-yi Saltanat-i Qajar.* Tehran: Ibn Sina, 1342 Shamsi.

Shaykh al-Islami, Javad. 'Muzaffar Ad-Din Shah Qajar,' *Rahnima-yi Kitab,* XIV, No. 1, Part 3 (1350 Shamsi), pp. 27-36.

Sur Israfil. 1907.

Tamaddun, Muhammad. *Uzai-yi Iran dar Jang-i Avval ya Tarikh-i Riza'iya.* Tehran: Islamiya Press, 1350 Shamsi.

Taymuri, Ibrahim. *Asr-i Bikhabari ya Tarikh-i Imtiyazat-dar Iran.* Tehran: Iqbal Press, 1332 Shamsi.

Yasi, Rashid. *Adabbiyat-i Mu'asir.* Tehran: Ibn Sina, 1352 Shamsi.

SECONDARY SOURCES

Adelson, Roger. *Mark Sykes: Portrait of an Amateur.* London: J. Cape, 1975.

Afshar, M. *La Politique Européenne en Perse: Quelques pages de l'histoire diplomatique.* Berlin: Librairie orientale 'Iran, scähr,' 1921.

Alder, G. J. *British India's Northern Frontier, 1865-95: A Study in Imperial Rivalry.* Imperial Studies, No.25. Published by the Royal Commonwealth Society. London: Longmans, 1963.

Algar, Hamid. *Mirza Malkum Khan: A Biographical Study in Iranian Nationalism.* Berkeley: University of California Press, 1973.

_____. *Religion and State in Iran, 1785-1906: The Role of the Ulema in the Qajar Period.* Los Angeles: University of California Press, 1969.

Allen, W. E. D. and Paul Muratoff. *Caucasian Battlefields: A History of the Wars on the Turco-Caucasian Border, 1828-1921.* Cambridge: Cambridge University Press, 1953.

Anderson, M. S. *The Eastern Question, 1774-1923.* London: Macmillan, 1966.

Avery, Peter. *Modern Iran.* New York: Praeger, 1967.

Bailey, Thomas A. *Woodrow Wilson and the Lost Peace.* New York: Macmillan, 1947.

Balfour, James M. *Recent Happenings in Persia.* Edinburgh: Blackwood & Sons, 1922.

Banani, Amin. *The Modernization of Iran, 1921-41.* Stanford: Stanford University Press, 1961.

Barker, A. J. *The Neglected War: Mesopotamia, 1914-1918.* London: Faber & Faber, 1967.

Berghahn, V. R. *Germany and the Approach of War in 1914.* New York: Macmillan, 1973.

Bill, J. A. *The Politics of Iran: Groups, Classes and Modernization.* Columbus, Ohio: Charles Merrill Pub. Co., 1972.

Binder, Leonard. *Iran: Political Development in a Changing Society.* Berkeley: University of California Press, 1964.

Browne, E. G. *A Literary History of Persia, 1500-1924.* Vol. 4. Cambridge: Cambridge University Press, 1959.

_____. *The Persian Revolution of 1905-1909.* London: Frank Cass & Co. 1966 [first ed., 1910].

Busch, Briton Cooper. *Britain, India and the Arabs, 1914-1921.* Berkeley: University of California Press, 1971.

_____. *Britain and the Persian Gulf, 1894-1914.* Los Angeles: University of California Press, 1967.

_____. *Mudros to Lausanne: Britain's Frontier in Western Asia, 1918-1923.* Albany: State University Press of New York, 1976.

Carr, E. H. *The Bolshevik Revolution, 1917-1923.* 2 vols. London: Macmillan & Co., 1930.

Cassar, George H. *The French and the Dardanelles: A Study of Failure in the Conduct of War.* London: George Allen & Unwin, 1971.

Chapman, Maybelle Kennedy. *Great Britain and the Baghdad Railway.* Smith College Studies in History. Vol. XXXI. 1948.

Chapman-Huston, Desmond M., ed. *Subjects of the Day: Being a Selection of Speeches and Writings by Earl Curzon of Keddleston.* Introduction by Earl of Cromer. New York: Macmillan, 1915.

Chirol, Valentine. *The Middle Eastern Question or Some Political Problems of Indian Defense.* New York: E. P. Dutton & Co., 1903.

Churchill, Roger Platt. *The Anglo-Russian Convention of 1907.* Iowa: Torch Press, 1939.

Churchill, Winston. *The World Crisis.* 6 vols. London: Butterworth, 1923-31.

Cohen, Stuart. *British Policy in Mesopotamia, 1903-1914.* St. Antony's Middle East Monographs, No. 5. London: Ithaca Press, 1976.

Cottam, Richard. *Nationalism in Iran.* Pittsburgh: University of Pittsburgh Press, 1964.

Curzon, George N. *Persia and the Persian Question.* 2 vols. New York: Barnes and Noble, Inc., 1966 [first ed., 1892].

———. *Russia in Central Asia in 1889 and the Anglo-Russian Question.* London: Longmans, Green & Co., 1889.

Dilks, David. *Curzon in India.* 2 vols. London: Rupert Hart-Davis, 1969-70.

Dugdale, Blanch L. *Arthur James Balfour, First Earl of Balfour.* 2 vols. London: Hutchinson, 1936.

Earle, Edward M. *Turkey, the Great Powers and the Baghdad Railway: A Study in Imperialism.* London: Macmillan, 1923.

Edwardes, Michael. *Playing the Great Game: A Victorian Cold War.* London: Hamish Hamilton, 1975.

Entner, Marvin L. *Russo-Persian Commercial Relations, 1828-1914.* University of Florida Monographs, No. 28, Fall 1965. Gainesville: University of Florida Press, 1965.

Farnie, D. A. *East and West of Suez, The Suez Canal in History, 1854-1956.* Oxford: Clarendon Press, 1969.

Fatemi, N. *Diplomatic History of Persia, 1917-23: Anglo-Russian Power Politics in Iran.* New York: Russell F. Moore Co., 1952.

———. *Oil Diplomacy: Powder Keg in Iran.* New York: Whittier Books, 1954.

Feis, Herbert. *Europe the World's Banker, 1870-1914: An Account of European Foreign Investment and the Connection of World Finance with Diplomacy Before the War.* New Haven: Yale University Press, 1930.

Fischer, Fritz. *Germany's Aims in the First World War.* Introduction by Hajo Holborn. New York: W. W. Norton & Co., 1967 (in Germany, 1961).

———. *World Power or Decline: The Controversy over Germany's Aims in the First World War.* Translated by Lancelot Farrar, Robert Kimber, and Rita Kimber. New York: W. W. Norton & Co. 1974.

Gail, Marzieh. *Persia and the Victorians.* London: George Allen & Unwin, 1951.

Gelfand, Lawrence E. *The Inquiry: American Preparations for Peace, 1917-1919.* New Haven: Yale University Press, 1963.

Gillard, David. *The Struggle for Asia, 1828-1914: A Study in British and Russian Imperialism.* London: Methuen, 1977.

Gleason, J. H. *The Genesis of Russophobia in Great Britain.* Cambridge: Mass.: Harvard University Press, 1950.

Gottlieb, W. W. *Studies in Secret Diplomacy During the First World War.* London: George Allen & Unwin, 1957.

Grabill, Joseph L. *Protestant Diplomacy and the Near East: Missionary Influence on American Policy, 1810-1927.* Minneapolis: University of Minnesota Press, 1971.

Graham, Gerald. *Great Britain in the Indian Ocean: A Study of Maritime Enterprise, 1810-1850.* Oxford: Clarendon Press, 1967.

Graves, P. P. *The Life of Sir Percy Cox.* London: Hutchinson, 1941.

Greaves, Rose Louise. *Persia and the Defence of India, 1884-1892: A Study of the Foreign Policy of the Third Marquis of Salisbury.* London: Athlone Press, 1959.

Guinn, Paul. *British Strategy and Politics, 1914-1918.* Oxford: Clarendon Press, 1965.

Gwynn, Stephen, ed. *The Letters and Friendships of Sir Cecil Spring-Rice.* London: Constable & Co., 1929.

Hinsley, Francis, ed. *British Foreign Policy under Sir Edward Grey.* Cambridge: Cambridge University Press, 1977.

Holt, P. M., Lambton, A. K. S., and Lewis, Desmond, eds. *The Cambridge History of Islam.* 2 vols. London: Cambridge University Press, 1970.

Hoskins, Halford Lancaster. *British Routes to India.* New York: Longmans, Green & Co., 1928.

Ingram, Edward. *The Beginning of the Great Game in Asia, 1828-1934.* Oxford: Clarendon Press, 1978.

Iran and Islam. C. E. Bosworth, editor. Edinburgh: Edinburgh University Press, 1971.

Issawi, Charles, ed. *The Economic History of Iran, 1800-1914.* Chicago: University of Chicago Press, 1971.

Jackson, Robert. *At War with the Bolsheviks: The Allied Intervention into Russia, 1917-1920.* London: Tom Stacey, 1972.

James, Robert R. *Gallipoli.* London: Pan Books, 1965.

Kazemzadeh, Firuz. *Russia and Britain in Persia, 1864-1914: A Study in Imperialism.* New Haven: Yale Univ. Press, 1968.

_____. *The Struggle for Transcaucasia, 1917-1921.* New York: Philosophical Library, 1951.

Keddie, Nikki R. *Religion and Rebellion in Iran: The Iranian Tobacco Protest of 1891-1892.* London: Frank Cass, 1966.

_____. *Sayyid Jamal ad Din al-Afghani: A Political Biography.* Berkeley: Univ. of California Press, 1972.

Kedourie, Elie. *The Chatham House Version and Other Middle Eastern Studies.* London: Weidenfeld & Nicolson, 1970.

_____. *In the Anglo-Arab Labyrinth: The McMahon-Husayn Correspondence and its Interpretations, 1914-1939.* Cambridge: Cambridge Univ, Press, 1976.

_____. and Sylvia Haim, editors. *Towards a Modern Iran: Studies in Thought, Politics and Society.* London: Frank Cass, 1980.

Kelly, J. B. *Britain and the Persian Gulf, 1795-1880.* Oxford: Clarendon Press, 1968.

Kent, Marian. *Oil & Empire: British Policy and Mesopotamian Oil, 1900-1920.* London: Macmillan, 1976.

Kumar, Ravinder. *India and the Persia Gulf Region, 1858-1907: A Study in British Imperial Policy.* London: Asia Publishing House, 1965.

Lafore, L. D. *The Long Fuse: An Interpretation of the Origins of World War I.* New York: Lippincott, 1965.

Lambton, A. K. S. *Landlord and Peasant in Persia: A Study of Land Tenure and Land Revenue Administration.* London: Oxford Univ. Press, 1953.

Landes, David. *Bankers and Pashas: International Finance and Economic Imperialism in Egypt.* Cambridge: Cambridge Univ. Press, 1958.

Langer, William. *The Diplomacy of Imperialism.* 3 vols. New York: Knopf, 1935.

_____. *European Alliances and Alignments, 1871-1890.* New York: Knopf, 1939.

_____. *The Franco-Russian Alliance, 1890-1894.* Cambridge: Harvard Univ. Press, 1929.

Lenczowski, George. *The Middle East in World Affairs.* Ithaca: Cornell Univ. Press, 1953.

_____. *Russia and the West in Iran, 1918-1948: A Study in Big Power Rivalry.* Ithaca: Cornell Univ. Press, 1954.

Liddell-Hart, B. H. *History of the First World War.* London: Book Club Associates, 1970 (first edition, 1930).

Louis, Wm R. *Great Britain and Germany's Lost Colonies, 1914-1919.* Oxford: Clarendon Press, 1969.

Lowe, C. J. and M. L. Dockrill. *The Mirage of Power.* 3 vols. London: Routledge and Kegan Paul, 1972.

_____. *The Reluctant Imperialists: British Foreign Policy, 1878-1902.* 2 vols. London: Routledge and Kegan Paul, 1967.

McDaniel, Robert A. *The Shuster Mission and the Persian Constitutional Revolution.* Minneapolis: Bibliotheca Islamica, 1974.

McLean, David. *Britain and Her Buffer State: The Collapse of the Persian Empire, 1890-1914.* London: Royal Historical Society, 1979.

Marder, Arthur. *The Anatomy of British Sea Power: A History of British Naval Policy in the Pre-Dreadnought Era, 1880-1905.* New York: Knopf, 1940.

_____. *From the Dreadnought to Scapaflow: The Royal Navy in the Fisher Era, 1904-1919.* London: Oxford Univ. Press, 1961.

Marlowe, John. *Late Victorian: The Life of Sir Arnold Talbot Wilson.* London: Cresset Press, 1967.

Marriott, Sir J. A. R. *The Eastern Question: An Historical Study in European Diplomacy.* Oxford: Clarendon Press, 1917.

Martin, Bradford. *German-Persian Diplomatic Relations, 1873-1912.* The Hague: Mouton & Co., 1959.

Mayer, Arno J. *Politics and Diplomacy of Peacemaking: Containment and Counter-revolution at Versailles, 1918-1919.* New York: Vintage, 1969.

Millman, Richard. *Britain and the Eastern Question, 1875-1878.* Oxford: Clarendon Press, 1979.

Miroshnikov, L. I. *Iran in World War I.* Moscow: Oriental Literature Publishing House, 1963.

Moberly, Brig.-Gen. F. J. *History of the Great War Based on Official Documents: The Campaign in Mesopotamia, 1914-1918.* 4 vols. London: H.M.S.O., 1927.

Monger, George. *The End of Isolation: British Foreign Policy, 1900-1907.* New York: Th. Nelson & Sons, 1963.

Monroe, Elizabeth. *Britain's Moment in the Middle East, 1914-1956.* London: University Paperbacks, 1963.

Nicolson, Harold. *Curzon: The Last Phase, 1919-1925. A Study in Post-War Diplomacy.* New York: Harcourt, Brace & Co., 1939.

_____. *Peacemaking, 1919.* New York: Grosset & Dunlap, 1965.

_____. *Sir Arthur Nicolson, Bart., First Lord Carnock: A Study in Old Diplomacy.* London: Constable, 1930.

Oberling, Pierre. *The Qashga'i Nomads of Fars.* Paris: Mouton, 1974.

Pierce, Richard. *Russian Central Asia, 1867-1917: A Study in Colonial Rule.* Berkeley: Univ. of California Press, 1960.

Platt, D. C. M. *Finance, Trade and Politics in British Foreign Policy, 1815-1914.* Oxford: Clarendon Press, 1968.

Rabinowitch, Alexander. *The Bolsheviks Come to Power: The Revolution of 1917 in Petrograd.* New York: W. W. Norton & Co., 1976.

Ramazani, Rouhollah. *The Foreign Policy of Iran, 1500-1941: A Developing Nation in World Affairs.* Charlottesville: Univ. Press of Virginia, 1966.

Ramm, Agatha. *Sir Robert Morier: Envoy and Ambassador in the Age of Imperialism, 1876-1893.* Oxford: Clarendon Press, 1973.

Rawlinson, Sir Henry. *England and Russia in the East: A Series of Papers on the Political and Geographical Condition of Central Asia.* London: John Murray, 1875.

Robbins, Keith. *Sir Edward Grey: A Biography of Lord Grey of Falloden.* London: Cassell, 1971.

Rolo, P. J. V. *Entente Cordiale: The Origins and Negotiations of the Anglo-French Agreement of 8 April 1904.* London: Macmillan, 1969.

Rose, Kenneth. *Superior Person: A Portrait of Curzon and His Circle in Late Victorian England.* London: Weidenfeld & Nicolson, 1969.

Rothwell, V. H. *British War Aims and Peace Diplomacy, 1914-1918.* Oxford: Clarendon Press, 1971.

Sachar, Howard. *The Emergence of the Middle East, 1914-1924.* New York: Knopf, 1969.

Shannon, Richard. *The Crisis of Imperialism, 1865-1915.* London: Paladin, 1974.

Silverlight, John. *The Victor's Dilemma: Allied Intervention in the Russian Civil War.* London: Barrie and Jenkins Ltd., 1970.

Sluglett, Peter. *Britain in Iraq, 1914-1932.* St. Antony's Middle East Monographs No. 4. London: Ithaca Press, 1976.

Steiner, Z. S. *Britain and the Origins of the First World War.* London: Macmillan, 1977.

_____. *The Foreign Office and Foreign Policy, 1898-1914.* Cambridge: Cambridge Univ. Press, 1969.

Sumner, B. H. *Tsardom and Imperialism in the Far East and Middle East, 1880-1914.* Vol 27, Proceedings of the British Academy. New York: Archon Books, 1968.

Sykes, Christopher. *Wassmuss: The German Lawrence.* New York: Longmans, Green & Co., 1936.

Sykes, Brig.-Gen. Sir Percy. *A History of Persia.* 2 vols. London: Macmillan, 1921.

Taylor, A. J. P. *The Struggle for Mastery in Europe.* New York: Oxford Univ. Press, 1971.

Trumpener, Ulrich. *Germany and the Ottoman Empire, 1914-1918.* Princeton: Princeton Univ. Press, 1968.

Ullman, Richard. *Anglo-Soviet Relations, 1917-1921.* 3 vols. Princeton: Princeton Univ. Press, 1961-72.

Waterfield, Robin. *Christians in Persia: Assyrians, Armenians, Roman Catholics and Protestants.* London: George Allen & Unwin, 1973.

Weber, Frank. *Eagles on the Crescent: Germany, Austria, and the Diplomacy of the Turkish Alliance, 1914-1918.* Ithaca: Cornell Univ. Press, 1970.

Williamson, Samuel. *The Politics of Grand Strategy: Great Britain and France Prepare for War, 1904-1914.* Cambridge: Harvard Univ. Press, 1969.

Wilson, Trevor. *The Downfall of the Liberal Party, 1914-1935.* New York: Collins, 1966.

Winstone, H. V. F. *Captain Shakespear: A Portrait.* London: J. Cape, 1976.

Woodward, Sir Ernest Llewellyn. *Great Britain and the War of 1914-1918.* London: Methuen & Co., 1967.

Yapp, M. E. *Strategies of British India: Britain, Iran, and Afghanistan, 1798-1850.* Oxford: Clarendon Press, 1980.

Zabih, Sepehr. *The Communist Movement in Iran.* Berkeley: Univ. of California Press, 1966.

PERIODICALS

Abrahamian, Ervand. 'Communism and Communalism in Iran: The *Tudah* and the *Firqah-i Dimukrat.*' *International Journal of Middle East Studies* 1 (Jan. 1970): 291-316.

_____. 'The Crowd in Iranian Politics, 1905-1953.' *Past and Present* 41 (1968):184-210.

Alder, G. J. 'Britain and the Defence of India: The Origins of the Problem, 1798-1815.' *Journal of Asian History* 6 (1972): 14-44.

_____. 'India and the Crimean War.' *Journal of Imperial and Commonwealth History* 2 (1973): 15-37.

_____. 'The Key to India?: Britain and the Herat Problem, 1830-1863.' *Middle Eastern Studies* 10 (1974): 186-209; 287-311.

Avery, Peter and J. P. Simmons. 'Persia on a Cross of Silver, 1880-1890.' *Middle Eastern Studies* 10 (Oct., 1974): 259-286.

Bakhash, Shaul. 'The Evolution of Qajar Bureaucracy: 1779-1879.' *Middle Eastern Studies* 7 (1971): 139-68.

Blacker, Capt. L. V. S. 'Wars and Travel in Turkestan, 1918-1920.' *Journal of the Royal Central Asiatic Society* 9 (1922): 4-20.

Brockway, Thomas. 'Britain and the Persian Bubble, 1888-1892.' *Journal of Modern History* 13 (March, 1941): 36-47.

Cohen, S. A. 'The Genesis of the British Campaign in Mesopotamia, 1914.' *Middle Eastern Studies* 12 (May, 1976): 119-32.

_____. 'Mesopotamia in British Strategy, 1903-1914.' *International Journal of Middle East Studies* 9 (1978): 171-81.

Cotes, Everard. 'Present Situation in the Persian Gulf.' *Contemporary Review* 85 (April, 1904): 480-486.

Cottam, Richard W. 'Political Party Development in Iran.' *Iranian Studies* 1 (Summer 1968): 82-95.

Cunningham, Allan. 'The Wrong Horse – A Study of Anglo-Turkish Relations before the First World War.' *St. Antony's Papers No. 17, Middle Eastern Affairs,* ed. by A. Hourani (London: Oxford University Press, 1965): 56-76.

Davis, H. W. C. 'The Great Game in Asia, 1800-1844.' Raleigh Lectures in History, *Proceedings of the British Academy* 12 (1926): 22-57.

Dermorgny, G. 'Les institutions de la police en Perse.' *Revue du Monde Musulman* 27 (1914): 183-237.

_____. 'Les réformes administratives en Perse. Les tribus de Fars.' *Revue du Monde Musulman* 22 (1913): 85-150; 23 (1914): 3-108.

Dillon, E. J. 'British Supremacy in the Persian Gulf.' *Contemporary Review* 85 (January 1904): 159-142.

Douglas, Maj.-Gen. J. A. 'The Bushire-Shiraz Road, 1918-1919.' *Journal of the Royal Central Asian Society* 10 (1923): 84-180.

Ducrocq, George. 'Les Allemands en Perse.' *Revue du Monde Musulman* 54 (June 1923): 53-199.

_____. 'La politique de gouvernement des Soviets en Perse: Le Bolshevisme et l'Islam.' *Revue du Monde Musulman* 52 (1922): 84-180.

Dunsterville, Maj.-Gen. L. C. 'Military Mission to North-West Persia, 1918.' *Journal of the Central Asian Society* 8 (1921): 79-98.

Edmonds, C. J. 'The Persian Gulf Prelude to the Zimmerman Telegram.' *Journal of the Royal Central Asian Society* 47 (January 1960): 58-67.

Ellis, C. H. 'Falsification of History: Review Article of *English Expansion in Iran, 1914-1920*. By L. I. Miroshnikov.' *Journal of the Royal Central Asian Society* 52 (1965): 53-56.

_____. 'Operations in Transcaspia, 1918-1919 and the 26 Commissars Case.' *St. Antony's Papers No. 6: Soviet Affairs Number Two*, ed. by David Footman (New York: Praeger, 1959): 129-153.

Elwell-Sutton, L. P. 'Parleying with the Russians in 1827.' *Journal of the Royal Central Asian Society* 39 (April 1962): 183-187.

Farmayan, Hafez F. 'The Forces of Modernization in Nineteenth Century Iran: A Historical Survey,' reprinted from *Beginnings of Modernization in the Middle East*, ed. by William R. Polk and Richard L. Chambers (Chicago: University of Chicago Press, 1968): 119-51.

_____. 'The Foreign Policy of Iran: A Historical Analysis, 559 B.C.-A.D. 1971.' Research Monograph No. 4, Middle East Center, University of Utah (Salt Lake: 1971).

Fas, G. 'Lettre de Tauris.' *Revue du Monde Musulman* 4 (1908): 360-369.

Ferrier, R. W. 'The Early Management Organization of British Petroleum and Sir John Cadman.' *Management Strategy and Business Development: An Historical and Comparative Study*, edited by Leslie Hannah (London: Macmillan, 1976): 130-47.

Floor, W. 'The Lutis – A Social Phenomenon in Qajar Persia.' *Die Welt des Islam* N.S., 13 (1971): 103-120.

Frechtling, L. E. 'The Reuter Concession in Persia.' *The Asiatic Review* 34 (July 1938): 519-533.

Gable, Richard W. 'Culture and Administration in Iran.' *Middle East Journal* 42 (Autumn 1959): 407-421.

Garrod, Oliver. 'The Qashqai Tribe of Fars. *Journal of the Royal Central Asian Society* 33 (July-October 1946): 293-306.

Garthwaite, Gene. 'The Bakhtiyari Khans, the Government of Iran and the British, 1846-1915.' *International Journal of Middle East Studies* 3 (January 1972): 23-44.

Gehrke, Ulrich. 'Germany and Persia up to 1919.' *Germany and the Middle East, 1835-1939*, Jehuda Wallach, ed. (Tel Aviv: Tel Aviv University Press, 1975): 104-116.

Ghilan. 'Le Club National de Tauris.' *Revue du Monde Musulman* 2 (March 1907): 1-9; 3 (August-September 1907): 106-117.

———. 'La décomposition du corps social en Perse.' *Revue du Monde Musulman* 4 (1908): 85-90.

———. 'La révolution à Tauris.' *Revue du Monde Musulman* 7 (1909): 287-294.

Goold, J. Douglas. 'Lord Hardinge and the Mesopotamia Expedition and Inquiry, 1914-1917.' *Historical Journal* 19 (1976): 919-45.

Greaves, Rose L. 'British Policy in Persia, 1892-1903 -I.' *Bulletin of the School of Oriental and African Studies* 28 (1965): 34-60.

———. 'British Policy in Persia, 1892-1903 – II.' *Bulletin of the School of Oriental and African Studies* 28 (1965): 284-07.

———. 'Some Aspects of the Anglo-Russian Convention and Its Workings in Persia, 1907-14 – I.' *Bulletin of the School of Oriental and African Studies* 31 (1968): 69-91.

———. 'Some Aspects of the Anglo-Russian Convention and its Workings in Persia, 1907-14 – II.' *Bulletin of the School of Oriental and African Studies* 31 (1968): 290-308.

Grey, Lt. Col. W. G. 'Recent Persian History.' *Journal of the Royal Central Asian Society* 13 (January 1926): 29-42.

Hambly, G. R. G. 'An Introduction to the Economic Organization of Early Qajar Iran.' *Iran* 2 (1964): 69-82.

———. 'Aqa Mohammad Khan and the Establishment of the Qajar Dynasty.' *Journal of the Royal Central Asian Society* 50 (1963): 161-173.

Haworth, Sir Lionel. 'Persia and the Persian Gulf.' *Journal of the Royal Central Asian Society* 16 (1929): 995-510.

Hogan, Michael. 'Informal Entente: Public Policy and Private Management in Anglo-American Petroleum Affairs, 1918-1924 .' *Business History Review* 48 (Summer 1974): 187-205.

Hurewitz, J. C. 'The Beginnings of Military Modernization in the Middle East: A Comparative Analaysis.' *Middle East Journal* 22 (Spring 1968): 144-158.

Ingram, Edward. 'An Aspiring Buffer State: Anglo-Persian Relations in the Third Coalition, 1804-1807.' *Historical Journal* 16 (1973): 509-33.

———. 'The Rules of the Game: A Commentary on the Defence of India, 1798-1929.' *Journal of Imperial and Commonwealth History* 3 (1975): 257-79.

Issawi, Charles. 'The Tabriz-Trabzon Trade, 1830-1900: Rise and Decline of a Route.' *International Journal of Middle East Studies* 1 (January 1970): 18-27.

Jones, Gareth. 'The British Government and the Oil Companies, 1912-1924: The Search for an Oil Policy.' *Historical Journal* 10 (1977): 647-72.

Kazemzadeh, Firuz. 'The Origin and Early Development of the Persian Cossack Brigade.' *The American Slavic and East European Review* 15 (October 1956): 351-363.

_____. 'Russia vs. Morgan Shuster.' *Ventures*, Magazine of the Yale Graduate School 4 (Fall 1964): 41-48.

_____. 'Russian Imperialism and Persian Railways.' *Harvard Slavic Studies: Russian Thought and Politics*, ed. by Hugh McLean, Martin E. Malia, and George Fischer (The Hague: Mouton & Co., 1957): 355-373.

Keddie, Nikki R. 'The Assassination of the Amin as-Sultaneh (Atabak-i Azam), 31 August 1907.' *Iran and Islam: in memory of the late Vladimir Minoisky*, ed. by C. E. Bosworth (Edinburgh: Edinburgh Univ. Press, 1971): 315-30.

_____. 'British Policy and the Iranian Opposition, 1901-1907.' *Journal of Modern History* 39 (September 1967): 266-82.

_____. 'The Origins of the Religious-Radical Alliance in Iran.' *Past and Present* 34 (July 1966): 70-80.

_____. 'Iranian Politics 1900-05: Background to Revolution – I.' *Middle Eastern Studies* 5 (January 1969): 3-31, 151-67, 234-51.

_____. 'The Iranian Power Structure and Social Change, 1800-1969: An Overview.' *International Journal of Middle East Studies* 2 (January 1971): 3-20.

_____. 'Religion and Irreligion in Early Iranian Nationalism.' *Comparative Studies in Society and History: An International Quarterly* 4 (April 1962): 265-95.

_____. 'The Roots of the Ulama's Power in Modern Iran.' *Studia Islamica* 29 (1969): 31-54.

Klein, Ira. 'The Anglo-Russian Convention and the Problems of Central Asia, 1907-1914.' *Journal of British Studies* 11 (1971): 126-47.

_____. 'British Intervention in the Persian Revolution, 1905-9.' *Historical Journal* 15 (1972): 731-52.

_____. 'British Policy and the Iranian Constitution, 1919-1920.' *The Historian* 36 (1974): 434-54.

_____. 'Prospero's Magic: Imperialism and Nationalism in Iran, 1909-11.' *Journal of Asian History* 14 (1980): 47-91.

Klieman, Aaron. 'Britain's War Aims in the Middle East in 1915.' *Journal of Contemporary History* 3 (1968): 237-53.

Kudsi-Zadeh, A. Albert. 'Iranian Politics in the Late Qajar Period: A Review.' *Middle Eastern Studies* 5 (October 1969): 250-57.

Lambton, A. K. S. 'The Case of Haji Nur al-Din, 1823-47: a Study in Land Tenure.' *Bulletin of the School of Oriental and African Studies* 30 (1967): 54-72.

_____. 'The Impact of the West on Persia.' *International Affairs* 3 (January 1957): 12-25.

_____. 'Land Reform and Rural Co-operative Societies in Persia, I and II.' *Journal of the Royal Central Asian Society* 56 (February and October 1969).

_____. 'Persia.' *Journal of the Royal Central Asian Society* 31 (January 1944): 8-22.

_____. 'Persian Political Societies 1906-1911.' *St. Antony's Papers No. 16, Middle Eastern Affairs No. Three*, ed. by A. Hourani (London: 1968): 41-89.

_____. 'Secret Societies and the Persian Revolution of 1905-6.' *St. Antony's Papers No. 4, Middle Eastern Affairs* No. One, ed. by A. Hourani (London: 1958): 43-60.

_____. 'The Tobacco Regie: Prelude to Revolution.' *Studia Islamica*, Part I, 22 (1965): 119-57.

_____. 'The Tobacco Regie: Prelude to Revolution.' *Studia Islamica*, Part II 23 (1965): 71-90.

Lenczowski, George. 'The Communist Movement in Iran.' *Middle East Journal* 1 (January 1947): 29-45.

Lockhart, Lawrence. 'The Constitutional Laws of Persia: An Outline of their Origin and Development.' *Middle East Journal* 13 (Autumn 1959): 372-88.

Loraine, M. B. 'A Memoir on the Life and Political Works of Maliku'l-Shu'ara Bahar.' *International Journal of Middle East Studies* 3 (April 1972): 140-68.

Lorentz, John H. 'Iran's Great Reformer of the Nineteenth Century: An Analysis of Amir Kabir's Reforms.' *Iranian Studies* 4 (Spring and Summer 1971): 85-103.

Machray, Robert. 'The Germans in Persia.' *Fortnightly Review* 105 (February 1916): 342-53.

_____. 'Persia and the Frustration of German Schemes.' *Fortnightly Review* 106 (July 1916): 34-44.

McDaniel, Robert A. 'Economic Change and Economic Resiliency in 19th Century Persia.' *Iranian Studies* 4 (Winter 1971): 36-49.

McLean, David. 'English Radicals, Russia, and the Fate of Persia, 1907-1913.' *English Historical Review* 93 (1978): 338-52.

McMahon, Col. Sir Henry. 'Recent Survey and Exploration in Seistan.' *The Geographical Journal* 28 (September 1906): 209-29.

Martchenki. 'Kutchuk Khan.' *Revue du Monde Musulman* 40-1 (September-December 1920): 98-116.

Malcolm Khan. 'Persian Civilisation.' *Contemporary Review* 59 (February 1891): 238-44.

Malleson, Maj.-Gen. Sir Wilfred. 'The British Mission to Turkestan, 1918-1920.' *Journal of the Royal Central Asian Society* 9 (1922): 96-110.

Mejcher, Helmut. 'British Middle East Policy, 1917-21: The Interdepartmental Level.' *Journal of Contemporary History* 8 (1973): 81-101.

_____. 'Oil and British Policy towards Mesopotamia, 1914-1918.' *Middle Eastern Studies* 8 (1972): 377-91.

Meredith, Colin. 'Early Qajar Administration: An Analysis of its Development and Functions.' *Iranian Studies* 5 (Spring-Summer 1971): 59-84.

Miller, William Green. 'Political Organization in Iran: From Dowreh to Political Party — I and II.' *The Middle East Journal* 23 (Spring and Summer 1969): 159-67, 343-50.

Millward, William G. 'Traditional Values and Social Change in Iran.' *Iranian Studies* 4 (1945):2-35.

Minorsky, V. 'The Tribes of Western Iran.' *Journal of the Royal Anthropological Institute* 80 (1945): 73-80.

_____. 'Les tsiganes Luli et les Lurs persans.' *Journal Asiatique* 218 (April-June 1931): 281-305.

Monger, G. W. 'The End of Isolation: Britain, Germany and Japan, 1900-02' [The Alexander Pinge Essay]. *Transactions of the Royal Historical Society*, Fifth Series, 13 (1963): 103-22.

Morris, L. P. 'British Secret Missions in Turkestan, 1918-19.' *Journal of Contemporary History* 12 (1977): 363-79.

Morrison, J. L. 'From Alexander Burnes to Frederick Roberts: A Survey of Imperial Frontier Policy.' [Raleigh Lectures]. *Proceedings of the British Academy*, 22 (1936): 117-206.

Noel, Capt. J. B. L. 'A Reconnaissance in the Caspian Provinces of Persia.' *The Geographical Journal* 57 (June 1921): 401-18.

Nikitine, B. 'Les Afsars de Urumiyeh.' *Journal Asiatique* 214 (January-March 1920): 67-123.

Norris, Capt. David. 'Caspian Naval Expedition, 1918-1919.' *Journal of Central Asian History* 10 (1923): 216-40.

Oberling, Pierre. 'British Tribal Policy in Southern Persia, 1906-1911.' *Journal of Asian History* 4 (1970): 50-79.

Pavlovitch, Michel. 'Le Brigade Russe en Perse.' *Revue du Monde Musulman* 15 (1911): 319-38.

_____. 'La Révolution Persane.' *Revue du Monde Musulman* 13 (1911): 312-33.

Philipp, Mangol Bayat. 'Mirza Aqa Khan Kirmani: A Nineteenth Century Persian Nationalist.' *Middle Eastern Studies* 10 (January 1974): 36-59.

Rabino, H. L. 'Notes sur la Perse.' *Revue du Monde Musulman* 26 (1914): 95-145.

Ramazani, R. K. '"Church" and State in Modernizing Society: The Case of Iran.' Supplement to the *American Behaviorial Scientist* 7 (December 1963): 26-8.

_____. 'Iran's Changing Foreign Policy: A Preliminary Discussion.' *Middle East Journal* 24 (Autumn 1970): 421-37.

Razi, Gholam Hossein. 'Genesis of Party in Iran: A Case Study of the Interaction Between the Political System and Political Parties.' *Iranian Studies* 3 (Spring 1970): 58-90.

_____. 'The Press and Political Institutions of Iran: A Content Analysis of Etala'at and Keyhan.' *Middle East Journal* 22 (Autumn 1968): 463-74.

Rothwell, V. H. 'Mesopotamia in British War Aims, 1914-1918.' *Historical Journal* 13 (1970): 273-94.

Savory, R. M. 'British and French Diplomacy in Persia, 1800-1810.' *Iran* 10 (1970): 31-44.

_____. 'Persia Since the Constitution.' *The Islamic Near East* ed. by D. Grant (1960): 243-61.

Shadman, S. F. 'A Review of Anglo-Persian Relations, 1798-1815.' *Journal of the Royal Central Asian Society* 31, Part I (January 1944): 23-9.

Sheikholeslami, A. Reza. 'The Role of the Sale of Offices in Qajar Iran, 1858-1896.' *Iranian Studies* 4 (1971): 104-15.

Spring, D. W. 'The Trans-Persian Railway Project and Anglo-Russian Relations, 1909-1914.' *Slavonic and East European Review* 54 (1976): 60-82.

Staley, Eugene. 'Business and Politics in the Persian Gulf: The Story of the Wonckhaus Firm.' *Political Science Quarterly* 38 (1933): 367-85.

Standish, F. J. 'British Maritime Policy in the Persian Gulf.' *Middle Eastern Studies* 3 (July 1967): 324-54.

_____. 'The Persian War of 1856-1857.' *Middle Eastern Studies* 3 (October 1966): 18-45.

Stanwood, Frederick. 'Revolution and the "Old Reactionary Policy": Britain in Persia, 1917.' *Journal of Imperial and Commonwealth History* 7 (1978): 144-65.

Steiner, Zara. 'The Foreign Office and the War.' *British Foreign Policy under Sir Edward Grey* (Cambridge: Cambridge University Press, 1977): 517-31.

_____. 'The Foreign Office under Sir Edward Grey, 1905-1914.' *British Foreign Policy under Sir Edward Grey* (Cambridge: Cambridge University Press, 1977): 22-69.

_____. Grey, Hardinge, and the Foreign Office, 1906-1910.' *Historical Journal* 10 (1967): 415-39.

Sykes, Major Percy. 'A Fourth Journey in Persia, 1897-1901.' *Geographical Journal* 19 (February 1902): 121-73.

_____. 'A Fifth Journey in Persia.' *Geographical Journal* 28 (December 1906): 560-92.

_____. 'A Seventh Journey in Persia.' *Geographical Journal* 45 (May 1915): 357-71.

_____. 'A Sixth Journey in Persia.' *Geographical Journal* 37 (January 1911): 1-19.

_____. 'Persia and the Great War.' *Geographical Journal* 43 (1931): 101-19.

_____. 'South Persia and the Great War.' *Geographical Journal* 58 (August 1921): 101-9.

Taqizadeh, Seyyed Hasan. 'Document: "The Background of the Constitutional Movement in Azerbaijan".' Translated by Nikki Keddie. *Middle East Journal* 14 (Autumn 1960): 456.

Thornton, A. P. 'British Policy in Persia, 1858-1890 – I.' *English Historical Review* 69 (October 1954): 554-79.

_____. 'British Policy in Persia, 1858-1890 – II.' *English Historical Review* 70 (January 1955): 55-71.

_____. 'The Reopening of the "Central Asian Question", 1864-9.' *History* 41 (1956): 122-36.

Tob, Col. J. K. 'The Malleson Mission to Transcaspia in 1918.' *Journal of the Royal Central Asian Society* 27, Part I (1940): 45-67.

Tunstall, W. C. B. 'Imperial Defence, 1897-1914.' *Cambridge History of the British Empire.* Vol. 3. Ernest Benians, et al., eds. (Cambridge: Cambridge University Press, 1959): 563-604.

Warman, Roberta. 'The Erosion of Foreign Office Influence in the Making of Foreign Policy, 1916-1918.' *Historical Journal* 15 (1972): 133-59.

Williams, Beryl. 'Great Britain and Russia, 1905 to the 1907 Convention.' *British Foreign Policy under Sir Edward Grey* (Cambridge: Cambridge University Press, 1977): 133-47.

_____. 'The Strategic Background to the Anglo-Russian Entente of August 1907.' *Historical Journal* 9 (1966): 360-73.

Wilson, Sir Arnold T. 'The Bakhtiari.' *Journal of the Royal Central Asian Society* 13, Part III (1926): 205-23.

Wolf, John B. 'The Diplomatic History of the Baghdad Railroad.' *The University of Missouri Studies: A Quarterly of Research* 11 (April 1936).
Yarshater, Ehsan. 'Persian Letters in the Last Fifty Years.' *Middle Eastern Affairs* 11 (November 1960): 298-306.
Zabih, Sepehr. 'Change and Continuity in Iran's Foreign Policy in Modern Times.' *World Politics* 23 (1970-71): 522-43.

UNPUBLISHED MATERIALS

Bakhash, Shaul. 'Reform and the Qajar Bureaucracy: 1858-1896.' Unpublished doctoral thesis, Oxford University, 1972.
Edmonds, C. J. Private interview on April 30, 1975, at Mr Edmond's home in Tunbridge Wells, England.
Garthwaite, G. R. 'The Bakhtiyari Khans: Tribal Disunity in Iran.' Unpublished doctoral dissertation, University of California at Los Angeles, 1969.
Haig, Lt.-Col. T. W. Unpublished Memoirs of Lt.-Col. Haig, Consul at Mashhed and Isfahan during the War. Middle East Library, St. Antony's College, Oxford, Great Britain.

INDEX

Abadan, 33
Afghanistan, 50, 52, 93, 101, 112, 181, 197, 241, 247
  German activities, 50, 89, 93, 97, 98
  incursions into India, 1, 3
  see also Anglo-Russian Convention, Eastern Cordon
Agreement see Anglo-Persian Agreement; Anglo-Russian Convention; Sipahsalar Agreement
Ahmad Shah, 31, 120, 121, 199
  abdication threat, 126
  assurances, 127-8, 237, 244, 245
  British pressure on, 79, 92, 114, 115, 116
  dismisses Samsam us-Saltana, 206
  dismisses Sipahsalar, 149
  European visit, 230, 232
  flight threat, 113, 119
  German influence on, 100
  and Mustaufi al-Mamaluk, 73
  and Peace Conference, 217, 220
  and Sipahsalar Agreement, 175
  and Vusuq ud-Daula, 178, 179, 189, 191, 211
  subsidy, 188, 189, 191, 203-4, 206, 220, 243, 248
Ahwaz, 64, 154
Ain ud-Daula, Sultan Abdul-Majid, politician, 71, 79, 84, 85, 92, 96, 120, 121, 150, 178, 188-9
  German backing, 69
  Prime Minister, 81-3, 189
  resignation, 91, 93, 191
Akhbar Mirza, politician, 150, 151, 228

see also Triumvirate
Ala us-Saltana, politician, 38, 39, 45, 47, 48, 70, 150, 185, 204
  Prime Minister, 179
  fall, 189
  subsidy request, 60
American Relief Commission, 202
Americans,
  exclusion from Iran, 216
Amin ud-Daula, 145
Anglo-Persian Agreement of 1919, 224-49
  abandonment, 248
  private arrangements, 238-40
  see also Peace Conference
Anglo-Persian Oil Company, 32, 33, 222, 239
Anglo-Russian Convention of 1907, 8-9, 14-20, 51, 63, 116n, 139, 172, 174, 182, 192, 193, 262n.14
  abrogation proposals, 114, 124, 180, 181, 189, 190, 194, 197, 200, 209, 226, 228
  spheres of influence, 8, 15, 60
Armored cars offer, 188, 196, 197, 198
Arms supply,
  Persian requests, 114, 123, 124, 125, 128, 131, 133, 137, 188, 190, 235
Assassinations, 185, 190, 199
Assim Bey, Turkish diplomat, 76, 77, 80-1
August Agreement see Sipahsalar Agreement
Azerbaijan, 20, 30, 36, 39-40, 43, 61
  Russian defeat, 44, 45-9
  see also Northern Persia

For Product Safety Concerns and Information please contact our EU
representative GPSR@taylorandfrancis.com
Taylor & Francis Verlag GmbH, Kaufingerstraße 24, 80331 München, Germany

www.ingramcontent.com/pod-product-compliance
Lightning Source LLC
Chambersburg PA
CBHW060147280326
41932CB00012B/1666